Q'EQCHI' MAYAN THEMATIC DICTIONARY - FIRST EDITION

Tusb'il Molob'aal Aatin Q'eqchi' ~ Inkles - Xb'een Xpuktasinkil

Q'EQCHI' MAYAN THEMATIC DICTIONARY

Tusb'il Molob'aal Aatin Q'eqchi' ~ Inkles

FIRST EDITION / Xb'een Xpuktasinkil

Q'EQCHI' MAYAN THEMATIC DICTIONARY - FIRST EDITION

Tusb'il Molob'aal Aatin Q'eqchi' ~ Inkles - Xb'een Xpuktasinkil

A Mayaglot book.

Online resources associated with this work are located at mayaglot.com.
Email communication can be sent to *info@mayaglot.com*.

Cover art credit: MINEDUC (Recursos Educativos del Portal Educativo, Ministerio de Educación Guatemalteca).

ISBN-13: 978-1514812280
ISBN-10: 1514812282
BISAC: Foreign Language Study / Native American Languages

TABLE OF CONTENTS

LI XSA' LI TASAL HU

DEDICATION

This humble work is dedicated to my parents, Brent and Carol Frazier. They love language and they love their children unconditionally—their charity never faileth.

XCH'OOLANINKIL

Ninq'axtesi li xch'aab'ilal li ch'ina k'anjel a'in cho'q reheb' inna' inyuwa', aj B'rent ut li xKarol Frazier xk'ab'a'eb'. A'aneb' neke'xra li aatinob'aal. Neke'xra ajwi' li ralal xk'ajoleb' chi anchal xch'ooleb'—li xrahomeb' maajoq'e na'oso'k.

AUTHOR'S NOTE

(Li naxch'olob' laj tz'iib'ahom re)

This book is intended to fill a gap not yet well covered by other published Q'eqchi' language materials. While in recent years professional linguists have produced a number of excellent Q'eqchi' grammars, vocabularies and bilingual lexicons, they almost always pair Q'eqchi' exclusively with Spanish. This means that native speakers of English or Q'eqchi' who don't speak Spanish must first acquire it before undertaking serious study in either language. It is my hope that this book might be a useful resource, for example, for the non-Spanish speaking medical or religious volunteer working in Q'eqchi' communities as well as for Q'eqchi' speakers seeking to work or study in English-speaking countries.

This goal of facilitating language learning has informed my choices on how to structure and develop this reference tool. For example, I have included some conveniences like illustrations, variant word forms, and occasional comments on how particular features of the language are used by modern speakers in an effort to make the book as user-friendly as possible. In essence, I have created the dictionary I wish I had had over 25 years ago when I first started studying Q'eqchi'. Ideally, it will be paired at some point with a good Q'eqchi' ~ English grammar for language students.

I have also included many additional items where possible such as neologisms developed by Q'eqchi' linguists from Q'eqchi' word stock to describe the modern world, alongside the many Spanish and even English loanwords that have also become embedded in the language. Some of the neologisms seem a bit strained or awkward, but many are quite elegant—in most cases they will be understood intuitively by native speakers even if they have not used the term before.

Q'eqchi' is still evolving as a written language and as such there is not universal agreement on spelling and punctuation conventions, let alone adoption of newly developed terms. Where possible I have included variant forms in terms of pronunciation, spelling and usage as they exist in the dialectal variations of Q'eqchi'. This effort is not exhaustive and I refer any interested readers to the bibliography at the back of this book for sources on additional work on dialectal variation in Q'eqchi'. Fortunately, due to the historical evolution of the language there is a high degree of mutual intelligibility (despite ongoing processes of divergence) and Q'eqchi' speakers from the lowlands and the highlands usually understand each other.

Users will note that the English used in this dictionary is largely of the Standard American variety, though there are some Britishisms too. (Q'eqchi' speakers in Belize might remind you that Belize only achieved its independence from Great Britain in 1981!)

This book is not an attempt to document a dying language. Q'eqchi' is alive and currently undergoing a dynamic expansion in its vocabulary, educational standards, and literary arts. With growing interest and activity on the part of native speakers to explore and develop their language as a primary manifestation of culture, it will be fascinating to see how the spoken and written language continues to progress in the coming years. No doubt there are errors in this book, typographical and otherwise, that have escaped hundreds (probably thousands) of hours of careful research. This is a first edition, and it will need to be updated and improved periodically. But with a nod to William Sedat, Father Esteban Haeserijn (and Voltaire) I say: *Il meglio è nemico del bene.* Tento xtaqlankil li ch'ina hu a'in sa' li qachoxach'och'.

Jeffrey B Frazier
June 21, 2015

ACKNOWLEDGMENTS

After spending two years of my youth as a missionary in Q'eqchi'-speaking areas of Guatemala, I always wanted to return someday in a meaningful way. For many years I didn't know how to do it—I didn't want to go back only as a tourist. It was a little bit of timely Providence that showed me how. Thank you Michael Penrose and Jim Carlisle for being in the right place at the right time. And thank you Bob Wells for following up when it could easily have dropped through the cracks. If I hadn't had the chance to work as an interpreter in the Faith in Practice medical clinics in the Petén, I might never have followed through on a lifelong goal to make a contribution, however simple, to the linguistic community of the Q'eqchi' Maya.

Thank you Gordon Romney for sending me to live with the Q'eqchi'—twice. And thank you Irene, Ava, and Alex. You indulged me with isolation during my sabbatical to work on this book, and sometimes even visited me in my man-cave. Thank you for your patience and understanding.

Lastly, much love to the developers of *Lexique Pro* lexicography software in Mali, West Africa, and SIL International—a truly selfless example of leveraging the power of the word.

FRIENDS OF Q'EQCHI'

Special thanks and warm regards to those who provided technical insight and/or financial support for this project: Michael Horlick, Liz Saint Rain, Kelly Nuttall, and others too shy to be mentioned here.

XB'ANTIOXINKIL

Nawaj xb'antioxinkil chijunileb' lin looy aj Q'eqchi'. Wankeb' k'ila poyanam xine'xtenq'a xtzolb'al li aatinob'aal Q'eqchi' chiru k'ila chihab' ut chekuy taxaq inmaak wi xsach sa' inch'ool wiib' oxib' eek'ab'a'.

Ninb'antioxi re aj Domingo Bol ut re aj Benjamin Rax (Senahú), jo' ajwi' re aj Alberto Coy (Seamay) ut laj Juan Can (Sacsuha). Ninb'antioxi re li xBlanca Azucena Noack Cajbon (intzolonel sa' li ch'ina tzoleb'aal Muqb'il B'e) jo' ajwi' laj Josué Oswaldo Xol Botzoc (Cobán), ut laj Ramón Chocooj (El Estor).

Aajel ru ajwi' xb'antioxinkil chiru laj Carlos Tiul ut chixjunil lix junkab'al sa' li xteepal Chupón chi re li palaw Izabal. Ninb'antioxi re li rixaqil Margarita de Tiul ut chijunileb' li ralal xk'ajoleb': Lucrecia Petrona, Ingris Mayaliy, Carlos Enrique, Kinberly Gabriela, ut Brayan Orlando. Ninb'antioxi eere ink'ulb'al sa' eerochoch ut lee ch'ina iklees wiib' oxib' kutan.

Sa' xchoyb'al, ninb'antioxi chiru li xNiik re...lix saasal ru lix nawom. Naq laa'in xwil li xk'anjel xink'e reetal li rusilal. Xb'aan naq a'an x'ala sa' inch'ool xb'aanunkil li molob'aal aatin a'in ut xk'eb'al jun ilb'al li usilal. At insaq'e, sa' junaq kutan tatink'ut chaawu laa k'ab'a' mayab'.

ABOUT THE Q'EQCHI' LINGUISTIC COMMUNITY

(Chi rix li xmolamil aatinob'aal Q'eqchi')

The Q'eqchi' are the predominant Maya group in the central highlands and northern lowlands of Guatemala. Geographically, Q'eqchi' is the largest Maya language community in Guatemala. Q'eqchi' is widely spoken in the northern Quiche', in Alta and Baja Verapaz, Isabal, Petén and to a lesser extent southern Belize and parts of Mexico and El Salvador (see Figure 1).

The Q'eqchi' language is part of the greater Quiche'an language family (see Figure 2). The ancestral territory of the Q'eqchi' runs from Coban and the mountain of Xucaneb in the west along the Sierra Yalijux and Cahabon river valley eastward to Lanquin / Cahabon and the mountain of Itzamna' in the east. Historically, the Q'eqchi' were a highland people, marginalized by more powerful groups: the Chol, Lacandon and Acalas whose ancient territory was a step lower in elevation. In the last hundred years the Q'eqchi' have increased numerically and geographically. They immigrated (or were forced) to the lowlands of Izabal and Belize and then to the lowlands of northern Alta Verapaz and the Peten. These migrations have made the Q'eqchi' language the widest spoken Maya language of Guatemala as understood by geographic area.

The Q'eqchi' Maya consider themselves heirs of the rich culture and history of the ancient Maya. The Q'eqchi' homeland encompasses the only Mayan territory never conquered militarily by the Spanish (Tezulutlan). The Q'eqchi' language is derived from Proto-Mayan and there are many examples of shared vocabulary between Proto-Mayan and Q'eqchi'. Although Q'eqchi' is a member of the Quiche'an language family, its geographic proximity through history to the Cholean languages of their closest neighbors also left its mark on their vocabulary and grammar.

In the classic period (ca. 200bc to 800ad) and into the post classic period, urban centers flourished in Chichen (between Chamelco and Santa Cruz), Chamelco, Coban, Ulpan, Chijolom and Lanquin. Today, some of these are only ruins, such as Chichen, Ulpan and Chijolom. Others continue as urban centers, for example: Chamelco, Coban and Lanquin.

Q'eqchi's nearest relative is Uspantec, a small language group west of the Rio Negro. Nothing much else is closely related to Q'eqchi'. Other Quiche'an languages seem to share more in common (the preceding passages are based largely on Cahill, 2014).

In sharp contrast to other Mayan linguistic communities where the indigenous language is on a path to extinction, Q'eqchi' is a thriving language (see Figure 3). Q'eqchi' is without a doubt the most rapidly expanding indigenous language in the Americas (Romero, 2012). Consider, for example:

- There are more than 1 million speakers; this places Q'eqchi' 2nd among all 30 living Mayan languages (CODISRA, 2010).

- The number of native speakers has more than doubled in the last 25 years.

- The current geographic footprint of the Q'eqchi' linguistic community (QLC) covers as much area as all other Guatemala Mayan groups combined.

- The area encompassed by the QLC is expanding within Guatemala, and includes a significant number of speakers in southern Belize and Mexico and El Salvador as well.

- Q'eqchi' has the highest proportion of monolingual speakers in all Guatemalan Mayan linguistic communities.

- Q'eqchi' has the highest rate of literacy among all Guatemalan Mayan linguistic communities. Reported at 10.3% in 2010, but still three times greater than K'iche', the next closest Mayan language (CODISRA, 2010).

- Q'eqchi' is culturally and linguistically assimilative, with a word stock reflecting absorption of words and concepts from other Mayan languages—both living and extinct. Q'eqchi' has a long history of assimilating other groups (indigenous and European) into its linguistic community.

- Since 1996, a number of native Q'eqchi' speakers have trained as professional linguists and published a large and growing body of professional descriptive and didactic linguistic resources.

- The language is in vigorous use, with standardization and literature being sustained through a widespread system of institutionally supported education (Lewis, 2014).

Figure 1 – Geography of Q'eqchi' Linguistic Community

Graphic credit: Dan Cole; Indigenous Geography Project, Smithsonian's National Museum of the American Indian.

Figure 2 – Mayan Language Tree

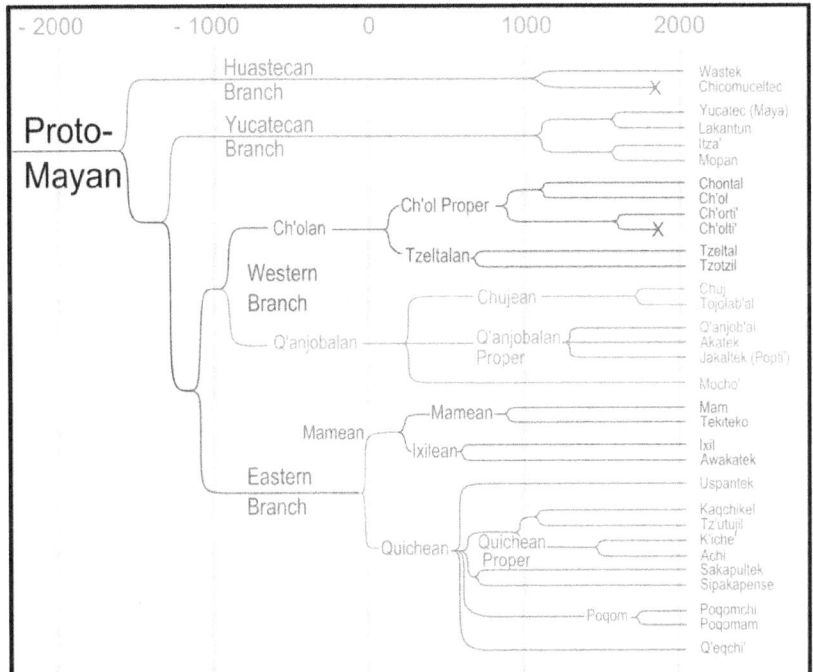

Source: A genealogy tree for the Mayan languages, based on an earlier tree by Maunus. From Wikimedia Commons, the free media repository. Permission is granted to copy, distribute and/or modify this document under the terms of the GNU Free Documentation License, Version 1.2 or any later version published by the Free Software Foundation.

Figure 3 – Place of Q'eqchi' Amongst World Languages

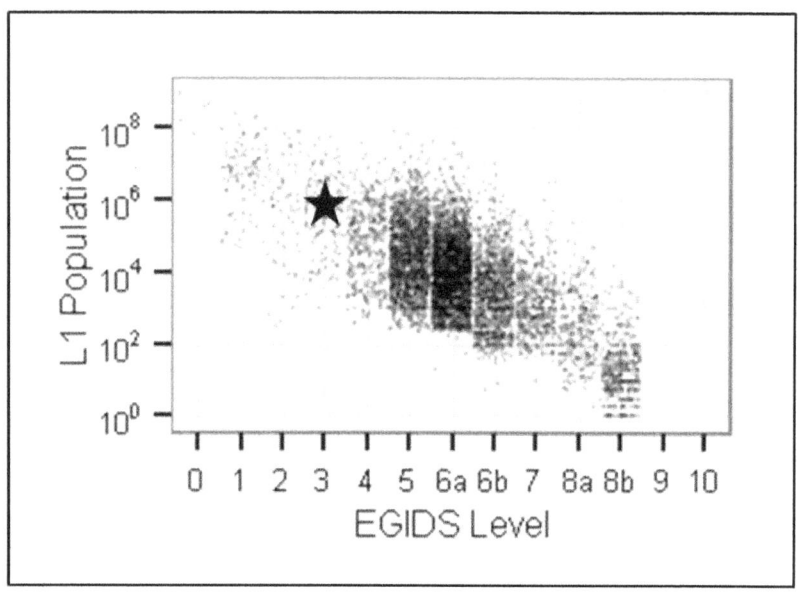

This graph shows the place of Q'eqchi' within the cloud of all living languages. Each language in the world is represented by a small dot that is placed on the grid in relation to its population (in the vertical axis) and its level of development or endangerment (in the horizontal axis), with the largest and strongest languages in the upper left and the smallest and weakest languages (down to extinction) in the lower right. The population value is the estimated number of first language (L1) speakers; it is plotted on a logarithmic scale (where $10^0 = 1$; $10^2 = 100$; $10^4 = 10,000$; $10^6 = 1,000,000$; $10^8 = 100,000,000$). The value for the development versus endangerment dimension is the estimated level on the EGIDS scale (Expanded Graded Intergenerational Disruption). The EGIDS level for Q'eqchi' in its primary country is 4 (Educational), meaning that the language is in vigorous use, with standardization and literature being sustained through a widespread system of institutionally supported education (Lewis, 2014).

HOW TO USE THIS BOOK

(Chan ru roksinkil li tasal hu a'in)

This book combines certain features of traditional bilingual dictionaries as well as vocabularies used for language learning. It is a thematic dictionary, since the arrangement of entries in the Q'eqchi'-to-English section is done by theme, rather than alphabetically. This approach offers advantages to students as a vocabulary builder, to writers as a thesaurus, and to linguists as an insight into the structure of the language.

There are three principal sections:

- Section I contains a simple introduction to Q'eqchi' orthography and pronunciation for English speakers that are new to Q'eqchi'.

- Section II is a thematic list of Q'eqchi' words followed by their parts of speech and English equivalent(s). Many of the entries are illustrated. Themes vary from basic nominal categories like *fruits* or *tools* to linguistic categories such as *verb-ending type* or notional categories such as *time* and *weather*.

- Section III is an alphabetical listing of the English words corresponding to all of the 8,500+ Q'eqchi' entries in Section II (as in a traditional dictionary).

While these structural choices increase the language-learning utility for native speakers of both Q'eqchi' and English (both young and old), they also reflect some tradeoffs. For the sake of space I did not include an alphabetical Q'eqchi'-to-English index and only a few examples of usage or word etymologies. I have, though, included a few helpful notes on grammatical usage and evidence for borrowed words where possible, as explained elsewhere and referenced in the appendix. I hope to include many more features in a future work in print, digitally, and accessible on the internet at *mayaglot.com.*

I
Q'EQCHI' MAYAN PRONUNCIATION GUIDE

Esilal Chi Rix Xyaab'asinkil Aatinob'aal Q'eqchi'

Q'EQCHI' MAYAN PRONUNCIATION GUIDE

(Esilal chi rix xyaab'asinkil aatinob'aal Q'eqchi')

All the Mayan languages are descended from Proto-Mayan, which is thought to have arisen some 5,000 years ago in the Western highlands of Guatemalan. The Mayan language family is a rather large one: there are 8 official Mayan languages in Mexico and 21 in Guatemala. In Guatemala, the four largest Mayan languages are Kaqchikel, K'ichee', Mam, and Q'eqchi', all with more than 500,000 speakers. As noted previously, Q'eqchi' is a flourishing language that is experiencing growth and expansion both in the number of speakers and the geographic territory of its linguistic community.

Modern Mayan languages, especially in Guatemala, are now written using a Latin alphabet which was first standardized by the Guatemalan Academy of Mayan Languages in 1986. Although the Mayan languages are largely mutually unintelligible, they all share some common features that distinguish them from other language groups. An interesting feature of Mayan languages is that they are ergative. Ergative languages are characterized by complex verb systems that treat the subjects of intransitive verbs differently from the subjects of transitive verbs. In this dictionary I have provided some convenient verb lists categorized by verb endings based on their base infinitive (or unconjugated) form, but generally do not further classify verbs by their transitive, intransitive, and reflexive, and other forms—information on these formations will be found in any good Q'eqchi' grammar.

In terms of sounds, Mayan languages have several glottalized or ejective consonants, and they also make distinctions between short and long vowels; these sound features are often the most difficult thing for new learners of Q'eqchi' to pick up, but they are essential in that they distinguish meaning.

The standard modern Q'eqchi' alphabet uses the following letters and symbols:

Upper case letters: A AA B' CH CH' E EE H I II J K K' L M N O OO P Q Q' R S T T' TZ TZ' U UU W X Y '

Lower case letters: a aa b' ch ch' e ee h i ii j k k' l m n o oo p q q' r s t t' tz tz' u uu w x y '

Unused letters: Letters in the English and Spanish alphabets not typically used in Q'eqchi' orthography: C c, D d, F f, G g, LL ll, Ññ, RR rr, V v, Z z.

Note: The letter B' in Q'eqchi' is always accompanied by the glottalization symbol ('), and all vowels can also be glottalized.

Examples of pronunciation

Q'eqchi' Vowels

Vowel	Pronunciation
a	Like the *a* in *father*.
aa	Like *a* only held longer.

e	Like the Spanish *e*, similar to the *a* in English *gate*.
ee	Like *e* only held longer.
i	Like the *i* in *police*.
ii	Like *i* only held longer.
o	Like the *o* in *note*.
oo	Like *o* only held longer.
u	Like the *u* in *flute*.
uu	Like *u* only held longer.

Q'eqchi' Diphthongs

Dipthong	Pronunciation
ay	Like English *eye*.
ey	Like *ey* in English *they*.
oy	Like *oy* in English *boy*.
uy	like the *uoy* in English *buoy*.

Q'eqchi' Consonants

Consonant Pronunciation

b'   Like *b* in *boy*, only more plosive. To English
          speakers, it sounds as if Maya speakers are
          'swallowing' the b sound, similar to the way *b*
          is pronounced in Vietnamese.

ch   Like *ch* in *chair*.

ch'   Like *ch*, only glottalized (pronounced with a
          slight pop or click.)

h   Like the *h* in *hay*.

j   Like the raspy *j* in Spanish *jalapeño*.

k   Like *k* in *key*.

k'   Like *k*, only glottalized (pronounced with a
          slight pop or click.)

l   Like *l* in *light.*

m   Like *m* in *moon*.

n   Like *n* in *night*.

p   Like the *p* in *pie*.

q   Like *k* only pronounced further back in the

throat. This is similar to the *q* in Arabic.

q'   Like *q*, only glottalized (pronounced with a slight pop or click.)

r   Like Spanish *r*, somewhat like the *tt* in English *butter.*

s   Like the *s* in *sun.*

t   Like the *t* in *tell.*

t'   Like *t*, only glottalized (pronounced with a slight pop or click.)

tz   Like *ts* in *cats.*

tz'   Like *tz*, only glottalized (pronounced with a slight pop or click.)

w   Like *gw* in *Gwen.* Some speakers pronounce it like the *qu* in *qui*ck (closer to the sound of the Q'eqchi' *k* followed by a *w*; alternatively, some pronounce it more like the *w* in the English *wheel* without an initial plosive.

x   Like *sh* in *shell.*

y   Like *y* in *yes.* Some speakers pronounce it more like the "ky" sound in *cute.*

'   A glottal plosive, like the one in the middle of the English exclamation "uh-oh". Represented in written Q'eqchi' using the apostrophe symbol.

Figure 4 – Pronunciation of Q'eqchi' (IPA symbols)

Vowels

a	aa	e	ee	i	ii	o	oo	u	uu
[a]	[aː]	[e]	[eː]	[ɪ]	[iː]	[o]	[oː]	[u]	[uː]

Diphthongs

ay	ey	oy	uy
[aj]	[ej]	[oj]	[uj]

Consonants

b	ch	ch'	h	j	k	k'	kw	ky	l	m	n	p
[ɓ]	[tʃ]	[tʃʼ]	[h]	[x]	[k]	[kʼ]	[gʷ]	[gʲ~dʲ]	[l]	[m]	[n]	[p]

q	q'	r	s	t	t'	tz	tz'	w	x	y	'
[q]	[qʼ]	[ɾ]	[s]	[t]	[tʼ]	[ts]	[tsʼ]	[gw]	[ʃ]	[j~kʲ]	[ʔ]

Note: All Q'eqchi' words are stressed on the final syllable. Pronunciation notes adapted from (Redish, 2014) and (Ager, 2014).

II

Q'EQCHI' MAYAN
THEMATIC DICTIONARY

Tusb'il Molob'aal Aatin
Q'eqchi' ~ Inkles

SEMANTIC DOMAINS

(Xch'uutalil Xyaalalil)

13

17

18

LANGUAGE CHARACTERISTICS & EXAMPLES

(Chan ru li aatinob'aal ut eb' li xk'utb'esinkil)

Ajl ut Ajlank / Math and Counting

Aatin chi rix Ajl / Math Terms

aj b'isonel na'leb' *n.* rate, ratio.

aj k'ihanel ajl *n.* coefficient.

aj naw'ajl *n agt.* mathematician.

ajl *n.* number, numeral.

ajlank *v.* to count.

ajleb'aal *n.* calculator.
Var: ajlab'al.

ajlil *n.* numeration.

araaw *n.* Arabic numeral. *From:* Spanish 'arábigo'.

b'ehul *n.* formula.

b'irleb'aal *n.* calculator.
Var: b'irlob'aal.

b'isb'il eetalil *n.* geometric figure, geometric shape.

b'isxuk *n.* protractor.

chi jachal *adv.* fractionally, by fraction.

chi lajetqil *adv phr.* by tens.

chi'ajlil *adv.* mathematically.

ch'utub'ank *n.* sum.

ch'uut *n.* set.

eetalb'irok *adj.* algebraic.

eetalb'irool *n.* algebra.

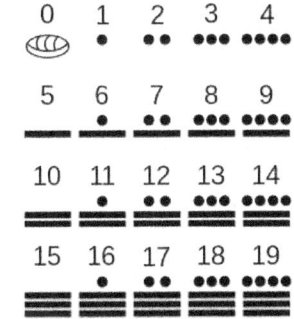

eetalil ajl mayab' *n.* Mayan numbers.

eetalpuk-ajl *n.* times, multiplication sign (x), multiplication symbol (x).

jachb'il'ajl *n.* fraction.

jachinb'il chi *adj.* divided by.

jachlil'ajl *n.* fractional, mixed number.

jaljookil ru ajl *n.* algebra.

jarjek'il *n.* denominator.

jeb'ib'aal *n.* divisor.

jeb'ok *v.* to subtract.

21

jeb'ok *n.* subtraction, remainder.

jeb'ok-ajl *n.* subtraction.

jech'-uhil *n.* asymmetry.

jek'ink *v.* to divide.

jek'iil *n.* numerator.

jun jachal *n.* a half.

jun kaajachal *n.* a quarter.

jun xka *n.* one fourth, a quarter.

jun xwaqxaqil *n.* one eighth.

junaj k'anjel *n.* linear function.

junajeetalb'irok *n.* monomial.

junpak'alil *adj.* reversible.

junqmayil *n.* base-twenty.

juntaq'eetil eetalil *n.* symmetric figure.

$$9 + \frac{5x}{2} = 4$$

juntaq'eetin k'anjel'ajl *n.* equation.

ka'eetalb'irok *n.* binomial.

01234
56789

kaxajl *n.* Arabic numeral.

kaxukutinb'il *n.* grid.

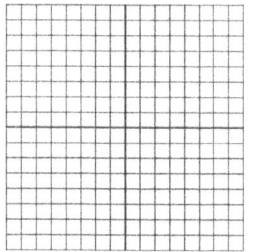

kaxukuutinb'ilhu *n.* graph paper.

kok'ajil xsa' *n.* frequency.

k'aalil *n.* base-twenty.

k'ila eetalb'irok *n.* polynomial.

k'ila'u *n.* polygon.

k'onoljuch' *n.* curved line.

k'ucha'alk'anjel *n.* formula.

lajetqil *adj.* base-ten.

lajetqil *n.* unit of ten.

laq'juch' *n.* parallel line.

laq'lookil juch' *n.* parallel line.

maachoyb'ach'uut *adj.* infinite.

maalajkch'uut *n.* infinite set.

molob'ank *n.* addition.

molool *n.* sum.

naw'ajl *n.* mathematics, math.

nawajlil *n.* numeracy.

nimajel *adj.* deductive.

ox'eetalb'irok *n.* trinomial.

oxjachal *n.* one third.

oxwahink *v.* to cube.

puktahil'ajl *n.* multiplication.

puktasinb'il *adj.* multiplied.

puktasinel *n.* multiplier.

puktasink *v.* to multiply.

puktasink ajl *v.* to multiply.

puktasink chi *phr.* multiplied by.

puktasink ib' *v phr.* to square.

puktasiil *n.* multiplication.

puktaal *n.* multiple.

q'eq'ookil juch' *n.* horizontal line.

q'ot-eetalil *n.* parabola.

raqro juch' *n.* perpendicular line.

reetal jach'ajl *n.* division symbol (/).

reetal molam ajl *n.* plus sign (+), addition symbol (+).

reetal puktasiil *n.* times, multiplication sign (x), multiplication symbol (x).

reetaljeb'ok-ajl *n.* minus sign (-).

reetaljek'ajl *n.* division symbol (/).

reetaltamok-ajl *n.* plus sign (+), addition symbol (+).

ro'wahink *v.* to raise to the fifth power.

roxch'otonel *adj.* antepenultimate, third to last. *Var:* roxch'otol.

rub'elal xraqik *adj.* penultimate, second to last.

salam *adj.* diagonal.

sumch'a'ajkilal *n.* equation.

tamok-ajl *n.* addition, total, sum.

tawrib' oxxukuut *n.* congruent triangle.

tiikaljuch' *n.* straight line.

tiikil juch'ul *n.* straight line.

tiik-uhil *n.* symmetry.

tzol *n.* row, line.

tzolil *n.* row, line.

xaqxo *adj.* vertical.

xaqxookil juch' *n.* vertical line.

xb'arxukil *n.* coordinate.

xch'oolil *n.* axis.

xjalanil *n.* variable.

xjartawahil *n.* frequency.

xjek'inkil *n.* division.

xjek'iil *n.* quotient.

xjultikankil *n.* formulation.

xk'anjel *n.* function.

xk'atq xraqik *n.* terminal side (of an angle).

xk'atq xtiklajik *n.* initial side (of an angle).

xmola *n.* sum.

xna'ajtz'uq *n.* abscissa.

xsa' *adj.* area, contents.

xsa' ruhil *n.* surface area.

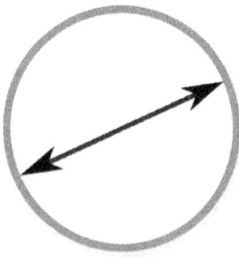

xsa'kotko *n.* diameter.

xsal *adj.* reversed.

xsutq'isinkil chi rix *adj.* reversible.

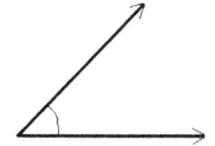

xtehelal *n.* angle.

xtiklajik *n.* start, beginning, origin.

xtiklajik xb'arxukil *n.* coordinate origin.

yamch'uut *n.* empty set.

yamyookil ch'uut *n.* empty set.

yanq *n.* space, interval.

yanqil *n.* intermediate point.

yanqxuk *n.* angle.

yijachal *n.* half.

yiib'ank ch'a'ajkilal *v phr.* to solve equations.

yiib'ank ch'a'ajkilal *n.* solution (to a problem).

Eb' li T'or'ajl / Cardinal Numbers (0-100)

(0.) maajun *num.* zero.

(1.) jun *num.* one.

(2.) wiib' *num.* two. *Var:* kiib'.

(3.) oxib' *num.* three.

(4.) kaahib' *num.* four.

(5.) oob' *num.* five. *Var:* hoob'.

(6.) waqib' *num.* six.

(7.) wuqub' *num.* seven.

(8.) waqxaqib' *num.* eight.
Var: wajxaqib'.

(9.) b'eleeb' *num.* nine.

(10.) lajeeb' *num.* ten.

(11.) junlaju *num.* eleven.

(12.) kab'laju *num.* twelve.

(13.) oxlaju *num.* thirteen.

(14.) kaalaju *num.* fourteen.

(15.) o'laju *num.* fifteen.
Var: ho'laju.

(16.) waqlaju *num.* sixteen.

(17.) wuqlaju *num.* seventeen.

(18.) waqxaqlaju *num.* eighteen.

(19.) b'eleelaju *num.* nineteen.

(20.) jun may *Var:* junk'aal. *num.* twenty. *From:* may 'to count' (Mixe-Zoquean) (4).

(21.) jun xka'k'aal *num.* twenty-one.

(22.) wiib' xka'k'aal *num.* twenty-two.

(23.) oxib' xka'k'aal *num.* twenty-three.

(24.) kaahib' xka'k'aal *num.* twenty-four.

(25.) oob' xka'k'aal *num.* twenty-five.

(26.) waqib' xka'k'aal *num.* twenty-six.

(27.) wukub' xka'k'aal *num.* twenty-seven.

(28.) waqxaq'ib' xka'k'aal *num.* twenty-eight.

(29.) b'eleb' xka'k'aal *num.* twenty-nine.

(30.) lajeeb' xka'k'aal *num.* thirty.

(31.) junlaju xka'k'aal *num.* thirty-one.

(32.) kab'laju xka'k'aal *num.* thirty-two.

(33.) oxlaju xka'k'aal *num.* thirty-three.

(34.) kaalaju xka'k'aal *num.* thirty-four.

(35.) o'laju xka'k'aal *num.* thirty-five.

(36.) waqlaju xka'k'aal *num.* thirty-six.

(37.) wuqlaju xka'k'aal *num.* thirty-seven.

(38.) waqxaqlaju xka'k'aal *num.* thirty-eight.

(39.) b'elelaju xka'k'aal *num.*
thirty-nine.

(40.) ka'k'aal *num.* forty.

(41.) jun roxk'aal *num.* forty-
one.

(42.) wiib' roxk'aal *num.* forty-
two.

(43.) oxib' roxk'aal *num.* forty-
three.

(44.) kaahib' roxk'aal *num.*
forty-four.

(45.) oob' roxk'aal *num.* forty-
five.

(46.) waq'ib' roxk'aal *num.*
forty-six.

(47.) wukub' roxk'aal *num.*
forty-seven.

(48.) waqxaq'ib' roxk'aal *num.*
forty-eight.

(49.) b'eleb' roxk'aal *num.*
forty-nine.

(50.) lajeeb' roxk'aal *num.* fifty.

(51.) junlaju roxk'aal *num.*
fifty-one.

(52.) kab'laju roxk'aal *num.*
fifty-two.

(53.) oxlaju roxk'aal *num.* fifty-
three.

(54.) kaalaju roxk'aal *num.*
fifty-four.

(55.) o'laju roxk'aal *num.* fifty-
five.

(56.) waqlaju roxk'aal *num.*
fifty-six.

(57.) wuqlaju roxk'aal *num.*
fifty-seven.

(58.) waqxaqlaju roxk'aal
num. fifty-eight.

(59.) b'elelaju roxk'aal *num.*
fifty-nine.

(60.) oxk'aal *num.* sixty.

(61.) jun xkaak'aal *num.* sixty-
one.

(62.) wiib' xkaak'aal *num.*
sixty-two.

(63.) oxib' xkaak'aal *num.*
sixty-three.

(64.) kaahib' xkaak'aal *num.*
sixty-four.

(65.) oob' xkaak'aal *num.*
sixty-five.

(66.) waqib' xkaak'aal *num.*
sixty-six.

(67.) wuqub' xkaak'aal *num.*
sixty-seven.

(68.) waqxaqib' xkaak'aal
num. sixty-eight.

(69.) b'eleb' xkaak'aal *num.*
sixty-nine.

(70.) lajeeb' xkaak'aal *num.*
seventy.

(71.) junlaju xkaak'aal *num.*
seventy-one.

(72.) kab'laju xkaak'aal *num.*
seventy-two.

(73.) oxlaju xkaak'aal *num.*
seventy-three.

(74.) kaalaju xkaak'aal *num.*
seventy-four.

(75.) o'laju xkaak'aal *num.*
seventy-five.

(76.) waqlaju xkaak'aal *num.*
seventy-six.

(77.) wuqlaju xkaak'aal *num.*
seventy-seven.

(78.) waqxaqlaju xkaak'aal
num. seventy-eight.

(79.) b'elelaju xkaak'aal *num.*
seventy-nine.

(80.) kaak'aal *num.* eighty.

(81.) jun ro'k'aal *num.* eighty-
one.

(82.) wiib' ro'k'aal *num.*
eighty-two.

(83.) oxib' ro'k'aal *num.*
eighty-three.

(84.) kaahib' ro'k'aal *num.*
eighty-four.

(85.) oob' ro'k'aal *num.* eighty-
five.

(86.) waqib' ro'k'aal *num.*
eighty-six.

(87.) wuqub' ro'k'aal *num.*
eighty-seven.

(88.) waqxaqib' ro'k'aal *num.*
eighty-eight.

(89.) b'eleb' ro'k'aal *num.*
eighty-nine.

(90.) lajeb' ro'k'aal *num.*
ninety.

(91.) junlaju ro'k'aal *num.*
ninety-one.

(92.) kab'laju ro'k'aal *num.*
ninety-two.

(93.) oxlaju ro'k'aal *num.*
ninety-three.

(94.) kaalaju ro'k'aal *num.*
ninety-four.

(95.) o'laju ro'k'aal *num.*
ninety-five.

(96.) waqlaju ro'k'aal *num.*
ninety-six.

(97.) wuqlaju ro'k'aal *num.*
ninety-seven.

(98.) waqxaqlaju ro'k'aal *num.* ninety-eight.

(99.) b'elelaju ro'k'aal *num.* ninety-nine.

(100.) o'k'aal *n.* one hundred.

Eb' li Jek'b'il Ajl / Distributive Numbers (1-20)

1. junqjunq *Var:* junqjunqatq. *n.* every one.

2. ka'kab' *Var:* ka'kab'atq. *n.* every other one.

3. ox'ox' *Var:* ox'oxatq. *n.* every third one.

4. kaaka *Var:* kaakatq. *n.* every fourth one.

5. o'otq *n.* every fifth one.

6. waqitq *n.* every sixth.

7. wuqutq *n.* every seventh.

8. wajxaqitq *Var:* waqxajqitq. *n.* every eighth.

9. b'eleetq *n.* every ninth.

10. lajeetq *n.* every tenth.

11. junqtaqlaju *n.* every eleventh.

12. kab'taqlaju *n.* every twelfth.

13. oxtaqlaju *n.* every thirteenth.

14. kataqlaju *n.* every fourteenth.

15. o'taqlaju *n.* every fifteenth.

16. waqtaqlaju *n.* every sixteenth.

17. wuqtaqlaju *n.* every seventeenth.

18. wajxaqtaqlaju *Var:* waqxaqtaqlaju. *n.* every eighteenth.

19. b'eletaqlaju *Var:* b'ele'taqlaju. *n.* every nineteenth.

20. junmaytq *n.* every twentieth.

Eb' li Tusb'a'ajl / Ordinal Numbers (1-100)

(1st.) xb'een *num.* first.

(2nd.) xkab' *num.* second.

(3rd.) rox *num.* third.

(4th.) xka *num.* fourth.

(5th.) ro' *num.* fifth.

(6th.) xwaq *num.* sixth.

(7th.) xwuq *num.* seventh.

(8th.) xwajxaq *Var:* xwaqxaq. *num.* eighth.

(9th.) xb'elee *num.* ninth.

(10th.) xlajee *num.* tenth.

(11th.) xjunlajuil *num.*
eleventh.

(12th.) xkab'lajuil *num.* twelfth.

(13th.) roxlajuil *num.*
thirteenth.

(14th.) xkaalajuil *num.*
fourteenth.

(15th.) ro'lajuil *Var:* rob'lajuil.
num. fifteenth.

(16th.) xwaqlajuil *num.*
sixteenth.

(17th.) xwuqlajuil *num.*
seventeenth.

(18th.) xwajxaqlajuil
Var: xwaqxaqlajuil. *num.*
eighteenth.

(19th.) xb'ele'lajuil
Var: xb'eleeb'lajuil or
xb'eleelajuil. *num.* nineteenth.

(20th.) xjunmayil
Var: xjunk'aalil. *num.* twentieth.

(21st.) xjun xka'k'aalil *num.*
twenty-first.

(22nd.) xkab' xka'k'aalil *num.*
twenty-second.

(30th.) xlajee xka'k'aalil *num.*
thirtieth.

(40th.) xka'k'aalil *num.* fortieth.

(50th.) xlajee roxk'aalil *num.*
fiftieth.

(60th.) roxk'aalil *num.* sixtieth.

(70th.) xlajee xkaak'aalil *num.*
seventieth.

(80th.) xkaak'aalil *num.*
eightieth.

(90th.) xlajee ro'k'aalil *num.*
ninetieth.

(100th.) ro'k'aalil *num.*
hundredth.

Jalaneb' Chik li Ajl / Other numbers

jun oq'ob' *n.* four hundred.

kiib' oq'ob' xkab' xchuy *n.*
one million.

lajeeb' oq'ob' *n.* four
thousand.

lajeeb' syent *n.* one thousand.
From: 10 ciento '10 hundred'
(Spanish) (1).

lajeek'aal *n.* two hundred.

lajeek'aal rox oq'oob' *n.* one
thousand. *Var:* lajeek'aal rox
roq'ob'.

lajeek'aal xwaqxaq roq'ob' *n.*
three thousand.

maasumal'ajl *n.* odd numbers.

o'k'aal xkab' roq'ob' *n.* five hundred.

o'lajuk'aal *n.* three hundred.

oob' chuy xwaq k'alab' *n.* one million.

oob' oq'ob' *n.* two thousand.

sumal'ajl *n.* even numbers.

Ajleb'aal Kutan ut Xq'ehil / Calendar and Time

ajleb'aal kutan *n.* calendar. *Var:* ajlab'al kutan.

akoost *n.* August. *From:* Spanish 'agosto'.

ak'il *adj.* new.

ak' *adj.* new.

al *adj.* young.

al po *n.* new moon.

anaqwan *n.* today.

anaqwan q'e kutan *n.* nowadays.

awril *n.* April. *From:* Spanish 'abril'.

b'ayjik *n.* delay.

b'ayok ib' *v.* to waste time.

b'isleb'hoonal *n.* chronometer.

b'yers *n.* Friday. *Var:* b'iyernes. *From:* viernes 'Friday' (Spanish) (1).

chalen q'e kutan *n.* eternity.

chaalel *n.* future.

chi q'eq *n.* evening, night.

chi ru li eq'la *adv phr.* in the morning.

chi ru li ewu *adv phr.* in the afternoon.

chi ru li hab' xnume' *adv phr.* last year.

chi ru li q'oqyin a'in *adv phr.* this evening.

chi ru li saqewk *adv phr.* in the early morning.

chi ru li xamaan chalk re *adv phr.* next week.

chi ru li xamaan xnume' *adv phr.* last week.

chi ru q'oqyin *adv phr.* at night, in the evening.

chihab' *n.* year.

ch'olq'e *n.* calendar.

ch'olq'e maayab' *n.* Maya calendar. *Var:* ch'olkutan maayab'.

ch'otonik *n.* end (temporal).

eneer *n.* January. *From:* Spanish 'enero'.

eq'la *n.* morning.

eq'la *adj.* early.

eq'laaho'k *n.* sunrise.

estasion *n.* season. *From:* estación 'the season' (Spanish) (1).

ewer *n.* yesterday.

ewer chi q'eq *n.* last night, yesterday evening.

ewer eq'la *n.* yesterday morning.

eweraq *n.* a day ago.

ewu *adj.* late.

ewu *n.* afternoon.

ewuuk *n.* sunset.

hab' *n.* year.

hab'al q'e *n.* winter.

hik'o *n.* early morning.

hoon chi q'eq *n.* tonight.

hoonal *n.* hour. *Var:* honal. *From:* jornal 'a day's wage' (Spanish) (2).

hoonal *n.* moment.

hoonalil *n.* schedule. *Var:* honalil.

hulaj *adv.* tomorrow. *Var:* wulaj.

hulaj chi eq'la *adv phr.* tomorrow morning.

hulaj chi q'eq *adv phr.* tomorrow evening.

hulaj ewu *adv phr.* tomorrow afternoon.

ik'ek' *n.* early morning.

ilb'ahoonal *n.* clock. *Var:* ilob'aal hoonal.

jo' wanaq *adv.* later.

jun kutan rub'elaj *n.* the day before.

jun wa'leb' *n.* midday.

junpaatil *n.* moment.

junxil *adj.* old, ancient.

juul *n.* July. *From:* Spanish 'julio'.

juun *n.* June. *From:* Spanish 'junio'.

jweews *n.* Thursday. *Var:* jweeb's. *From:* jueves 'Thursday' (Spanish) (1).

kab'ej *n.* the day after tomorrow.

kab'ejer *n.* two days ago, day before yesterday.

kaajer *n.* four days ago. *Var:* ko'ejer.

kiib' kutan chi rix *n.* two days later.

ko'ej *n.* in four days.

kutan *n.* time.

k'asal *n.* minute.

k'ojlajik *n.* beginning.

lajeeb' hab' *n.* decade.

leb'eb'nak *adj.* slow.

li hab' chalk re *n.* next year.

li po a'in *n.* this month.

li po ak xnume' *n.* last month.

li po chalk re *n.* next month.

li xamaan a'in *n.* this week.

luuns *n.* Monday. *From:* lunes 'Monday' (Spanish) (1).

mama' *adj.* old.

maars *n.* March. *From:* Spanish 'marzo'.

maarts *n.* Tuesday. *From:* martes 'Tuesday' (Spanish) (1).

maay *n.* May. *From:* Spanish 'mayo'.

miercools *n.* Wednesday. *Var:* **myeers.** *From:* miércoles 'Wednesday' (Spanish) (1).

moqon *n.* future.

najkutan *n.* afternoon.

najt kutan *adj.* late.

najter *adj.* old, ancient.

najter q'e kutan *n.* former times, olden days.

najto'k *v.* to be late.

naq ta ewuuq *adv phr.* at dusk.

naq ta saqewq *adv phr.* at dawn.

naq tk'e tuktu q'oqyin *adv phr.* at midnight.

naq tk'e waleb' *adv phr.* at noon.

naab'al honal *adj.* for a long time.

nowyemr *n.* November. *Var:* **nob'yemb'r.** *From:* Spanish 'noviembre'.

oktuuwr *n.* October. *Var:* **oktuub'wr.** *From:* Spanish 'octubre'.

ok'aal hab' *n.* century.

oso'jik *n.* end (temporal).

otoony *n.* autumn, fall (season). *From:* otoño 'autumn' (Spanish) (1).

oxej *adv.* in three days.

oxejer *adv.* three days ago.

oor *n.* hour. *From:* hora 'the hour' (Spanish) (1).

pewreer *n.* February. *Var:* **peb'reer.** *From:* Spanish 'febrero'.

po *n.* month.

pohol *n.* month.

primab'eer *n.* spring (season). *From:* primavera 'spring' (Spanish) (1).

priim *n.* dawn, early morning. *From:* prima 'first canonical hour' (Spanish) (1).

q'iil *n.* time.

rajlal xamaan *adv phr.* every week.

raqik *n.* end (temporal).

reloj *n.* clock. *From:* reloj 'the clock or watch' (Spanish) (1).

riil *adj.* slow.

ro'ilpo *n.* May.

roxilpo *n.* March.

ruujik *v.* to cease.

sa' najter q'e kutan *adv phr.* anciently.

saq'ehil *n.* summer.

saaj *adj.* young.

saaw *n.* Saturday. *From:* sábado 'Saturday' (Spanish) (1).

sektiyemr *n.* September. *From:* Spanish 'septiembre'.

seeb'ank *v.* to hurry.

sut *n.* time.

taqik *n.* time.

tikkehil kutan *n.* spring (season).

tiklajik *n.* beginning.

tiklaak *v.* to begin.

timil *adj.* slow.

tisyemr *n.* December. *Var:* **risyemr; risymb'r.** *From:* Spanish 'diciembre'.

tiixil po *n.* full moon.

toj eq'la *adv.* earlier.

toje' *adv.* a moment ago, recently.

toje' *adj.* recent.

tomiin *n.* Sunday. *Var:* **domiin; romink.** *From:* domingo 'Sunday' (Spanish) (1).

tuqtu q'ojyin *n.* midnight.

tuqtu waleb' *n.* noon.

uq'mil k'uthoonal *n.* watch, wristwatch.

wej *adv.* in four days.

wosol *n.* chill. *Var:* woso.

wuqub'ix *adv.* in seven days.

wuq'ix *n.* week.

xamaan *n.* week. *From:* semana 'the week' (Spanish) (1).

xb'elehilpo *n.* September.

xb'een kutan *n.* Monday.

xb'een waleb' *n.* afternoon.

xb'eenilpo *n.* January.

xchi hab' *n.* age.

xjunlajuhilpo *n.* November.

xkab'aljuhilpo *n.* December.

xkab'ilpo *n.* February.

xkab'kutan *n.* Tuesday.

xkakutan *n.* Thursday.

xkaapo *n.* April.

xkutankil yo'lajik *n.* date of birth, birthday.

xlajehilpo *n.* October.

xoronikpo *n.* full moon.

xq'ehil kutan *n.* calendar.

xraqik hab'alq'e *n.* autumn, fall (season).

xwaqkutan *n.* Saturday.

xwaqxaqpo *n.* August.

Eb' li Q'ekutan / Geologic Eras

mayer q'e *n.* Archean era, Archaeozoic era.

q'e *n.* era, eon.

q'ekutan *n.* era, eon.

ro' q'ekutan *n.* Cenozoic era.

rox q'ekutan *n.* Paleozoic era.

xb'een q'ekutan *n.* Precambrian era.

xka q'ekutan *n.* Mesozoic era.

xwaq q'ekutan *n.* Anthropozoic era, Anthropocene.

Ajsink-U ut Hilaal / Entertainment and Leisure

B'atz'iil ut Ajsink-U / Arts & Entertainment

aj b'aanunel *n agt.* protagonist, subject.

aj hiltesinel *n agt.* usher.

aj k'aak'anel *n agt.* ticket taker.

aj yehonel *n agt.* narrator.

ajsib'aal'u *n.* recreation, fun, recess.

ajsink u *v phr.* to entertain, enjoy.

ajsink-u *n.* entertainment, diversion.

b'atz'iil *n.* art.

b'onb'il q'esnalna'leb' *n.* work of art.

b'uuleb' *n.* raffle, lottery.

b'uuleb'aal *n.* lottery.

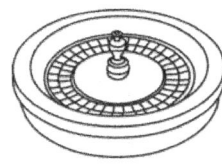

b'uulik *n.* raffle, lottery, gambling.

b'uuluk *n.* lottery.

eek' jalam'uuch *n.* moving picture, movie.

eek'mu *n.* film, movie.

eetalmu *n.* cinema, movie theater.

hilaal *n.* break, recreation.

hoonalhilaal *n.* recreation, fun, recess.

ileb' *n.* screen (TV).

ileb'aalmu *n.* cinema, movie theater.

jahok u *v phr.* to entertain, amuse, distract.

jalam'uuch *n.* film, movie.

ka'xaqab'aal *n.* renown, fame.

k'oj *n.* mask.

k'utb'ahom *n.* theatrical production.

k'utb'esib'aal *n.* theater.

k'utb'esink *v.* to perform, present.

k'utb'il *adj.* theatrical.

k'uub'anb'il k'anjel *n.* program (TV).

k'uub'ank *n.* program (TV).

lemaal *n.* screen (TV).

pak'b'il ismal *n.* wig.

pumb'uul *n.* raffle, lottery.

raqalilk'utb'esink *n.* scene.

rochochil ilob'aal mu *n.* cinema, movie theater.

rochochil k'utb'esink *n.* arts center.

sahob'k'utleb'aal *n.* staging, set.

tojleb'aal *n.* box office, ticket window.

xajleb'aal *n.* disco, nightclub.

xaqxo jalam'uuch *n.* still life.

xhoonal asjsink-u *n.* recreation, fun, recess.

xlemul kaxmuhel *n agt.* movie screen, silver screen.

xna'aj ajsink u *n.* recreation center.

xna'aj k'utleb'aal *n.* art gallery.

xq'ehil hilaal *n.* vacation.

xyik'utb'esink *n.* set, stage.

yaljot'ok *n.* adventure.

yalok hu *v phr.* to bet.

yalok hu *n.* lottery.

B'atz'unk ut B'atz'uul / Sports and Games

aj aanilanel *n agt.* athlete, runner.

aj b'atz'unel *n agt.* athlete, sportsman.

aj b'atz'unel b'olotz oq *n agt.* soccer player, footballer.

aj b'atz'uneleb' *n.* team.

aj b'olotz *n agt.* ballplayer, soccer player, footballer.

aj b'olotz chakach *n agt.* basketball player.

aj ch'e'ol b'aqlaq ch'iich' *n agt.* cyclist.

aj ilonel *n agt.* spectator.

aj jolominel b'atz'unk *n agt.* coach.

aj muqa'l *n agt.* swimmer.

aj numxinel *n agt.* swimmer.

aj ramonel b'olotz *n agt.* goalie, goalkeeper.

aj tuqub'anel *n agt.* referee.

ajsink u li tib'elej *v phr.* to exercise, play sports.

atib'aal *n.* pool, swimming pool.

aanilak *v.* to run. *Var:* alinak.

b'atb'een'aq *n.* knee guard, knee pad.

b'atz'ub'aal *n.* playing field.

b'atz'uul *n.* toy, game.

b'aanunk *v.* to practice.

b'ololch'iich' *n.* whistle
(object).

b'olotz *n.* ball.

b'olotz chakach *n.* basketball.

b'olotz meex *n.* foosball table.

b'olotz oq *n.* soccer, soccer
ball.

b'olotz sum uq'ib'k *n.*
volleyball.

b'olotz-uq' *n.* basketball.

champa *n.* net.

ek'asink chi oq *v phr.* to pedal.

jomal *n.* playing field.

kaxb'olol *n.* whistle (object).

kelkookil soq' *n.* net.

keelsoq' *n.* net.

kutuk q'e'che' *n.* javelin throw.

kutuk suriil *n.* discus throw.

k'ajk'amonkmetzew *n.* trophy.

k'as *n.* goal.

k'ayib'aal b'atz'uul *n.* toy
store.

k'ehok k'as *v phr.* to win.

k'ilab'atz'unk *n.* athleticism.

lapok *v.* to kick.

pisk'ok *v.* to jump, leap.

pitzok *v.* to jump, leap.

lapok chi oq *v phr.* to kick.

maatanej *n.* trophy.

mitzt'orotz *n.* marbles.

mitz' b'olotz *n.* marbles.

potz'b'aqib'k *n.* boxing.

puulesink *v.* to throw.

q'aqt *n.* dice.

q'ochleb'aal *n.* gym, gymnasium.

muqa'lik *v.* to dive, scuba dive. *Var:* muqa'alik.

najtil pisk'ok *n.* long jump.

numxib'aal *n.* pool, swimming pool.

numxik *n.* swimming.

okeb'aal b'olotz *n.* goalposts. *Var:* okleb'aal b'olotz.

perperink *v.* to pedal.

ramok *v.* to catch, block, prevent.

ramtzelek *n.* shin guard.

rupelhu *n.* kite.

sak'lemb'ilb'olotz *n.* volleyball.

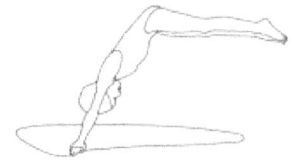

pisk'leb'aal *n.* diving board.

sururu *n.* top.

sururub'atz'uul *n.* top.

sutisink *v.* to spin.

tojl *n.* ticket.

tusb'il chunleb'al *n.* bleachers, stands.

t'i'ok *v.* to kick.

t'orlemtz' *n.* marbles.

t'uuyleb' *n.* hammock, swing. *Var:* **t'uyleb'.**

tzakib'k *v.* to win.

tz'eqok *v.* to throw.

tz'eqok *v.* to lose (a game).

tz'eqok *n.* defeat.

xaab'ank *v.* to kick.

xb'aanunkil *n.* action, execution, practice.

xchaq'rab'il *n.* rules.

xmaatanil li yalok u *n.* trophy.

xmolamil b'atz'unk *n.* team.

yeq'ok *v.* to kick.

Sa' li Nimq'e / At the Fair or Party

aj b'eenel chi ru b'aqb'il k'aam sa iq' *n agt.* tightrope walker.

aj ch'uch' *n agt.* clown.

aj eek' *n agt.* magician.

aj k'ay ki'ilsaqb'ach *n agt.* ice cream vendor.

aj k'ay ki'tuux *n agt.* cotton candy vendor.

aj nawal *n agt.* magician.

aj seeb'alk'utb'esink *n agt.* acrobat.

aj t'uyanel *n agt.* trapeze artist.

aj xajonel *n agt.* ballerina, dancer.

ajsink u *v phr.* to entertain, enjoy.

b'eek chi tustu *v phr.* to parade.

b'eenink *v.* to invite.

b'onb'il u *n.* painted face.

b'oqok *v.* to summon, call, invite.

b'uulink *v.* to raffle.

b'uulink maatan *v phr.* to raffle a prize.

b'uulink tumin *v phr.* to raffle money.

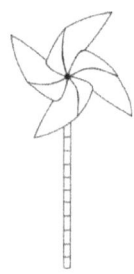

ch'ina ral simaj *n.* pinwheel.

ch'uch'ib'leb'aal *n.* circus.

eetz'aal *n.* costume, disguise.

jahok u *v phr.* to entertain, amuse, distract.

jolool *n.* slide, chute, slippery place.

jutzutzu *n.* fireworks, bottlerocket.

kab'il kaxlan wa *n.* sweet roll.

kaxmuheb'aal ch'uch'ib'leb'aal *n.* circus tent.

ki'ilsaqb'ach *n.* ice cream.

ki'tuux *n.* cotton candy.

kotkookil b'atz'uul *n.* Ferris wheel.

k'amom *n.* packet.

k'ilimb'il saa'us *n.* churro.

k'orechtul *n.* plantain chip.

k'utb'aatal *n.* costume, disguise.

maatan *n.* gift, prize, surprise.

milmich' hu *n.* streamer.

mixpirik *n.* the day before a party.

moqx *n.* popcorn. *Var:* moqs.

mu *n.* parasol.

nimq'e *n.* party, fair. *Var:* ninq'e.

nimq'ehink *v.* to party.

pam'iq' *n.* balloon.

poyb'atz'uul *n.* marionette, puppet.

puk'um *n.* piñata.

pumb'uul *n.* revolving drum.

q'axtesink *v.* to present, give.

sa' memil *n.* mime.

se'eel winq *n.* clown.

seeb'ch'oolil *n.* acrobatics.

si *n.* gift.

sumsihink *v.* to exchange (gifts).

tusilb'eek *n.* parade.

tz'aab'il kaxlan wa *n.* French toast.

tz'aab'il ki'ik q'een *n.* fruit slices.

uutz'u'ujinb'il eetz'unk *n.* costume, disguise.

uutz'u'ujinb'il saa'us *n.* piñata.

uutz'u'ujink *v.* to decorate.

xajleb' *n.* dance. *Var:* xajl.

xajok *v.* to dance.

xk'aj hu *n.* confetti.

xna'aj payas *n.* circus.

xpunit aj eek' *n.* magician's hat.

Sa' li Rochoch Xul / At the Zoo

aj k'amolb'e *n agt.* guide, director.

aj k'aak'anel *n agt.* keeper.

aj k'utunel b'e *n agt.* guide, director.

aj maxxul *n.* primate.

aj nawxul *n agt.* zoologist.

aj q'unb'esihonel xul *n agt.* animal trainer.

b'ateey *n.* feed tray.

ch'uut *n.* group.

koral ch'iich' *n.* metal bars, cage.

nimla xna'ajkar *n.* fish tank.

ramleb' *n.* railing.

rochoch tz'ik *n.* aviary.

rochoch xul *n.* zoo.

xna'aj ha' *n.* watering hole.

xna'aj k'ila xul *n.* zoo.

xna'ajkar *n.* fishbowl.

xna'ajleb'aalxul *n.* zoo.

xtz'alam xul *n.* animal cage.

Ak'il Nawk'anjelahom / Modern Technology

ab'ib'aal aatin *n.* radio (receiver).

ab'ib'aalson *n.* radio (receiver).

aj b'ironel *n.* calculator.

aj ha'resinel *n.* solvent.

ajleb'ilha' *n.* water meter.

ajsib'aal hoonal *n.* alarm clock.

ajsinel *n.* alarm clock.

anyooj *n.* spectacles, glasses. *From:* anteojos 'glasses' (Spanish) (1).

b'ateriiy *n.* battery. *From:* batería 'the battery' (Spanish) (1).

b'eek xb'aan choxach'och' *n.* space travel.

b'irleb'aal *n.* calculator. *Var:* b'irlob'aal.

b'isb'ametz'ew *n.* electric meter.

b'isleb'hab' *n.* barometer.

b'isleb'tiq *n.* thermometer.

b'omb'iiy *n.* light bulb. *From:* bombilla 'bulb' (Spanish) (1).

chajb'a'esil *n.* alarm.

chak'oq *n.* tripod.

chapleb' aatin *n.* tape recorder.

chapleb'jalam'u *n.* video camera, security camera.

puktasib'aalhu *n.* photocopier, copy machine, copier.

pumleb'ha' *n.* water tank.

q'och-eetalil *n.* film.

raqb'ametz'ew *n.* electric switch, switch, interruptor.

raqleb' saqen *n.* power switch, light switch.

raqmetz'ew *n.* electricity.

raqmetz'eweb' *n.* escalator.

ray *n.* radio. *From:* radio 'the radio' (Spanish) (1).

repolmu *n.* overhead projector, projector.

repom *n.* overhead projector, projector.

repsaqenk *n.* flash.

roqechil k'at *n.* electric tower.

roqkaxlan xam *n.* electric current.

saqenlem *n.* glass.

teleb'ision *n.* television. *From:* televisión 'television' (Spanish) (1).

tokxaml *n.* match.

tuqb'ametz'ew *n.* thermostat, regulator, controller.

tz'iib'leb' ch'iich' *n.* typewriter.

xaml *n.* electricity.

xlaawil ha' *n.* water tap, faucet.

xmetz'ew tiik *n.* kinetic energy.

xna'aj ha' *n.* water tank.

xokleb' mu *n.* video camera.

yaaw *n.* tap, faucet. *From:* llave 'the key' (Spanish) (1).

yolojch'iich *n.* robot.

yoob' *n.* invention.

yoob'anb'il *adj.* invented.

yu'am ch'iich *n.* robot.

Ak'il Xb'aanunkil Raaxiik' / Modern Warfare

ach'ab'ank *v.* to liberate, free, let go.

aj kolom *n agt.* hero.

aj kookox *n agt.* soldier.

aj pleet *n agt.* fighter. *From:* Spanish 'pleito'.

aj puub' *n agt.* soldier.

aj tuqtuukilnel *n agt.* pacifist.

aj tz'alam *n agt.* captive, prisoner.

aj yalonel *n agt.* warrior.

ak'il xb'aanunkil raaxiik' *n.* modern warfare.

b'atz'unk puub'ak *v phr.* to target shoot.

b'eetak'aak'alenel *n.* patrol.

b'eetak'aak'alenk *v.* to patrol.

b'oom *n.* bomb. *From:* bomba 'the bomb' (Spanish) (1).

ch'e'ok *v.* to fight.

ch'impo' *adj.* violent.

ch'iich' *n.* armour.

eb' aj puub' *n.* army.

echanink *n.* victory.

eelelik *v.* to retreat, flee.

josq' *adj.* violent, aggressive.

jukub' re pleetik *n.* warship, battleship.

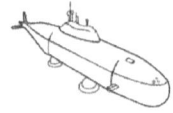

jukub' re rub'elha' *n.* submarine.

kab'l najt xteram *n.* tower.

kach'in puub' *n.* handgun.

kalkab' *adv.* in peace.

kampameent *n.* camp. *From:* campamento 'camp' (Spanish) (1).

kamsib'aal *n.* weapons.

kamsink-ib' *n.* war.

kamsiil *n.* weapons.

katunink *v.* to make war.

ketok *v.* to beat, hit, strike.

ketok *n.* victory.

kok' puub' *n.* pistol, revolver.

kolb'ajolom *n.* helmet.

k'ilapotz' puub' *n.* machine gun.

k'uluk *n.* attack.

k'uub'ank *v.* to arm, set up, assemble.

lak'am *n.* shield. *Var:* lakam. *From:* lakam 'banner' (Yucatecan, Ch'olan, possible) (2).

makaan *n.* sword. *From:* macana 'the club' (Spanish) (1).

maal *n.* battle-axe.

min'isink *v.* to loot, sack, plunder.

minyamtesink *v.* to loot, sack, plunder.

nimla ch'iich' *n.* sword.

paraq'aq'a *n.* machine gun.

pleet *n.* battle, war. *From:* pleito 'fight' (Spanish) (1).

pleetik *n.* combat.

poqsxaml *n.* gunpowder, powder.

potz'ok *v.* to strike, hit, beat.

po'ok *v.* to destroy.

preex *n.* captive, prisoner. *Var:* **pereex**. *From:* preso 'captive' (Spanish) (1).

puub' *n.* firearm, gun, rifle.

puub'ak *v.* to shoot.

puub'ank *v.* to shoot.

q'axtesink ib' *v phr.* to surrender, give up.

rajtziil *n.* enemy.

rampalaw *n.* marines.

raaxiik' *n.* war, battle.

raaxiik' *n.* quarrel.

rixnaq'puub' *n.* shell, bullet casing.

rixxnaq'puub' *n.* bullet shell.

rochochil aj puub' *n.* barracks.

ru'uj puub' *n.* cannon.

sachok *v.* to destroy.

sahil ch'oolej *n.* peace.

soldaa *n.* soldier. *Var:* **sola**. *From:* soldado 'soldier' (Spanish) (1).

sutuxink *v.* to surround.

tawasink *v.* to injure.

taaqinel *n.* guard.

temb'il *n.* blow.

tikb'il *n.* challenge.

tikok *v.* to challenge.

tikonel *n.* challenger.

toch'ok *n.* hurt, harm.

toor *n.* tower. *Var:* **tore**. *From:* torre 'tower' (Spanish) (1).

tuqtuukilal *n.* peace.

t'ane'k *n.* defeat, fall, rendition.

tz'eqok *n.* defeat.

uk'alpunit *n.* helmet.

winqilal *n.* bravery.

xb'oolpuub' *n.* cannon.

xeq'ok *v.* to stab. *From:* *xeq', xek' 'to stab or pierce' (Ch'olan) (2).

xerek' winq *n.* young men.

xe'xke rib' *v phr.* to surrender.

xib'enk *v.* to threaten.

xik'onel *n.* enemy.

xna'aj puub' *n.* holster.

xnaq' puub' *n.* cartridge, magazine.

xnaq'puub' *n.* bullet.

yalok *n.* war, battle.

yalok *v.* to fight.

Choxach'och'il B'eek / Space Travel

aj b'e chahim *n.* satellite.

aj b'e choxa *n agt.* astronaut.

aj b'eenel sa' po *n agt.* astronaut.

aj ch'e'ol b'oq'ch'iich' iq' *n agt.* astronaut.

b'eenelchahim *n.* satellite.

b'oq'ch'iich' iq' *n.* space capsule.

chahimch'iich' *n.* satellite.

chahimch'iich' aj na'onel ru li ruchich'och' *n.* weather satellite.

choxach'och' *n.* universe, cosmos.

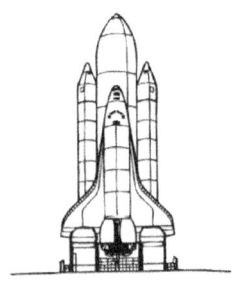

jukub' iq' *n.* space shuttle, spaceship.

k'achleb'aal sa' po *n.* lunar module, lunar capsule.

k'ochlaak sa' li po *n.* moon landing.

maaruuchich'och' *n.* extraterrestrial.

maawa' re ruchich'och' *n.* extraterrestrial.

na'leb'aal ch'iich' iq' *n.* space station.

48

puraq' *n.* space suit.

purik aq' aj b'eenel sa' po *n.* space suit.

raq' aj b'eenel sa' po *n.* space suit.

Esilal Nawk'anjelahom / Information Technology

aj yiib'om ulul ch'iich' *n agt.* computer programmer.

anum ch'iich' *n.* fax machine, fax.

aroow *n.* at symbol (@). *From:* Spanish 'arroba'.

aatinob'aal ch'iich' *n.* telephone, phone.

b'oqleb' *n.* cell phone, cell (phone), cellular (phone).

b'oqleb' *n.* telephone, phone.

b'oqleb'aal *n.* telephone, phone.

b'oqleb'aal ch'iich' *n.* telephone, phone.

chahimch'iich' re puktesink esil *n.* communications satellite.

chochtz'iib' *n.* floppy disk, diskette.

ch'ik-ib' *n.* interference.

ch'ilb'oqleb' *n.* cell phone, cell (phone), cellular (phone).

ch'ilb'oqleb' *n.* cell phone, cell (jail).

ch'ohib'aal *n.* mouse pad.

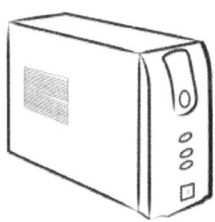

ch'olk'anjelob'aal *n.* processor, central processing unit, CPU.

esil sa' tz'iib' *n.* text message.

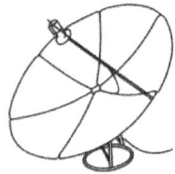

esilsek' chahimch'iich' *n.* satellite dish.

eeqajil *n.* backup copy.

eetal *n.* cursor.

eetaltaql *n.* icon.

jalam'uuch *n.* photo.

Var: jalam'u.

jalam'uuchleb'aal ch'iich' *n.* photocopier, copy machine, copier.

jekb'ametz'ew *n.* powerstrip, circuit board.

jwal kach'in xkutum *n.* weak signal.

kaxmu'eetalil *n.* computer screen, monitor, display.

k'atb'il-eetalil *adj.* scanned.

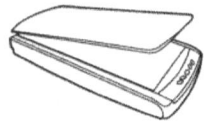

k'atleb'-eetalil *n.* scanner.

k'atok-eetalil *v.* to scan.

k'osleb' *n.* zip drive.

k'ul'esilal *n.* beeper.

k'uuleb'jalam'uuch *n.* photo album.

k'uulhu *n.* file, archive.

mak'aam b'oqleb' *n.* cordless phone.

metz'ewib'aalb'oqleb' *n.* charger, phone charger.

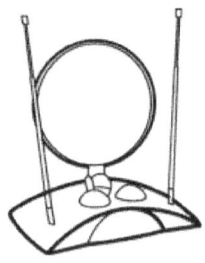

misik'ch'iich' *n.* antenna.

mitz'jalam'u *n.* thumbnail photo.

50

muhil'esil *n.* fax.

muhilsik'leb' *n.* internet.

muhiltaql *n.* email.

num'esil *n.* fax.

numch'o *n.* cursor.

numjalam'uuch *n.* scanner.

numleb' kaxlanxaml *n.* semiconductor.

numsinel *n.* conductor.

numsink *v.* to transmit.

pukleb'hu *n.* printer.

puktasib'aal esil *n.* media, means of communication.

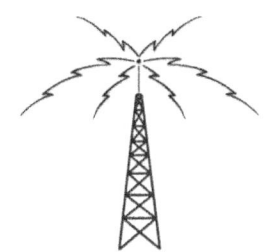

puktasib'aal kab'l najt xteram *n.* radio tower.

puktasib'aalhu *n.* printer, imprint.

puktasiil *n.* printer.

rajlil b'oqleb' *n.* phone number.

raatik'aamch'iich' tenamit *n.* public telephone.

reetalil tz'iib'aal *n.* email address.

roopilch'iich' *n.* cable.

ru tz'iib'leb' *n.* key (of keyboard).

ru ululch'iich' *n.* keyboard.

rululil *n.* hard disk.

sum ajlil *n.* binary system.

sur chapleb'aal *n.* CD-ROM, compact disk, disk, CD.

surchoch *n.* disk.

tarjeet re b'oqleb' *n.* phone card.

teleef *n.* telephone, phone.
From: teléfono 'the telephone' (Spanish) (1).

tojb'il b'oqleb' *n.* payphone.

tojhuil b'oqleb' *n.* prepaid phone card.

tzolom chi rix ululch'iich' *n.* computer science.

tz'iib'leb' *n.* keyboard.

tz'uy tz'iib'esil *n.* beeper.

ulul ch'iich' *n.* computer or PC.

ululil xokleb' *n.* floppy disk, computer disk.

xche'e'b'al *n.* keyboard.

xkutum b'oqleb' *n.* cell phone signal.

xk'aamal b'oqleb'aal *n.* phone line.

xk'aamal kaxmu *n.* cable television.

xk'ub'lal xsa' *n.* operating system.

xlemul kaxmuhel *n.* screen (TV).

xmisik' kaxmu *n.* television antenna.

xmisik' puktasib'aal *n.* radio antenna.

xna'aj xokleb' *n.* floppy disk, computer disk.

xokleb' *n.* file.

xokok *v.* to file, save.

xramb'al xxulel yajel *n.* antivirus.

xya'al puktasiilhu *n.* ink, printer ink.

yaab'aal *n.* siren, ring (phone).

Ak'il Nawsutam / Modern Science

ha'ilyol *n.* nitroglycerine.

hesok *v.* to refine.

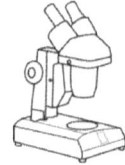

ileb'aalmitz' *n.* microscope.

ilob'aal chahim *n.* telescope.

jalb'ehil saqen *n.* refraction, light refraction.

kawalil chi ru raaxiik' *n.* disaster prevention, emergency preparedness.

kawresil *n.* stimulus.

kawsik kaxaml *n.* electrical resistance.

k'uyum k'at *n.* electrical resistance.

metz'ewanb'il *adj.* catalytic.

na'lenk *n.* discovery.

na'ok *n.* to discover.

numsiilk'anjel *n.* radioactivity.

ta'ok *n.* to discover.

tehok ru *n.* to discover.

tiqkaxlan xaml *n.* proton.

tiikil kaxlanxaml *n.* electron.

xhesb'al *n.* refinement.

xjalalik ru *n.* catalysis.

xkolb'al rix li loq'laj che'k'aam *n.* resource conservation.

xk'anjel *n.* function.

xmetz'ew k'a'aq ru *n.* potential energy.

xnumsinkil *n.* radiation.

xrajikraxil *n.* photosynthesis.

xsak'om tiqkaxlanxaml *n.* positive electric charge.

xsak'om tiikil kaxlanxaml *n.* negative electric charge.

Nawchahim / Astronomy

aj ilol chahim *n agt.* astronomer.

aj nawchahim *n agt.* astronomer.

ak'chahim *n.* nova.

b'ookatq *n.* gases.

b'ookil *adj.* gaseous.

b'utzchahim *n.* comet.

chahim *n.* star.

chahimpek *n.* meteor.

choqlil tzoqchahim *n.* nebulous galaxy.

choxach'och' *n.* universe, cosmos.

ch'uut chahim *n.* constellation.

jiskotko tiwok *n.* annular eclipse.

junaj tzoqchahim *n.* compact galaxy.

juntz'ap tiwok *n.* total eclipse.

jus chahim *n.* shooting star.

kaqchahim *n.* Venus, morning star. *Var:* kaqi chahim.

kehil chahim *n.* neutron star.

kototiil tzoqchahim *n.* spiral galaxy.

kutan chahim *n.* morning star.

k'ajchahim *n.* meteor.

k'on tzoqchahim *n.* elliptical galaxy.

moyk ru li saq'e *n.* eclipse.

muluq'utchahim *n.* comet.

muqlaak kutan *n.* eclipse.

muqlaak po *n.* lunar eclipse.

muqlaak saq'e *n.* solar eclipse.

muqpo *n.* lunar eclipse.

muqsaq'e *n.* solar eclipse.

nach'ilchahim *n.* Ursa Minor.

nawchahim *n.* astronomy.

naxtiw rib' li saq'e ut li po *n.* eclipse.

nimlachahim *n.* planet.

numlentz' saqen *n.* meridian.

numsiilk'anjel *n.* radioactivity.

po *n.* moon. *From:* *poy'a 'moon' (Mixe-Zoquean) (3).*

pukchahim *n.* supernova.

puukchahim *n.* asteroid.

q'eq'ookil eetalil *n.* equator.

ralsaq'e *n.* planet.

raxmoyinil tzoqchahim *n.* blue galaxy.

ro' ralsaq'e *n.* Jupiter.

ruuchich'och' *n.* world, Earth.

saqb'e *n.* Milky Way.

saqonaqilchahim *n.* galaxy.

saq'e *n.* sun.

satuurn *n.* Saturn. *From:* Spanish 'Saturno'.

sutrib' *n.* rotation.

sutrix *n.* revolution.

suutalnawom *n.* cosmology.

suutilal *n.* orbit.

tiwok posaq'e *n.* eclipse.

tzoqchahim *n.* galaxy.

tzoqtzokilchahim *n.* constellation.

wankilal saq'e *n.* solar system.

wuqchahim *n.* Ursa Major.

xb'e ruuchich'och' *n.* orbit.

xb'e'chahim *n.* orbit.

Var: xb'eechahim.

xb'ele' ralsaq'e *n.* Pluto.

xb'een *n.* surface.

xb'een ralsaq'e *n.* Mercury.

xche' kaqixaml *n.* infrared light.

xche' saq'e *n.* ultraviolet light.

xch'ool *n.* nucleus.

xch'oolil *n.* axis.

xch'uutulal chahim *n.* constellation.

xhoplalil *n.* black hole.

xk'otchahim *n.* meteorite.

xmetz'ew raalal *n.* gravity.

xmetz'ew xyi li ruchich'och' *n.* gravity.

xnumsinkil *n.* radiation.

xtumb'choxa *n.* planet.

xtuqlajik q'e *n.* equinox.

xtusulal ruuchich'och' *n.* solar system.

xtzoq saq'e *n.* Milky Way.

xulab' *n.* Venus.

xwaq ralsaq'e *n.* Saturn.

xwaqxaq ralsaq'e *n.* Neptune.

xwuq ralsaq'e *n.* Uranus.

xyalojikeb' li saq'e ut li po *n.* eclipse.

Ninqi K'utleb'ruuchich'och' / Macrogeography

eetaj palaw *n.* Atlantic Ocean.

jayal *n.* direction.

junajroqil *n.* compass.

junpak'alpalaw *n.* Europe.

kehilch'och' *n.* cold climate.

kelam *n.* longitude.

keehil siraal *n.* glacial zone.

keekehil siraalch'och' *n.* temperate zone.

k'ab'a'na'jej *n.* toponym.

k'ixkoot *n.* compass.

numlentz' saqen *n.* meridian.

pak'alilch'och' *n.* continent.

palaw kariiw *n.* Carribean sea.

q'otch'och'ilpalaw *n.* Mediterranean Sea.

releb' iq' *n.* north. *Var:* releb'aal iq'; releb'l iq'.

releb' saq'e *n.* east. *Var:* releb'aal saq'e; releb'l saq'e.

reetalil ch'och' *n.* map.

rokeb' iq' *n.* south. *Var:* rokeb'aal iq'; rokeb'l iq'.

rokeb' saq'e *n.* west. *Var:* rokeb'aal saq'e; rokeb'l saq'e.

roq ab'yayala *n.* South America.

taqe'q q'eq'ookot eetalil *n.* Tropic of Cancer.

taq'a q'eq'ookot eetalil *n.* Tropic of Capricorn.

tasal ruuchich'och' *n.* tectonic plates.

tiqwal siraalch'och' *n.* tropics, sun belt.

tiqwalch'och' *n.* hot climate.

tiikal *n.* direction.

tuulan palaw *n.* Pacific Ocean.

xhelam *n.* latitude.

xjolom ab'yayala *n.* North America.

xk'atqil *n.* latitude.

xnajtil roq *n.* longitude.

xsiraal taq'eq *n.* arctic circle.

xtaqe'qil ruuchich'och' *n.* north pole.

xtaq'ahil ruuchich'och' *n.* south pole.

xtuqlajik q'e *n.* equinox.

xt'oram ruuchich'och' *n.* globe.

xtz'uq junajroqil *n.* cardinal directions.

xye ab'yayala *n.* North America.

xyi ab'yayala *n.* Central America, Mesoamerica.

yiib'ejilch'och' *n.* Central America, Mesoamerica.

Poyanimil Nawyu'am / Human Biology

aj nawyu'amilal *n agt.* biologist.

ajsiil *n.* protein.

alab'metz'ew *n.* mitochondria.

alk'uula'al *n.* fetus.

b'olsutaal'eek' *n.* axon.

b'onkik' *n.* hemoglobin.

ch'emna'yu'am *n.* prokaryotic cell.

ch'uut ich'mul *n.* nervous system.

hilhookilna'yu'am *n.* homeostasis.

ich'mej *n.* nerve.

iyajib'aal *n.* chromosome.

jek'cha'alil chi rix *n.* exocrine gland.

jek'cha'alil chi sa' *n.* endocrine gland.

jek'muriil *n.* meiosis.

jek'pojk'ok *n.* meiosis.

julel *n.* vacuole.

junilna'yu'am *adj.* unicellular.

kaqkik' *n.* hemoglobin.

kaqkil mitz'kotkik' *n.* red blood cells.

kawub'l *n.* protein.

kok'cha'al *n.* organelle, inner cell components.

kolb'a'ich'mulej *n.* meninges.

k'ilana'yu'am *adj.* pluricellular, multicellular.

k'ub'lb'eeleb'aal na' yu'am *n.* endoplasmic reticulum.

k'uub'aal sam *n.* pituitary gland.

k'uub'aal xeeb' *n.* sebaceous gland.

k'uub'suutaalkik' *n.* circulatory system.

latztz'in *n.* dextrine.

mitz'cha'al *adj.* microscopic.

mitz'k'amk'ot *n.* ribosome.

mitz'k'icha'al *n.* microorganism.

na'yu'am *n.* cells.

nawyu'am *n.* biology.

pojk'ok *n.* mitosis.

poyanimil nawyu'am *n.* human biology.

ralyu'amej *n.* embryo.

ratz'amilq'olch'iich' *n.* nitrate.

saqkil mitz'kotkik' *n.* white blood cells.

sooto'y *n.* digestive system.

tz'aqalna'yu'am *n.* eukaryote.

tz'ilol *n.* vacuole.

xb'een pojk'ok *n.* prophase.

xchaqijik *n.* dendrite.

xka pojk'ok *n.* telophase.

xk'anjel *n.* function.

xk'ub'lal ich'mul ak re *n.* parasympathetic autonomic nervous system.

xk'ub'lal ich'mul yal jo' *n.* autonomic nervous system.

xk'ub'lal ich'mulej xtaq rib' *n.* autonomic nervous system.

xmurinkil rib' *n.* mitosis.

xna'yu'am *n.* cell (biological).

xpaayil kawub'l *n.* enzyme.

xtuslal'ich *n.* central nervous system.

xtzuumal xna'yu'am *n.* cell membrane.

xtz'aqob'cha'al *n.* gland.

xwaxil rumetz'ew *n.* adrenaline.

xxulel kik'el *n.* red blood cells.

xya'alna'yu'am *n.* cytoplasm.

xyich'ool xna'yu'am *n.* cell nucleus, nucleus.

xyihil xk'ub'lal ich'mulej *n.* central nervous system.

xyihil xk'ub'lal ich'mulej *n.* neuron.

yu'am *n.* life.

yu'amej *n.* life.

Nawyu'amilsutaal / Ecology

ak'ob'resink *adj.* renewable.

ak'oresiil *adj.* recyclable.

b'ook-iq' *n.* oxygen.

b'ookol *n.* oxygen.

choxach'och' *n.* nature. *Var:* ru choxach'och'.

chun *n.* lime (stone).

ch'och' *n.* land, soil. *From:* ch'och' 'earth, land' (Q'anjob'alan) (4).

eechej *n.* resource.

eechej che'k'aam *n.* natural resources. *Var:* eechel che'k'aam.

eechej ch'och' *n.* natural resources.

ha' *n.* water.

ilok ib' *n.* sustainability.

iq' *n.* wind.

ka'awb'il *n.* reforestation.

ka'awk *v.* to reforest, reseed.

ka'oksink *v.* to recycle, reuse.

kik'che' *n.* rubber, latex.

kolb'il che'k'aam *n.*
ecological preserve.

k'iche' *n.* woods, forest.

k'uub'wank *n.* ecosystem.

loq'alil sutam *n.* ecological
values.

petrool *n.* petroleum. *From:*
petróleo 'petroleum' (Spanish) (1).

puukalche'k'aam *n.* flora.

puukalxul *n.* fauna.

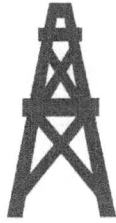

q'olch'och' *n.* oil, petroleum.

rawimal ch'och' *n.* natural
resources.

rin *n.* rubber.

roq saq'e *n.* sunshine.

ruuchiha' *n.* hydrosphere.

sib'eel *n.* carbon.

sutam *n.* environment, area.
Var: suutaal.

usil k'a'aq re ru *n.* raw
materials.

xb'een tasal iq' *n.*
atmosphere, troposphere.

xcha'al *n.* elements.

xch'ajom hab' *n.* alluvial
erosion.

xch'ajom iq' *n.* wind erosion.

xch'ajom saqb'ach *n.* glacial
erosion.

xch'och'il *n.* climate.

xka'awb'il *adj.* reforested.

xka'oksinkil *n.* recycling,
reuse.

**xkolb'al rix li loq'laj
che'k'aam** *n.* resource
conservation.

Amaq'il ut Awab'ejil / Society and Governance

ab'ink *v.* to obey.

ab'liltenamit *adj.* international.

ach'ab'ilal *n.* liberalism.

aj ch'oolanel *adj.* responsible.

aj k'anjel sa' chaq'rab' *n agt.*
civil servant.

aj k'uub'anelchaq'rab' *n.* representative, legislator.

aj mayab' *n.* Maya.

aj mitz-u *n.* Chinese.

aj q'an'isul *n.* American.

aj raholtenamit *adj.* patriotic.

aj taqlanel *n agt.* dictator.

aj tz'ilpoyanam *n agt.* census taker.

ajaw *n.* king, lord.

ajawilxoy *n.* crown.

ajb'il *n.* request.

amaq'il *n.* society.

amaq'il loq'alil *n.* social values.

awab'ej *n.* government.

awab'ej *n.* chieftain, president.

awab'ejilal *n.* government.

awab'ejink *v.* to rule, govern.

aatin *n.* announcement.

b'axton *n.* walking stick. *From:* bastón 'stick used for walking or ceremonial purposes' (Spanish) (1).

ch'och'el *n.* native country.

ch'och'el sululel *n.* culture.

ch'uutal tenamit *n.* United States.

echkab'al *n.* neighbor, inhabitant.

esil *n.* announcement.

esilal *n.* guideline, notice, information.

eeqaj *n.* substitute, retribution.

eetalil *n.* nameplate, sign.

hab'ilhu *n.* birth certificate.

hu chi ru chaq'rab' *n.* government identification, ID.

hutojxoyiil *n.* community beautification tax, city improvement tax.

huxaqalil *n.* government identification, ID.

ixajaw *n.* queen.

jolomil *n.* chieftain.

jolomilal *n.* administration, board of directors.

jolomilk'aleb'aal *n.* civic leadership committee.

jultikob'lhu *n.* agenda.

jultik'anjel *n.* agenda.

junajil *n.* solidarity, unity.

junpak'alpalaw *n.* Europe.

juntaq'eetil *n.* equity, equality.

juntaq'eetil amaq'il *n.* social equality.

kamab'k *n.* mutual help, volunteer work, assistance.

kok'anjel *n.* duty, chore.

komonil *n.* community.

komonilk'anjel *n.* cooperative.

komonilwank *n.* socialism.

komontenq' *n.* cooperation.

k'a'aq re ru li tenamit *n.* public services.

k'ajk'amontzolok *n.* title.

k'amch'oolanink *n.* responsibility.

k'amolb'e *n.* administration, board of directors.

k'ehok *v.* to give, permit. *From:* k'eh 'to give (as a present or libation) (Tzeltal) (3).

k'ila'aatinob'aal *adj.* multilingual.

k'ilana'leb' *adj.* multicultural.

k'ilpoyanimil *adj.* multiethnic, diverse.

k'iilayehom b'aanuhom *n.* multiculturality, diversity.

k'ojarib'aal *n.* throne.

k'uluk ib' *v phr.* to meet.

k'uub'leb'chaq'rab' *n.* congress.

loq'al *n.* worthy, dignitary.

loq'al wankilal *n.* identity.

loq'alil *n.* worthiness, dignity.

loq'alil na'leb' *n.* cultural values.

loq'altenamit *adj.* civic.

loq'-ilok *n.* identity.

mama' tenamit *n.* city.

meej *n.* Mexico.

molam *n.* association.

mu'us *adj.* foreign.

na'leb' xe'toon *n.* custom.

najt xtenamit *n.* stranger.

najtil poyanam *n.* stranger.

nimalraqb'leb'aatin *n.* supreme court.

nimla tenamit *n.* country, city.

nub'aal *n.* boundary, border, property line. *Var:* nub'ajl; **nub'aj.** *From:* nub' 'to join' (Ch'olan) (2).

oxloq'il *n.* respect.

oxloq'il na'leb' *n.* culture.

papelseya *n.* birth certificate. *From:* papel de sello 'sealed document' (Spanish) (1).

patz'b'il *n.* request.

pereera *n.* birth certificate. *From:* fe de edad 'birth certificate' (Spanish) (1).

poqlenk *v.* to register.

poyanimil *n.* humanity.

poopirk *v.* to rule, govern, reign.

qana' *n.* lady.

qawa' *n.* sir.

qaana' *n.* goddess.

rab'in ajwal *n.* princess.

re tenamit *adj.* public.

rehil loq'alil *n.* personal values.

reetalil xyo'lajik *n.* birth certificate.

reetaltenamit *n.* patriotic symbols.

rochoch ruuchilawab'ej *n.* state capital, state house, departmental government.

rochochil ab'lil tenamit *n.* embassy.

rochochil aj k'uub'anel chaq'rab' *n.* congress.

rochochil'awab'ej *n.* palace.

roq ab'yayala *n.* South America.

ruhan *n.* power.

ruq'b'chaq'rab' *n.* decree, order, ruling.

ruuchil ab'l tenamit *n.* ambassador.

ruuchilawab'ej *n.* governor, ruler, delegate.

sachom *n.* budget. *Var:* sachomq.

sahil wank *n.* harmony (social).

sumlaak chi ru chaq'rab' *n.* civil marriage.

sutq'isinb'il *n.* repatriate.

sutq'iik *v.* to repatriate, revert, return.

sutruuchich'och' *adv.* internationally.

sutruuchich'och'ink *v.* to internationalize.

taqlank *v.* to rule, govern.

taqlank *v.* to command, order.

tawloq'aal *n.* civilization.

tawok u *v phr.* to meet.

tenamit *n.* village, town. *From:* tena:mitl 'wall' (Nahuatl) (1).

tenamitil *n.* people.

teneb'aal *n.* obligation.

tenq'ank *v.* to help, protect.

tenq'aal *n.* cooperation.

tenq'aal *n.* help, assistance.

teepalpoopol *n.* municipality.

toj chi ru awab'ej *n.* taxes.

triiw *n.* clan. *From:* tribu 'the clan' (Spanish) (1).

tusk'anjel komonil *n.* community projects.

tz'ilpoyanam *n.* census.

usilal *n.* favor.

uuchininkil *n.* representativity.

wankil *n.* power.

wankilal *n.* kingdom.

waril *n.* guest.

xaqab'ank aatin *n.* contract.

xaq-aatin *n.* contract.

xaaqalhu *n.* government identification, ID.

xch'ajom ajwal *n.* prince.

xch'olch'ookil amaq'il *n.* social security.

xhuhul tenamit *n.* government identification, ID.

xjolom ab'yayala *n.* North America.

xjolomiltenamit *n.* capital.

xjuntaq'eetil xwinqul *n.* gender equality.

xk'ulub'poyanam *n.* human rights, civil rights, rights. *Var:* xk'ulub'eb' poyanam.

xk'uyb'al *n.* tolerance.

xmolamil k'iila tenamital *n.* United Nations.

xna'ajil tz'iib'ahom k'ab'a'ej *n.* civil registry.

xnimal raqb'a chaq'rab' *n.* supreme court.

xoq'jaw *n.* queen.

xtenamitil *n.* nationality.

xtenamitil ilob' *n.* national identity.

xtenq'ankil *n.* help, assistance.

xtz'iib'ankil li yo'lajik *n.* birth registry.

xuq' *n.* walking stick, baton. *Var:* xuq'y; xuq'l. *Note:* A symbol of authority in Q'eqchi' local government.

xye ab'yayala *n.* North America.

xyi ab'yayala *n.* Central America, Mesoamerica.

yehol'esilal *n.* bulletin, news.

yiib'ejilch'och' *n.* Central America, Mesoamerica.

yo'lajik *n.* birth.

yo'lhu *n.* birth certificate.

yu'aminb'il *n.* customs.

Junajch'oolej / Democracy

aj jolominel *n agt.* authority.

aj jolominel k'aleb'aal *n.* mayor, town leader.

aj juch'unel *n agt.* voter.

aj okenel chi awab'ejink *n agt.* candidate.

aj tenamit *n.* citizen.

aj yalol u chi awab'ejink *n agt.* politician.

b'oot *n.* election. *From:* vota 'the vote' (Spanish) (1).

b'ootib'k *n.* ballot.

ch'uut awab'ejilal *n.* political party.

eeqajink *v.* to represent.

juch'uk *v.* to vote.

junajch'oolej *n.* democracy.

k'ulub' *n.* rights.

k'ulub'em *n.* rights.

nawchaq'rab'ik *n.* legislation.

pukta'esil *n.* propaganda.

q'unb'esink *v.* to campaign.

sahilwank *n.* democracy.

sik'ok-u *n.* election, choice.

uuchilej *n.* representative.

uuchilink *v.* to represent.

xaqab'ank *v.* to elect, vote, name, propose, nominate.

xb'ehil ru k'anjel *n.* bureaucracy, agenda.

xb'eenil awab'ej *n.* president.

xb'eenil poopol *n.* mayor.

xchaq'rab' li tenamit *n.* constitution.

xjolomil awab'ejilal *n.* cabinet (presidential).

xkab'awa'b'ejil *n.* vice president.

xkab'il awab'ej *n.* vice president.

xk'ub'ankil ru chaq'rab' *n.* bill (legislative).

xwankilal b'aanunel *n.* executive power.

xwankilal chaq'rab'inel *n.* legislative power.

xwankilal raqonel *n.* judicial power.

yehokb'aanunk *n.* campaign.

B'eek ut B'eleb'aal / Travel and Transportation

aj b'eresinelch'iich' *n agt.* pilot, driver, chauffeur.

aj b'eenel *n agt.* passenger.

aj ch'e'ol ch'iich' *n agt.* pilot, driver, chauffeur.

aj kawaayach'iich' *n.* motorist.

aq'ab'ank *v.* to brake.

b'eek *v.* to travel, walk.

Var: b'ehek.

b'eenink *v.* to travel around, travel.

b'iismetz'ew *n.* amp meter.

b'ookha' *n.* methane.

b'ookhumha' *n.* kerosene.

b'ookilxaml *n.* propane.

chi nim *adv phr.* to the right.

chi tz'e *adv phr.* to the left.

ch'oolmetz'ew *n.* motor.

eek'metz'ew *n.* motor.

hiltasib'aalch'iich' *n.* parking lot.

homtol'iq' *n.* inner tube.

humb'ookilha' *n.* gasoline, gas,

humb'ookilha' *n.* kerosene.

iq'ob'aal *n.* inner tube.

iq'xaml *n.* propane.

jumha'elch'iich' *n.* gasoline, gas,

kawaayach'iich'inb'il *adj.* motorized.

kax'olb' *n.* lubricant, cooking oil.

kax'olb' poych'iich' *n.* motor oil.

kuukb'eleb'ch'iich' *n.* body work, metal carriage insert.

k'atolch'iich' *n.* catalytic converter.

k'ehob'a iq' *n.* air pump.

k'eleb' iq' *n.* air pump.

k'uub'kutha' *n.* water pump.

k'uulmetz'ew *n.* accumulator, storage battery.

leplepb'aal *n.* pedal.

lit'b'e *n.* brakes.

mama' kaax *n.* steamer trunk.

masleb'ha' *n.* windshield wiper.

metz'ewil *n.* speed, velocity.

najtil *n.* distance.

numilhu *n.* passport.

olb'lit'b'e *n.* brake fluid.

olb'xaqleb' *n.* brake fluid.

pasaaj *n.* fare. *From:* Spanish 'pasaje'.

patz'num *n.* turn signal.

patz'numleb' *n.* turn signal.

paak'ilal *n.* model, make.

pitzk' *n.* spring (metal).

qishumha' *n.* diesel.

q'ochb'il noq' ch'iich' *n.* coil.

ralpuub' *n.* gas dispenser.

raq'metz'ewanb'il eeb' *n.* escalator.

raanil *n.* speed, velocity.

releb'aalsib' *n.* exhaust pipe.

ruk'a ch'iich' *n.* gasoline, gas, diesel, fuel.

ruk'a'il lit'olb' *n.* brake fluid.

sob'olal *n.* dent.

tamleb'aal metz'ew *n.* battery.

tuqtiq *n.* radiator.

tzub'pajha' *n.* water pump.

tz'amb'ahilch'iich' *n.* chassis.

tz'ilb'akax'olb' *n.* oil filter.

tz'ileb' olb' *n.* oil filter.

wosleb' *n.* radiator.

xaqleb' *n.* brakes.

xche'el kaxolb' ch'iich' *n.* dipstick.

xch'ool ch'iich' *n.* motor.

xkax'olb' poych'iich' *n.* oil, motor oil.

xkumb'il ruk'a' poych'iich' *n.* gas pump.

xk'aamal *n.* belt, strip, drive belt.

xna'aj eetalil *n.* dashboard.

xna'aj iq' *n.* air compressor, compressor.

xtaab'il xsa' *n.* fan belt.

xya'al b'eleb'aal *n.* gasoline, gas, diesel, fuel.

xya'al ch'iich' *n.* gasoline, gas, diesel, fuel.

yuuk'isib'aal *n.* carburetor.

Choxahil B'eek / Air Travel

aj b'eenel *n agt.* passenger.

aj ch'e'ol so'sol ch'iich' *n agt.*
aviator, airplane pilot.

aj k'anjel sa' so'sol ch'iich'
n agt. flight attendant.

aj k'ehol purik *n.* airline.

b'elahom iiq *n.* luggage tram.

chalik *n.* arrival.

choxahilb'eeleb' *n.* space
shuttle.

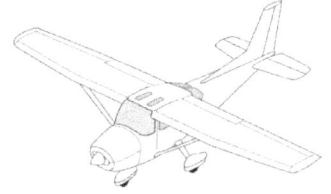

ch'ina so'sol ch'iich' *n.* light
airplane.

elk *n.* departure.

elk sa' najtil tenamit *n.*
international departures.

elk yal sa' xteep tenamit *n.*
domestic departures.

esilal re elk *n.* departing
flights information.

k'ayib'aal b'oleet *n.* ticket
office.

k'aak'aleb'aal *n.* control tower.

k'ochlaak *v.* to land, alight.
Var: **k'ojlaak.**

k'ochleb'aal *n.* airport.

k'ochleb'aal ch'iich' *n.*
runway, landing strip.

na'elk *n.* departures.

**na'ilman xhuhil re najtil
tenamit** *n.* international
check-in.

nak'ulun *n.* arrivals.

nawso'solch'iich' *n.* aviation.

numkawyaab' *adj.* supersonic.

pamb'eeresinb'il *n.* blimp,
dirigible, zeppelin.

purik *v.* to fly.

rupik *v.* to fly. *Var:* **rupupik.**

so'sol ch'iich' *n.* airplane.

sururu *n.* propeller.

tiikil k'ayib'aal *n.* duty free shop.

tulux ch'iich' *n.* helicopter.

xb'ay chaq *adj.* delayed.

xhuhil purik *n.* airfare.

xhuhil purik *n.* plane ticket, boarding pass.

xik so'sol ch'iich' *n.* airplane wing.

xjayal xb'e *n.* airline.

xna'aj so'sol ch'iich' *n.* airport, hangar.

xna'aj taks *n.* taxi stand.

xraqman ru *adj.* cancelled.

xye so'sol ch'iich' *n.* airplane tail, tail wing.

Ch'och'il B'eek / Overland Travel

ach'ab'alhu *n.* license.

amb'ulaans *n.* ambulance.
From: Spanish 'ambulancia'.

b'aqlaq ch'iich' *n.* bicycle.

b'e *n.* road.

b'eleb'aal *n.* transport.

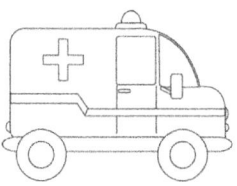

b'eleb'aal yaj *n.* ambulance.
Var: b'eeleb'yaj.

b'eleb'aalch'iich' *n.* bus.

b'eleb'poyanam *n.* bus.

b'eeche' *n.* boardwalk.

b'eek *v.* to travel, walk.
Var: b'ehek.

b'eeresink *v.* to drive.

b'isikleet *n.* bicycle. *From:* bicicleta 'bicycle' (Spanish) (1).

chak'chotk *v.* to run.

ch'ina b'eleb'aal ch'iich' *n.* car.

ch'ina elajinel *n.* turn signal.

ch'ina iiqob'aal ch'iich' *n.* pickup truck.

ch'ina poy ch'iich' *n.* SUV (sport utility vehicle).

68

ch'iich' *n.* car.

ilb'a'ixlem *n.* rear-view mirror.

ilb'anumleb' *n.* traffic signal.

iiqaal *n.* backpack.

iiqaal *n.* cart, wheelbarrow.

jalb'e *n.* path.

jayab'aalb'e *n.* steering wheel.

jek'inel *n.* distributor.

ka'yab'aal ixkej *n.* rear-view mirror.

kamyon *n.* truck. *From:* Spanish 'camión'.

kamyoneet *n.* bus. *From:* camión 'the bus' (Spanish) (1).

kareton *n.* cart, wagon. *From:* carretón 'cart' (Spanish) (1).

kareet *n.* cart. *From:* Spanish 'carreta'.

kawaaya ch'iich' *n.* motorcycle.

kawaayink *v.* to ride (a horse).

kaxsoq' *n.* backpack.

kolten *n.* bumper.

k'aleb'aal poy ch'iich' *n.* Jeep.

k'anti'ch'iich' *n.* train.

k'aak'aleb'aal ch'iich' *n.* police car.

k'ehol numleb' *n.* traffic signal.

k'iche'b'aalik *v.* to travel through the mountains.

k'iche'b'aalik *v.* to travel through the forest.

k'ub' *n.* gearshift.

lemaal'ix *n.* rear-view mirror.

lep ch'iich' *n.* hood.

letzool *n.* backpack.

liseens *n.* driver's license. *From:* licencia 'driver's license' (Spanish) (1).

masleb'ha' *n.* windshield wiper.

mesb'a lem *n.* windshield.

motzo'ch'iich' *n.* trailer truck, semi truck, eighteen-wheeler, box truck.

moot *n.* motorcycle. *From:* moto 'motorcycle' (Spanish) (1).

nimb'e *n.* road.

nimla iiqob'aal ch'iich' *n.* box truck.

nuchkawaay ch'iich' *n.* scooter.

numleb'aal *n.* road, street, route, path, passage.

paattzim *n.* motorcycle.

pekilnimb'e *n.* dirt road, unpaved road.

poy ch'iich' *n.* bus.

q'a *n.* bridge.

q'axleb'aal *n.* footbridge, walkway, gangway, catwalk.

rajlilb'eleb'ch'iich' *n.* license plate.

reetalil b'eleb'aal ch'iich' *n.* license plate.

roq *n.* wheel.

roq poy ch'iich' *n.* wheel, tire.

rueed *n.* wheel. *From:* rueda 'the wheel' (Spanish) (1).

ruqb'e *n.* path.

saajil poy ch'iich' *n.* minivan.

taqe'k chi rix kawaay *v phr.* to ride, go horseback riding, mount a horse.

teken ch'iich' *n.* truck.

tolb'ech'iich' *n.* wheel, tire.

toltol *n.* cart, wheelbarrow.

tool *n.* tire.

tren *n.* train. *From:* tren 'the train' (Spanish) (1).

tz'akalb'e *n.* pavement.

xaqch'iich' *n.* license plate.

xb'aalil *n.* axle.

xb'eelil *n.* wheel.

xcha'aleb' b'eleb'aal ch'iich' *n.* car parts.

xche'el lep ch'iich' *n.* hood support.

xche'el tiikob'aal b'e *n.* steering wheel.

xch'e'b'al *n.* steering wheel.

xk'ihal b'eleb'aalch'iich' *n.* traffic.

xna'aj iiq *n.* trunk.

xook'il ch'iich' *n.* tow truck.

xraqilal xsa' *n.* delivery truck.

xtoch'ol b'eleeb'aal ch'iich' *n.* car accident.

Ha'il B'eek / Water Transport

aj b'ehenel *n agt.* navigator.

aj b'eresinel jukub' *n agt.* sailor, rower.

aj iiqom *n.* ferry.

aj jolominel b'eeleb' *n agt.* captain.

b'aark *n.* boat, ship. *From:* barco 'the boat' (Spanish) (1).

b'eek chi ru ha' *v phr.* to sail.

b'eel *n.* sail. *Var:* b'ela. *From:* vela 'the sail' (Spanish, Portuguese, ?) (1).

b'eeresink jukub' *v phr.* to row.

b'oolha' *n.* wave.

ch'ina jukub' *n.* small boat.

eetaj palaw *n.* Atlantic Ocean.

hilob'jukub' *n.* port.

jaq'e'k *v.* to drown.

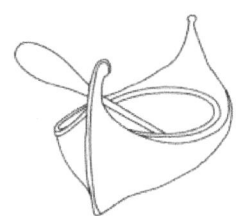

jukub' *n.* canoe, outrigger, boat.

jukub'iiq *n.* ferry.

juyuk *v.* to row. *From:* *juy 'to move' (Ch'olan) (2).

kanaleet *n.* oar. *From:* canaleta 'short, broad oar' (Spanish) (1).

kaxjukub' *n.* motorboat.

kojl *n.* paddle.

kojlenk *v.* to row.

mama' jukub' *n.* ship.

much' jukub' *n.* launch.

muqa'lik *v.* to dive, scuba dive. *Var:* muqa'alik.

numleb'ha' *n.* canal.

numxik *v.* to swim.

nuq'unk *v.* to sink.

ok chi ha' *v phr.* to drown.

pach'lenk *v.* to splash.

pach'ok *v.* to splash.

palaw kariiw *n.* Carribean sea.

paleet *n.* paddle, oar. *From:* paleta 'paddle' (Spanish) (1).

pamamnak *v.* to float.

paq'e'k *v.* to drown.

paq'e'k *n.* drowning.

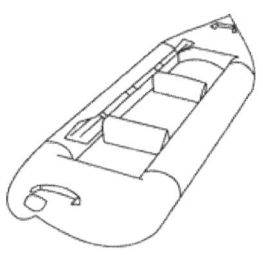

poyte' *n.* raft. *From:* pooyte' 'raft' (Yucatecan, Ch'olan, possible) (2).

poyte'ib'k *v.* to raft.

q'otch'och'ilpalaw *n.* Mediterranean Sea.

rachok *v.* to splash.

repok *v.* to splash.

sob'e'k *v.* to sink, fall.

sub'e'k *v.* to sink. *From:* *suhp' 'to sink' (Ch'olan) (2).

sururu *n.* propeller.

tuulan palaw *n.* Pacific Ocean.

t'ilob'aal *n.* anchor.

xaqleb'jukub' *n.* dock.

xaqleb'jukub' *n.* port.

xik'jukub' *n.* rudder.

xnimalpalaw *n.* ocean, sea.

xolk'ok *v.* to drown.

xookilch'iich' *n.* anchor.

xxaqleb'aal jukub' *n.* dock.

B'ihomal ut Neb'a'il / Wealth and Poverty

ab'l *adj.* somebody else's, other people's. *Var:* ab'.

b'ihom *adj.* rich, wealthy.

b'ihomal *n.* wealth, riches.

b'ihomink *v.* to be rich.

chapok *v.* to take, grasp, hold.

echanink *v.* to earn.

elab'k *v.* to succeed.

elab'k *n.* success.

eechanink *v.* to own, possess.

eechank *v.* to take possession of.

eechej *n.* possessions.

ink'a' xq'ulub'ank *v phr.* to refuse.

jalan aj e *adj.* somebody else's.

jalb'eetink *v.* to lend.

jalok *v.* to lend.

jek'ok *v.* to distribute, share. *Var:* jek'ink. *From:* *jek' 'break off, divide' (Yucatecan, Ch'olan, possible) (2).

kaqcha *adj.* unfortunate, poor.

kok' neb'a' *n.* beggar.

k'a'aq re ru *n.* thing.

k'a'atq ru *n.* thing.

k'aak'alenk *v.* to keep.

k'ehok *v.* to give, permit. *From:* k'eh 'to give (as a present or libation) (Tzeltal) (3).

k'uluk *v.* to get.

neb'a' *adj.* poor.

neb'a'il *n.* poverty.

neb'a'irk *v.* to slowly go broke.

neb'a'o'k *v.* to go broke.

q'ajsink *v.* to give back.

q'unuk *v.* to hold.

rajb'al ru *n.* need, necessity.

sachok *v.* to lose.

sihink *v.* to share.

sik'ok *v.* to look for, seek.

tawok *v.* to get, find.

73

tob'ok *v.* to let go.

toq'ob' ru *adj.* poor.

tz'eqok ib' *v phr.* to lose (a possession).

wan aj eechal re *adj.* owned.

wan aj eere *adj.* private.

wank e *v phr.* to have.

wotzok *v.* to share.

xokok *v.* to keep.

K'ayink ut Loq'ok / Commerce

ab'lilk'ayink *v.* to export.

chaab'il xtz'aq *n.* a good value.

huhil-loq'om *n.* receipt, invoice.

jalok *v.* to trade, barter.

komontoj *n.* value-added tax, VAT.

kotzko *adj.* cheap.

kotzko xtz'aq *n.* sale, bargain.

kub'enaq xtz'aq *n.* sale, bargain.

kub'enaq xtz'aq *adj.* inexpensive, cheap.

k'alomal *n.* goods.

k'asok *v.* to owe.

k'ayink *v.* to sell.

k'uub'k'ay *adj.* industrial.

loq'ok *v.* to buy, purchase.

loq'om *n.* purchase.

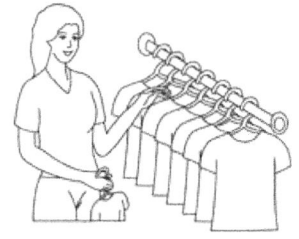

lukleb'aal *n.* clothes rack.

numsink kutan *v phr.* to earn a living.

nuumel ula' *n.* client.

okenk *n.* opportunity.

rosojik k'ay *n.* clearance sale.

rusilal *n.* benefit.

sik'ok ib' *v phr.* to earn.

taqlilk'ay *n.* export, exportation.

toj *n.* tax, tribute, VAT.

tojok *v.* to pay.

tzakink *v.* to earn.

xchapliikroqruq'b' *n.* mortgage.

xhuhil li aatik'aam ch'iich' *n.* telephone bill.

xhuhil li ha' *n.* water bill.

xhuhil li k'uulank *n.* deposit receipt.

xhuhil li saqen *n.* electric bill.

xhuhil loq'om *n.* receipt, invoice.

xhuhil purik *n.* airfare.

xhuhil tojok *n.* payment plan.

xhuhilk'uluk *n.* receipt, invoice.

xtz'aq *n.* value, price.

xwech'b'al xtz'aq *v phr.* to bargain, haggle.

Tumin / Money

aj ajlanel *n agt.* accountant.

aj b'irom tumin *n agt.* accountant.

aj eechal k'uuleb'aal tumin *n agt.* banker.

aj xokol tumin *n agt.* bank teller, teller.

ajlilkomontoj *n.* tax identification number.

ajlilk'uultumin *n.* bank account.

b'ayom *n.* debt.

ch'iich'tumin *n.* coin.

ch'uut tumin *n.* savings account.

eeqajsachomj *n.* voucher, travel allowance.

hu xaqb'anb'il xwankil *n.* IOU, promissory note.

huhiltumin *n.* bills, banknotes.

jun ketzal *n.* one quetzal.

jun senta *n.* one cent, penny. *From:* Spanish 'centavo'.

jun tuxtun *n.* fifty cents, half dollar.

junq eechej *n.* per capita income.

kok' tumin *n.* coin.

kweent *n.* bill. *From:* cuenta 'the bill or account' (Spanish) (1).

k'as *n.* debt.

k'as *n.* account.

k'asib'k *n.* loan.

k'ehok juch' *n.* endorsement.

k'o'al *n.* treasure, savings.

k'ohaal *n.* piggy bank, money box.

k'uul tumin *n.* bank account.

lajeb' ketzal *n.* ten quetzals.

lajeb' senta *n.* ten cents, a dime.

loq'al *adj.* valuable.

loq'leb' *n.* money.

o'k'aal ketzal *n.* one hundred quetzals.

o'laju xk'ak'aal senta *n.* twenty-five cents, a quarter.

oob' ketzal *n.* five quetzals.

oob' senta *n.* five cents, nickel.

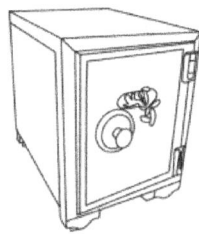

pak'b'il tz'ak *n.* safe.

perhub'aal *n.* cardholder.

po *n.* wages, monthly pay.
From: *poy'a 'moon' (Mixe-Zoquean) (3).

pu'ak *n.* money, metal.
Var: pu'aq; pwaq.

q'uq' *n.* quetzal.

rajliltoj *n.* tax identification number.

raltoj *n.* bonus, award.

raltumin *n.* interest.

sachok *v.* to spend.

sachom *n.* bill, tab, expense.

terto xtz'aq *adj.* expensive.

to' *n.* loan.

to'nink *v.* to lend, loan.
Var: to'onink.

to'nink *v.* to borrow.
Var: to'onink.

tojleb'hu *n.* check.

tumin *n.* money.

xhuhil tojok *n.* payroll.

xhuhiltoj *n.* IOU, promissory note.

xhuhiltumin *n.* check.

xk'eb'al xhuhul tojleb' *v phr.* to write a check.

xk'ulb'al xtz'aq *v phr.* to charge.

xloq'al *n.* value, price.

xna' tumin *n.* account.

xna'aj huhil tumin *n.* wallet.

xna'aj tumin *n.* purse.

xtasal xhuhil tumin *n.* savings passbook, checkbook.

xtz'aq *n.* value, price.

Chankeb' ru li Poyanam / Human Traits

Eek'ahom / Feelings

anchal ch'oolej *n.* excitement, enthusiasm.

anchal xmetzew *n.* elation.

atawank *v.* to want.

ch'inank ch'ool *v phr.* to regret, be sorry.

eek'ahom *n.* feeling, sentiment.

eek'aal *n.* feeling, sentiment.

hob'ok *n.* insult.

jatz'uuchink *v.* to hate.

josq'il *n.* anger, fury, wrath.

kiib'ch'oolink *v.* to regret, be sorry.

kosa *adj.* uncomfortable.

moyok xutaan *v phr.* to hide one's shame.

numsach'ool *n.* emotion.

numsaxch'ool *adj.* emotional.

po'jik *n.* anger.

q'axal us *adj.* good, very good.

ru ch'oolej *n.* moods.

sachb'ach'ool *n.* emotion.

se' *n.* smile.

se'ek *v.* to laugh, smile.

se'se'il ch'oolej *n.* sense of humor.

waxerk *n.* anger.

woqxeel *n.* ebullience, boiling point.

xaqalch'ool *n.* attitude.

xik'uchink *v.* to hate.

xiw *n.* fear, fright, dread. *From:* xiw 'to fear' (Q'anjob'alan) (3).

xiw xiw *adj.* dangerous.

xiwxiw *n.* danger.

xutaan *n.* shame, embarrassment.

xutaanal *adj.* ashamed, embarrassed.

xya'al u *n.* tear.

yaab'ak *v.* to cry, shriek.

yot'ik *n.* anxiety.

yot'ok ch'ool *v phr.* to regret, be sorry.

77

Rahok ut Rahilal / Love and Pain

ajok *n.* desire, attraction.

anchal xch'ool *n.* passion.

atawank *n.* longing, temptation.

aylok *v.* to cry out (in pain).

aakan *n.* agony.

aakanak *v.* to have nightmares.

aatinank *v.* to have sexual relations.

chaq'al ru *adj.* beautiful, pretty.

ch'a'ajkilal *n.* annoyance.

ch'i'ch'i' *n.* agitation.

ch'ina us *adj.* beautiful, pretty.

ch'inaak ch'ool *n.* frustration.

ch'ool re *n.* hope.

ch'um ch'ool *n.* ardent desire.

ink'a' tuqtu xch'ool *n.* insecurity.

jachkab'al *n.* divorce.

jachok-ib' *n.* divorce.
Var: jachoj ib'.

jipo'k *n.* infatuation.

josq'ok *n.* irritation.

junajihom *n.* union.

junes *adj.* alone.

junesal *n.* isolation.

junesal *adj.* alone.

juntaalil *n.* loneliness.

kamenaq xch'ool *n.* dejection.

kaqal *n.* envy, jealousy.

kaqi atawank *n.* envy.

kaq'ok *v.* to blush, turn red.

kawil ch'ool *n.* optimism.

k'a'uxl *n.* sorrow, grief.

k'a'uxlak *n.* anguish.

k'atok oq *v phr.* to commit adultery.

k'ehom uhej *n.* amusement.

k'utuk josq'il *n.* ferocity.

laq'ab'ank *n.* union.

loq'onink *n.* adoration.

lub'k ch'oolej *n.* depression.

maajewank *n.* humiliation.

maak *n.* guilt.

maasahil wank *n.* unhappiness.

mek'onk *v.* to embrace, hug.
From: mek' 'to embrace' (Yucatecan, Ch'olan, possible) (1).

molok *v.* to choose.

muxuk *n.* adultery.

muxuk sumlajik *n.* adultery.

nawok chi yaal *n.* apprehension.

ochb'eninb'il *adj.* together.

ok k'a'uxl *n.* distress.

oxloq'ink *v.* to love, appreciate, respect.

payok *v.* to whisper sweetly.

payok *v.* to fall in love, entrust.

payom *n.* object of a suitor's affection.

po'ok ch'ool *v phr.* to displease.

q'alunk *v.* to embrace, hug.

q'alunk ib' *v phr.* to hug each other.

q'etq'etil *n.* bitterness.

q'oq *n.* pain, sadness.

q'unal *n.* fondness.

q'unil *n.* tenderness.

ra *adj.* painful.

rahil *n.* pain.

rahil ch'ool *adj.* sad.

rahil ch'oolej *n.* grief.

rahil ch'oolejil *n.* sadness, gloom.

rahilal *n.* pain, difficulty. *Var:* raylal.

rahink *v.* to want.

raho'k *v.* to hurt, suffer.

raho'k xch'ool *v phr.* to get sad, sadden.

rahob'k *n.* disappointment.

rahok *n.* love.

rahok *v.* to love.

rahom *n.* love.

rahro *adj.* beloved.

rilb'al xtoq'ob'al *n.* compassion.

sa' komonil *adj.* together.

sachb'ach'oolej *n.* amazement, astonishment.

sachjik *n.* mistake.

sahil *n.* liking.

sahil ch'oolejil *n.* happiness, contentment.

sahilal *n.* affection.

sahilank *n.* delight, pleasure, enjoyment. *Var:* saylank.

sahob'resink ch'ool *v phr.* to please.

sapsapink ib' *n.* despair.

sik'ok u *v phr.* to choose.

sowenal *n.* jealousy.

sowenk *n.* jealousy, zeal.

sumenk ru aatin *v phr.* to promise.

sumlajik *n.* wedding.

sumlaak *v.* to marry.

suunal *n.* boyfriend, girlfriend.

suunuhom *n.* boyfriend, girlfriend.

tihok u *v phr.* to choose.

tiqwok' *n.* arousal.

tiik xch'ool *adj.* faithful, just, righteous.

toq'ob'al u *n.* pity, compassion.

tuq'ixq *n.* virgin, young woman. *Var:* t'ujixq.

tz'eqtanank *n.* contempt.

tz'eqtanaank *n.* rejection.

tz'eqtaanank *v.* to reject.
  Var: tz'eqtanank.

tz'ub'uk u *v phr.* to kiss.

utz'uk u *v phr.* to kiss.

wankil *n.* pride.

xib'esink *n.* fright.

xik aak'a'uxl *n.* caring.

xikenaq xch'ool *adj.* in love.

xik' ilok *n.* hate, hatred, disgust, disdain.

xsum aam *n.* boyfriend, girlfriend, soul mate.

xsum ch'ool *n.* boyfriend, girlfriend.

xulil'aatin *n.* flirtatious remark, flattering compliment.

yib'ok *v.* to be disgusted.

yot'ek ch'oolej *n.* dismay.

yo'nink *v.* to hope.

yumb'eetak *v.* to fornicate.

Ru Ch'oolej / Moods

aj b'atz'unel *adj.* playful.

aj q'em *adj.* lazy.

aj'aj ru *adj.* alert.

ch'a'aj ru *adj.* annoyed.

ch'a'aj treek'a *adj.* uncomfortable.

ch'ich'i re *adj.* grumpy, impatient.

ch'ina xch'ool *adj.* dejected.

hob'il *adj.* offended.

josq' *adj.* angry.

junesal *adj.* lonely.

junesalil *n.* independence.

junesalil *adj.* independent.

kamenaq xch'ool *adj.* depressed.

kaw xch'ool *adj.* proud.

kosa xch'ool *adj.* disappointed, disillusioned.

k'ahil ch'oolej *n.* pessimism.

k'ojk'o xch'ool *adj.* happy, content.

k'ojla xch'ool *adj.* pleased.

k'uul ru *adj.* sad, self-absorbed.

maak'a' naraj wi' *adj.* indifferent, listless.

maausilanb'il *adj.* happy.

moymo ru *adj.* dizzy.

nab'anyoxin *adj.* thankful, grateful.

nach'a'ajko' *adj.* upset.

nasach xch'ool *adj.* surprised, impressed.

naxiwak *adj.* terrified.

q'axal q'un *adj.* mild, meek.

q'etq'et *adj.* proud.

ra xch'ool *adj.* sad, gloomy.

rataw chi us *adj.* excited.

sa xch'ool *adj.* content, glad, happy.

sa' xyaalal *adj.* wary.

sachaamil xch'ool *adj.* surprised, astonished.

sachenaq ru *adj.* confused, puzzled.

sachenaq xch'ool *adj.* amazed.

sahil ch'ool *adj.* happy.

tawajenaq *adj.* tired, weary.

titz'jenaq *adj.* bored.

tk'a'uxlaq *adj.* thoughtful.

toch'ool *adj.* hurt.

tuqtu xch'ool *adj.* content.

tuulan *adj.* mild, meek.

twulaq chi ru *adj.* delighted.

tz'aqal ru *adj.* positive.

tz'eqtananb'il *adj.* humiliated, rejected.

us li naraj *adj.* positive.

usilanb'il *adj.* happy.

xiwajenaq *adj.* scared, afraid, alarmed. *Var:* xuwajenaq.

xul aj al *adj.* mischievous, naughty.

xulil *adj.* mischievous, naughty.

xutaanaq *adj.* ashamed, embarrassed.

yo xiw *adj.* scared, afraid.

yo xjosq'il *adj.* furious.

yo xk'a'uxl *adj.* worried.

yo xsik *adj.* edgy.

yo xwara *adj.* sleepy.

Usil Na'leb' / Positive Traits

aj b'e *adj.* adventurous.

aj cheek *adj.* mature.

aj kayanel *adj.* curious.

aj kuyunel *adj.* calm.

aj k'anjel *adj.* hard-working.

aj num aatin *adj.* talkative.

aj se' *adj.* amusing.

atawal *adj.* ambitious.

chab'il xch'ool *adj.* kind.

ch'aj *adj.* clean.

ch'aj ch'aj *adj.* very clean.

ch'ajmich'aj *adj.* clean.

ch'ajom *adj.* young.

ch'iq *adj.* ambitious.

ch'olch'o nak'anjelak *adj.* organized.

ch'ukch'u xk'a'uxl *adj.* intelligent.

jot'b'il *adj.* combed.

kaw *adj.* strong.

kaw rib' *adj.* brave, courageous, robust, energetic, vigorous.

kaw xmetz'ew *adj.* strong.

kawresil-ib' *n.* self-esteem.

maak'a' naxch'e' *adj.* honest.

na'oxloq'in *adj.* respectful.

nache'ch'ot *adj.* extrovert.

nakayan *adj.* curious.

nakuyuk *adj.* broad-minded.

napaab'an *adj.* obedient.

narataw *adj.* ambitious.

natz'ilok chi us *adj.* meticulous.

nawk'anjelil *n.* professionalism.

naxyoob' rib' *adj.* courageous.

nimal *n.* greatness.

q'un *adj.* humble, tender.

q'un xch'ool *adj.* gentle, peaceful, attentive.

sa *adj.* pleasing.

sa na'aatinak *adj.* friendly.

sa' xse'enkil *adj.* funny, entertaining.

sa' yaal na'aatinak *adj.* realistic.

sak'a *adj.* diligent.

sak'ahil *n.* diligence. *Var:* sak'ahal.

saq ru *adj.* clean.

se'se' ru *adj.* light-hearted.

seeb' *adj.* audacious.

teeto xk'a'uxl *adj.* considerate.

tijb'il *adj.* educated.

tiik ru *adj.* serious.

tiik xch'ool *adj.* faithful, just, righteous.

tiikilal *n.* honesty.

tk'ul ach'ool *adj.* charming.

tuqtu ru *adj.* easy-going.

tustu ru *adj.* organized.

tusul *adj.* organized.

tuulan *adj.* humble, quiet, peaceful.

t'e'b'il *adj.* combed.

t'uj *adj.* spotless.

usilalch'ool *adj.* generosity.

waklesinelch'ool *adj.* motivating.

wan rusil *adj.* useful.

wan xna'leb' *adj.* wise, smart, intelligent.

wankil *adj.* brave.

xaaqilalk'utuk *adj.* masterly.

xchaq'al u *n.* beauty.

xtuulanil *n.* humility.

yal maatoch' *adj.* sensitive.

Yib' aj Na'leb' / Negative Traits

aj atawanel *adj.* greedy.

aj kaqal *adj.* envious.

aj pix *adj.* stingy, petty.

aj sik'onel xyib'al ru *adj.* pessimistic.

aj taqlanel *adj.* bossy.

aj tik'ti' *n agt.* liar.

aj xiw *adj.* shy, cowardly.

aj yop *adj.* cowardly.

aj yoob'anel aatin *adj.* boastful.

b'alak' *adj.* dirty.

ch'ich'i re *adj.* grumpy, impatient.

ch'iq' rik'in k'a re ru *adj.* impatient.

hirook *adj.* disorganized.

ink'a' na'ab'in *adj.* rebellious.

ink'a' na'eek'an *adj.* introverted.

ink'a' na'oken *adj.* passive.

ink'a' na'oxloq'in *adj.* disrespectful.

ink'a' nanawman k'a tb'aanu *adj.* unpredictable.

ink'a' t'e'b'il *adj.* uncombed.

ink'a' us xna'leb' *adj.* dishonest.

jip *adj.* obstinate, stubborn, lazy.

jip *adj.* stupid, foolish, clumsy.

jo'maajo' *adj.* ugly.

jok *adj.* lazy.

jun chi aatin *adj.* gullible.

ka'pak'al u *adj.* hypocritical.

kalajenaq *adj.* drunk. *From:* *kal 'to get drunk' (Yucatecan, Ch'olan, possible) (2).

kaq ru xch'ool *adj.* mean, selfish.

lab' *adj.* bad.

lolob' *adj.* vulgar.

lolom re *adj.* toothless.

maa'al'ixq *n.* sterile (woman).

maa'alwinq *n.* sterile (man).

maak'a' naraj wi' *adj.* insensitive.

maak'a' rusil *adj.* unuseful.

maak'a' xkuyum *adj.* ruthless, vicious.

maak'a' xk'as chi rix *adj.* irresponsible.

maak'a' xmetz'ew *adj.* weak.

maak'a' xna'leb' naxk'ut rib' *adj.* naive.

maak'a' xxutaan *adj.* rude, insolent.

mem *adj.* mute.

moko naxsume ta jo'yaal *adj.* unreliable.

moymo ru xtib'el *adj.* sullen.

nach'a'ajko' *adj.* annoying.

nakujkut *adj.* nosy.

namunta *adj.* arrogant, vain.

nasach sa' xch'ool *adj.* forgetful.

nataqlan *adj.* dominant.

naxik xch'ool *adj.* absent-minded.

naxkuj rib' *adj.* cheeky.

naxk'e reeqaj naxk'ul *adj.* vindictive.

naxk'uula ra sa' xch'ool *adj.* spiteful.

ninqilwank *n.* irresponsibility.

ninqilwankil *adv.* irresponsibly.

ninqiwank *adj.* irresponsible.

numjip *adj.* stubborn.

numlab'al *n.* cruelty.

numtaak *adj.* proud.

pes *adj.* dirty.

pix *adj.* stingy.

pixilk'a'uxl *n.* egocentrism.

84

q'emkun *adj.* lazy.

q'emkunal *n.* laziness.

q'etq'etil *adj.* negative.

q'eel *adj.* old.

rahob'tesink wank *n.* vulnerability.

sik *adj.* lame, paralyzed.

sowen *adj.* jealous. *Var:* sowem.

t'inis *n.* heavyset person.

t'omt'o re *adj.* toothless.

t'onos *adj.* fat.

t'ont'on xyaab' *adj.* clamorous.

tzukinb'il ru *adj.* disorganized.

tz'aqal re ru naraj *adj.* strict.

tz'i'b'eetal *adj.* abject, vile.

tz'i'ej *adj.* immoral.

wech' re *adj.* fussy.

wenb'enk ib' *v.* to brag, boast, show off.

xa'b'eetal *adj.* ugly.

xik' ru *adj.* strange.

xiwxiwil *n.* insecurity.

yajti'ox *n.* idiot.

yal k'a' naxb'aanu *adj.* restless.

yal naxkuti rib' *adj.* impulsive, rash.

yal sa' re naxik *adj.* talkative.

yal yalok re *adj.* insecure.

yib' ru *adj.* ugly, bad. *Var:* yib'i ru.

yib' yib' *adj.* revolting.

yib'ob'aal ru *adj.* dirty.

yiib'na'leb' *adj.* negative.

yo rix *adj.* moody, ill-tempered.

Chi rix li Kab'l / Around the House

b'onb'il ochoch *n.* painted house.

kaxmuheb'aal *n.* tent.

kab'l *n.* house. *Var:* kab'.

k'imal kab'l *n.* straw hut.

ochoch *n.* house.

ochochil *n.* habitation.

paapa'x *n.* hut. *Var:* papa'ax.

po'lem kab'l *n.* hut, cabin.

Xcha'al Ochoch / House Parts

arko *n.* arch. *From:* arco 'the arch' (Spanish) (1).

b'aqsotz' *n.* rafter.

b'entaan *n.* window. *From:* ventana 'the window' (Spanish) (1).

b'oqleb'aal *n.* doorbell.

champa *n.* doorpost. *From:* jamba 'the doorpost' (Spanish) (1).

ch'och' *n.* floor.

ch'uukib'aal *n.* window.

eeb' *n.* step. *From:* *e'ehb' 'the ladder' (Ch'olan) (2).

kantaaw *n.* lock. *From:* candado 'the lock' (Spanish) (1).

kapoteer *n.* peg. *From:* capotera 'peg ?' (Spanish) (1).

kaxlankaq' *n.* false ceiling, sub ceiling.

kuuk *n.* wall.

k'aan *n.* latch, door-bolt.

k'imal kab'l *n.* thatch.

k'imalch'iich' *n.* tin roofing sheet. *Var:* k'imch'iich'.

k'ub' *n.* handle, lever.

k'ulb'lem *n.* security door.

laaw *n.* key. *From:* llave 'the key' (Spanish) (1).

lem *n.* window pane.

lokoch *n.* peg.

lukub'al *n.* peg.

nat'leb' *n.* latch, door-bolt.

okeb'aal *n.* door, gate, entry, entrance. *Var:* okleb'aal; rokleb'aal.

oqech *n.* post, pole, beam, column.

oqechch'iich' *n.* metal beam.

pak'b'il *adj.* earthen, made of clay.

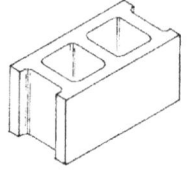

pak'b'il tzak *n.* clay brick, cinder block.

pweert *n.* door, gate. *From:* puerta 'the door' (Spanish) (1).

q'ut *n.* adobe.

ramch'iich' *n.* shutters.

re kab' *n.* door, gate.

rokeb' xlaawil kab'l *n.* door lock.

rokeb'aal saqen *n.* window, skylight.

ru ch'och' *n.* floor.

ru tz'ak *n.* wall.

ru tz'amb'a *n.* ceiling.

saqenk'im *n.* ceiling light, transparent roof panel, skylight.

taqleb'aal *n.* steps.

tz'ak *n.* wall. *From:* *tz'ahk 'wall' (Ch'olan) (1).

tz'amb'a *n.* ridgepole, beam. *From:* tz'am 'beam' (Western Mayan) (3).

tz'apleb' *n.* lock.

tz'apokeb'ch'iich' *n.* security door, metal door.

xan *n.* brick, adobe.

xb'e ch'o *n.* rafter.

xb'een kab'l *n.* roof.

xna'aj xam *n.* fireplace.

Xna'ajeb' li Kab'l / House Places

cha'jleb'aal *n.* laundry room.

chi re xam *n.* kitchen, cookhouse.

eeb' *n.* staircase.

hilaal *n.* living room.

jaleb'aal *n.* hall.

kuukch'iich' *n.* balcony.

kwaart *n.* room. *From:* cuarto 'the room' (Spanish) (1).

k'ub' *n.* fireplace.

k'uub'leb'aal *n.* kitchen, cookhouse.

neb'a *n.* patio.

neb'aal *n.* yard, court, atrium.

neb'aal kab'l *n.* front yard.

ramleb'ch'iich' *n.* balcony.

rub'el kab'l *n.* basement.

tz'akal'ochoch *n.* terrace.

wa'leb'aal *n.* dining room.

warib'aal *n.* bedroom, dormitory.

xb'een che' *n.* attic.

xb'een tasal kab'l *n.* ground floor.

xmu kab'l *n.* hallway.

xna'aj b'eleb'aal ch'iich' *n.* garage.

xna'aj k'a'aq re ru *n.* utility room.

xna'aj k'anjeleb'aal *n.* workshop.

xna'aj k'ula'al *n.* baby room.

xna'aj k'uleb'aal *n.* cellar.

xna'aj tzolok *n.* study.

xna'aj xam *n.* cookhouse.

xramleb' ilob'aal *n.* balcony.

Atinleb'aal / Bathroom

atib'aal *n.* bathroom, shower.

b'arxab'on *n.* bar soap.

ch'ejej *n.* tile.

hu re li k'otak *n.* toilet paper.

ji'b'al e *n.* brush.

johob'a mach *n.* razor.

johok *v.* to shave.

jooleb' *n.* razor.

jooleb'mach *n.* razor.

k'otleb'aal *n.* toilet, latrine.

laasp re xtz'uumal e *n.* lipstick.

lem *n.* mirror.

lemtz'un xan *n.* tile.

nawaaj *n.* razor. *From:* navaja 'knife' (Spanish) (1).

noq' re uuch e *n.* dental floss, floss.

releb'tz'ajha' *n.* drain.

roq ha'il tzaj *n.* drain.

sasalxab'on *n.* shampoo.

sepiiy *n.* brush. *From:* cepillo 'the brush' (Spanish) (1).

setleb' ixi'ij *n.* nail clippers.

sob'sob'k'uub' *n.* sponge.

sununkil b'ook *n.* lotion, perfume.

tapon *n.* stopper. *From:* from tapón (Spanish).

teeleb'ha' *n.* faucet, water tap.

tiqwal ha' *n.* hot water.

tuwaay *n.* towel. *From:* toalla 'the towel' (Spanish) (1). *Var:* **tohaay**.

t'ikr re chaqob'resink uq *n.* hand towel.

tz'eqleb'aal *n.* toilet.

woqx *n.* foam, bubble.

woqx re joohok *n.* shaving cream.

xab'on *n.* soap. *From:* jabón 'the soap' (Spanish) (1).

xampu *n.* shampoo. *From:* English 'shampoo'.

xileet *n.* razor blade. *From:* French "Gillete".

xiyab' *n.* comb, hairbrush.

xna'aj b'an *n.* medicine cabinet.

xna'aj ha' re atink *n.* bathtub.

xna'aj xab'on *n.* soap dish.

xsununkil sa' tel *n.* deodorant.

xteeb'al ha' *n.* faucet, water tap.

yulb'ilb'on *n.* nail polish.

K'uub'leb'aal / Kitchen

ak'ach *n.* kettle.

almul *n.* basket. *From:* almud 'basket ?' (Spanish) (1).

b'anha' *n.* chlorine, bleach.

b'ut'leb' *n.* funnel.

chakach *n.* basket.

chiqleb' *n.* pans.

chiqleb' *n.* stove.

chupuk *v.* to extinguish, blow out.

ch'ajleb' *n.* sink.

ch'ajleb' sek' *n.* dishwasher.

ch'ajleb'aal sek *n.* dishwasher.

ch'inkumb' *n.* pail.

ch'iich' re setok *n.* cleaver.

ch'och' uk'al *n.* clay pot, earthenware.

estuuf *n.* stove. *From:* estufa 'the stove' (Spanish) (1).

hux *n.* whetstone.

jisleb' *n.* grater.

jokleb' *n.* spoon.

jorinkleb' *n.* toaster.

jotzleb' *n.* peeler.

joomuk'al *n.* pot.

joor *n.* oven. *From:* Spanish 'horno'.

ka' *n.* grinding stone.

kaqcha *n.* firewood.

kaxjoom *n.* washbasin, washbowl.

kaxkojl *n.* mixer.

kaxlan chiqleb' *n.* stove.

kaxxaml *n.* stove.

kaax *n.* drawers. *From:* Spanish 'cajas'.

keho'k *v.* to freeze.

kehob'resib'aal *n.* freezer.

kehob'resilb'aal *n.* refrigerator, fridge.

keeleb'aal *n.* refrigerator, fridge.

kok' ch'iich' re wa'ak *n.* cutlery, silverware.

k'atink *v.* to burn.

k'atk *v.* to burn.

k'atok *v.* to burn.

k'ehok xam *v phr.* to light.

k'ileb'aal *n.* toaster.

k'orechib'aal *n.* toaster.

k'orleb' *n.* toaster.

k'ulb'a tz'aj *n.* apron.

laat *n.* tin, can, canister. *From:* lata 'tin or can' (Spanish) (1).

lechleb' *n.* lighter.

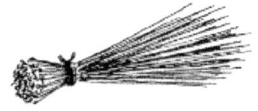

mesleb' *n.* broom.

metz'ewilpuch'leb' *n.* washing machine.

meet *n.* glass, bottle, container. *From:* limeta 'bottle of wine' (Spanish) (1).

mikro oont *n.* microwave oven.

mul *n.* garbage, trash.

mulel *n.* garbage, trash.

nat'b'il uk'al *n.* pressure cooker.

nimla lek *n.* ladle.

pak'b'il *n.* pottery.

pomleb' *n.* grill, roasting pan.

pomleb'aal tzakahemq *n.* microwave oven.

pomok *v.* to broil, grill, roast, fry.

poqxab'on *n.* detergent.

porselaan *n.* porcelain. *From:* Spanish 'porcelana'.

poos *n.* match. *From:* fósforo 'the match' (Spanish) (1).

puch'leb' *n.* washbasin, washbowl.

puch'leb'aal ch'iich' *n.* washing machine.

puq'leb' *n.* blender, mixer.

q'ixaml *n.* stove.

releb'aal sib' *n.* chimney.

releb'sib' *n.* chimney.

reepri *n.* refrigerator, fridge. *From:* Spanish 'refrigeradora'.

reetalil k'uub'ank *n.* recipe.

saqb'achleb'aal *n.* freezer.

si' *n.* firewood.

soq' *n.* net bag, rope net.

tamb'aha' *n.* washbasin, washbowl.

tasal *n.* shelf.

t'anruche' *n.* shelf.

tz'ab'ok *v.* to light.

tz'alamche' re setok *n.* cutting board.

tz'aptz'ookil uk'al *n.* pressure cooker.

tz'ileb' *n.* strainer, colander, sieve.

xb'ehil sib' *n.* chimney.

xhuhuil'esil *n.* recipe book.

xna'aj elaat *n.* freezer.

xna'aj kape *n.* coffee maker.

xna'aj tzakahemq *n.* pantry.

xta ru sa'ej *n.* apron.

xxaaril kape *n.* coffee pot.

xxaaril te *n.* teapot.

yatz'leb' *n.* juicer, juice press.

yuuleb' *n.* mixer, beater.

Xna'aj K'anjeleb'aal / Workshop

b'on *n.* paint.

b'oot *n.* bucket, pail. *From:* Spanish 'bote'.

chaab' *n.* watering can.

chupleb'xaml *n.* fire extinguisher.

ch'ina k'arch'iich' *n.* hacksaw.

eswaayr *n.* square. *From:* Spanish 'escuadra'.

hitb'arch'iich' *n.* screwdriver. *Var:* jitob'arch'iich'.

hitleb' kotox ch'iich' *n.* screwdriver.

hopleb' *n.* drill, hole punch.

hopleb'che' *n.* drill, hole punch.

hopleb'tz'ak *n.* drill.

iiqaal *n.* cart, wheelbarrow.

jachleb'aal che' *n.* chainsaw.

ji'leb' *n.* sandpaper.

ji'leb' *n.* file, rasp.

jotzleb' *n.* chisel, awl, scraper.

kaxchaj *n.* flashlight.

kaaxukuutleb' *n.* square.

lekleb' *n.* shovel. *Var:* lek.

lekleb'ch'och' *n.* shovel.

machb'onleb' *n.* brush.

meex re k'anjelak *n.* workbench.

pikleb' *n.* chisel.

rastriiy *n.* fork, pitchfork, rake. *From:* rastrillo (Spanish) (1).

rochochil k'anjel *n.* workshop.

tikil che' *n.* ruler.

toltol *n.* cart, wheelbarrow.

tuqb'iis *n.* level.

tuqleb' *n.* level.

t'ojleb' *n.* hammer.

tz'alamch'iich' *n.* machete.

xeer *n.* saw. *From:* sierra 'the saw' (Spanish) (1).

xk'aamal saqen *n.* extension cord.

Xna'aj K'a'aq re ru / Utility Room

aq' re puch'e'k *n.* laundry.

heleb' puch'um *n.* clothesline.

ji'leb'aal *n.* iron.

ji'leb't'ikr *n.* iron.

jiq'leb'mul *n.* vacuum cleaner.

kub'eet *n.* bucket. *From:* Spanish 'cubeta'.

kumb'i'uk'al *n.* bucket.

saqi aq' *n.* clean laundry.

tz'alam re ji'ok aq' *n.* ironing board.

xb'anol suq *n.* bug spray, insecticide.

xchakachil aq' *n.* laundry basket.

xchakachil mul *n.* wastebasket, trash can, garbage can.

xb'eeresib'aal k'ula'al *n.*
baby walker.

xna'aj mul *n.* wastebasket,
trash can, garbage can.

xra'al ch'o *n.* mousetrap.

<u>Xna'aj K'ula'al / Baby Room</u>

ab' *n.* swing.

b'atz'uul *n.* toy, game.

xkoral k'ula'al *n.* crib, cradle.

xwaresib'aal k'ula'al *n.*
cradle.

<u>Xna'aj Ula' / Living Room</u>

kaxtzukxul *n.* stuffed animal,
plush toy.

pak'b'il k'uula'al *n.* doll.

panyal *n.* diaper. *From:* Spanish
'pañuelo'.

paach *n.* baby bottle. *From:*
pacha 'the rubber nipple' (Spanish)
(1).

poy'al *n.* doll.

tu'unil *n.* baby bottle.

t'ikr re maqab' *n.* baby bib.

tzojtzoj *n.* baby rattle.

tz'alamch'aat *n.* crib, cradle.

ab' *n.* hammock.

aj *n.* mat, reed.

alfoombr *n.* rug, carpet. *From:*
alfombra 'the rug' (Spanish) (1).

apusinel na'ajej *n.* fan.

apuul *n.* fan.

b'eexam *n.* torch.

b'omb'il eetalil *n.* painting.

chunleb'aal *n.* chair.

ilob'aal hoonal *n.* wall clock.
Var: ileb'honal.

ilob'aal mu *n.* video.

jalam u *n.* picture.

kanteel *n.* candle. *Var:* kandeel.
From: candela 'the candle'
(Spanish) (1).

kanxam *n.* lamp, lantern,
torch.

kaxmu *n.* television, TV.

kaxwaal *n.* fan.

k'ojarib' *n.* chair.

lampr *n.* lamp, lantern, torch.
From: lámpara 'the lamp' (Spanish)
(1).

lemaal'esil *n.* television or TV.

luhasib'aal *n.* heater.

nimla tem *n.* easy chair.

potztem *n.* couch, sofa.

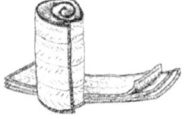

poop *n.* mat.

pumleb'yaab' *n.* stereo.

rochochil tasal hu *n.*
bookcase.

ruhiltz'ak *n.* rug, carpet.

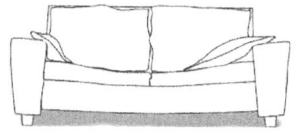

soq'il chunleb' *n.* couch, sofa.

sulem *n.* light bulb.

tem *n.* chair, bench.

t'uuyleb' *n.* hammock, swing. *Var:* **t'uyleb'**.

uutz'u'uj *n.* candle.

waal *n.* fan. *From:* *wahl 'the fan' (Yucatecan, Ch'olan, ?) (2).

xam *n.* lamp, lantern, torch.

xjaar uutz'u'uj *n.* vase.

xn'aj sek' *n.* sideboard.

xn'aj xchahil may *n.* ashtray.

xna'aj hu *n.* bookcase.

xna'aj lemal eetalil *n.* videocassette.

xna'aj uutz'u'uj *n.* vase, flowerpot.

xna'ajtasalhu *n.* bookcase.

xnaq' saqen *n.* light bulb.

xwalub'aal kab'l *n.* ceiling fan.

Warib'aal / Bedroom

aq ru ch'aat *n.* bedding.

chapleb' saqen *n.* plug, socket, outlet (electrical).

chupleb' saqen *n.* light switch, power switch.

ch'aat *n.* bed.

ch'aat re junesal *n.* single bed.

ch'ina meex warib'aal *n.* night table, night stand.

isb' *n.* blanket.

jayil'isb' *n.* sheet.

jolom ch'aat *n.* headboard.

kaax *n.* trunk, box. *From:* Spanish 'caja'.

nimla ch'aat *n.* double bed.

ramleb' saqen *n.* curtain, drape, blind.

rix sok jolom *n.* pillowcase.

roq ch'aat *n.* footboard.

ru ch'aat *n.* mattress, blanket, bedding. *Var:* **ruuch'aat**.

ru warib'aal *n.* bedspread, comforter.

saqenb'aal *n.* lamp. *Var:* **saqen**.

sok jolom *n.* pillow, cushion.

warib' *n.* bed.

xna'aj aq' *n.* dresser, chest of drawers, wardrobe.

xsokel ru ch'aat *n.* mattress.

xta ru ch'och' *n.* rug.

Wa'leb'aal / Dining Room

b'aas *n.* drinking glass. *From:* Spanish 'vaso'.

b'elaal tzakahemq *n.* tray.

isib'aal tapon *n.* corkscrew.

kok' kaxlan wa *n.* rolls.

kuchaar *n.* spoon. *From:* Spanish 'cuchara'.

lanb'alwa *n.* napkin. *Var:* lamb'awa.

lanleb' *n.* napkin.

meex *n.* table. *From:* mesa 'the table' (Spanish) (1).

pikleb' *n.* fork.

pulaat *n.* dish. *From:* Spanish 'plato'.

ru meex *n.* tablecloth.

sek' re kape *n.* coffee cup.

teeleb' *n.* opener. *Var:* teheleb'.

teeleb' laat *n.* can opener.

teeleb' meet *n.* bottle opener, corkscrew.

xna'aj atz'am *n.* salt shaker.

xna'aj kanteel *n.* candlestick.

xna'aj kape *n.* coffee pot.

xna'aj k'aj kab' *n.* sugar bowl.

xna'aj k'aj pens *n.* pepper shaker.

xna'aj murinb'il sa us *n.* salad bowl.

xtameex *n.* tablecloth.

xt'ikrul wa *n.* napkin.

Chi rix li Kab'l / Outside the House

chirleb' *n.* watering can.

ch'ina b'e *n.* path, walkway.

eskaleer *n.* ladder. *From:* escalera 'ladder, stairs' (Spanish) (1).

eeb' *n.* ladder. *From:* *e'ehb' 'the ladder' (Ch'olan) (2).

hoyal *n.* hose.

job'che' *n.* trough.

kira'sleb' *n.* watering can.

mu *n.* sunshade.

na'aj re muhenk *n.* garden shed.

pach'aya' *n.* grass, lawn.

pim *n.* shrub, bush, weeds.

re b'e *n.* fence gate.

releb'aal ha' *n.* fountain.

rokeb'aal b'eleb'aal ch'iich' *n.* driveway.

roos *n.* rose bush. *From:* Spanish 'rosal'.

ru xaml *n.* charcoal.

ruutz'uujil kab'l *n.* flower bed.

setleb' pach'aya' *n.* lawnmower.

setleb' uutz'u'uj *n.* pruning shears.

taqleb'aal *n.* ladder.

tz'alam *n.* garden-house.

xb'eleb'aal ha' *n.* hose.

xna'aj esilhu *n.* mailbox.

xna'aj uutz'u'uj *n.* flowerbed, flower garden.

xneb'a' rix kab'l *n.* back yard.

Ech'alal ut Rehil Ilob' / Kinship and Identity

amaq' *n.* clan.

ixqilal *n.* femininity, females.

oxloq' ilob' *n.* cultural identity.

poyanam *n.* human.

poyanamilal *n.* ethnic group.

puukalil *n.* generation.

ralch'och'il *n.* ethnicity.

reetalil iyajil *n.* family tree.

sa' k'ilawank *adj.* intercultural.

teneb'anb'il sa' junkab'lal *n.* family chores.

winqilal *n.* manhood, masculinity, males.

wotzb'aanuhem *n.* interculturality.

xch'uutulal ilob' *n.* ethnicity.

xe'toon *n.* ancestors.

xpaayil tenamitil *n.* ethnic group.

Tz'aqal Qatib'el / Blood Relatives

al *n.* son, child.

alal *n.* son. *From:* *alal 'child' (Ch'olan) (2).

alaleb' *n.* children.

alib' *n.* daughter-in-law (of a man or woman).

amaq'il tenamit *n.* relatives.

anab' *n.* sister (older, of a male).

anab'ej *n.* older sibling.

as *n.* brother (older).

as e *n.* cousin.

asb'ej *n.* older sibling.

asb'ej *n.* brother (generic).

b'alk *n.* sibling-in-law.

b'alk ixq *n.* sister-in-law.

b'alk winq *n.* brother-in-law.

b'eelom *n.* husband.

chaq'na' *n.* older sister.

chaq'na' *n.* sister (older, of a female). *Var:* chaq'b'ej.

chaq'na'b'ej *n.* older sibling.

cha'al *n.* relative.

ch'i'p *n.* last son.

ech alalb'ej *n.* sibling-in-law.

hi' *n.* son-in-law (of a man or woman).

hi'om e *n.* parents-in-law.

ikan *n.* uncle, mother's brother.

ikan na' *n.* aunt. *Var:* ikanna'.

ikaq'b'ej *n.* sibling's child.

inna' inyuwa' *n.* parents (my).

itz'in *n.* brother (younger).

itz'in ixq *n.* sister (younger, of a male or female).

ixa'an *n.* grandmother.

ixqi i *n.* granddaughter.

ii *n.* granddaughter, grandson.

iib'ej *n.* grandchild.

iitz'in *n.* younger brother, younger sister.

iitz'inb'ej *n.* younger sibling.

iitz'in'e *n.* cousin (younger). *Var:* iitz'in we.

junkab'al *n.* family. *Var:* junkab'lal.

ka'na' *n.* stepmother.

ka'yuwa' *n.* stepfather.

kab' alal *n.* stepson.

ka' ralal *n.* stepdaughter.

ko' *n.* daughter. *From:* ko' 'grandmother; sister of the mother of the father' (Ch'olan) (2).

komon *n.* relative, partner, associate. *From:* común 'common' (Spanish) (1).

mam *n.* great grandchild.

mama' *n.* grandfather.

mel *n.* grandparents.

mel *n.* grandfather, great grandfather.

na' *n.* mother.

na' eechej *n.* aunt.

na'chin *n.* grandmother.

neb'a' *n.* orphan.

ral chaq'na' *n.* niece, nephew.

ral we *n.* nephew.

ralal ikan *n.* niece.

ralal xk'ajol *n.* descendants.

ranab' xyuwa' *n.* father's sister.

rab'in *n.* daughter.

ruk' *n.* relative.

taat *n.* father.

teelom i *n.* grandson.

wiheb' *n.* grandchildren.

xb'een alal *n.* first-born.

xchaq'na' na' *n.* mother's sister.

xikin i *n.* great-grandchild.

xikin mama' *n.* great-grandfather.

xikin xa'an *n.* great-grandmother.

xkab' alal *n.* stepson.

xkab' na' *n.* stepmother.

xkab' rab'in *n.* stepdaughter.

xkab' yuwa' *n.* stepfather.

xka' alalb'ej *n.* stepdaughter.

xna' wechb'een *n.* mother-in-law.

xna'chin inna' *n.* great-grandmother.

xna'chin inyuwa' *n.* great-grandfather.

xna' ixaqil *n.* mother-in-law (of a man).

xna' b'eelom *n.* mother-in-law (of a woman).

xrab'in we *n.* niece.

xrabin iitz'in *n.* niece (from a younger sibling).

xrab'in as *n.* niece (from an older sibling).

xyuwa' b'eelomej *n.* parents-in-law.

xyuwa' ixaqilb'ej *n.* parents-in-law.

xyuwa' ixaqil *n.* father-in-law (of a man).

xyuwa' b'eelom *n.* father-in-law (of a woman).

yum *n.* son (of a mother).

yumej *n.* son (of a mother).

yuwa' *n.* father.

yuwa'b'ej *n.* father.

yuwa'b'ejeb' *n.* parents.

yuwa'chin *n.* grandfather.

yuwa'chinb'ejeb' *n.* grandparents.

Poyanam ut Na'no Ru / People and Acquaintances

ab'lil poyanam *n.* foreigner.

aj maatan *n agt.* heir.

aj mu's *n.* Ladino, foreigner. *Note:* Word adopted from other Mayan languages.

amiiw *n.* friend. *From:* Spanish 'amigo'.

as itz'in *n.* neighbor.

b'ab'ay *n.* baby.

chankilal *n.* gender, sex (gender), genre.

cheekel winq *n.* elder (male).

ch'ajom *n.* boy, young man. *From:* *ch'ajom 'young man' (Yucatecan, Ch'olan, possible) (2).

ch'ajomal *n.* youth.

ch'ina ixqa'al *n.* girl. *Var:* ch'inaxqa'al.

ch'ina teelom *n.* boy.

echaalal *n.* partner.

ech-aatin *n.* close friend.

echkab'al *n.* neighbor, inhabitant.

eeqaj *n.* namesake.

ixaqil *n.* wife.

ixaqilb'ej *n.* wife.

ixq *adj.* female.

ixq *n.* woman.

ixqa'al *n.* young woman. *Var:* xqa'al; qa'al.

junaqlil *n.* individual.

junaatal alalb'ej *n.* only child.

kach'in *n.* baby.

kaxlan winq *n.* Ladino, foreigner.

kok'al *n.* children.

komonil *n.* member.

kristian *n.* person, people. *Var:* kristiaan; kristyan; kristyaan. *From:* Spanish 'cristiano'.

k'ajol *n.* child.

k'ehal *n.* crowd.

k'ultiq *n.* connection.

latzlut *n.* Siamese twins, conjoined twins.

lo'y *n.* friend. *Var:* looy.

lo'yil *n.* friendship.

lut *n.* twins. *From:* *lut 'the twins' (Yucatecan, Ch'olan, possible) (2).

malka'an *n.* widow. *Var:* xmalka'an.

mama' *n.* elder (male).

na'chinb'ej *n.* godmother.

nuumel ula' *n.* client.

ochb'een *n.* companion. *Var:* ochb'en.

paab'ajel *n.* confidant.

poyanam *n.* person, people.

saaj al *n.* boy.

saaj ixqa'al *n.* girl.

sumsuukil *n.* married man, married woman.

suunal *n.* boyfriend, girlfriend.

suunuhom *n.* boyfriend, girlfriend.

te'elch'ool *n.* widower.

teelom *adj.* male (of humans).

teelom *n.* man. *From:* *tehlom 'young man' (Ch'olan) (2).

tiix *adj.* old.

tiix *n.* elder, old man, old woman. *From:* *ti'ix 'old woman' (Ch'olan) (2).

tiixil ch'ajom *n.* confirmed bachelor.

tuq'ixq *n.* virgin, young woman. *Var:* t'ujixq.

tz'ob'ay *n.* namesake.

waltatyox ixq *n.* goddaughter.

waltatyox winq *n.* godson.

winq *n.* man.

xma'al ixq *n.* barren woman.

xsum aam *n.* boyfriend, girlfriend, soul mate.

xsum ch'ool *n.* boyfriend, girlfriend.

yuwa'chinb'ej *n.* godfather.

Xsum K'ab'a'ej / Q'eqchi' Surnames

Ak *sur. From:* ak' ('new') (B1).

Akb'al *sur.*

Akte' *sur. From:* akte' (a thorny palm tree) (B1).

Asij *sur. From:* 'asij' (a type of cicada.) (B1).

Ax *sur. From:* A tree, valuable for its hard red wood. (B1).

Aaqam *sur. From:* agouti (dasyprocta) (Span 'cotuza') (B1).

B'a *sur. From:* Spanish 'taltuza' (a type of mole). (B1).

B'aq *sur. From:* b'aq ('bone'). (B1).

B'atz' *sur. From:* b'atz ('monkey'). (B1).

B'eeb' *sur.*

B'in *sur.*

B'ol *sur.*

Chamam *sur. From:* cha ('ashes'). (B3).

Che' *sur. From:* che' ('tree'). (B1).

Chitay *sur.*

Chok *sur.*

Choko' *sur.*

Cholom *sur.*

Chun *sur. From:* chun ('lime'). (B1).

Ch'en *sur. From:* ch'een ('mosquito'). (B1).

Ch'o *sur. From:* ch'o ('mouse'). (B1).

Ch'ok *sur. From:* choq ('cloud'). (B1).

Ch'oko'oj *sur. From:* cho'k'oj ('bat'). (1).

Ch'ub' *sur. From:* ch'ub' ('wasp'). (B1).

Hub' *sur.*

Ik *sur. From:* ik ('chile'). (B1).

Ixim *sur. From:* ixim ('corn'). (B1).

Jalal *sur. From:* jal ('change'). (B3).

Jolom *sur. From:* jolom ('head'). (B1).

Jolomna' *sur. From:* jolom na' ('head' and 'mother' or 'perhaps'). (B3).

Jukub' *sur. From:* jukub' ('canoe'). (B1).

Kab' *sur. From:* kab' ('sweet'). (B3).

Kak *sur.*

Kakaw *sur. From:* kakaw ('cacao'). (B1).

Kal *sur.*

Kan *sur.*

Katun *sur.*

Kaw *sur.*

Kej *sur. From:* kej ('deer'). (B1).

Kol *sur.*

Kuk'ul *sur. From:* k'ul ('receive'). (B3).

Kun *sur.*

Kus *sur.*

Kuwa' *sur.*

K'anti' *sur. From:* k'anti' ('snake'). (B1).

K'as *sur.*

K'i'ix *sur.*

K'im *sur. From:* k'im ('straw' or 'thatch'). (B1).

K'inich *sur.*

K'ol *sur.*

K'oy *sur. From:* k'oy ('chewing gum'). (B1).

K'u *sur. From:* k'u ('volcano'). (1).

K'uk'ul *sur. From:* kuk ('squirrel'). (B3).

Laj *sur.*

Makin *sur.*

Maqs *sur. From:* maqs ('pumice'). (B1).

Max *sur. From:* max ('monkey') (Span 'mico'). (B1).

Maxena *sur.*

May *sur. From:* may ('tobacco' or 'poison'). (B1).

Mes *sur. From:* mes ('wipe' or 'scrub'). (B1).

Mo' *sur. From:* mo' ('macaw') (Span 'guacamaya'). (B1).

Och *sur.*

Oxom *sur. From:* ox ('three'). (B3).

Pa' *sur.*

Pa'aw *sur. From:* aw ('sow'). (B3).

Pana' *sur.*

Paqay *sur.*

Pek *sur. From:* pek ('stone'). (B1).

Pix *sur. From:* pix ('tomato'). (B1).

Po'ow *sur. From:* po' ('rot'). (B3).

Poq *sur. From:* poq ('powder'). (B1).

Poop *sur. From:* poop ('straw mat'). (B1).

Putul *sur. From:* tul ('plantain'). (B3).

Q'a'al *sur. From:* al ('young boy'). (B3).

Q'an *sur. From:* q'an ('yellow'). (B1).

Q'ol *sur. From:* q'ol ('bead' or 'necklace'). (B1).

Rax *sur. From:* rax ('green' or 'blue'). (B1).

103

Sakb'a *sur.*

Sakil *sur. From:* sakil (the seed of plants like melons or squashes). (B1).

Sakul *sur. From:* saq ('white'). (B3).

Sam *sur. From:* sam ('snot'). (B1).

Sawi' *sur.*

Seb' *sur. From:* seb' ('clay'). (B1).

Si' *sur. From:* si' ('firewood'). (B1).

Sis *sur.*

Sub' *sur. From:* sub (a thorny tree). (B1).

Sun *sur.*

Teni' *sur. From:* ten ('hammer'). (B3).

Teyul *sur.*

Tiul *sur.*

Tok' *sur. From:* tok' ('flint'). (B1).

Tun *sur. From:* tun (a hollow wooden musical instrument). (B1).

Tupil *sur.*

Tux *sur.*

Tuut *sur.*

T'ot' *sur.*

T'ox *sur.*

Tzalam *sur. From:* tzalam ('prison'). (B1).

Tzib' *sur.*

Tzib'oy *sur.*

Tz'i' *sur. From:* tz'i' ('dog'). (B1).

Tz'ub' *sur. From:* tz'ub' ('kiss'). (B1).

Xaq *sur. From:* xaq ('leaf'). (B1).

Xe' *sur. From:* xe' ('root'). (B1).

Xi' *sur.*

Xol *sur. From:* xolb' ('flute'). (B1).

Xoy *sur. From:* xoy (a certain weed, also an adornment). (B1).

Xuk *sur. From:* xuk ('corner' or 'angle'). (B1).

Yalib'at *sur.*

Yaxkal *sur. From:* yax ('pincers'). (B3).

Yoob'anb'il K'ab'a'ej / Q'eqchi' Nicknames

B'ex *nick.* Sebastián.

B'it *nick.* Victor. *Var:* **B'itol.**

Kax *nick.* Lucas.

Konsep *nick.* Concepción.

Ku' *nick.* Domingo.

Kux *nick.* Marcos.

Laj *nick.* Alejandro.

Las *nick.* Lázaro.

Len *nick.* Elena.

Lex *nick.* Andrés.

Liik *nick.* Federico.
Liin *nick.* Marcelina.
Liin *nick.* Marcelino.
Lo *nick.* Pablo.
Lool *nick.* Lola.
Lu' *nick.* Pedro.
Lus *nick.* Luz.
Mar *nick.* María.
Mat *nick.* Matilde.
Max *nick.* Tomás.

Mek *nick.* Miguel.
Nat *nick.* Natividad.
Nich *nick.* Dionisio.
Pet *nick.* Petrona.
Rap *nick.* Rafael.
Rik *nick.* Ricardo.
Rob' *nick.* Roberto.
Room *nick.* Rómulo.
Rup *nick.* Ruperto.
Xiwan *nick.* Juan.

Kawilal ut Yajel / Health and Sickness

aatinak rik'in yaj *n.* psychotherapy.
b'ach'al *n.* sprain. *Var:* b'ach'b'il.
b'anleb'aal *n.* clinic, health center.
b'anok *v.* to cure, heal.
b'eleb'aal tem *n.* wheelchair.
b'iqb'ilb'an *n.* ointment.
b'uqux *n.* bump.
chaqi ix *n.* dry skin.
chuq'ub' *n.* hiccough, hiccup.
ch'ich'i'il *n.* stress.
hilank *v.* to rest.
hiil *n.* rest.

jiq'ok ch'ool *v phr.* to breathe deeply.
jiq'ok iq' *v phr.* to breathe rapidly.
jochol *n.* scrape.
kaqpech'in *n.* inflamed, swollen.
kaqxot'ink *n.* red face.
kawal *adj.* healthy.
kawb'aqel *n.* calcium.
kawresinel ch'ool *n.* stimulant.
ke *n.* cold.
k'aj atz'am b'an *n.* bath salts, effervescent salts.

105

k'atal *n.* burn.

k'irtesink *v.* to cure.
Var: **k'irtasink.**

loq'leb'aal b'an *n.* pharmacy, drugstore.

lub'lu *adj.* weak, tired.
Var: **lub'lub'.** *From:* lub' 'tired' (Ch'olan) (4).

may *n.* cigarette, cigar.

may *n.* poison.

mayib'k *v.* to smoke.

metz'ew ich'mulej elkik' *n.* systolic blood pressure.

metz'ew ich'mulej okik' *n.* diastolic blood pressure.

mitz'k'icha'al *n.* microorganism.

nat'ich'mul *n.* blood pressure.

nawcha'al'ixq *n.* gynecology.

nawch'oolej *n.* cardiology.

nawrub'elalink *v.* to diagnose.

nimank ru *v phr.* to worsen.

nimlab'anleb'aal *n.* hospital.

numsink-al *n.* miscarriage.

ojb'ak *v.* to cough.

paq'ek *n.* choking.

patkik' *n.* coagulation (blood).

pojel *n.* pus.

pojk *n.* pus. *Var:* **poj.**

porha' *n.* rash, blister.

poxe'k *n.* blister.

pujkik' *n.* hemmorhage.

q'un *adj.* weak.

ramb'al ru yajel *n.* first aid.

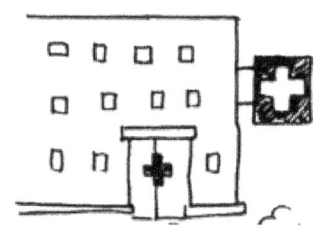

rochochil yaj *n.* hospital.

sa' yu'am *adj.* pregnant.

saqb'et *n.* pallor.

saqb'etin *adj.* pale.

saqb'yino'k *v.* to fainting.

saqijoj *n.* cyst.

saqkirin *adj.* pale.

saqleb' *n.* disinfectant.

saqleb' *n.* leper. *Var:* **saqlep.**

saqmoy *adj.* colorless.

sarampyon *n.* measles. *From:* Spanish 'sarampión'.

saan *n.* wound, sore.

sik *n.* paralytic.

sik'l *n.* cigarette, cigar.

sik'lik *v.* to smoke.

sipook *n.* swelling, inflammation.

siipilal *n.* swelling, inflammation. *Var:* **siip.**

sununkil b'an *n.* ointment.

teb'elal *n.* swelling.

tiq *n.* fever.

tiq'ilal *n.* wound, sore. *Var:* **tiiq'**; **tiq'il.**

tiwb'il *n.* bite.

toqolal *adj.* broken. *Var:* **toqol.**

tuxl *n.* scabies.

t'anliik *v.* to fall sick.

tz'eqok kik' *n.* bleeding, loss of blood, blood loss.

tz'eqok k'ula'al *n.* miscarriage.

usaak *v.* to improve, get better.

xa'aw *n.* vomit.

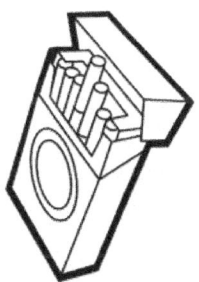

xaqmay *n.* cigarette.

xawak *n.* vomit.

xb'ookil-iq' *n.* oxygenation.

xb'ooxil saqb'ach *n.* ice bag, icepack.

xb'ooxil tiqwal ha' *n.* hot-water bottle.

xka'ha'resinkil *n.* rehydration.

xmetz'ew ich'mulej elkik' *n.* systolic blood pressure.

xraqik *n.* outcome.

xtib' jolom *n.* worry, preoccupation.

xtiwom xul *n.* insect bite.

xxulel yajel *n.* bacteria.

xyajelil *adj.* pathological.

yaj *adj.* sick, ill.

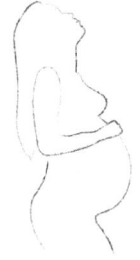

yaj aj ixq *adj.* pregnant.

yajel *n.* sickness, illness, disease.

yajel nab'onok *n.* epidemic.

yajel naxb'on rib' *n.* epidemic.

yajel qatib'el *n.* health problems.

yajelil *n.* sickness, illness, disease.

yajerk *v.* to get sick, sicken.

yeq *adj.* crippled, lame.
Var: **yeeq**.

yok'ol *n.* cut.

yok'olal *n.* injury, wound, sore.

yo'rahil *n.* handicapped.

yu'amil *n.* pregnancy.

yu'amil *n.* life expectancy.

Aj Nawk'anjel Yajel / Medical Professionals

aj aatinanel rik'in yaj *n agt.* psychotherapist.

aj b'anonel *n agt.* doctor, physician.

aj cho'onel *n agt.* surgeon.

aj ilol kamenaq *n agt.* coroner, medical examiner.

aj ilolyaj *n agt.* nurse.

aj ilom yaj *n agt.* paramedic.

aj k'ayinel b'an *n agt.* pharmacist, chemist.

aj nawb'an *n agt.* pharmacologist.

aj nawcha'al'ixq *n agt.* gynecologist.

aj nawch'oolej *n agt.* cardiologist.

aj nawkomonyajel *n agt.* epidemiologist.

aj nawk'anjel yajel *n agt.* medical professional.

aj nawtuqch'ool *n agt.* psychologist.

aj tenq' re b'anok *n agt.* nurse.

aj xokol'al ixq *n agt.* midwife.

aj xokonel *n agt.* obstetrician.

loktor *n.* physician, doctor.
From: doctor 'physician or doctor' (Spanish) (1).

xtenq' aj b'anonel *n agt.* nurse.

Sa' li Uuch Eleb'aal / At the Dentist

aj ilol'uuch-e *n agt.* dentist.
Var: **aj ilol ruuch e**.

aj isihom ruuch e *n agt.* dentist.

aj tenq'anel risihom uuch e
n agt. dental assistant.

aj tiikob'resinel'uuch-e *n agt.*
orthodontist.

b'utb'il uuch e *n.* filling
(dental).

chunleb'aal *n.* dental chair.

eek'ch'iich' *n.* X-ray machine.

ji'leb'-e *n.* toothbrush.

ka' *n.* molar.

k'anjeleb'aal ruuch e *n.*
dental instrument.

lit'ob'l uuch e *n.* braces.

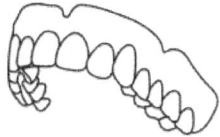

pak'b'il ruuch e *n.* denture.

ruutz'u'ujinkil *n.* crown
(dental).

uuch eleb'aal *n.* dental clinic,
dentist office.

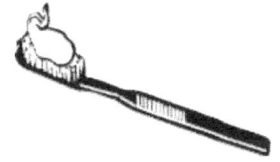

xji'b'al ruuch e *n.* toothbrush.

xq'emal ruuch e *n.*
toothpaste.

xtib'el xtoon ruuch e *n.*
gums, gum tissue.

xul e *n.* cavity.

xulum *n.* broken tooth.

xxab'onil ruuch e *n.*
toothpaste.

Sa' li B'anleb'aal / At the
Hospital

ab'ib'leb'aal aam *n.*
stethoscope.

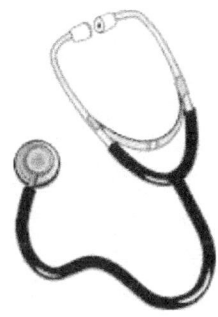

ab'ib'leb'aal yajel *n.*
stethoscope.

ab'ib'leb'aal'ch'ool *n.* stethoscope.

alab'tesib'aal *n.* maternity ward.

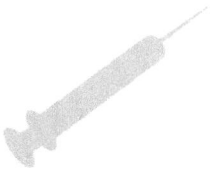

b'akuun *n.* injection, shot, vaccination. *From:* vacuna 'the vaccination' (Spanish) (1).

b'atok *v.* to pack, wrap.

b'eleb'aal tem *n.* wheel chair.

b'isleb'aal *n.* scale.

b'ojok tiq'il *n.* suture.

b'ookol *n.* oxygen.

chaqihob' t'ikr *n.* towel.

cho'ok *n.* operation.

chunt'ikr *n.* cast.

ch'ajleb'aal uq'b' *n.* sink.

Var: ch'ajleb'aal uq'm.

ch'ina chunleb' *n.* bench.

ch'ina ch'aat *n.* cot, stretcher.

ch'ina eetalil *n.* nametag.

ch'ina meex *n.* night table.

eek'ch'iich' *n.* X-ray machine.

eetalil yaj *n.* patient chart.

hulak *n.* visit.

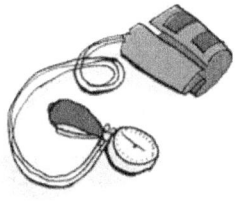

ich'leb'ch'iich' *n.* sphygmomanometer, blood pressure meter.

ich'mulb'an *n.* oral rehydration solution, ORS.

ilok *v.* to examine, check.

ink'a' jultik re *adj.* unconscious.

jultikleb' *n.* call button, buzzer.

junpaatilsachk *adj.* unconscious.

kamna'aj *n.* morgue.

kawub'l kik' *n.* IV, intravenous line.

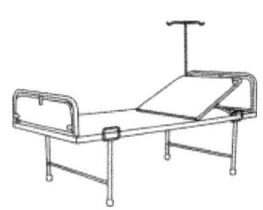

kaxch'aat *n.* hospital bed.

kaxkukay *n.* otoscope.

kaxlan tem *n.* wheel chair.

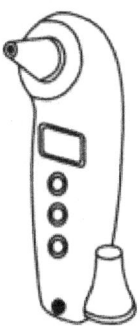

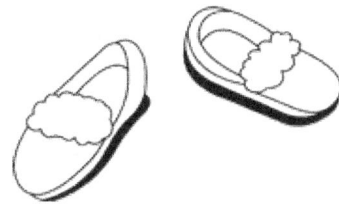

kaxlan xam *n.* otoscope.

kaxsuk *n.* incubator.

kelkookil tem *n.* bench.

kub'sib'aal ru'uj aq' *n.* tongue depresser.

kutb'il b'an *n.* injection, shot.

kutuk *v.* to inject.

kuux *n.* needle. *From:* Spanish 'aguja'.

k'uub'anb'il b'an *n.* oral rehydration solution, ORS.

masleb'ix *n.* towel.

mochleb' ismal *n.* hairnet.

musiq' *n.* respiration. *Var:* musiq'ak.

na'aj re oyb'enink *n.* waiting room.

numsinb'il'eetalil *n.* X-ray.

oyb'eb'aal *n.* waiting room.

pere'xaab' *n.* slipper. *Var:* per xaab'.

potzt'ikr *n.* towel.

q'otq'ookil sek' *n.* bedpan.

ramleb' *n.* bedrail.

ramleb' saqen *n.* curtain, drape, blind.

raq' aj b'anonel *n.* hospital gown.

raq' yaj *n.* hospital robe.

re wartesink *n.* anesthesia.

resilal yajel *n.* medical record.

reetalil b'aq *n.* X-ray plate.

reetalil kik' *n.* blood test.

rilom aj b'anonel *n.* check-up.

ruq' ch'aat *n.* bed crank.

sa' kab'l *n.* room.

sweer *n.* IV, intravenous solution.

tasal hu re ula' *n.* appointment book, visitor log.

tasl *n.* screen (dividing).

toltem *n.* wheel chair.

tz'ileb' rix yajel *n.* lab, laboratory. *Var:* tz'ileb'aal yaj.

tz'ileb'aal *n.* lab, laboratory. *Var:* tz'ileb'aal yaj.

tz'iraych'iich' *n.* call button, buzzer.

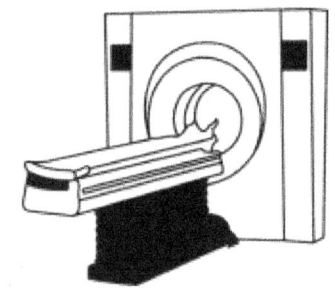

tz'ub'ch'iich'b'il eek'ch'iich' *n.* MRI machine, magnetic resonance imaging.

uk'metz'ewilb'an *n.* oral rehydration solution, ORS.

ula' *n.* visitor, guest.

ula' *n.* visit.

ula'ak *v.* to visit.

ula'anink *v.* to receive visitors.

ula'ank *v.* to visit.

wartesiilb'an *n.* anesthesia.

xb'eeleb'aal yaj *n.* wheelchair.

xb'otb'al chi chunt'ikr *v phr.* cast.

xb'ook iq *n.* oxygen.

xiitink tiq'il *n.* suture.

xjalam'uuchil *n.* X-ray.

xk'anjelob'aal aj b'anonel *n.* surgical instruments.

xmesul cho'ok *n.* operating table.

xna'aj b'an *n.* first aid kit.

xna'aj kamenaq *n.* morgue.

xna'aj nimqal yaj *n.* ICU, intensive care unit.

xsek'ul tz'aj *n.* bedpan, chamber pot.

xtiklajik li yajel *n.* symptoms, disease onset.

xtoltolil b'an *n.* medicine cart.

yaj *n.* patient.

yeksyon *n.* injection, shot. *From:* inyección 'the injection' (Spanish) (1).

yees *n.* plaster. *From:* Spanish 'yeso'.

Sa' li K'ayib'aal B'an / At the
Pharmacy

aj tuqub'anel sa' *n.* antacid,
decongestant.

alkohol *n.* alcohol (isopropyl).
From: Spanish 'alcohol'.

b'an *n.* medicine, remedy.

b'an ha' *n.* sterilized water.

b'an re ixkej *n.* skin cream.

b'an re naq' u *n.* eye drops.

b'an re ojb' *n.* cough drops.

b'an re wark *n.* sleeping pills.

b'an uk'b'il *n.* syrup.

b'an xk'atom saq'e *n.*
sunburn lotion.

b'ane'k *n.* treatment.

b'anol u *n.* ointment.

b'anxxulelyajel *n.*
antibacterial.

b'aqil b'an *n.* suppository.

b'ir *n.* bandage.

b'irb'o *adj.* bandaged,
wrapped.

b'itamin Se *n.* vitamin C.

b'otb'an *n.* capsule, caplet.

b'otb'il b'an *n.* capsule, caplet.

b'otb'il hu *n.* paper roll.

b'ot'leb' *n.* bandage.

chiq'ch'ool *n.* amphetamine.

chunilb'an *n.* antibiotic,
penicillin.

ch'ikb'ilb'an *n.* suppository.

ch'ina b'an *n.* tablet, pill.

huhil sut *n.* tissues, Kleenex.

jaq'ilb'an *n.* air freshener.

jerink *n.* syringe. *From:* Spanish
'jeringa'.

jiq'leb'aal b'an *n.* inhaler.

ka' paay ru *n.* compound.

kawub'lb'an *n.* vitamin.

kaanilb'an *n.* drug, narcotic.

kok' t'ikr *n.* gauze.

kuriit *n.* Band-Aid. *From:*
Spanish 'curita'.

kutleb' *n.* syringe.
Var: kutleb'b'an.

poqilsunob'l *n.* talcum powder, talc.

putzputzb'an *n.* talcum powder, talc.

puutz'leb'aal *n.* nebulizer, spray.

kuutiil *n.* crutch.

k'aj atz'am b'an *n.* bath salts, effervescent salts.

k'aj sut *n.* gauze.

k'aj t'ikr *n.* gauze.

k'ayib'aal b'an *n.* pharmacy, drugstore, chemist.

k'iila b'an *n.* medicine.

k'uulchob' *n.* drawer.

letzb'il b'an *n.* patch.

mertyolaat *n.* iodine. *From:* Spanish 'mertiolate'.

mitz'meetil b'an *n.* vial.

nuq'b'ilb'an *n.* tablet, pill.

olb'il b'an *n.* oil, ointment.

pastiiy *n.* pill, tablet. *From:* pastilla 'pill, tablet' (Spanish) (1).

pomaat *n.* ointment. *From:* Spanish 'pomada'.

poqb'an *n.* talcum powder, talc.

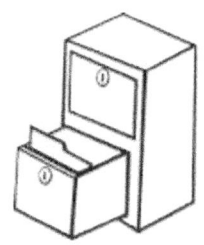

ralmeex *n.* drawer. *From:* Spanish 'mesa'.

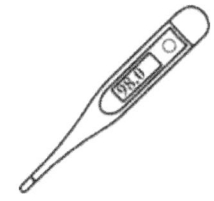

re b'isok tiq *n.* thermometer.

re chajok sa' e *n.* toothbrush.

re chajok tiqil *n.* disinfectant.

re kotzok siip *n.* anti-inflammatory.

re kotzok xrahil *n.* analgesic.

re kubsink rahil *n.* sedative.

re lanok tiq'il *n.* bandage.

re raxkehob' *n.* cold tablets.

re wotz'ok *n.* anti-itch cream.

re xkotzb'al xrahil *n.*
painkiller.

re xkub'sinkil xrahil *n.*
painkiller.

re xmay *n.* antibiotic.

reetalil b'an *n.* prescription.

sunob'resiil *n.* cosmetics.

sut *n.* sling.

tusleb'aal k'ay *n.* shelves.

tuxil noq' *n.* cotton swab.
Var: **tuux noq'; tuuxil noq'.**

t'oq't'ookil b'an *n.* ointment.

tz'uqb'il b'an re sa' u *n.* eye
drops.

tz'uqleb' b'an *n.* eyedropper.

uk'b'il b'an *n.* cough syrup.

uq'unil b'an *n.* cream,
ointment.

xb'iisul b'an *n.* dose.

xche'el li b'otb'il hu *n.* paper
towel dispenser, roll paper
dispenser.

xhuhul b'an *n.* prescription.

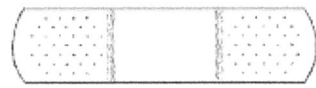

xiitleb' b'an *n.* bandage,
Band-Aid.

xjultikankil *n.* formulation.

xlemul k'ayib'aal *n.* glass
cabinet, display case.

xna'aj k'ay *n.* display shelves.

yulb'ilb'an *n.* pomade.

Yajel ut Ch'a'jkil / Diseases
and Ailments

amamnak *v.* to feel itchy.

atz'umxox *n.* chickenpox.

aakanak *v.* to have difficulty
breathing at night.

b'uq' kux *n.* mumps.

b'ux *n.* syphilis.

b'uxo'k *v.* to be syphilitic.

chachib' *n.* skin rash.

chak'aanil *n.* allergy.

chaqi'oqil *n.* rickets.

joj *n.* skin infection.

jolomb'ej *n.* cold, flu.

jolomb'ej *n.* headache.

kanser *n.* cancer.

kaqi yajel *n.* fever, typhoid.

kaqlamj *n.* measles.

kaqyajel *n.* AIDS.

katzkatz aj ja'aj *n.* dry cough.

katzkatz kux *n.* cough.

keho'ktib'elej *n.* hypothermia.

kik'sa' *n.* dysentery.

kuxb'ej *n.* cough, tuberculosis.

k'atom *n.* burn.

k'atom saq'e *n.* sunburn.

lub'ik *n.* vertigo, dizziness.

lub'k *n.* fainting spell.

lub'k *v.* to tire, get tired.

lub'k chi ru saq'e *n.* sunstroke.

lub'k ch'oolej *n.* depression.

luqaak *n.* polio.

maxelyu'am *n.* AIDS.

maak'a'il wara *n.* insomnia.

muchkej *n.* cramp.

ninqixox *n.* chickenpox, smallpox.

numay *n.* rickets.

nume' sa' *n.* diarrhea.

nume'sa'xa'aw *n.* cholera.

numt'ikt'ot-aam *n.* hypertension.

ojb' *n.* flu, cough. *Var:* oj.

papeer *n.* mumps. *From:* Spanish 'paperas'.

pat *n.* corn (cutaneous).

pojkun *n.* gonorrhea.

puchil *n.* anemia. *Var:* puchilk.

puchirk *v.* to become anemic.

q'anil *n.* hepatitis.

q'anyajel *n.* hepatitis.

q'aak *n.* infection. *Var:* q'a'k.

q'aayajel *n.* cancer.

ra chu' *n.* urinary pain.

rahil jolom *n.* headache, migraine.

rahil ruuch a' *n.* leg pain.

rahil ruuch e *n.* toothache.

rahil sa' xik *n.* earache.

rahil sa'ej *n.* stomach ache.

rahil u *n.* conjunctivitis.

rahil xalaa'it *n.* backache.

raxkihob' *n.* malaria. *Var:* raxkehob'.

sa'ej *n.* stomach ache.

sa'ej *n.* diarrhea.

saqb'yino'k *n.* fainting spell.

saqkirin *n.* anemia. *Var:* saq kirink.

saqleb' rix *adj.* leprotic.

saqlep *n.* skin spots (white).

sob'yajel *n.* cancer.

toqol *n.* fracture.

toqol a' *n.* broken leg.

wa *n.* acne.

wax ru *n.* rabies.

wax'ilom *n.* hallucination.

wotz'ok *n.* itch.

x'am ja'aj *n.* asthma.
Var: amja'aj.

xkuntz'i' *n.* eye inflammation.

xlub'ik li ch'ool *n.* heart attack, infarct.

xmaxel *n.* virus.

xo't' *adj.* blind.

xox *n.* spot, blemish.

xsik ke *n.* shiver, chill, shudder.

xtib' jolom *n.* headache.

xtib'l sa'ej *n.* colic.

xxaqliik aamej *n.* heart attack.

xyajel kik' *n.* leukemia.

xyajel pospo'oy *n.* tuberculosis, TB.

xyajelpospo'oy *n.* bronchitis.

xyajelxnaq'ja'aj *n.* tonsillitis.

yalaalt'ikt'ot-aam *n.* hypotension.

yeqo'k *v.* to limp.

yib'onik sa' sa'ej *n.* stomach acid.

yot'e'k sa'ej *n.* constipation.

yu'uk ichmul *n.* muscle tear.

K'anjel / Work

ab'en *n.* parcel, package.

aj pech'onel *n.* interviewer.

aj q'unob'tesinel *n agt.* conventioneer.

ch'olna'leb' *n.* orientation.

esilnawom *n.* resumé, curriculum vitae, CV.

hupatz'om *n.* application, written request.

hutz'aam *n.* application, written request.

kub'siil *n.* task, job, chore.

k'ehok k'anjel *v phr.* to hire.

k'uleb'aal *n.* reception.

laatz'al *n.* occupation, commitment.

nimru'ajk'anjel *n.* professional.

taqlil *n.* assignment, errand, commission.

tenq' *n.* task, job, chore.

titz'ok *n.* interview.

tusk'anjel *n.* plan.

tusk'anjelank *v.* to plan.

tz'aqal'ajk'anjel *n.* professional.

tz'aqalil hab' *n.* legal adult.

xb'ehil k'anjel *n.* career.

xhuhil tojok *n.* payroll.

xna'leb'ankil k'anjel *n.* job orientation.

yalok q'e *n.* effort.

Eb' li K'anjel / Jobs and Professions

aj ajlanel *n agt.* accountant.

aj awinel *n agt.* farmer.

aj aanilanel *n agt.* athlete, runner.

aj aatinanel *n agt.* announcer.

aj aatinanel rik'in yaj *n agt.* psychotherapist.

aj b'anonel *n agt.* doctor, physician.

aj b'atz'iil *n agt.* artist.

aj b'atz'unel *n agt.* athlete, sportsman.

aj b'atz'unel b'olotz oq *n agt.* soccer player, footballer.

aj b'e choxa *n agt.* astronaut.

aj b'ehenel *n agt.* navigator.

aj b'eresinel jukub' *n agt.* sailor, rower.

aj b'eresinelch'iich' *n agt.* pilot, driver, chauffeur.

aj b'esonel *n agt.* hairdresser.

aj b'eenel sa' po *n agt.* astronaut.

aj b'eetaql *n agt.* messenger.

aj b'ichanel *n agt.* singer.

aj b'irom tumin *n agt.* accountant.

aj b'ojonel *n agt.* tailor.

aj b'ojonel ixq *n agt.* seamstress.

aj b'olotz *n agt.* ballplayer, soccer player, footballer.

aj b'onol xaab' *n agt.* shoeshiner.

aj b'ononel *n agt.* painter.

aj b'ononel kab'l *n agt.* housepainter.

aj b'uub'anel *n agt.* organizer.

aj chamalnawom *n agt.* scientist.

aj chapol'esil *n agt.* cameraman.

aj chaponel *n agt.* police, policeman, police officer.

aj chi'resilnel *n agt.* adviser, counselor.

aj cho'onel *n agt.* surgeon.

aj chupulxam *n agt.* fireman.

aj ch'e'ol b'aqlaq ch'iich' *n agt.* cyclist.

aj ch'e'ol b'oq'ch'iich' iq' *n agt.* astronaut.

aj ch'e'ol ch'iich' *n agt.* pilot, driver, chauffeur.

aj ch'e'ol so'sol ch'iich' *n agt.* aviator, airplane pilot.

aj e re *n agt.* author.

aj eechal k'uuleb'aal tumin *n agt.* banker.

aj hiltesinel *n agt.* usher.

aj ilol chahim *n agt.* astronomer.

aj ilol kamenaq *n agt.* coroner, medical examiner.

aj ilol k'ila tasal hu *n agt.* librarian.

aj ilol k'ula'al *n agt.* babysitter.

aj ilol mayer kab'k *n agt.* archaeologist.

aj ilol okeb'aal *n agt.* janitor.

aj ilol uutz'u'uj *n agt.* gardener.

aj ilol wakax *n agt.* cowboy, cattleman, herder, herdsman.

aj ilol xna'aj ketomq *n agt.* farmer.

aj ilol'uuch-e *n agt.* dentist. *Var:* aj ilol ruuch e.

aj ilolketomq *n.* pastor (animals), shepherd.

aj ilolk'anjel *n agt.* supervisor.

aj iloltenamit *n agt.* police, policeman, police officer.

aj ilolyaj *n agt.* nurse.

aj ilom aj k'anjel *n agt.* supervisor.

aj ilom kamenaq *n agt.* undertaker.

aj ilom xul *n agt.* veterinarian.

aj ilom yaj *n agt.* paramedic.

aj isihom jalam'uuch *n agt.* photographer.

aj isihom ruuch e *n agt.* dentist.

aj jalom uuchinel *n agt.* sketch artist.

aj jek'ol preens *n agt.* newspaper boy.

aj jolominel b'atz'unk *n agt.* coach.

aj jolominel b'eeleb' *n agt.* captain.

aj jolominel k'aleb'aal *n.* mayor, town leader.

aj jultikahonel *n agt.* prompter, commentator.

aj kanab'om esilhu *n agt.* letter carrier, mailman.

aj kar *n agt.* fisherman.

aj kaxlanwahinel *n agt.* baker.

aj kelonel *n agt.* hauler, carrier.

aj k'alom *n agt.* farmer.

aj k'amol iiq *n agt.* porter, bellboy.

aj k'amolb'e *n agt.* guide, director.

aj k'anjel *n agt.* worker, laborer.

aj k'anjel re k'a' re ru *n agt.* craftsman.

aj k'anjel sa' chaq'rab' *n agt.* civil servant.

aj k'anjel sa' kab'l *n agt.* housewife.

aj k'anjel sa' kab'l *n.* maid.

aj k'anjel sa' so'sol ch'iich' *n agt.* flight attendant.

aj k'ay *n agt.* sales clerk, salesman, merchant.

aj k'ay ch'iich' *n agt.* ironmonger.

aj k'ay kar *n agt.* fishmonger.

aj k'ay tib' *n agt.* butcher.

aj k'ay xe' ru che' *n agt.* vegetable seller.

aj k'ay xxe' pim *n agt.* grocer.

aj k'ayinel *n agt.* merchant, salesman.

aj k'ayinel b'an *n agt.* pharmacist, chemist.

aj k'aak'alehom ketomq *n agt.* herdsman, herder.

aj k'aak'alenel *n agt.* police, policeman, police officer.

aj k'aak'alom *n agt.* security guard.

aj k'ehol esil *n agt.* journalist, reporter.

aj k'ehol na'leb' *n agt.* counselor.

aj k'ehonel tzakahemq *n agt.* waiter.

aj k'ulul ula' *n agt.* receptionist, secretary.

aj k'utunel *n agt.* teacher.

aj k'utunel b'e *n agt.* guide, director.

aj k'utunel re xnimal tzoleb'aal *n agt.* college professor.

aj k'uub'anel kab'l *n agt.* architect.

aj k'uub'anel poych'iich' *n agt.* mechanic.

aj k'uub'anel tzakahemq *n agt.* chef, cook.

aj letzolsimb'ha' *n agt.* plumber.

aj limoox *n agt.* beggar. *From:* limosna 'the offering or donation' (Spanish) (1).

aj loq'onel *n agt.* merchant.

aj mesol ru xaab' *n agt.* shoeshiner.

aj mesunel *n agt.* street sweeper.

aj molol'esil *n agt.* journalist, reporter.

aj naw'ajl *n agt.* mathematician.

aj nawb'an *n agt.* pharmacologist.

aj nawcha'al'ixq *n agt.* gynecologist.

aj nawchahim *n agt.* astronomer.

aj nawch'oolej *n agt.* cardiologist.

aj nawhiik *n agt.* seismologist.

aj nawkomonil *n.* sociologist.

aj nawkomonyajel *n agt.* epidemiologist.

aj nawk'anjel *n agt.* professional.

aj nawk'anjel yajel *n agt.* medical professional.

aj nawk'uhil *n agt.* vulcanologist.

aj nawpoyanam *n agt.* anthropologist.

aj nawtijok *n agt.* pedagogue.

aj nawtuqch'ool *n agt.* psychologist.

aj nawtus'aatin *n agt.* lexicographer.

aj nawxul *n agt.* zoologist.

aj nawyu'amilal *n agt.* biologist.

aj numsihom k'aj' esil *n agt.* telegrapher.

aj pak'ol *n agt.* potter.

aj pak'onel *n agt.* potter, sculptor.

aj pech'ol che' *n agt.* woodcarver, carpenter.

aj pech'onel *n agt.* sculptor.

aj peech' *n agt.* carpenter.

aj poch'onel *n agt.* miller.

aj puch'unel *n agt.* laundress.

aj puub' *n agt.* security guard, armed guard.

aj q'unb'esihonel xul *n agt.* animal trainer.

aj raqol chaq'rab' *n agt.* judge.

aj raqol'aatin *n agt.* judge, adjudicator.

aj se' k'al *n agt.* peasant.

aj seeb'alk'anjel *n agt.* engineer.

aj tenol ch'iich' *n agt.* blacksmith.

aj tenq' *n agt.* barman, manservant.

aj tenq' re b'anok *n agt.* nurse.

aj tenq' sa' li raxiik' *n agt.* fireman.

aj tenq'anel *n agt.* assistant.

aj tiikob'resinel'uuch-e *n agt.* orthodontist.

aj tzilol'ix *n agt.* researcher, investigator.

aj tzilonel *n agt.* researcher, investigator.

aj tzolonel *n.* teacher.

aj tz'ak *n agt.* mason, bricklayer.

aj tz'ilonel *n agt.* detective.

aj tz'iib' *n agt.* secretary, scribe.

aj tz'iib' *n agt.* writer.

aj tz'iib'ahom *n agt.* author.

aj tz'iib'anel esil *n agt.* reporter.

aj uutz'u'ujinel *n agt.* decorator.

aj wajb' *n agt.* musician.

aj waklesihom ch'uut *n agt.* social worker.

aj xaqab'anel *n agt.* presenter.

aj xiitinelch'iich' *n agt.* mechanic.

aj xokol mul *n agt.* garbage collector.

aj xokol tumin *n agt.* bank teller, teller.

aj xokol'al ixq *n agt.* midwife.

aj xokonel *n agt.* obstetrician.

aj yakonel *n agt.* shopkeeper, merchant.

aj yehomb'aanuhem *n agt.* historian.

aj yehonel *n agt.* narrator.

aj yehonel'uxk *n agt.* commentator.

aj yib'anel eetalil aq' *n agt.* clothing designer, fashion designer.

aj yiib'ank xaqab'ank *n.* construction worker.

aj yiib'om ch'iich' *n agt.* mechanic.

aj yiib'om ha' *n agt.* plumber.

aj yiib'om q'ol *n agt.* jeweller.

aj yiib'om reloj *n agt.* watchmaker.

aj yiib'om saqen *n agt.* electrician.

aj yiib'om ulul ch'iich' *n agt.* computer programmer.

aj yiib'om xaab' *n agt.* shoemaker, cobbler. *Var:* aj yiib'ahom xaab'.

kaan ru ixq *n.* prostitute.

k'ayihom rib' *n.* prostitute.

moos *n.* servant, slave. *From:* mozo 'lad, manservant' (Spanish) (1).

peech'ab'k *n.* carpentry.

tz'akkab'l *n.* masonry.

xb'eenil tijonel *n.* director.

yakonel *n.* merchant.

yal'ajot'onel *n.* adventurer.

yiib'anel *n.* artist, artisan.

yiib'ank xaqab'ank *n.* construction.

yoob'k'a'aq *n.* author, inventor. *Var:* yoob'k'a'aj.

Eb' li K'anjelob'aal / Tools

alalch'iich' *n.* plumb.

alpek'iich' *n.* key.

asaron *n.* hoe. *From:* azadón 'the hoe' (Spanish) (1).

awleb' *n.* stake.

awleb' *n.* digging stick, yamstick.

b'alent'ojiil *n.* screw.

b'aqb'il k'aham ch'iich' *n.* chain.

b'aqch'iich' *n.* rebar.

b'arch'iich' *n.* screw.

b'atb'een'aq *n.* knee guard, knee pad.

b'ekol ch'och' *n.* tractor. *Var:* b'ekleb' ch'och'.

b'isleb' *n.* measuring tape.

b'isleb' iq' *n.* air gauge.

b'isleb' sek' *n.* measuring cup.

b'isleb'hab' *n.* rainfall meter.

b'itool *n.* head pad.

b'ola *n.* rolling pin. *Var:* b'ol.

b'olb'okiil ch'iich' *n.* metal tube, metal pipe.

b'onleb' *n.* brush, paintbrush.

b'oq'leb'ch'iich' *n.* crowbar.

b'otz'leb' *n.* screwdriver.

b'oot *n.* bucket, pail. *From:* Spanish 'bote'.

b'ukleb'aal *n.* mixer.

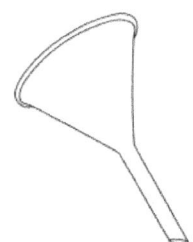

b'ut'leb' *n.* funnel.

chapleb' *n.* vise.

chapleb' *n.* nail.

chapleb'metz'ew *n.* plug, outlet.

chapteeleb' *n.* keychain.

chaab' *n.* watering can.

chupleb'xaml *n.* fire extinguisher.

ch'ina k'arch'iich' *n.* handsaw.

ch'ina k'arch'iich' *n.* hacksaw.

ch'ina maal *n.* cleaver.

eetalnum'iq *n.* weather vane.

eetaal *n.* measuring tape.

helleb'aal *n.* clothesline.

hitb'arch'iich' *n.* screwdriver. *Var:* **jitob'arch'iich'**.

hitleb' kotox ch'iich' *n.* screwdriver.

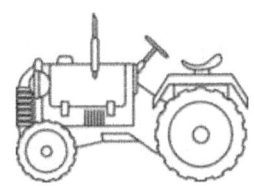

hixch'iich' *n.* tractor.

homch'iich' *n.* metal tube.

hompaq' *n.* plastic tube.

hopleb' *n.* drill, hole punch.

hopleb'che' *n.* drill, hole punch.

hopleb'hu *n.* paper punch, hole punch.

hopleb'tz'ak *n.* drill.

ilob'aal *n.* visor.

iiqaal *n.* cart, wheelbarrow.

jachleb' *n.* saw.

jaqleb' *n.* opener, key.

ji'leb' *n.* sandpaper.

ji'leb' *n.* file, rasp.

ji'leb' *n.* whetstone.

ji'leb' t'ikr *n.* iron (for clothing).

ji'leb'aal *n.* ironing board.

ji'leb'che' *n.* plane.

ji'leb'ch'iich' *n.* file, rasp.

ji'leb'tz'ak *n.* trowel.

jit'aal *n.* buckle.

jit'iil *n.* screw.

jit'leb' *n.* nut (fastener), fastener.

jiileb' *n.* plumb line.

jochleb' *n.* rake.

jochleb'mul *n.* rake.

jorleb'pek *n.* sledgehammer.

jotzleb' *n.* chisel, awl, scraper.

jookleb' *n.* hoe. *Var:* jokleb'.

joom *n.* basin.

jusk'aam *n.* cord, line.

ka't'oj *n.* rivet.

kachiimp *n.* pipe. *From:* cachimba 'the pipe' (Spanish) (1).

karetiiy *n.* wheelbarrow. *From:* Spanish 'carretilla'.

kaxchaj *n.* flashlight.

kaxemel *n.* washbasin, washbowl.

kaaxukuutleb' *n.* square.

ke'leb'aal *n.* windmill.

kelk'arch'iich' *n.* saw. *Var:* k'arch'iich'.

klaawx *n.* nail. *Var:* kalawx.
From: clavos 'the nails' (Spanish)
(1).

kok'poli'n *n.* rolling pin.

koral ch'iich' *n.* bar (metal).

kotoxch'iich' *n.* nut (fastener),
fastener.

kukb' *n.* water jar.

kulb't'ojom *n.* steel nail.

kumb' *n.* barrel, cask.

k'ahamch'iich' *n.* wire.
Var: k'aamch'iich'; k'aham
ch'iich'.

k'ajche' *n.* sawdust.

k'ajpek *n.* gravel.

k'anjelob'aal *n.* tool,
instrument. *Var:* k'anjeleb'aal.

k'arhu *n.* sandpaper.

k'atzleb' *n.* pliers.

k'aam *n.* string.

k'ix k'ahamch'iich' *n.* barbed
wire.

k'ixleb' *n.* screwdriver.

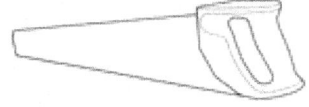

k'ixsetleb' *n.* saw.

k'ob'leb' *n.* awl, drill.

k'ochkaq'l *n.* scaffolding.

k'onk'ookil ch'iich' *n.* sickle,
scythe.

k'uhilpek *n.* gravel.

k'uxch'iich' *n.* pliers, pincer.

k'uub'kutha' *n.* water pump.

laas *n.* lasso. *From:* lazo 'the
lasso' (Spanish) (1).

lekleb' *n.* shovel. *Var:* lek.

lekleb'ch'och' *n.* shovel.

lemtz'b'on *n.* varnish.

leplepb'aal *n.* pedal.

lochte'b'aal *n.* scaffolding.

lukleb' *n.* pegboard.

machb'onleb' *n.* brush.

masleb'tz'ak *n.* mop.

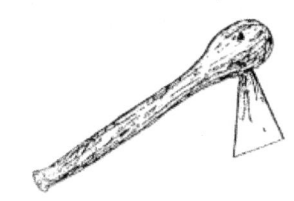

maal *n.* axe.

mesol lem *n.* squeejee, wiper.

mokooch *n.* tarp, dropcloth.

nat'b'iltz'ap *n.* bottle cap.

nat'leb' *n.* press, pressing machine.

nat'leb' okeb'aal *n.* lock, padlock.

nub'leb'aal *n.* plug, outlet.

orkeet *n.* fork, pitchfork. *From:* horqueta 'pitchfork' (Spanish) (1).

patb' *n.* club.

paal *n.* shovel, spade. *From:* pala 'shovel, paddle' (Spanish) (1).

pek'iich' *n.* lock.

pikleb' *n.* pickaxe.

pitzk' *n.* spring (metal).

poq re tz'akab'ak *n.* cement.

pormon *n.* chisel, awl. *Var:* **formon.** *From:* formón 'awl or chisel' (Spanish) (1).

puub'b'on *n.* paintgun.

puub'xaml *n.* blowtorch.

puutzink *v.* to spray.

q'eqitz'aakalb'e *n.* asphalt, tar.

q'esyaxch'iich' *n.* tongs.

q'otleb'ch'iich' *n.* wrench, crescent wrench.

q'otol *n.* shackle.

q'unleb' *n.* sandpaper.

ralteeleb' *n.* latchkey.

rastriiy *n.* fork, pitchfork, rake. *From:* rastrillo (Spanish) (1).

rix *n.* case, sheath.

rixch'iich' *n.* case, sheath, scabbard.

roq *n.* end piece, handle, grip.

roopilch'iich' *n.* cable.

seruch *n.* saw. *From:* Spanish 'serrucho'.

setleb' *n.* scissors, shears.

simb'ch'iich' *n.* pipe (metal).

simb'plaast *n.* pipe (plastic), PVC.

simb'tz'uum *n.* hose.

sirk'arch'iich' *n.* electric saw. *Var:* surk'arch'iich'.

sob'sob'k'uub' *n.* sponge.

soq'ch'iich' *n.* chicken wire.

sub'inch'iich' *n.* nail.

surjachleb'che' *n.* electric saw.

sursu *n.* wheel.

tamleb'aalha' *n.* barrel, cask.

taqleb' *n.* scaffolding, platform.

taqleb'aal *n.* scaffolding, platform.

taqsiil *n.* jack.

taab' *n.* tumpline, head strap.

tenleb' *n.* hammer, mallet.

teeleb' *n.* key.

tixeer *n.* scissors, shears. *From:* tijera 'scissors' (Spanish) (1).

tiikalxaqab'aal *n.* plumb.

tiikisib'aal *n.* pedal.

toltol *n.* cart, wheelbarrow.

torniiy *n.* screw. *From:* tornillo 'the screw' (Spanish) (1).

tuntuukir t'ikr *n.* towel.

tuqb'iis *n.* level.

tuqleb' *n.* level.

t'ojleb' *n.* hammer.

t'ojom *n.* nail.

tzub'pajha' *n.* water pump.

tz'akleb' *n.* trowel.

tz'alamche' *n.* board.

tz'alamch'iich' *n.* machete.

tz'apb'al re *n.* cap.

tz'apil *n.* cap.

tz'apleb' *n.* cover, lid, top.

tz'ileb' *n.* strainer, colander, sieve.

tz'uum *n.* whip.

xeer *n.* saw. *From:* sierra 'the saw' (Spanish) (1).

xhumalilche' *n.* shaving.

xiitleb'ch'iich' *n.* soldering iron.

xkaxon aj b'onol xaab' *n.* shoeshiner kit.

xkaxonil k'anjeleb'aal *n.* toolbox.

xkukil li puutzink *n.* fumigation pump, fumigator.

xk'aamal *n.* belt, strip, drive belt.

xk'ilul kaxlan wa *n.* bread pan.

xlek aj tz'ak *n.* trowel.

xlokochil t'ikr *n.* hanger.

xmeexul li peech'ab'k *n.* work bench. *Var:* xmeexul li peech'b'k.

xna'aj iq' *n.* oxygen tank.

xna'aj puch'um *n.* wash basin (clothing).

xtaab'il *n.* belt, strip.

xukub'k'ix *n.* safety pin, pin.

xxik *n.* handle.

yaxch'iich' *n.* pliers.

yunta *n.* yoke. *From:* yunta 'the yoke' (Spanish) (1).

yutleb'ch'iich' *n.* clamp.

yuul *n.* mix.

Naw'awk / Agriculture

aj awinel *n agt.* farmer.

aj k'aleb'aal *n agt.* farmer, fieldworker.

aq *n.* hay, grass. *From:* *ak, aq 'grass, hay' (Ch'olan) (2).

aq' *n.* vine.

aq'ink *v.* to dig.

aros *n.* rice. *From:* arroz 'rice' (Spanish) (1).

asuukr utz'ajl *n.* sugarcane.

awinq *n.* plant.

awib'aal *n.* field.

awleb'aal *n.* field.

awo *adj.* planted, sown.

awok *v.* to plant, sow.

b'anpim *n.* herbicide.

b'antz'ipxul *n.* insecticide.

b'ekok *v.* to dig.

b'ooyx *n.* ox, yoke (of oxen). *From:* buey 'the ox' (Spanish) (1).

cho'leb' ch'och' *n.* plowed land, tilled land.

cho'ok jul *n.* ditch, furrow.

choqlenk *v.* to burn.

ch'epok *v.* to thresh.

ch'ol *n.* furrow.

ch'oqom *n.* harvest. *Var:* ch'oqok.

hirok *v.* to sow.

humuk *v.* to burn.

is *n.* sweet potato.

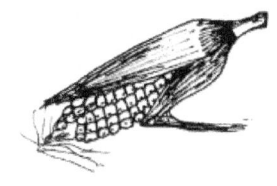

ixim *n.* maize, corn.

iximaak *v.* to thresh. *Var:* iximak.

iyaj *n.* seed.

iyajiil *n.* seedbed.

joom *n.* gourd.

jul *n.* ditch, pit.

jun'al iyaj *n.* monocotyledonous seed.

jur'ichaj *n.* chard.

kawil k'aam *n.* hemp.

kok' ixim *n.* millet, sorghum.

kok'awinq *n.* orchard, garden.

kok'k'aleb'aal *n.* hamlet, small village, collection of country houses.

koral *n.* fence. *From:* corral 'the fence, the space in front of the house' (Spanish) (1).

k'al *n.* field, cornfield. *From:* k'al 'cornfield' (Tzeltal) (4).

k'aleb'aal *n.* countryside, field.

k'anjelank *v.* to cultivate.

k'anjelob'aal *n.* tool, instrument. *Var:* k'anjeleb'aal.

k'aam keenq' *n.* green bean.

k'i *n.* growth.

k'iham *n.* abundance.

k'im *n.* hay, straw.

k'iik *v.* to grow.

k'um *n.* gourd, squash, pumpkin.

lajtesib'aalxul *n.* insecticide.

lut-al iyaj *n.* dicotyledonous seed.

may *n.* tobacco.

metz'ew *n.* strength, force.

mu' *n.* seedbed.

naw'awk *n.* agriculture, agronomy.

neb'aal *n.* field.

pahok jul *n.* ditch, furrow.

pech'ok *v.* to carve. *From:* pech' 'to carve in wood' (Ch'olan) (2).

pikok *v.* to dig. *From:* *pik 'to dig' (Ch'olan) (2).

poqsiyajink *n.* pollination.

qeer *n.* furrow.

q'ap *n.* green bean, string bean.

q'em *n.* fertilizer.

q'een *n.* leaf.

q'ol *n.* sap.

q'olok *v.* to harvest.

q'olom *n.* harvest.

raxonb'an *n.* fertilizer.

rix *n.* husk.

riximul kaxlan wa *n.* wheat.

rochochil hal *n.* granary.

roq ha' *n.* ditch.

roq waj *n.* cornstalk.

setok *v.* to mow.

seb'aad *n.* barley. *From:* cebada 'the barley' (Spanish) (1).

seel *n.* gourd, squash.

sol *n.* husk (grain), plaque.

suurk *n.* furrow. *From:* surco 'the furrow' (Spanish) (1).

suut *n.* furrow.

tam *n.* hay.

torol'ichaj *n.* cabbage.

triiw *n.* wheat. *From:* trigo 'the wheat' (Spanish) (1).

t'orol *n.* grain.

tzol *n.* furrow. *From:* *tzohl 'line, row' (Yucatecan, Ch'olan, possible).

tz'in *n.* cassava, manioc.

utz'aal *n.* sugarcane.

waj *n.* cornfield.

waqlajuk'aam *n.* lot, plot, terrain. *Note:* From 'Sixteen cords," or the size corresponding to the unit of measure called "manzana" in Guatemala.

xb'anil xxulil awimq *n.* insecticide.

xk'anjelankil li ch'och' *n.* farming.

xna'aj hal *n.* granary.

xna'aj ketomq *n.* corral.

xna'aj kok'awinq *n.* orchard, garden.

xnaq' *n.* seed.

xna'aj aros *n.* rice paddy.

xokok *n.* harvest.

xoral *n.* field, plot, terrain.

xoralwakax *n.* corral.

xq'emal ru li ch'och' *n.* fertilizer.

xq'emulch'och' *n.* fertilizer.

xtzakahemq ch'och' *n.* fertilizer.

xxib'enkil k'al *n.* scarecrow.

ya'al *n.* sap. *From:* ya'al 'sap' (K'iche'an) (4).

Xna'ajeb' li K'anjeleb' / Workplaces

b'esleb'aal *n.* barbershop.

b'it'b'it'leb'aal *n.* beauty salon.

ch'ina k'uleb'aal *n.* service window.

ja'leb'aal *n.* kiosk.

kab'lak *n.* construction site.

kaxlan wahib'aal *n.* bakery.

kayib'aal *n.* shop, store.

k'aleb'aal *n.* countryside, field.

k'anjel *n.* work, profession, job.

k'ayib'aal kape *n.* cafe, cafeteria.

k'ayib'aal kaxlan wa *n.* bakery.

k'ayib'aal k'anjelob'aal *n.* hardware store.

k'ayib'aal tasal hu *n.* bookstore.

k'ayib'aal uutz'u'uj *n.* florist, flower shop.

k'ayib'aal xaab' *n.* shoe store.

k'ayib'aalhu *n.* bookstore.

k'ayib'aalhumb'ookilha' *n.* gas station.

k'uub'leb'aal *n.* workshop.

k'uuleb'aal *n.* warehouse.

k'uuleb'aaltumin *n.* bank. *Var:* k'ulab'aal.

loq'b'ilch'och' *n.* farm, plantation.

mama' rochochil aq'ej *n.* department store.

nimla k'ayib'aal tzakahemq *n.* restaurant.

nimlawa'leb'aal *n.* restaurant.

ochochnaal *n.* hotel.

peech'leb'aal *n.* woodshop.

rochoch ketomq *n.* farm.

rochochil b'oqleb' *n.* call center.

rochochil li yiib'leb'aal xaab' *n.* shoe workshop, shoemaker's, cobblery.

rochochil ruk'a' poych'iich' *n.* gas station.

rochochil tasal hu *n.* library.

sisib'aaltib' *n.* barbeque stall.

uk'leb'aal kape *n.* cafe, cafeteria.

wa'leb'aal *n.* restaurant, diner.

waj *n.* cornfield.

xna'ajeb' li k'anjeleb' *n.* workplaces.

xna'aj yiib'ank xaqab'ank *n.* construction site.

xna'ajeb' cheek *n.* nursing home.

yiib'leb'aal *n.* workshop.

Maak ut Chaq'rab' / Crime and Justice

ach'abaak *n.* acquittal.

aj b'aanun re *adj.* guilty.

aj kuutunel *n agt.* witness.

aj na'onel chaq'rab' *n agt.* attorney, lawyer.

aj raqol chaq'rab' *n agt.* judge.

aj raqol'aatin *n agt.* judge, adjudicator.

aj tik'ti' *n agt.* liar.

b'alaq' *n.* fraud, deceit.

b'alaq'ik *n.* bribery.

b'alaq'ik *v.* to lie (tell falsehoods).

b'eeresink yib' aj k'ay *n.* drug trafficking.

b'ololch'iich' *n.* whistle (object).

chapb'il *n.* hostage.

chapok *v.* to arrest.

chaq'rab' *n.* law, justice.

ch'a'jkilal *n.* court case.

ch'olob'ank *v.* to swear (an oath), inform.

elq' *n.* burglary, theft. *Var:* eelq'.

elq'ak *v.* to steal.

elq'ak sa' josq'il *n.* assault.

eetalil maak *n.* evidence.

ink'a' xsumenkil *v phr.* to deny.

ixi'jink *v.* to steal.

jalmuqank *v.* to deny, hide. *Var:* jalmuqink.

jalok ru yaal *v phr.* to forge.

jalok ru yaal *n.* forgery.

jitok *v.* to accuse.

jitom *n.* indictment.

jitonel *n.* plaintiff.

jitb'il *n.* defendant.

jochok *v.* to steal.

kamij winq *n.* homicide.

kamk tojb'a maak *n.* death penalty.

kamsink *v.* to murder.

kamsink chi uk'b'il *v phr.* to poison.

kamsiik *n.* murder.

kaxb'olol *n.* whistle (object).

kok' maak *n.* misdemeanor.

kole'k *n.* protection.

kolok *n.* custody.

kolok *v.* to defend, protect.

kuyuk maak *v phr.* to forgive, acquit.

k'a'uxlanb'il k'atok *n.* arson.

k'ajk'amunk *v.* to reward.

k'ajk'amunkil *n.* reward, recompense.

k'ajtesink *v.* to punish.

k'ehok sa' sahilal *v phr.* to release.

k'ehok sa' tzalam *v phr.* to imprison.

k'ehok xiw *n.* threat.

k'ehok xiw *v phr.* to threaten.

k'ob'ok chi ch'iich' *v phr.* to stab.

k'utb'esil *n.* proof.

lemaank sa' muqmu *v phr.* to spy.

maq'ok *n.* mugging.

maq'ok sa' b'alaq' *n.* swindle.

maak *n.* crime, fault.

maakonel *adj.* guilty.

maak'a' xmaak *adj.* innocent, not guilty.

moko yaal ta *adj.* wrong, untrue.

muquk poyanam *n.* kidnapping.

muxuk *n.* rape, sexual assault, violation.

muxuk *v.* to rape, violate.

muult *n.* fine. *From:* multa 'the fine' (Spanish) (1).

nimalraqb'leb'aatin *n.* supreme court.

nimlamaak *n.* offense.

pak'ok aatin *v phr.* to lie (tell falsehoods).

patz'ok *v.* to interrogate.

paaltil *n.* error.

poyanam wan aatin chirix *n.* suspect.

poopol *n.* court.

puut *n.* prostitute. *From:* Spanish 'puta'.

puutink *n.* prostitution.

q'ab'anb'il *n.* defendant.

q'ab'ank *v.* to accuse.

q'ab'ankil *n.* accusation.

raqb'a' aatin *n.* judgment.

raqleb'aatin *n.* court.

raqok aatin *v phr.* to judge, adjudicate.

raqok aatin *n.* trial, justice.

raqok aatin chi rix *v phr.* to convict, condemn.

raqonel chaq'rab' *n.* jury.

raschaq'rab' chi rix tojb'amaak *n.* penal code.

sachalkil *n.* error.

sachk *n.* error.

somenkil *n.* oath.

sumenk aatin *n.* oath.

takchi' *n.* bad advice.

takchi' *n.* blackmail.

teneb'anb'ilkamk *n.* death penalty.

teneb'ankil sa' xb'een *v phr.* to convict.

tenok chi che' *v phr.* to beat up.

testiig *n.* witness. *From:* testigo 'the witness' (Spanish) (1).

tik'ti' *n.* lie, falsehood.

tik'ti'ink *v.* to lie (tell falsehoods).

tiq'eek *n.* accident.

titz'e'k *n.* appeal.

tiikilwank *n.* justice.

toch'ok *n.* assault.

toch'ok *v.* to assault.

toch'ol *n.* injured party.

tojb'a maak *n.* punishment.

tojl *n.* fine.

tojleb' re maak *n.* bail.

tojleb'aal maak *n.* penalty, punishment.

tojmaak *n.* fine.

tojok maak *v phr.* to serve a sentence.

tojok maak *n.* sentence.

tumin re uuchil *n.* ransom.

tzapliik junelik *n.* life sentence.

tziib'aak *v.* to search.

tz'alam *n.* prison, jail, iron bars.

tz'apok *v.* to lock up.

tz'aqtaanank *v.* to condemn.

tz'ilok maak *n.* justice.

uq'mink *v.* to steal.

wank sa' ilb'il *adj.* on parole, on probation.

wank sa' raqb'a aatin *adj.* on trial.

wank sa' xyaalal *n.* safety.

xhuhultojb'amaak *n.* sentence.

xkolb'al rix junkab'al *n.* family services.

xkomon rib' *n.* accomplice, accessory.

xkux uq'b' ch'iich' *n.* handcuffs.

xk'aamal sa' aj puub' *n.* policeman's belt.

xk'ub'laal tojb'a maak *n.* prison system, corrections.

xk'ub'leb'aalchaq'rab' *n.* legislative system.

xk'ulub'poyanam *n.* human rights, civil rights, rights. *Var:* xk'ulub'eb' poyanam.

xk'uub'lalraqleb'aatin *n.* judicial system.

xk'uub'laltojb'amaak *n.* penitentiary system, prison system, corrections.

xminb'al ru *n.* rape.

xnimal raqb'a chaq'rab' *n.* supreme court.

xraqlil xsa' tz'alam *n.* cell (jail), jail cell.

xsum *n.* accomplice.

yehok aatin sa' chaq'rab' *n.* witness statement.

yehok aatin sa' chaq'rab' *v phr.* to testify.

yehok maak *v phr.* to plead guilty.

yehom *n.* testimony.

yik'ti'ink *v.* to lie (tell falsehoods).

Xpaayileb' Yib' aj Poyanam / Types of Bad Guys

aj b'alaq' *n agt.* briber, extortionist.

aj elq' *n agt.* burglar, thief.

aj elq' *n agt.* kidnapper.

aj elq' karteer *n agt.* pickpocket.

aj jalonel *n agt.* forger.

aj kalajel *n agt.* alcoholic.

aj kamsinel *n agt.* assassin, murderer.

aj k'ay yib' aj b'an *n agt.* drug dealer.

aj maq'onel *n agt.* mugger, swindler.

aj maak chi ru chaq'rab' *n agt.* delinquent.

aj muxunel *n agt.* rapist.

aj naark *n agt.* drug trafficker. *Var:* aj narko. *From:* Spanish 'narcotraficante'.

aj takchi' *n agt.* blackmailer.

aj tochonel *n agt.* assailant.

aj yumb'eet *n agt.* fornicator.

jochonel *n.* thief. *From:* joch-on-el 'the thief' (Ch'olan) (4).

pereex *n.* convict. *Var:* **preex**. *From:* Spanish 'preso'.

piyok *n.* thief.

yib' aj poyanam *n.* bad guy.

Oob'eb' Li Eek'ob'aal / The Five Senses

Ab'ib'aal / Hearing

ab'ib'aal *n.* hearing, sense of hearing.

ab'ink *v.* to listen, hear.

ab'ink *n.* hearing.

eek'ank *n.* noise.

ink'a' na'aatinak *adj.* quiet.

kaw *adj.* loud.

kaw xyaab' *adj.* loud.

k'irnak *adj.* quiet.

sumyaab' *n.* echo.

tz'uyink *v.* to groan.

xik' naxye *adj.* noisy, sensational, controversial.

xkuxb'il *n.* sound, noise.

xuxb' *n.* whistle (sound).

yaab' *n.* cry.

yaab' *n.* sound, noise.

Eek'ob'aal / Touch

b'aqx *adj.* wet.

b'iqok *v.* to rub, handle.

b'urux *adj.* rough.

chaqi *adj.* dry.

ch'e'ok *v.* to touch, feel.

ch'epok *v.* to pinch.

ch'uyuk *v.* to pinch.

eek'ob'aal *n.* touch, sense of touch, feeling, tact.

ixkej *n.* touch, sense of touch, tact. *Var:* **ixej**; **ixb'ej**.

ji'ji' *adj.* smooth.

jilok *v.* to rub, handle.

jochok *v.* to pinch.

jutz' *adj.* pointed.

jutz' ru'uj *adj.* pointed.

kaw *adj.* hard.

ke *adj.* cold, chilly.

k'urux *adj.* rough. *From:* *k'urux
'curly' (Ch'olan) (2).

luub' *adj.* wet.

pitz'ok *v.* to squeeze, press.

potzpotz *adj.* soft.

purux *adj.* rough.

q'es *adj.* pointed, sharp.

q'es ru *adj.* rough.

q'ix *adj.* hot.

q'ixnal *n.* heat.

q'ochq'och *adj.* soft.

q'oyok *v.* to scratch, scrape.

q'un *adj.* soft, smooth.

raap *adj.* wet.

roq'roq' *adj.* soft.

room *adj.* blunt. *From:* romo
'blunt' (Spanish) (1).

tiq *adj.* hot.

tiq *adj.* warm.

tiwok *v.* to eat, bite.

tiik *adj.* smooth.

turux *adj.* rough.

t'aqt'aq *adj.* damp, wet, humid.

t'oqx *adj.* wet.

tz'uuq *adj.* wet.

xeb'ok *v.* to pinch. *From:* *xeb'
'to pinch' (Yucatecan, Ch'olan,
possible) (2).

xq'esnal *n.* sharpness.

xujxuj *adj.* dry.

yab'yab' *adj.* soft.

yolyol *adj.* smooth.

yotyot *adj.* hard.

yuq'yuq' *adj.* soft.

Ileb'aal / Sight

ileb'aal *n.* sight, sense of sight,
vision.

ilob'aal *n.* view.

ilob'aal xsa'u *n.* sight, sense
of sight, vision.

ilok *v.* to see.

ka'yank *v.* to look, observe.

kootal *n.* silhouette.

k'ehok eetal *v phr.* to observe.

lemlotk *v.* to shine.

lemtz' *adj.* bright.

muhej *n.* shadow (of animate being).

muhelil *n.* silhouette.

q'anq'an *adj.* brilliant.

raxk'urin *adj.* light (not dark).

rik'ok *v.* to blink.

saqen *adj.* light (not dark).

tuh *adj.* dark.

xk'utum xaml *n.* reflection (light).

yuqyuqink *v.* to blink.

Utz'leb'aal / Smell

chu *adj.* stinking, smelly.

jaq'b'ab' *n.* perfume.

kis *n.* fart, flatulence.

k'ajo' sununkil *adj.* fragrant.

k'isk'is *n.* bad odor.

sunob'l *n.* perfume.

sununk *adj.* fragrant.

utz'uk *v.* to smell, sniff.

utz'leb'aal *n.* smell, sense of smell.

utz'leb'aal *n.* smell.

utz'uk *n.* smell.

Yaleb'aal / Taste

chaqi'el *n.* thirst. *Var:* chaq'ieel; chaqi e.

ch'am *adj.* sour, rancid.

hulak chi uhej *v phr.* to taste.

ki' *adj.* sweet.

k'a *adj.* bitter.

k'a *adj.* sour.

k'aak'a *adj.* very bitter.

k'ipitz'in *adj.* salty.

k'oylenk *v.* to chew.

k'uxuk *v.* to chew.

num atz'am *adj.* very salty.

nuq'uk *v.* to swallow. *From:* *nuq' 'throat' (Western Mayan) (4).

pitz'pitz' *adj.* salty.

ra re *adj.* acidic.

remrem *adj.* sour, brackish.

req'ok *v.* to lick.

rub'rub' *adj.* sour.

sa *adj.* tasty, delicious, rich.

sahil *n.* flavor.

saasa *adj.* tasty.

yaleb'aal *n.* taste, sense of taste.

yalok *v.* to try, taste, savor.

yalok xsahil *v phr.* to taste.

Paab'aal ut Najter Na'leb' / Faith and Tradition

aj ilol tijob'aal *n agt.* sacristan.

aj iiqanel *n agt.* pallbearer.

aj kolom *n agt.* hero.

aj k'ehol kuult *n agt.* pastor (religious).

aj k'ehol miix *n agt.* priest.

aj maak *n agt.* sinner.

aj paab'anel *n agt.* adherent, believer.

aj paab'anel *adj.* faithful, believing.

aj santil paab'anel *n agt.* saint.

aj tiikilal *n agt.* saint.

apoostl *n.* apostle. *From:* Spanish 'apóstol'.

arsob'iisp *n.* archbishop. *From:* Spanish 'arzobispo'.

artal *n.* altar. *From:* altar 'the altar' (Spanish) (1).

atawank *n.* longing, temptation.

ayuunink rix *v phr.* to fast. *From:* ayunar 'to fast' (Spanish) (1).

aalenk *v.* to induce, tempt.

b'ichleb' *n.* songbook, hymnal.

b'oqok *v.* to summon, call, invite.

chaq'rab' *n.* commandment, moral principle. *Var:* chaq'rab'il.

chimam *n.* priest.

choxa *n.* heaven. *Var:* choxaal.

choxahil wank *n.* paradise.

ch'ina xukup *n.* crucifix.

ch'inank ch'ool *v phr.* to repent.

ch'uttenq' *n.* collection (of donations).

ek'ank ib' *n.* repentance.

ermiit *n.* temple. *From:* ermita 'holy place' (Spanish) (1).

eetal *n.* symbol, sign.

eetalkamenaq *n.* gravestone, headstone.

eetil *n.* foolishness.

hilaal *n.* pew, bench.

hilob'aal kutan *n.* day of rest.

huhilkub'ha' *n.* baptismal certificate.

iklees *n.* church. *Var:* iglees. *From:* iglesia 'church' (Spanish) (1).

ink'a us *adj.* bad.

ink'a' us *adj.* wrong.

jalam'uuch *n.* idol, holy image, statue.

jaljookil ru aatin *n.* parable.

julel kamenaq *n.* grave.

kab'yo'lajik *n.* resurrection.

kapiiy *n.* chapel, temple. *From:* capilla 'the chapel' (Spanish) (1).

kaxlan pom *n.* incense.

kaaxukuut *n.* painting.

kolok *v.* to rescue, save.

konb'eent *n.* convent. *From:* Spanish 'convento'.

krus *n.* cross. *Var:* kurus. *From:* cruz 'the cross' (Spanish) (1).

kub'iha' *n.* baptism.

kuyuk *v.* to tolerate.

kuyuk maak *v phr.* to forgive, acquit.

kuyuk sa' *n.* fast.

kuyuk sa' *v phr.* to fast.

kuult *n.* church services. *From:* Spanish 'culto'.

k'ajk'amunkil *n.* reward, recompense.

k'ajolb'ej *n.* son (of god).

k'atleb'aal pom *n.* incense burner.

k'ehok limoox *v phr.* to give alms.

k'eelenk *v.* to preach.

k'utuk eetalil *v phr.* to make the sign of the cross.

lajetqil *n.* tithing.

lochok *v.* to light. *Var:* lechok.

loq'alil *n.* values.

loq'alil *n.* worthiness, dignity.

loq'onink *v.* to worship.

loq'oniik *v.* to take communion.

loq'tasalhu *n.* bible.

mayr *n.* nun. *From:* Spanish 'madre'.

maak *n.* sin.

miix *n.* mass. *From:* Spanish 'misa'.

mu *n.* spirit.

muhel *n.* spirit.

muqb'aanunb'il *adv.* mysteriously.

muqleb'aal *n.* cemetery.

muqmuukil *adj.* mysterious.

muqmuukilal *n.* mystery.

musiq'ej *n.* spirit.

na'aj uutz'u'uj *n.* flower vase.

najter na'leb' *n.* tradition.

najterilk'utb'esink *adj.* traditional.

ne'b'aal *n.* entry platform.

nimank u *n.* praise.

nimla tijob'aal *n.* cathedral.

nimla t'ikr *n.* cloak, vestment.

ob'iisp *n.* bishop. *From:* Spanish 'obispo'.

osob'tesinb'il *adj.* holy, blessed.

osob'tesink *v.* to bless.

oxloq' *adj.* sacred.

oxloq'il hu *n.* prayer book.

oxloq'il na'aj *n.* altar.

oxloq'ilal *n.* morality.

oyb'enink *v.* to wait.

paqleb' *n.* pall.

pastor *n.* pastor. *From:* Spanish 'pastor'.

patz'ok b'aanunk *v phr.* to exhort.

patz'ok limoox *v phr.* to ask for alms.

payr *n.* priest. *From:* padre 'father, priest' (Spanish) (1).

paab'ank *v.* to obey, believe.

paab'aal *n.* faith.

paab'aal *n.* religion.

paap *n.* pope. *From:* Spanish 'papa'.

pixcal *n.* sacristan.

pom *n.* incense.

q'axal chaab'il *adj.* right (correct).

rahil kutan *n.* holy week, Easter.

rajikab'aal *n.* rebirth.

rajikru *v.* to be reborn.

rajleb' tij *n.* rosary.

rajom *n.* mission.

ramleb' *n.* curtain.

ramleb'aal lem *n.* stained glass.

raqalil li paab'aal *n.* article of faith.

raq' qaawa' *n.* cloak, vestment.

rixkil paab'aal *n.* nun.

ruutz'u'ujil ru b'e *n.* flower carpet.

sachb'ach'oolej *n.* miracle.

santil hu *n.* bible. *From:* Spanish 'santo'.

santil musiq'ej *n.* holy spirit.

saant *n.* saint. *From:* Spanish 'santo'.

sik'ok maak *v phr.* to sin.

sumwank *n.* covenant.

sununkil k'ol *n.* incense.

taqlankil *n.* mission, mandate.

terq'usink k'ab'a' *n.* praise.

tij *n.* prayer.

tij *n.* doctrine.

tije'k *v.* to be indoctrinated.

tijob'aal *n.* church, chapel, temple.

tijok *v.* to pray.

tijok *v.* to indoctrinate.

tiik xch'ool *adj.* faithful, just, righteous.

tojleb'aal maak *n.* hell.

tyox *n.* god. *Var:* yos. *From:* dios 'God' (Spanish) (1).

tzemok *v.* to covet.

tzoleb' *n.* doctrine.

tz'aamank limoox *v phr.* to ask for alms. *From:* Spanish 'limosna'.

tz'i'ej na'leb' *n.* immoral practices.

us *adj.* good.

uxtanank *n.* charity.

wa'tesink *v.* to perform rituals.

wa'tesiik *v.* to receive rites.

wankil *adj.* holy.

wiq'laak *v.* to kneel.

xaqab'ank *v.* to raise.

xb'aanunkil mayejak *v phr.* to worship.

xb'eenil aj tij *n.* priest.

xch'ool nataqlank re *n.* free will, free agency.

xch'uut aj b'ichk *n.* choir.

xilik' *n.* fairy, elf.

xna'aj kampaan *n.* bell tower.

xna'aj punitch'iich' *n.* bell tower.

xna'aj qaawa' *n.* altar.

xnimal winq *n.* hero.

xotonk *v.* to confess. *Var:* **xootonk**.

xootonib'aal maak *n.* confessional.

xootonink *v.* to confess.

xsok oq *n.* carpet.

xtaql xch'ool *n.* free will, free agency.

xtaql xch'ool li tyox *n.* god's will.

xukup *n.* cross.

xyehok maak *n.* confession.

yaal *adj.* true.

yaal *n.* truth.

yaalal *n.* truth, righteousness.

yo'laak xka'wa *v phr.* to be reborn.

yot'o'k *v.* to repent.

Na'leb' Mayab' / Maya Tradition

aj eek' *n agt.* magician.

aj nawal *n agt.* magician.

aj q'e *n agt.* fortune teller, spiritual guide.

anum *n.* demon.

anumal *n.* ghost.

awas *n.* bad luck, taboo.

awasinel *n.* sorcerer, witch.

aamej *n.* soul, spirit.

b'alamq'e *n.* sun god.

b'atxaqam *n.* mummy.

ch'i' *n.* bad omen.

ch'olwinq *n.* caveman, troglodyte.

ch'oolej *n.* soul, spirit.

ch'utub'eetalil *n.* iconography.

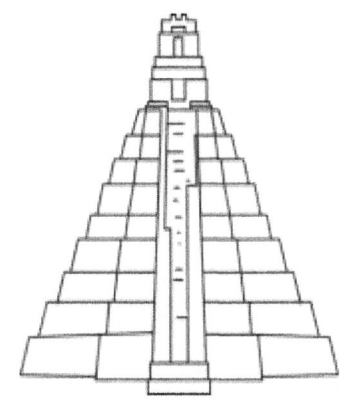

jutz'il na'aj *n.* pyramid (monument).

jutz'ochochilpek *n.* pyramid (monument).

kok' xul *n.* fairy, elf.

mayab' *adj.* Maya. *Note:* Perhaps from original Mayan name for the Yucatan (ma'ya'ab) meaning "few, not many", or "we have none" referring to its sparse population or alternatively its lack of gold (as sought by the Spaniards).

mayej *n.* sacrifice.

mayejak *v.* to make an offering.

maa'us *n.* demon.

maa'us *adj.* bad.

maa'us aj winq *n agt.* the devil.

maay *adj.* Maya.

maayil *adj.* Mayan, Maya.

nawalil *n.* magic.

ox'ukab'l *n.* pyramid (monument).

qaawa' *n.* god, lord.

ralch'och' *n.* indigenous, Maya. *Var:* ral ch'och'. *Note:* Literally 'son of the land'. Term the Q'eqchi' use to refer to themselves. (Aj Q'eqchi' traditionally refers to a speaker of the Q'eqchi' language, not a tribe or ethnicity.)

ranumal q'ojyin *n.* fairy, elf.

147

rax muhel *n.* good luck.

sachb'ach'oolej *adj.* magical, miraculous.

seeraq' *n.* legend.

sik'ok-eetalil *n.* iconography.

tuul *n.* magic.

tuulanel *n.* sorcerer, witch.

tza *n.* demon, devil.

tzaqal winq *n.* indigenous, Maya. *Note:* Literally 'authentic man'. Term the Q'eqchi' use to refer to themselves. (Aj Q'eqchi' traditionally refers to a speaker of the Q'eqchi' language, not a tribe or ethnicity.)

tzuultaq'a *n.* mountain spirit.

tz'ak-eetalil *n.* stela.

tz'iib'uuchil *n.* ideograph.

xb'alb'a *n.* hell, underworld. *Var:* b'alb'a; xib'alb'a.

xq'ehinkil *n.* omen.

yaal winq *n.* indigenous, Maya. *Note:* Literally 'true man'. Term the Q'eqchi' use to refer to themselves. (Aj Q'eqchi' traditionally refers to a speaker of the Q'eqchi' language, not a tribe or ethnicity.)

yoob'kink *n.* improvisation.

yoob'k'a'uxl *n.* myth.

Xpaayileb' li Paab'aal / Types of Faith

aj ateey *n agt.* atheist. *From:* Spanish 'ateo'.

aj juliis *adj.* Jewish.

aj k'atol mayej *n agt.* Maya priest.

aj mayej *n.* Maya spiritualist.

aj mormon *adj.* Mormon.

ch'olwinq *n.* unconverted (archaic).

juliis *n.* Jew.

kapiiy *n.* Protestant.

katoolk *n.* Catholic. *Var:* katolika.

kristyaan *n.* Christian.

kristyaanil paab'aal *n.* Christian faith.

maak'a' xyos *n.* atheism.

musulman *n.* Muslim.

Ruhil ut Xb'onil / Shape and Color

Ruhil ut Reetalil / Shapes and Forms

b'ach'b'o *adj.* crooked.

b'alxuk *n.* triangle.

b'aq'al *n.* oval.

b'aral *n.* cylinder.

b'arxuk *adj.* rhomboid, diamond-shaped.

b'ech' *adj.* crooked. *From:* *b'ech' 'roll up' (Yucatecan, Ch'olan, possible) (2).

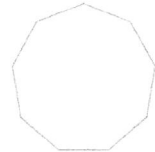

b'eleexuk *n.* nonagon.

b'isb'il eetalil *n.* geometric figure, geometric shape.

b'olb'o *n.* cylinder.

b'olb'o *adj.* cylindrical.

b'uq' *adj.* convex.

b'uq'b'u *adj.* convex.

chanchanil eetalilatq *n.* similar figures.

chankatq ru *n.* form.

eetalil *n.* figure.

eetalilatq *n.* figures.

helhookil eetalilatq *n.* flat figures, plane figures.

hopo *adj.* hollow.

jachsirso *n.* semicircle.

jech' *adj.* crooked.

jech'xuk *n.* corner, angle.

juch' *n.* line.

juch'uk *v.* to trace.

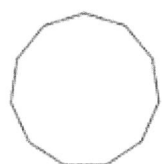

junlajuxuk *n.* hendecagon.

juntaq'eetil eetalil *n.* symmetric figure.

jutz' kaaxukuut *n.* pyramid (four-sided).

jutz' oxxukuut *n.* pyramid (three-sided).

jutz'-eetalil *n.* pyramid.

jutz'ju *n.* cone.

juutz' *n.* cone.

ka'suut *n.* box.

kaw ru *adj.* solid.

kaaxukuut *n.* square.

kaaxukuut *adj.* square.

kelkookil kaaxukuut *adj.* rectangular.

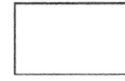

kelkookilkaaxukuut *n.* rectangle.

kotko *n.* circle.

k'atq *n.* side.

k'ob'b'il *n.* hole.

k'onk'o *adj.* crooked. *From:* k'on 'twisted' (Ch'olan) (2).

liq'lo *adj.* crooked.

loot' *n.* corner.

na'aj *n.* place.

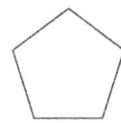

o'xukuut *n.* pentagon. *Var:* ho'xukuut; o'xuk.

ox'u *n.* pyramid.

oxxukuut *n.* triangle.

pak'al *n.* side.

perpo *adj.* flat.

q'e'q'o *adj.* horizontal.

q'es *adj.* pointed, sharp.

q'otq'o *adj.* round, circular.

q'otq'o *adj.* curved, twisted.

q'oot *adj.* curved, twisted.

q'oot *n.* curve.

rilb'al *n.* form, structure.

rok'ox *adj.* crooked.

ru *n.* side.

ru'uj *n.* top.

ruutaq'a *adj.* flat.

sa' *n.* bottom.

sa' xyi *n.* middle.

salsookil kaaxukuut *n.* rhombus, diamond.

siq'il *adj.* crooked.

siril *n.* circle.

sirso *n.* circle. *Var:* surso.

sursu *adj.* round, circular.

tach'to *adj.* flat. *From:* tach' 'be flat' (Ch'olan) (2).

tawrib' oxxukuut *n.* congruent triangle.

tiik *adj.* straight.

t'ort'o *adj.* spherical, round.

t'ort'o *n.* sphere.

t'ort'ookil *adj.* spherical.

tzelam *n.* edge.

tzol *n.* row, line.

tzolil *n.* row, line.

tzoltzo *adj.* lined up.

tz'uq *n.* point.

waqxaqxuk *n.* octagon.

waqxaqxuk-u *n.* octahedron.

waqxuk *n.* hexagon.

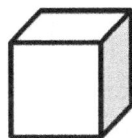

waqxukuut *n.* cube.
Var: **waxaqxukuut.**

wuqxuk *n.* heptagon.
Var: **wuqxukuut.**

xaqamkaaxuk *n.* rhombus, diamond.

xjech'lal *n.* angle.

xmar *n.* edge.

xmar *n.* end (spatial).

xtehelal *n.* angle.

xuk *n.* corner. *From:* xuhk' 'corner' (Yucatecan, Ch'olan, possible) (2).

xxuk *n.* angle.

xyirib' *adj.* concentric.

yanqxuk *n.* angle.

yi *n.* half.

yi *n.* middle.

yiib'ej *n.* middle. *Var:* yib'ej.

yiisirso *n.* semicircle.

yokos *adj.* crooked.

Xpaayil B'onol / Colors and Shades

b'on *n.* color.

b'onol *n.* color.

chaacha *adj.* gray.

chiin *adj.* orange.

chupchu *adj.* dull.

kaq *adj.* red.

kaq kaq *adj.* scarlet.

kaq moyin *adj.* mauve.

kaq saqin *adj.* pink.

kaqiq'an *adj.* orange.

kaqjorin *adj.* bright red.

kaqyojin *adj.* brown.

kutaniru *adj.* transparent.

moymo *adj.* dark.

nalemtz'un *adj.* shiny, golden.

q'an *adj.* yellow.

q'an kaqin *adj.* orange.

q'anb'uyin *adj.* yellowish.

q'anch'ik' *adj.* copper.

q'anjorin *adj.* golden.

q'anmalaw *adj.* yellowish.

q'antzoq'i *adj.* yellowish.

q'eq *adj.* black.

q'eqmoyin *adj.* brown.

q'eqmoyin *adj.* purple.

rax *adj.* green.

rax ju'in *adj.* blue. *Var:* raxrax; rax.

rax moyin *adj.* navy blue.

rax moyin *adj.* dark green.

rax q'u'in *adj.* blue.

raxjo'in *adj.* sky blue.

raxmo'in *adj.* bluish.

raxmo'in *adj.* greenish.

raxpotz'in *adj.* cerulean, sky blue.

raxtint *adj.* violet.

raxtz'o'in *adj.* blue.

saq *adj.* white.

saqen *adj.* light, clear.

saqen ru *adj.* transparent.

saqikaq *adj.* pink.

saqirax *adj.* cerulean, sky blue.

saqjorin *adj.* whitish.

saqmoy *adj.* colorless.

saqpotz'in *adj.* silver.

saqpotz'in *adj.* very white.

saqpuk'in *adj.* very white.

turans *adj.* peach.

tz'ib' *adj.* reddish-gray.

xchamal xb'onol *n.* color tone.

Ruuchich'och' / The Natural World

Che' ut Che'k'aam / Trees and Vegetation

arkute' *n.* oak.

b'ob' *n.* palm tree. *From:* b'ob' 'a certain plant with large leaves' (Yucatecan, Ch'olan, ?) (4).

chaj *n.* pine.

chakalte' *n.* cedar.

chamal pim *n.* weeds.

che' *n.* tree, wood.

che'eb' *n.* trees.

che'k'aam *n.* vegetation.

chik che' *n.* bush, shrub.

chiin *n.* orange tree.

ch'ina ruq' *n.* twig.

ichaj *n.* grass.

inup *n.* ceiba.

ji *n.* oak.

kala' *n.* palm tree.

kok' che' *n.* plants.

kok' pim *n.* scrub, brush, bush.

k'atk'al *n.* scrub, brush.

k'aamal pim *n.* creeper vine.

k'isis *n.* cypress.

k'ix *n.* thorn, spine.

la *n.* nettle.

mansaan *n.* apple tree.

muy che' *n.* cedar.

nimank *v.* to grow.

nokal *n.* walnut tree. *From:* Spanish 'nogal'. *Var:* **nohal.**

panchool *n.* nettle. *From:* panchola ('a type of nettle' ?) (Spanish) (1).

peetaq *n.* cactus.

pim *n.* wild grass.

q'eqi che' *n.* ebony tree.

q'ooqil ik'e *n.* aloe vera.

ra' che' *n.* forked branch.

raqan *n.* trunk (fruit bearing).

rix *n.* bark.

rix che *n.* bark.

roq *n.* tree trunk.

roq' *n.* stem.

ru *n.* fruit.

ru chaj *n.* cone.

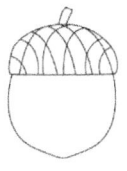

ru ji *n.* acorn.

ruq' *n.* branch.

ruq' che' *n.* branch. *Var:* **ruq'b' che'.**

simb' *n.* bamboo.

sipres *n.* cypress. *From:* Spanish 'cipres'.

siyab'aal *n.* biotope.

sutz'uj *n.* cedar.

sutz'ujl *n.* mahogany.

toon *n.* tree trunk, stump.

tul *n.* banana tree.

xaq *n.* leaf. *Var:* **xxaq**.

xaqchaj *n.* needle (of a tree).

xaal che' *n.* forked branch.
From: xaal che' 'forked branch'
(Yucatecan, Ch'olan, possible) (2).

xche'el noq' *n.* cotton tree.

xche'el pim *n.* stem, stalk.

xch'uylal *n.* segment.

xe' *n.* root, bulb, trunk. *Var:* **xxe'**.

xeek' *n.* palm tree. *From:*
*xeek'el 'a type of palm or palm
tree' (Western Mayan) (2).

xk'ix *n.* thorn.

xtoonal ruq'b' *n.* tree trunk.

xtuxmel *n.* sprout, shoot.

xxaq *n.* leaves.

xxaq pim *n.* fern.

xxaqeb' *n.* leaves.

xxe'il *n.* roots.

ya'al *n.* sap. *From:* ya'al 'sap'
(K'iche'an) (4).

Eb' li Ch'iich' / Metals

chaab'il ch'iich' *n.* precious
metal.

ch'iich' *n.* metal. *Note:* Ch'iich'
is said of anything metal, often
with an additional descriptor for
clarification of size, dimension
or function.

ch'iich' *n.* iron.

ka'xik *n.* gold.

kulb'ch'iich' *n.* steel.

lemtz'ch'iich' *n.* aluminum.

mo' *n.* rust, oxidation.

mo'onk *v.* to rust, oxidize.

plaat *n.* silver. *From:* plata 'silver'
(Spanish) (1).

pu'akink *v.* to work metal.

q'an ch'iich' *n.* bronze,
copper.

q'an pwaq *n.* gold, yellow
gold. *Var:* q'anpuhak;
q'anpuhaq.

q'anich'iich' *n.* gold. *Var:* q'an
ch'iich'.

q'anmuch'iich' *n.* rhodium.

rax ch'iich' *n.* lead (metal).

saqch'iich' *n.* aluminum.

saqi ch'iich' *n.* silver.

saqi pwaq *n.* silver, white gold. *Var:* saqpuhak; saqpuhaq.

saqmuch'iich' *n.* palladium.

seeb'ajch'iich' *n.* aluminum.

sink *n.* zinc.

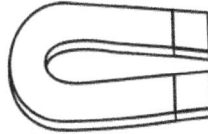

tz'ub'ch'iich' *n.* magnet.

Ru Choxa / Atmosphere

choxa *n.* sky. *Var:* choxaal.

iq' *n.* wind.

iq' *n.* air.

metz'ewil iq' *n.* atmospheric pressure.

raq xtasalil'iq' *n.* exosphere.

rox tasal'iq' *n.* mesosphere.

ru choxa *n.* atmosphere.

ruuchiha' *n.* hydrosphere.

xamlt'or *n.* ionosphere.

xb'een tasal iq' *n.* atmosphere, troposphere.

xka tasal'iq' *n.* thermosphere.

xkab' tasal iq' *n.* stratosphere.

xkab't'or *n.* metasphere.

Uutz'u'uj / Flowers

amapool *n.* poppy. *From:* Spanish 'amapola'.

asuseen *n.* lily. *From:* Spanish 'azucena'.

atz'um *n.* flower.

atz'umak *v.* to flower.

jasmin *n.* jasmine. *From:* Spanish 'jazmin'.

junq'aal uutz'u'uj *n.* flower bouquet, bouquet.

kalawx *n.* carnation. *From:* Spanish 'clavel'.

karayool *n.* gladiola. *From:* Spanish 'gladiola'.

k'ix'atz'um *n.* rose.

k'onon *n.* sunflower.

k'onop *n.* magnolia.

markariit *n.* daisy. *From:* Spanish 'margarita'.

orteens *n.* hortensia. *From:* Spanish 'hortensia'.

poqsiyaal *n.* pollen.

roq xwinkil atz'um *n.* filament (flower).

roq-atz'um *n.* style (flower).

roos *n.* rose. *From:* Spanish 'rosa'.

ru'uj atz'um *n.* stigma (flower).

saqihix *n.* white orchid, monja blanca.

uutz'u'uj *n.* flower.

xb'aar li qaawa' *n.* gladiola.

xcha'al uutz'u'uj *n.* flower petal.

xtorol ru uutz'u'uj *n.* bud.

xxaq atz'um *n.* sepal.

xxaq xcha'al uutzu'uj *n.* flower petal.

Xcha'alil Ruuchich'och' / Geographic Features

b'ook *n.* steam. *From:* *b'ook 'the smell' (Yucatecan, Ch'olan, possible) (2).

b'ookha' *n.* methane.

b'oolha' *n.* wave.

cha *n.* ash.

chamal jul *n.* precipice.

chaqi ch'och' *n.* desert.

chi re ha' *n.* shore.

choq *n.* cloud. *Var:* choql. *From:* *tyoq 'cloud' (Greater Tzeltalan) (3).

ch'ina ha' *n.* spring, well (water).

ch'ina k'iche' *n.* grove.

ch'ina nima' *n.* creek.

ch'ina ochoch *n.* island.

ch'och' sutsu chi ha' *n.* island.

ch'och'il b'e *n.* dirt path.

ch'och'ilha' *n.* island.

e *n.* edge.

helo *n.* plain.

hilob'aal k'iche' *n.* oasis.

hopolal *n.* hole.

jolool *n.* slide, chute, slippery place.

ju'e'k *v.* to erode.

jul *n.* hole.

julpek *n.* cave.

kaqlaaq' *n.* rainbow. *Var:* kaqla.

156

kaq'naab' *n.* lake, lagoon. *Var:* **k'aqnab'**; **kaqnab'**.

ke *n.* ice.

kelkookil tzuul *n.* hills, range, mountain range, mountain ridge.

kontineent *n.* mainland. *From:* continente 'the mainland or continent' (Spanish) (1).

kootal *n.* silhouette.

kumb' *n.* spring, well (water).

k'ab'a'na'jej *n.* toponym.

k'ajob' *n.* dew.

k'ak'naab' *n.* spring, well (water). *From:* k'ahk'-naab' 'the sea' (Yucatecan, Ch'olan, possible) (2).

k'anha' *n.* swamp.

k'iche' *n.* mountain.

k'iche'b'aal *n.* jungle.

k'u *n.* volcano.

laatz' *n.* strait.

maqs *n.* pumice.

metz'kelob' *n.* magnetism.

mu *n.* shadow, shade.

muhelil *n.* silhouette.

muhul *n.* island.

neb'a ha' *n.* island.

nima' *n.* river, stream.

nimla kaqnab' *n.* lake.

nimla rokeb' palaw *n.* gulf.

ninqi che' *n.* forest.

numleb'ha' *n.* canal.

ochoch pek *n.* cave.

ox'ukab'l mayab' *n.* Maya pyramid.

pach'il ha' *n.* waterfall.

pahal *n.* opening.

pajaj ha' *n.* waterfall.

palaw *n.* ocean, sea, lake. *From:* palaw 'sea' (Ch'olti') (3).

pek *n.* stone, rock.

pek ha' *n.* ice.

pekal *n.* stone, rock.

pekil ha' *n.* reef.

pekil nima' *n.* river rock.

pekilha' ch'och' *n.* glacier.

po'lem *n.* ruins, abandoned house. *Var:* **polem**. *From:* *po'lem 'abandoned house or ruin' (Ch'olti') (2).

poqs *n.* dust.

potreer *n.* pasture, meadow, paddock. *From:* potrero 'pasture' (Spanish) (1).

pumpuukil ha' *n.* lake, pond, lagoon.

puub' tzuul *n.* volcano.

raq'xam *n.* flame. *Var:* raq'xaml.

rarehilpoq *n.* sulphur.

re ha' *n.* beach.

re palaw *n.* coast, seashore.

rokeb' palaw *n.* bay.

roq ha' *n.* stream, brook.

roq ha' *n.* river.

roq taq'a *n.* plain, prairie.

roqtaq'a *n.* basin, catchment area, watershed.

ru taq'a *n.* valley.

ru'uj ch'och' *n.* peninsula.

ru'uj tzuul *n.* summit, peak.

ruq' nima' *n.* tributary.

ruq'b'ich'och' *n.* peninsula.

rusos *n.* waterfall.

ruuxam *n.* embers, coals, charcoal.

samahi' *n.* sand. *Var:* samayib'.

saqen *n.* light.

saqi pek *n.* marble.

saqoonak *n.* cave.

sabaan *n.* savannah. *From:* sabana 'the savannah' (Spanish) (1).

saab' *n.* swamp.

saab' ha' *n.* marsh, swamp.

seb' *n.* clay.

sib' *n.* smoke.

siwan *n.* cave, abyss.

sib'j *n.* charcoal.

sulul *n.* mud.

suut ha' *n.* whirlpool.

taq'a *n.* valley, plain, prairie.

tiqwal *n.* steam. *From:* tikwal 'heat' (Ch'olan) (3).

tok' *n.* flint.

tuq *n.* spring, well (water). *Var:* tuqb'.

t'anleb'aalha' *n.* waterfall.

tzoltzookiltzuul *n.* hills, range, mountain range, mountain ridge.

tzuul *n.* mountain, hill.

tz'ajn *n.* grime, dirt, filth, muck.

uk'leb'aal *n.* spring.

uk'leb'aal ha' *n.* water well.

uq'e'k *v.* to erode.

uq'e'k *n.* fault (geologic), erosion.

uq'ul *n.* landslide.

uul *n.* landslide.

uul *n.* ravine, gully.

uul *n.* cliff, precipice.

uul ch'och' *n.* cliff.

uul pek *n.* cliff.

wa *n.* clay.

woqxkum *n.* lava.

xa'awku *n.* lava.

xam *n.* fire. *Var:* xaml.

xb'e ha' *n.* channel.

xb'een tzuul *n.* summit, peak.

xchamal taq'a *n.* abyss.

xch'ajom *n.* erosion.

xch'och palaw *n.* island.

xhopolal *n.* opening.

xiik' *n.* gully, ravine.

xjul taq'a *n.* abyss.

xkawil roq ha' *n.* rapids.

xk'uhil *adj.* volcanic.

xmar choxa *n.* obsidian.

xmaal kaaq *n.* obsidian.

xmu che' *n.* shade (under trees).

xnimalpalaw *n.* ocean, sea.

xokaq'ab' *n.* rainbow.

xpisk' ha' *n.* waterfall.

xrepom palaw *n.* wave.

xtz'akeb' xe'toon *n.* ruins.

xtz'iral ch'och' *n.* crevice.

xulk'ukil nima' *n.* waterfall.

xyampi ha' *n.* island.

xyanq tzuul *n.* gorge, canyon.

yo'leb'aal ha' *n.* fountain.

yo'lejeb'ha' *n.* fountain.

Xq'ehil / Weather

aak'ab' *n.* darkness. *Var:* ak'ab'.
From: *ahk'ab' 'night' (Yucatecan, Ch'olan, possible) (1).

b'achal hab' *n.* rain with hail.

b'isketiiq *n.* degrees.

b'ut *n.* flood.

choq ru *adj.* foggy.

chu' ke *n.* dew.

chu'ke *n.* dew.

hab' *n.* rain.

hab'al *n.* rain.

hiik *n.* earthquake.

iq' xsa' *adj.* windy.

kaqsut-iq' *n.* storm, hurricane.

kawil hab' *n.* downpour, shower.

kaaq *n.* storm, thunder.

ke *adj.* cold, chilly.

kehilch'och' *n.* cold climate.

kok' ruhil hab' *n.* drizzle.

kutan *adj.* clear.

kutan *n.* day, weather.
  Var: kutank.

kutankil hab' *adj.* rainy.

lan lan *adj.* humid.

lemskaaq *n.* lightning bolt.

luulu *adj.* mild, cool, lukewarm.

muqb'il *adj.* cloudy, overcast.

musmus *adj.* very fine.

musmus hab' *n.* mist.

nub'un *adj.* cloudy.

palawhiik *n.* undersea earthquake.

paynum *adj.* fast.

pekb'ach *n.* ice.

priim *n.* dawn, early morning.
  From: prima 'first canonical hour' (Spanish) (1).

q'ojyin *n.* night, evening.
  Var: q'oqyin.

q'ojyin *adj.* dark.

rachhab' *n.* precipitation.

raq'kaaq *n.* lightning.

repom *n.* lightning.

repom kaaq *n.* thunderstorm.

saqb'ach *n.* hail, ice.

saq'ehil *n.* drought, dry spell.

saq'ehil kutan *n.* sunny.

sujen *n.* frost. *Var:* sujew.

sujew *n.* mist, fog.

tiq *adj.* warm.

tiqkehil *n.* temperature.

tiqwal saq'e *adj.* hot.

tiqwalch'och' *n.* hot climate.

tuntunkil choq *n.* fog.

t'aqt'aq *adj.* damp, wet, humid.

xa'awilk'u *n.* eruption.
Var: **xxa'aw k'u.**

xchu' ke *n.* snow. *Var:* **xchu'i keh.**

xlanlanil *n.* humidity.

xq'ehil *n.* season.

xrepom kaaq *n.* lightning bolt, bolt of lightning. *Var:* **xrepoom kaaq.**

xrepomkaaq *adj.* electrocuted.

xteram *n.* degrees.

xtiqwalil *n.* temperature.

xyaab' kaaq *n.* thunder.

yamyo ruhil kutan *adj.* cloudless, clear.

yo hab' *adj.* rainy.

Sa' Tenamit / In Town

aj ab'ine'leb' *n.* crowd.

aj ab'l tenamit *n agt.* tourist.

aj b'e *n agt.* passer-by, migrant, traveler, pilgrim.

aj b'e *n agt.* tourist.

aj b'eenel *n agt.* pedestrian.

aj ch'upul xaml *n agt.* fire brigade.

aj k'ay kok'toq' *n agt.* gum seller.

aj k'uub'anel poych'iich' *n agt.* mechanic.

aj numelb'e *n agt.* pedestrian.

ajsib'aal u *n.* park.

amaq' tenamit *n.* crowd.

b'atz'unleb'aal *n.* stadium.

b'esleb'aal *n.* barbershop.

b'it'b'it'leb'aal *n.* beauty salon.

chajb'a'e *n.* loudspeaker.

chinamiit *n.* gallery.

ch'ina huhiljelool *n.* paper bag.

ch'ina kaaxukuutil lem *n.* streetlight.

ch'utamil *n.* meeting, encounter.

ch'uutleb'aal *n.* meeting place, meeting hall.

ch'uutleb'aalkab'l *n.* meeting place, meeting hall.

elkleb'aal *n.* exit.

elkleb'aal sa' junpaat *n.* emergency exit.

eetalil jalam u *n.* monument.

eetalil patz'e'k *n.* monument.

eetalmu *n.* cinema, movie theater.

hilob'eleb'aal ch'iich' *n.* bus station, terminal.

hiltasib'aalch'iich' *n.* parking lot.

ileb'aalmu *n.* cinema, movie theater.

iiq *n.* suitcase, luggage, large bag.

ja'leb'aal *n.* kiosk.

ja'leb'aal'u *n.* park.

ja'leb'ch'ool *n.* park.

kaxlan wahib'aal *n.* bakery.

kaxlan xamlel b'e *n.* traffic light.

kaxtzuychampa *n.* plastic bag.

kayib'aal *n.* shop, store.

ki'b'ach *n.* ice cream.

ki'il saqb'ach saa'us *n.* ice cream.

k'ayib'aal b'an re ketomj *n.* veterinary store.

k'ayib'aal b'atz'uul *n.* toy store.

k'ayib'aal kape *n.* cafe, cafeteria.

k'ayib'aal kaxlan wa *n.* bakery.

k'ayib'aal kok' tenb'il ch'iich' *n.* jewelry store.

k'ayib'aal k'anjelob'aal *n.* hardware store.

k'ayib'aal k'areru *n.* candy store.

k'ayib'aal saa'us *n.* fruit shop.

k'ayib'aal tasal hu *n.* bookstore.

k'ayib'aal tib' *n.* butcher shop.

k'ayib'aal uutz'u'uj *n.* florist, flower shop.

k'ayib'aal xaq ut xe' pim *n.* greengrocer.

k'ayib'aal xaab' *n.* shoe store.

k'ayib'aalhu *n.* bookstore.

k'ayib'aalhumb'ookilha' *n.* gas station.

k'ayiil *n.* market.

k'ehok sahil ch'ool *v phr.* to greet.

k'ila poyanam *n.* crowd.

k'ulb'aq'qax'ib' *n.* roundabout, traffic circle.

k'utb'a numleb' *n.* traffic light.

k'utul numeb'aal *n.* traffic light.

k'uuleb'aaltumin *n.* bank. *Var:* k'ulab'aal.

lit'leb'aal *n.* barrier.

loq'leb'aal *n.* shop, store.

mama' rochochil aq'ej *n.* department store.

mul *n.* litter.

na'ajej *n.* location, place.

neb'a' *n.* tramp, beggar.

nimaltzoleb'aal *n.* university.

nimla b'e *n.* road.

nimla kab'l *n.* building.

nimla k'ayib'aal *n.* department store.

nimla k'ayib'aal *n.* grocery store, supermarket.

nimla k'ayib'aal tzakahemq *n.* restaurant.

nimla ochoch *n.* building.

nimlawa'leb'aal *n.* restaurant.

nimqi kab'l *n.* buildings.

ninqi'ochoch *n.* building.

ochochnaal *n.* hotel.

pak'b'il poyanam *n.* statue.

pak'yu'amha' *n.* fountain.

poyanamb'iltz'ak *n.* statue.

poopol kab'l *n.* city hall.

pujha'nel ch'iich' *n.* fire truck.

puktasib'aal aatin *n.* loudspeaker.

ral punitch'iich' *n.* little bell.

re tenamit *n.* outskirts.

reb'e *n.* sidewalk. *Var:* re b'e; reeb'e.

reetalil b'e *n.* traffic sign.

rochoch aj titz'ol toj *n.* toll booth.

rochochil awa'b'ejink *n.* national palace.

rochochil ilob'aal mu *n.* cinema, movie theater.

rochochil k'utb'esink *n.* arts center.

rochochil ruk'a' poych'iich' *n.* gas station.

rochochil tasal hu *n.* library.

rochochil tumin *n.* bank.

roqb'e *n.* street.

ruhib'e *n.* cobblestone.

ruq'b'e *n.* avenue.

sa' uleb'aal *n.* eyewear shop.

sahil ch'oolib'k *v phr.* to greet.

saqb'ach ha' *n.* snowcone, shaved ice.

sisib'aaltib' *n.* barbeque stall.

taks *n.* taxi.

tenamitil teepal *n.* urban center.

teep *n.* district, neighborhood, sector, canton.

t'ujleb'aal *n.* beauty salon.

tz'ub'pajha' *n.* fire truck.

uk'leb'aal *n.* water fountain, drinking fountain.

uk'leb'aal kape *n.* cafe, cafeteria.

wa'leb'aal *n.* restaurant, diner.

wakax kab'l *n.* kiosk.

warb'etaal *n.* boarding house.

xajleb'aal *n.* disco, nightclub.

xaqleb'aal ch'iich' *n.* bus stop.

xb'eleb'aal poyanam *n.* crosswalk.

xb'een ochoch *n.* rooftop terrace.

xhilob'aal b'eleb'aalch'iich' *n.* parking meter.

xlemul k'ayib'aal *n.* glass cabinet, display case.

xmolam aj kolonel *n.* rescue unit.

xmu mama' k'ayib'aal *n.* mall entrance.

xna'aj aj ilol tenamit *n.* police station.

xna'aj aj k'ehol esil *n.* information office.

xna'aj b'eleb'aal ch'iich' *n.* bus station.

xna'aj cha *n.* ashtray.

xna'aj esil *n.* billboard.

xna'aj hu *n.* trash can, wastepaper bin.

xna'aj k'utleb'aal *n.* art gallery.

xna'aj taql *n.* mailbox.

xna'aj uutz'u'uj *n.* flowerbed, flower garden.

xna'ajeb' cheek *n.* nursing home.

xnimal neb'aal *n.* plaza, square.

xnimal ru tzoleb'aal *n.* university.

xnumik poyanam *n.* crosswalk.

xpuchleb'aal tenamit *n.* laundromat.

xteepal tenamit *n.* district, neighborhood, sector, canton.

xtoltolil ki'il saqb'ach saa'us *n.* ice cream cart.

xxanil b'e *n.* cobblestone street.

xxaal b'e *n.* crossroads. *Var:* **xxaali b'e.**

xxuk b'e *n.* street corner, corner.

xyi *n.* center.

xyi tenamit *n.* downtown.

yeechi'ink *n.* commercial, ad, advertisement.

Sum'aatinank Ib' / Speech and Communication

aj ka'aatin *n agt.* bilingual, polyglot.

aj k'ila'aatin *n agt.* polyglot.

aj pukaatin *n.* broadcaster.

aatinab'aal *n.* media, means of communication, communications.

aatinak *v.* to speak, talk, chat.

aatinak chi rix *v phr.* to opine, give one's opinion.

aatinak-ib' *n.* monologue.

aatinamank *v.* to speak, talk.

aatinank *v.* to consult.

aatinob'aal *n.* language, tongue.

aatinom *n.* speech. *Var:* **aatin.**

chajok e *v phr.* to shout.

chaq'b'enk *v.* to answer.

chaq'om *n.* answer, echo.

ch'anaak *n.* silence.

ch'anch'o *n.* silence.

ch'iilank *v.* to scold.

ch'ool'aatin *v.* to paraphrase.

esilank *v.* to announce.

hasb'ak *v.* to whisper, mumble.

ja'ajul *n.* voice.

jalb'esiil'aatin *n.* dialect.

jiq'jiq'ink ib' *v phr.* to whisper.

ka'aatin *adj.* bilingual.

kawyehink *n.* recital, recitation.

kulku *adj.* silent, quiet.

k'a'uxlal *n.* comment.

k'a'uxlil *n.* motto.

k'ab'a'ink *v.* to call (a name), name.

k'anasink rix *v phr.* to boast.

k'ehok eetal *v phr.* to take note of, notice, realize.

lolob' aatin *n.* bad words.

lotz re *v phr.* to stutter, stammer.

muqmukil aatin *n.* secret.

muqmukilna'leb' *n.* secret.

murink *v.* to separate, segregate, break down, fragment. *Var:* **xmurb'al.**

nim sa' xkux *adj.* hoarse.

nimob'eresink ib' *v phr.* to boast.

oq'lok *v.* to howl.

patz'ok *v.* to ask, beg, plead, survey, inquire.

patz'om *n.* question.

q'ichok e *v phr.* to shout. *From:* q'ich 'to open the mouth to laugh' (Q'anjob'alan) (3).

q'usuk *v.* to scold, warn, reprimand.

ralab'aatinob'aal *n.* dialect.

sak'ok aatin *n.* murmurs, offensive words, slurs.

seb'esink *v.* to threaten.

seeraq'ik *v.* to speak, talk, tell stories, narrate. *Var:* **saaraq'ik; saraq'ik; seraq'ik.**

sihokna'leb' *v.* to suggest.

sumchi'ib'k *v.* to exchange (words).

sumenk *v.* to answer, respond, reply.

sumenk-ib' *adj.* reciprocal.

sumyaab' *n.* echo.

tat re *v phr.* to stutter, stammer.

tiikil'aatin *adj.* colloquial.

tos e *n.* speech impairment.

t'ilb'a'u'ji'aq *n.* tongue twister.

t'ilru'uj'aq *n.* tongue twister.

tz'i'ej aatin *n.* obscenity.

tz'uq kawyaab' *n.* accent mark.

wech'ok *v.* to describe.

wech'ok *n.* description.

Var: **xwech'b'al rix.**

xib'enk *v.* to threaten.

xik' aj aatin *n.* dirty words.

xtuqlal'aatinob'aal *n.* grammar.

xuxb'ak *v.* to whistle.

Var: **xuxb'ank.** *From:* xuxub' 'to whistle' (Yucatecan, Ch'olan, possible) (2).

xyaab'asinkil *n.* pronunciation.

xyeb'al *n.* communication.

xyeeb'al *n.* conference.

yaab'asink *v.* to recite, dictate, pronounce.

yaab'aatin *n.* accent, accentuation.

yehok *v.* to say, communicate.

yoob'ank aatin *n.* gossip, rumor.

yoob'k'ab'a' *n.* nickname.

Aatinob'aal sa' Yiib'ejilch'och' / Central American Languages

achi *lang.* Achi (Baja Verapaz).

akateko *lang.* Akatek (Huehuetenango).

aatinob'aal maay *n.* Mayan languages.

chalchitan *lang.* Chalchitek (Huehuetenango).

chuj *lang.* Chuj (Huehuetenango).

ch'orti' *lang.* Chorti (Chiquimula, Zacapa).

inkles *lang.* English. *From:* Spanish 'inglés'.

itza' *lang.* Itza (El Petén).

jakalteka *lang.* Jakaltek [aka Popti] (Huehuetenango).

kaqchikel *lang.* Kaqchikel (Chimaltenango, Guatemala, Baja Verzpaz, Sacatepéquez, Sololá, Suchitepéquez).

karifuna *lang.* Garífuna (Izabal).

kastiiy *lang.* Spanish, Castilian. *From:* Spanish 'castellano'.

kaxlan aatin *lang.* Spanish, Castilian, foreign language. *From:* Spanish 'castellano'.

kaxlanchi' *lang.* Spanish, Castilian, foreign language. *From:* Spanish 'castellano'.

k'iche' *lang.* K'iche (El Quiché, Huehuetenango, Quetzaltenango, Retalhuleu, Sololá, Suchitepéquez Totonicapán, San Marcos, Chimaltenango).

mam *lang.* Mam (Huehuetenango, Quetzaltenango, San Marcos, Retalhuleu).

mopan *lang.* Mopan (El Petén).

popti *lang.* Popti [aka Jakaltek] (Huehuetenango).

poqomam *lang.* Poqomam (Escuintla, Guatemala, Jalapa).

poqomchi' *lang.* Poqomchi (Alta Verapaz, Baja Verapaz, El Quiché).

q'anjob'al *lang.* Qanjobal (Huehuetenango).

q'eqchi' *lang.* Q'eqchi' (Alta Verapaz, Baja Verapaz, El Quiché, Izabal, El Petén, Belize).

sipakapense *lang.* Sipakapa (San Marcos).

tektiteko *lang.* Tektitek (Huehuetenango).

tz'utujil *lang.* Tz'utujil (Sololá, Suchitepéquez).

xinka *lang.* Xinca (Santa Rosa, Jutiapa).

T'ikr ut Xsahob' ru / Clothing and Adornments

aq' *n.* uniform.

aq' ch'ot ruq' *n.* vest.

aq' re atink *n.* swimsuit, bathing suit.

aq' re b'atz'unk *n.* sportswear.

aq' re sa' aq'ej *n.* slip.

aq' re wark *n.* pyjamas.

aq'ej *n.* clothing.

atiyach' *n.* bathing suit, swimsuit.

b'atb'a ib' *n.* coat.

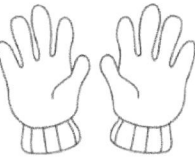

b'atb'a uq' *n.* glove.

b'atz-aq' *n.* jersey, team jersey.

b'atz'unk b'aatal *n.* camisole.

b'aatal *n.* clothing.

b'eq *n.* tie, necktie.

b'estiiy *n.* dress. *From:* Spanish 'vestido'.

b'eel *n.* veil. *Var:* **b'elo**. *From:* velo 'the veil' (Spanish) (1).

b'een'aqej *n.* knee pad, knee patch.

b'otb'il aq' *n.* skirt.

b'otonx *n.* button. *From:* botones 'the buttons' (Spanish) (1).

b'ools *n.* bag, purse. *From:* Spanish 'bolsa'.

b'oox *n.* pocket. *From:* *box 'round container' (Yucatecan, Ch'olan, possible) (2).

chakeet *n.* jacket. *From:* Spanish 'chaqueta'.

chapleb'ismal *n.* hair pin.

chapleb't'ikr *n.* button.

chet-aq' *n.* skirt.

ch'ina yax ch'iich' *n.* clip.

ch'ot b'estiiy *n.* miniskirt.

ch'ot t'ikr *n.* undershirt.

ch'otlepon *n.* shirt, t-shirt.

ch'otwex *n.* shorts, briefs.

isb' *n.* poncho.

isink aq' *v phr.* to get undressed, undress.

jisil t'ikr *n.* ribbon.

jit'leb'wex *n.* belt.

junxaqalil t'ikr *n.* suit.

jur aq' *n.* nightgown.

jut aq' *n.* overcoat.

jut t'ikr *n.* overcoat.

jut-aq' *n.* dress.

kamiis *n.* shirt. *From:* camisa 'shirt' (Spanish) (1).

kamiis ixq *n.* blouse.

kaxlanuuq *n.* skirt. *Var:* kax'uuq.

kaxpo'ot *n.* blouse.

kem *n.* cloth.

kok' aq' re ixq *n.* panties, underwear.

kok' aq' re winq *n.* underpants, underwear.

kok' sut *n.* handkerchief.

kopmokooch *n.* cape.

korb'aat *n.* tie. *From:* Spanish 'corbata'.

kotchapleb' *n.* button.

k'aamal sa' *n.* sash. *Var:* k'aamalsa'ej; k'aamasa'.

k'ehok aq' *v phr.* to get dressed.

k'erex *n.* zipper.

lamb'a tu' *n.* bra, brassiere.

lanb'aja'aj *n.* scarf.

lantu' *n.* bra, brassiere.

laan *n.* wool. *From:* lana 'wool' (Spanish) (1).

lemtz'ti'kr *n.* silk.

lepon *n.* shirt (woman's).

lep-punit *n.* visor.

loon *n.* canvas. *From:* Spanish 'lona'.

loonil wex *n.* jeans, blue jeans.

mama' pimil t'ikr *n.* coat.

muheel *n.* umbrella.

mut aq' *n.* shorts.

nayl *n.* nylon. *From:* Spanish 'nylon'.

nimla siinch *n.* belt. *From:* cincho 'belt' (Spanish) (1).

noq' *n.* cotton.

paraaw *n.* umbrella. *From:* Spanish 'paraguas'.

peeraj *n.* shawl.

po'ot *n.* blouse (typical Mayan).

potzwex *n.* sweatpants, sweats.

punit *n.* hat, cap.

q'ixleb'aq' *n.* jacket.

q'ixt'ikr *n.* sweater, jacket.

q'unil t'ikr *n.* flannel.

re t'ikr *n.* lace.

re xch'ool wex *n.* fly (of pants).

riiqankil *n.* suspender.

roq wex *n.* pant leg.

ru aq' *n.* pattern (clothing).

ruq'b' *n.* sleeve.

ruq'm aq' *n.* cuff.

sa' ruq' aq' *n.* cuff.

seet *n.* silk. *From:* seda 'the silk' (Spanish) (1).

sok xb'een'aq *n.* knee pad, knee patch.

soq'keep *n.* beret, cap.

soq'punit *n.* beret.

sumal'aq' *n.* change of clothes.

sut *n.* handkerchief, rag.

ta *n.* fur.

tiqb'al *n.* clothing, clothes.

tiqb'al *n.* dress.

tiqok ib' *v phr.* to put on.

t'ikr *n.* clothing, cloth.

t'upuy *n.* headband, headdress. *From:* t'upuy 'the headband' (Ch'olti') (2).

tz'apleb' *n.* zipper.

tz'uleb' *n.* ribbon.

tz'uumal *n.* leather. *Var:* tz'uum.

tz'uumil chakeet *n.* fur coat.

uuq *n.* skirt (typical indigenous).

warib'aq *n.* pyjamas.

warib'aal aq *n.* pyjamas.

wex *n.* trousers, pants.

wex ch'ot roq *n.* shorts.

wex re loon *n.* jeans, blue jeans.

xb'ak'b'al wex *n.* belt.

xb'asalal *n.* pant cuff.

xb'aatal ja'aj *n.* scarf.

xch'ina ch'iich'ul *n.* buckle.

xik'sotz' *n.* umbrella.

xkux aq' *n.* collar.

xkux ruq' aq' *n.* shirt cuff.

xk'aamal *n.* suspender.

xk'aamal uuq *n.* drawstring (for a skirt).

xk'ob'lal *n.* hole.

xlanb'al xb'een'aq *n.* knee pad, knee patch.

xnimal *n.* size, dimension.

xnimal roq *n.* length.

xnimal ru *n.* width.

xputz't'ikr *n.* rag.

xsa' xaab' *n.* insole.

xsok b'itom *n.* head pad.

xta *n.* wrap, wrap-around.

xta a' *n.* knee-high stocking.

xta b'aatal *n.* underwear.

xta jolom *n.* cap.

xta oq *n.* sock, stocking.

xta uq' *n.* glove. *Var:* xta uq'b'; xta uq'm.

xta-uuq *n.* underskirt, petticoat, slip.

xtehelal xkux *n.* low neck.

xxik aq' *n.* loop.

xyach'winq *n.* underwear, brief.

xyi *n.* waistband.

xyi aq' *n.* belt.

yach' *n.* underwear, brief, panty.

yaalt'ikr *n.* shirt.

yutkux *n.* tie, necktie.

yutleb' *n.* hair tie, hair band.

yut'ismal *n.* hair pin.

Chaab'il Eechej / Jewelry

aj tenol ch'iich' *n agt.* jeweller.

aj yiib'om q'ol *n agt.* jeweller.

aj yiib'om reloj *n agt.* watchmaker.

b'ot *n.* ring.

ch'ina sursukil ch'iich' *n.* ring.

jutz'un pemech *n.* mother-of-pearl.

ka'xik *n.* earring.

kok' tenb'il ch'iich' *n.* jewelry.

lemtz'pek *n.* diamond.

matq'ab' *n.* ring. *From:* matk'ab' 'ring' (Ch'olan) (4).

nat'leb'ismal *n.* diadem, tiara, hairband.

pulseer *n.* bracelet. *From:* pulsera 'the bracelet' (Spanish) (1).

q'ol *n.* pearl, bead.

q'ol *n.* chain.

q'ol *n.* necklace.

q'ol *n.* jewel.

q'ol'uq' *n.* bracelet.

ruutz'u'ujil aq' *n.* adornment, accessory, decoration.

tiqilal *n.* link (in a chain).

xpemechil palaw *n.* sea shell.

xsahob' ru *n.* adornment.

Eb' li Xaab' / Footwear

aanilxaab' *n.* tennis shoes.

b'atb'al oq *n.* sock, stocking.

b'onxaab' *n.* shoe polish.

b'oot *n.* boot. *From:* bote 'the boot' (Spanish) (1).

b'ootaxaab' *n.* boots.

jurxaab' *n.* boot.

kok' tzelek xaab' *n.* ankle boot.

kok' xaab' *n.* sneakers.

mesleb' xaab' *n.* shoe brush.

perxaab' *n.* sandal.

potzxaab' *n.* tennis shoes.

raq'xaab' *n.* tongue (of a shoe).

reetalil xaab' *n.* shoe mold, shoetree.

rit xaab' *n.* heel (of a shoe).

sa' roq xaab' *n.* sole (footwear).

tzelek xaab' *n.* boot.

tz'apb'al oq *n.* sock, stocking.

xaab' *n.* shoe.

xk'aamal xaab' *n.* shoelace.

xlemtz' xaab' *n.* shoe polish.

xta xaab' *n.* sock, stocking.

Xb'aanunkil T'ikr / Clothes Making

aj b'ojonel *n agt.* tailor.

aj b'ojonel ixq *n agt.* seamstress.

b'ak'ok *v.* to tie.

b'arb'arink *v.* to roll.

b'ekleb' k'ix *n.* needle (sewing).

b'ojleb' *n.* sewing machine.

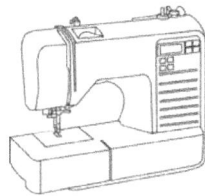

b'ojleb' ch'iich' *n.* sewing machine.

b'ojleb'aal *n.* sewing workshop.

b'ojok *v.* to sew.

b'ojom *n.* seam.

b'onok *v.* to dye, paint, stain.

chirok *v.* to spread out.

ch'int'ojiil *n.* tack, thumbtack.

hitok *v.* to untie, untangle, unravel. *From:* *hit 'to untie' (Ch'olan) (3).

jit'aal *n.* buckle.

jutz'b'ojleb' *n.* needle (sewing).

jutz'kutleb' *n.* needle (hypodermic).

kemleb' *n.* loom.

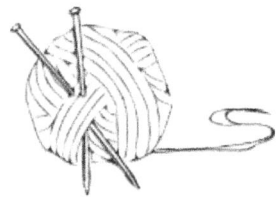

kemok *v.* to weave, braid, plait, knit.

kok' kuux *n.* pin.

kuux *n.* needle. *From:* Spanish 'aguja'.

kuuxink *v.* to sew.

k'aamak *v.* to spin.

k'ehok b'otonx *v phr.* to sew on buttons.

k'ixok *v.* to untie.

k'olok *v.* to shorten. *Var:* k'osok.

k'uub'ch'iich'b'ojleb' *n.* sewing machine.

k'uub'ch'iich'kem *n.* loom.

noq' *n.* thread.

peteet *n.* spindle. *Var:* pet'eet'.

pixlenk *v.* to tangle.

q'ooch *n.* roll.

ranok chi noq' *v phr.* to stitch.

re t'ikr *n.* lace.

rela' t'ikr *n.* scrap of cloth.

reetalil *n.* pattern.

rinrin *n.* elastic band.

setok *v.* to trim, cut.

tachweel *n.* tack, thumbtack. *From:* Spansish 'tachuela'.

t'ikr *n.* clothing, cloth.

t'ikr loon *n.* denim.

t'oklal *n.* knot.

t'ok' *n.* knot.

tz'uluk *n.* plait, braid. *Var:* tz'ulum. *From:* *tz'ul 'to weave (mat arch)' (Ch'olti') (2).

xb'asb'al *n.* fold.

xb'asb'al sa' xyi *n.* crease.

xche'el noq' *n.* bobbin, spool.

xiitink *v.* to mend, darn.

xkolb'al ru'uj uqb' *n.* thimble.

xna'aj kuux *n.* pin cushion.

xnoq'inkil li akuux *v phr.* to thread a needle.

xtok' *n.* knot. *Var:* t'oklal.

xtusb'al xsa' *n.* pleat.

xukub'k'ix *n.* safety pin, pin.

xyuch'inkil xsa' *n.* gather.

yiib'ank sa' ru t'ikr *v phr.* to sew buttonholes, sew eyelets.

Tzakahemq ut K'uub'ank / Food and Cooking

al *adj.* unripe.

aseet *n.* oil. *Var:* aseyt. *From:* aceite 'the oil' (Spanish) (1).

b'ich'ok *v.* to peel, skin.

b'ik'b'ik' *adj.* greasy.

b'iq'e'k *v.* to choke.

b'otwa *n.* taco.

b'uch *n.* corn (prepared for grinding).

chaqi'el *n.* thirst. *Var:* chaq'ieel; chaqi e.

chaqiq re *adj.* thirsty.

chaqi'eel *v.* to be thirsty.

chaq' *adj.* ripe.

chaq' chi us *adj.* well done.

chikleb' *n.* fork.

chiqb'il *adj.* cooked.

chiqb'il tib' *n.* stew.

chiqok *v.* to cook.

chiron *n.* pork rind.

ch'um *n.* hunger.

ch'ume'k *v.* to be hungry.

hab'ok *v.* to chew.

ichaj tzakahemq *n.* salad.

isink xkehil *v phr.* to defrost.

jichok *v.* to grate, scrape.

jiq'e'k *v.* to choke.

jochok *v.* to scrape. *From:* *joch 'to take off, peel off' (Yucatecan, Ch'olan, possible) (2).

jokok *v.* to scrape, scoop.

jot'ok *v.* to scrape.

jotzok *v.* to peel.

junajink *v.* to stir, mix.

juylek *v.* to beat, whip.

kab' *n.* candy, sweets.

kab' *n.* caramel.

kakaw *n.* cocoa.

kaq ik *n.* turkey soup.

kax'olb' *n.* lubricant, cooking oil.

kaxlanq'ib' *n.* cooking oil.

kaalt *n.* soup, broth. *From:* caldo 'soup or broth' (Spanish) (1).

ke'b'il pix *n.* tomato sauce.

ke'ek *v.* to grind.

keresink *v.* to chill.

kees *n.* cheese. *From:* queso 'the cheese' (Spanish) (1).

kich'kich'ink *v.* to scrub.

kilinb'il paaps *n.* french fries.

kok' poch ob'en *n.* mini tamale.

kolb'ach'ool *n.* snack, refreshment.

kuut *n.* bunch.

k'ay *n.* spice.

k'ilink *v.* to fry.

k'orechkaxlanwa *n.* toast.

k'orkik'xe' *n.* enchilada.

k'oy *n.* gum.

k'oylenk *v.* to chew.

k'ook' *n.* lard.

k'ub'k'u *adj.* cooked.

k'uxuk *v.* to chew.

k'uub'anb'il olb' *n.* butter.

k'uub'aak *adj.* cooked.

loqlotk *v.* to boil.

manteek *n.* grease, fat, butter. *From:* manteca 'lard' (Spanish) (1).

mayonees *n.* mayonnaise, mayo. *From:* Spanish 'mayonesa'.

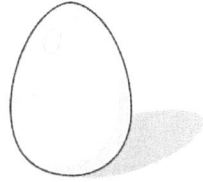

mol *n.* egg. *Var:* molb'.

nub'resink *v.* to rinse.

nuq'uk *v.* to swallow. *From:* *nuq' 'throat' (Western Mayan) (4).

ob'en *n.* tamale.

olb' *n.* lard, fat, grease, oil. *Var:* q'olb'.

paast *n.* pasta. *From:* Spanish 'pasta'.

piitza *n.* pizza. *From:* English 'pizza'.

pomb'il *adj.* roasted, grilled.

pomb'il paaps *n.* baked potatoes.

puq'b'il paaps *n.* mashed potatoes.

puq'b'il pix *n.* tomato sauce.

putz'ink *v.* to liquify.

qirok *v.* to scrape.

q'an *adj.* ripe.

q'aaneq *adj.* rotten.

q'em *n.* dough, cornmeal.

q'emrasink *v.* to knead.

q'emtu' *n.* cheese.

q'emya'altu' *n.* cheese.

q'ix ha' *n.* hot water.

ramb'atz'aj *n.* smock, apron.

raqink *v.* to chop.

rax *adj.* unripe.

rax *adj.* raw.

ru ut xe' pim *n.* vegetables.

ruuch che'k'aam *n.* vegetable.

sasob'resink *v.* to thicken.

saa'us *n.* candy.

sib'ha' *n.* carbohydrates.

sisank *v.* to roast, fry.

sob'ok *v.* to crush, grind, dent.

soop *n.* soup. *From:* Spanish 'sopa'.

supq'een *n.* vegetable.

tayarin *n.* noodles. *From:* Spanish 'tallarines'.

tenok *v.* to crush, grind. *From:* *ten 'to hammer, flatten' (Ch'olan) (2).

tib'el wa *n.* food, meal.

tiwok *v.* to eat, bite.

tiikob'resink *v.* to season.

toj al *adj.* unripe.

toj rax *adj.* rare.

toq' *n.* gum.

t'oqtzak *n.* mayonnaise, mayo.

tzakahem *n.* food, meal.
   Var: tzakahemq; tzekeem.

tzakank *v.* to eat, feed.
   Var: tzekank.

tz'ilok *v.* to sieve, strain. *From:* tz'iil 'to sieve or strain' (Mopan) (4).

tz'okaak *v.* to be hungry.

tz'okaaq *adj.* hungry.

tz'ub'uk *v.* to suck, absorb.

tz'uqresink *v.* to soak.

uk'ak *v.* to drink.

uq'unink *v.* to liquify.

wa *n.* meal.

wa *n.* tortilla.

wa re eq'la *n.* breakfast.

wa re ewu *n.* supper.

wa re wa'leb' *n.* lunch.

wa'ak *v.* to eat.

wa'al *n.* food.

wa'ok *v.* to eat.

we'ej *n.* hunger, famine. *From:* *wi'ij ('hunger' ?) (Yucatecan) (3).

we'ejil *n.* scarcity.

we'ejink *v.* to go hungry.

woqxink *v.* to boil.

woqxink chi timil *v phr.* to simmer.

xab'onink *v.* to wash with soap.

xb'anol *n.* spice, seasoning.

xe' ru che' *n.* vegetable.

xjunes tz'ej *adj.* boneless.

xnaq' kakaw *n.* cocoa bean.

xokleb' *n.* fork.

xokxoxch'ool *adj.* concentrated.

xorok *v.* to make tortillas.

xq'anal mol *n.* yolk.

xsahob' tzakahemq *n.* spice, seasoning.

xtz'aqob' wa' *n.* dessert.

xtz'aqob'l ajsiil *n.* carbohydrates.

xujwahiltib' *n.* tostada.

xxeeb'ul pim *n.* margarine.

xxulel palaw *n.* seafood.

xya'al ik *n.* broth.

xya'al kab' *n.* honey.

xya'al pix *n.* salsa.

xya'al tib' *n.* gravy.

xyuutzakahemq *n.* spice, seasoning.

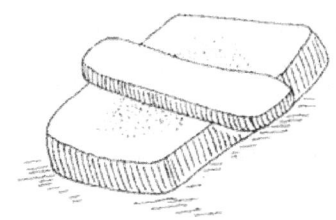

yab'ok *v.* to crush, grind.

yatz'ok *v.* to milk.

ya'al *n.* soup.

yo'yookilal *n.* nonperishable.

yolq'em *n.* lard, fat, grease, oil.

yoq'ok *v.* to knead.

yulenb'il molb' *n.* scrambled eggs.

yuq'uq'nak *adj.* ripe.

yuulink *v.* to dilute, blend.

Eb' li Tib' / Meats

b'utb'il paayil tib' aaq *n.* longaniza.

b'utb'iltib' chorizo.

b'utb'iltib' *n.* sausage, cold cuts.

b'utb'iltib'aaq *n.* chorizo.

choriis *n.* pork sausage. *From:* Spanish 'chorizo'.

ch'och' *n.* liver.

jamon *n.* ham. *From:* Spanish 'jamón'.

kaxlan xut' *n.* hamburger.

ke'b'il tib' *n.* ground meat.

ketomq *n.* fowl.

kilinb'il *adj.* fried.

kilinb'il kaxlan *n.* fried chicken.

kilinb'il tib' *n.* steak, beefsteak.

kostiiy *n.* ribs. *From:* Spanish 'costillas'.

k'aamk'ot *n.* tripe.

k'ook' *n.* fatty meat.

moronk *n.* blood sausage.

pihamb'r *n.* cold cuts. *From:* Spanish 'fiambre'.

pomb'il tib' *n.* roast beef.

salchiich *n.* sausage, hot dog. *From:* salchicha 'the sausage' (Spanish) (1).

saaseb' *n.* liver.

setinb'il tib' *n.* ground meat.

sisanb'iltib' *n.* grilled meat.

sulutz *n.* marrow.

tib' *n.* meat. *Var:* **chib'**.

t'ort'ookil tib' *n.* meatballs.

xkok' xch'al xul *n.* menudo.

xorb'il tib' *n.* ham.

xsaqal kaxlan *n.* chicken breast.

xtib'el ak'ach *n.* turkey.

xtib'el aaq *n.* pork.

xtib'el kaxlan *n.* chicken.

xtib'el kej *n.* venison.

xtib'el ru'uj aq' *n.* tongue.

xtib'el wakax *n.* beef.

xujanb'iltib' *n.* pork rinds.

xul k'iche' *n.* game.

Jorinb'il Kaxlan Wa / Baked Goods

atz'aminb'ilkaxlanwa *n.* French bread.

jorinb'il *adj.* baked, toasted.

kaxk'oyem *n.* cracker.

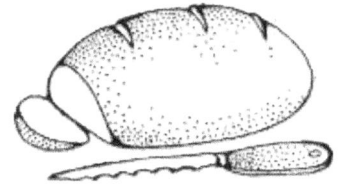

kaxlan wa *n.* bread.

kaxlan wahib'aal *n.* bakery.

kaxlank'uluj *n.* cake.

k'aj *n.* flour.

k'ajil kaxlanwa *n.* flour.

k'ayib'aal kaxlan wa *n.* bakery.

pomleb'aal *n.* oven.

potzkaxlanwa *n.* rolls.

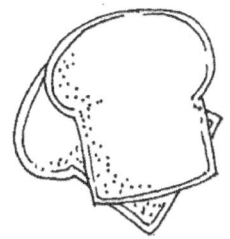

setb'ilkaxlanwa *n.* sliced bread.

siip kaxlan wa *n.* French bread.

tz'in *n.* manioc bread.

uutz'u'jinb'ilkaxlanwa *n.* cake.

xelexkaxlanwa *n.* cupcake.

xk'aj ariin *n.* flour (wheat).

xoyk'uluj *n.* cake.

xpoqsil kaxlanwa *n.* flour.

xsiiptz'ub' kaxlan wa *n.* yeast.

xujsaa'us *n.* cookie.

Ki'il Q'een / Fruits

ab'aal *n.* cherry, plum.

asetuun *n.* olive. *From:* aceituna 'the olive' (Spanish) (1).

chiin *n.* orange.

ch'ol tul *n.* plantain.

ch'op *n.* pineapple.

iko *n.* fig. *Var:* igo. *From:* higo 'the fig' (Spanish) (1).

iyaj *n.* seed.

kaxlant'usub' *n.* grape. *Var:* uub'.

kaxq'ooq' *n.* watermelon. *Var:* kaqiq'ooq'.

ki'il q'een *n.* fruit.

kook *n.* coconut. *From:* coco 'coconut' (Spanish) (1).

kranaa *n.* pomegranate. *From:* Spanish 'granada'.

181

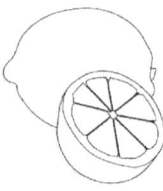

lamuunx *n.* lemon, citrus fruit. *Var:* **lamuux; lamunx**. *From:* limón 'the lemon' (Spanish) (1).

maniiy *n.* peanut. *Var:* **maniik**. *From:* mani 'the peanut' (Spanish) (1).

mank *n.* mango. *Var:* **maank**. *From:* Spanish 'mango'.

mansaan *n.* apple. *From:* manzana 'apple' (Spanish) (1).

mandariin *n.* tangerine. *From:* Spanish 'mandarina'.

melon *n.* melon. *From:* Spanish 'melón'.

mem'riiy *n.* quince. *From:* Spanish 'membrillo'.

met' tokan *n.* strawberry.

nispr *n.* medlar. *From:* Spanish 'níspero'.

nwes *n.* nut. *From:* nuez 'the nut' (Spanish) (1).

o *n.* avocado.

pata *n.* guayaba.

pechtokan *n.* strawberry.

perees *n.* strawberry. *From:* Spanish 'fresa'.

peer *n.* pear. *From:* Spanish 'pera'.

pix *n.* tomato.

putul *n.* papaya.

q'aajenaq *adj.* spoiled.

q'unixholob'oob' *n.* mango.

raxki' *n.* pear.

ru almeentr *n.* almonds. *From:* Spanish 'almendras'.

ru che' *n.* fruit.

ru peetaq *n.* fruit of the cactus.

sakil *n.* seed.

sakil k'um *n.* pumpkin seed.

sandiiy *n.* watermelon. *From:* Spanish 'sandía'.

saqi tul *n.* plantain.

sayi' *n.* plantain.

saa'us *n.* fruit.

serees *n.* cherry. *From:* Spanish 'cereza'.

sirweel *n.* plum. *From:* Spanish 'ciruela'.

tokan *n.* blackberry, mulberry.

toronj *n.* grapefruit. *From:* Spanish 'toronja'.

tul *n.* banana. *Var:* q'un tul.

turans *n.* peach. *Var:* lorans. *From:* Spanish 'durazno'.

t'usub' *n.* grape. *Var:* uub'.

u *n.* fruit.

utz'ajl *n.* sugarcane.

uuw *n.* grape. *From:* Spanish 'uva'.

wach'iil *n.* tamarind.

xnaq' *n.* seed.

K'ila sek' ut Tzakleb' / Crockery and Utensils

b'itzilch'iich' *n.* knife.

b'otb'okilsek' *n.* glass.

ch'ina ch'iich' *n.* knife.

ch'iich' sek' *n.* tin cup, tin plate.

ch'och' sek' *n.* plate.

helhokil sek' *n.* plate. *From:* sek' 'plate' (approximate form) (Western Mayan) (2).

kaxsu *n.* thermos.

konxik' *n.* clay frying pan.

k'ila sek' *n.* crockery.

k'ileb'aal *n.* pan.

k'ileb'aal *n.* frying pan.

k'ilolb' *n.* frying pan.

k'uuleb'aaltiq *n.* thermos.

lekleb' *n.* spoon, ladle. *Var:* lek.

mansek' *n.* saucepan.

per'uk'al *n.* saucepan.

platiiy *n.* saucer. *From:* platillo 'saucer' (Spanish) (1).

puk'xaar *n.* jug, pitcher.

sekch'iich' *n.* knife.

sek' *n.* cup, dish, bowl. *From:* sek' 'plate' (approximate form) (Western Mayan) (2).

taas *n.* cup. *From:* taza 'the cup' (Spanish) (1).

tz'ob'leb' *n.* extracter.

tz'ub'leb' *n.* straw.

uk'al *n.* pot.

uk'leb'lem *n.* cup, glass, drinking glass.

uq'unleb'aal *n.* blender.

wa'leb' sek' *n.* cup, plate.

xartin *n.* pan, frying pan. *From:* sartén 'the pan' (Spanish) (1).

xaar *n.* mug.

xaar *n.* jug, pitcher. *From:* jarro 'jug' (Spanish) (1).

xaaril ha' *n.* water jug.

Ru ut Xxe' Pim / Vegetables

al ixim *n.* sweet corn.

arb'eej *n.* pea, peas. *From:* Spanish 'arvejas'.

aselk *n.* chard. *From:* Spanish 'acelga'.

aapy *n.* celery. *From:* Spanish 'apio'.

b'rookl *n.* broccoli. *From:* Spanish 'brócoli'.

ch'ima *n.* guisquil (type of squash).

espinaak *n.* spinach. *From:* Spanish 'espinaca'.

ik'oy *n.* guicoy (type of squash).

kaqxe' *n.* radish.

karwans *n.* chick peas, garbanzo beans. *From:* Spanish 'garbanzos'.

kax'isk'i'ij *n.* celery.

kaxche'kenq' *n.* pea, peas.

kaxch'i'kay *n.* artichoke.

kaxlan is *n.* potato.

kaxlan q'een *n.* pepper.

kenq' *n.* bean.

ki'il ik *n.* chili pepper.

kik'xe' *n.* beet.

kok' samat *n.* cilantro.

koliplor *n.* cauliflower. *From:* Spanish 'coliflor'.

k'ux *n.* ear of corn.

lechuuk *n.* lettuce. *From:* Spanish 'lechuga'.

naaw *n.* turnip. *From:* Spanish 'nabo'.

okox *n.* mushroom.

paaps *n.* potato, sweet potato. *Var:* **paps**. *From:* papas 'potatoes' (Spanish) (1).

pepiin *n.* cucumber. *From:* Spanish 'pepino'.

q'anxe' *n.* carrot.

q'ap *n.* green bean, string bean.

raxwak' *n.* broccoli.

remolaach *n.* beet. *From:* Spanish 'remolacha'.

repooy *n.* cabbage. *From:* Spanish 'repollo'.

samat *n.* wild cilantro.

sanahoor *n.* carrot. *From:* Spanish 'zanahoria'.

saqmot *n.* cauliflower.

saqwak' *n.* cauliflower.

saqxe' *n.* turnip.

seb'ooy *n.* onion. *From:* cebolla 'the onion' (Spanish) (1).

tuxim *n.* onion.

tzaksu *n.* eggplant.

tz'aktz'um *n.* loroco (edible herb).

woch ichaj *n.* lettuce.

Uk'a' / Drinks

b'iin *n.* wine. *From:* vino 'the wine' (Spanish) (1).

b'oj *n.* fermented drink.

b'onb'ilha' *n.* Kool-Aid.
Var: **b'omb'ilha'**.

champan *n.* champagne. *From:* French 'champagne'.

ch'amb'ul *n.* fermented mush drink.

ch'amch'am *adj.* very fermented.

ch'amok' *v.* to ferment.

ha' *n.* water.

kalha' *n.* alcoholic drink.

kape *n.* coffee. *From:* café 'coffee' (Spanish) (1).

kaxlan b'oj *n.* alcohol, spirits.

kaxlanha' *n.* soft drink, carbonated drink, soda.

kaxuk'a' *n.* soft drink.

kehil ha' *n.* cold water.

kokakool *n.* Coca Cola, Coke. *From:* English 'Coca Cola'.

k'isk'im *n.* lemon tea.

leech *n.* milk. *From:* leche 'milk' (Spanish) (1).

matz' *n.* mush, porridge.

puq'b'il *n.* milkshake.

q'em ha' *n.* cornmeal drink.

q'eqil b'iin *n.* red wine.

ron *n.* rum. *From:* Spanish 'ron'.

saqi b'iin *n.* white wine.

saqjuy *n.* mush, porridge.

serwees *n.* beer. *Var:* **serb'ees**. *From:* cerveza 'beer' (Spanish) (1).

te *n.* tea. *From:* té 'tea' (Spanish) (1).

tiqwal kakaw *n.* hot chocolate.

traaw *n.* liquor, shot. *From:* Spanish 'trago'.

tzo'xul ha' *n.* beer. *Note:* 'El gallo' is a popular brand of beer in Guatemala. The bottles have a rooster logo on the front.

uk'a' *n.* drink.

uq'un *n.* mush, porridge.

waqib' ru *n.* six-pack.

wiisk *n.* whiskey. *From:* English 'whiskey'.

xya'al *n.* juice.

xya'al chiin *n.* orange juice.

xya'al ch'op *n.* pineapple juice.

xya'al lamunx *n.* lemonade.

xya'al mansaan *n.* apple juice, cider, apple cider.

xya'al pix *n.* tomato juice.

xya'al tu' *n.* milk.

yuki'q'een *n.* cocktail.

Xk'anjelob'aal K'uub'leb'aal / Kitchen Tools

b'isleb' sek' *n.* measuring cup.

b'itzilch'iich' *n.* knife.

b'ukleb'aal *n.* mixer.

ch'ina ch'iich' *n.* knife.

ch'ina maal *n.* cleaver.

kaxka' *n.* blender.

ke'leb'aal tib' *n.* meat grinder.

keleb'aal *n.* mill (grain).

k'uub'poch'leb' *n.* mill (grain).

pitz'leb' *n.* juice press.

poch'leb' *n.* mill (grain).

rokeb'l sib' *n.* oven vent.

ruq' ka' *n.* pestle.

sekch'iich' *n.* knife.

yax *n.* tongs. *From:* *yax 'the crab' (Ch'olan) (2).

Xsahob' Tzakahemq / Seasonings

alb'aak *n.* basil. *From:* Spanish 'albahaca'.

anis *n.* aniseed. *From:* Spanish 'anís'.

anx *n.* garlic.

asapran *n.* saffron. *From:* Spanish 'azafrán'.

asuukr *n.* sugar. *From:* azúcar 'sugar' (Spanish) (1).

atz'am *n.* salt.

atz'am aapy *n.* celery salt. *From:* Spanish 'apio'.

b'inaayr *n.* vinegar. *Var:* ninayr. *From:* Spanish 'vinagre'.

b'oj ha' tzakahemq *n.* vinegar.

ik *n.* chili pepper.

isk'i'ij *n.* mint, spearmint.

jolom q'een *n.* garlic.

jonjoli *n.* sesame seeds. *From:* Spanish 'ajonjolí'.

kalawx q'een *n.* clove spice.

kaneel *n.* cinnamon. *From:* Spanish 'canela'.

keb'il pix *n.* ketchup.

kulantr *n.* coriander. *From:* Spanish 'cilantro'.

k'ajkab' *n.* sugar.

oreek *n.* oregano. *From:* Spanish 'orégano'.

pens *n.* pepper.

perejil *n.* parsley. *From:* Spanish 'perejil'.

putz'b'il *n.* sauce.

putz'b'il pix ik *n.* hot sauce, picante sauce, salsa.

romeer *n.* rosemary. *From:* Spanish 'romero'.

rub'aarb' *n.* rhubarb. *From:* Spanish 'ruibarbo'.

sununkil pim *n.* herbs.

t'orol pens *n.* peppercorn.

tz'i' k'iche' *n.* wild cardamom.

xanxiiwr *n.* ginger.

xaxaq lawrel *n.* bayleaf. *From:* Spanish 'laurel'.

xayaw *n.* annatto.

xb'anol tzakahemq *n.* condiment.

xsahob' tzakahemq *n.* spice, seasoning.

Tz'iib'ak ut Esilhu / Writing and Correspondence

Esilhu / Correspondence

aj kanab'om esilhu *n agt.* letter carrier, mailman.

aj k'ulul re *n agt.* receiver, recipient.

aj taql'esil *n agt.* sender.

aj taqlanel re *n agt.* sender.

chaq'rab'ink *n.* farewell.

chaq'rab'ink *v.* to say goodbye, bid farewell.

esil nayehman sa' li hu *n.* message (written).

esil tz'iib'anb'il sa' li hu *n.* body text.

esilhu *n.* letter, flyer, poster.

eetal *n.* postage stamp.

eetaltoj *n.* postage, stamp.

188

jalam'uuchil taql *n.* postcard.

juch' *n.* signature.

junpaatil'esil *n.* telegram.

kaxt *n.* seal, stamp. *Var:* **kaaxt**.

kaaxtink *v.* to seal, stamp.

k'ab'a' *n.* name.

k'ab'a'ej *n.* name. *From:* k'aab'a' 'name' (Yucatecan, Ch'olan, possible) (2).

k'aj'esil *n.* telegram.

k'amb'il esilhu *n.* parcel.

k'osok *v.* to summarize.

mochok *v.* to fold.

nayeeman sa' li esilhu *n.* letter body.

nums'esilb'aal *n.* post office, telegrapher.

numsib'aal k'aj' esil *n.* telegraph machine.

ochochib'aal *n.* address.

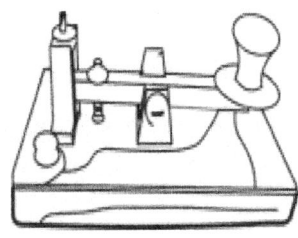

pitz'leb'taql *n.* telegraph.

reetalil ochoch *n.* address.

rix esilhu *n.* envelope.

rix taqlhu *n.* envelope.

rochochil esilhu *n.* post office.

sahil ch'oolej *n.* greeting.

taql *n.* post, mail.

taqlhu *n.* document.

tarjeet postal *n.* postcard. *From:* tarjeta postal 'postcard' (Spanish) (1).

tiimbr *n.* postage, stamp. *From:* timbre 'postage stamp' (Spanish) (1).

t'oqb'on *n.* wax seal.

tz'iib'anb'ilhu *n.* document.

xb'e li po *n.* date. *Var:* xb'epo.

xchampa aj kanab'om esilhu *n.* mailbag.

xhuhil resil kamk *n.* burial notice.

xjayalil *n.* address. *Var:* xjayal.

xjuch' li nataqlan re *n.* signature of sender.

xkaxonil esilhu *n.* mailbox, post office box, PO Box.

xkoxtalil li esilhu *n.* mailbag.

xk'ab'a' li nataqlan re *n.* name of sender, sender.

xk'ab'a' li taak'ulu'q re *n.* name of recipient, addressee, recipient.

xk'oslal *n.* summary.

xna'aj b'ar wi' wan li taak'ulu'q re *n.* address of recipient.

xna'aj esilhu *n.* mailbox.

xtojb'al relik *n.* stamp, postage.

Li Hu ut li Tz'iib'ak / Books and Writing

ab'aqhu *n.* carbon paper.

aj e re *n agt.* author.

aj k'ehol esil *n agt.* journalist, reporter.

aj molol'esil *n agt.* journalist, reporter.

aj tz'iib'ahom *n agt.* author.

aj uutz'u'ujinel aatin *n agt.* poet.

alab'tesink *v.* to reproduce.

anaqwankil'uxk *n.* present tense.

astz'iib' *n.* upper case, capital letter.

b'alq'hu *n.* flipchart.

b'anb'alil esil *n.* newspaper.

b'asb'il tasalhu *n.* pamphlet.

b'onleb' *n.* crayon, marker.

chahim'eetalil *n.* asterisk.

chapleb'hu *n.* paper clip.

chaq'aliltz'iib' *n.* calligraphy.

chaab'iltz'iib' *n.* calligraphy.

chuntz'iib'l *n.* chalk.
   Var: chuntz'iib'.

ch'ina tashu'esil *n.* magazine.

ch'inajelool *n.* briefcase.

ch'inaaljuch' *n.* dash, hyphen.

ch'inq'ejuch *n.* hyphen, dash.

ch'ol *n.* chapter.

ch'ol'aatin *n.* paragraph.

ch'ol'aatin *n.* sentence.

ch'ol'uutz'ujinb'il aatin *n.* verse.

ch'olob'aal'aatin *n.* glossary.

ch'olob'aalna'leb' *n.* encyclopedia.

ch'olob'ihom *n.* predicate.

ch'oltz'iib' *n.* alphabet.

ch'utub'eetalil *n.* iconography.

esilalil *n.* bibliography.

esilhu *n.* newspaper.

esilhu *n.* note.

esilk'anjel *n.* report.

etalink *v.* to copy.

eek'anb'iltz'iib' *n.* fable.

eetalilul *n.* symbolism.

eetalkawyaab' *n.* accent mark.

eetaltz'iib' *n.* glyph.

ha'il tz'iib'leb' *n.* pen.

hopleb'hu *n.* paper punch, hole punch.

hu *n.* book.

hu *n.* paper. *Note:* [hu] is said of anything made of paper, sometimes with an additional descriptor for clarification. **Eb' li tzolom neke'tz'iib' eb' li xtzolomil sa' li xtz'iib'leb'aal hu.** « The students write their assignments in their notebooks. »

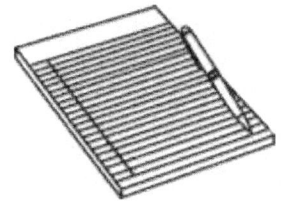

huhil *n.* paper.

hupatz'om *n.* application, written request.

hutz'aam *n.* application, written request.

ilok ru hu *v phr.* to read.

itz'intz'iib' *n.* lower case letter.

jalam'uuchink *v.* to photocopy.

jalam'uuchleb' *n.* photocopier, copy machine, copier.

jalam'uuchleb'aal ch'iich' *n.* photocopier, copy machine, copier.

jalam'uuchu *n.* photocopy.

jalok-aatin *n.* translation, interpretation.

jolomil na'leb' *n.* title.

jotzleb' tz'iib'leb' che' *n.* pencil sharpener.

jultikaal *n.* form.

jultikob'lhu *n.* agenda.

jultik'anjel *n.* agenda.

ka'muluq'utiltz'uq *n.* quotes, quotation marks.

ka'sutink *v.* to reproduce.

ka'tz'iib'ank *v.* to rewrite.

ka'tz'uq *n.* colon.

kanhub'aal *n.* briefcase.

karton *n.* cardboard. *From:* from Spanish 'cartón'.

kaxchampa *n.* briefcase.

kaxt *n.* seal, stamp. *Var:* kaaxt.

kaxukuutinb'ilhu *n.* graph paper.

kaaxtinb'il hu *n.* bond paper.

kaaxtink *v.* to seal, stamp.

kik' tz'iib' *n.* pen.

k'a'uxlal *n.* editorial.

k'aj'aatin *n.* particle.

k'ajtz'iib' *n.* particle.

k'amleb'aal *n.* briefcase.

k'onk'okiltz'uq *n.* comma.

k'ontz'uq *n.* comma.

k'ontz'uq *n.* parentheses, brackets.

k'osb'il *adj.* summarized.

k'osok *v.* to summarize.

k'uk'umtz'iib' *n.* pen.

k'ulb'atz'iib' *n.* synaleph, linkage of syllables.

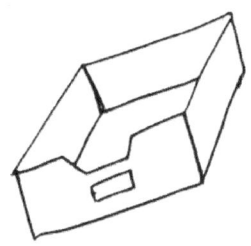

k'uulb'ahu *n.* in-box.

k'uuleb'jalam'uuch *n.* photo album.

k'uulhu *n.* file, archive.

k'uut *n.* letterhead.

lemtz'juch'leb'aal *n.* fluorescent marker.

liib'r *n.* book. *From:* libro 'the book' (Spanish) (1).

luttz'uq *n.* colon.

luttz'uqyaab' *n.* dieresis.

mayertz'iib' *n.* hieroglyphic, glyph.

mayertz'iib' maay *n.* Mayan glyph.

molob'aal aatin *n.* dictionary, lexicon.

moqonil'uxk *n.* future tense.

na'leb'ank tz'iib' *v phr.* to edit, redact, write up.

na'leb'aal tasal hu *n.* encyclopedia.

nat'leb'hu *n.* paper clip.

nat'yaab' *n.* glottal, glottalization.

nawil hu *n.* newspaper.

nawtz'iib'ak *n.* orthography.

nimaljuch' *n.* parentheses.

nimaljuch' *n.* parentheses, brackets.

numenaqil'uxk *n.* past tense.

nut'leb'hu *n.* newsprint.

perhu *n.* card.

periood *n.* newspaper. *From:* periódico (Spanish) (1).

pimilhu *n.* cardboard.

pukhub'aal *n.* print house, printer's, publisher.

pukleb'hu *n.* mimeograph.

puktasib'aalhu *n.* photocopier, copy machine, copier.

puktasinb'il *adj.* published.

puktasink *v.* to edit.

puktasink esil *v phr.* to publish.

q'inixtz'iib' *n.* cursive.

raqal'aatin *n.* sentence.

raqalk'a'uxl *n.* paragraph.

raqaltz'iib' *n.* verse.

raqleltz'uq *n.* period.

raqtz'uq *n.* period.

raqyanq *n.* semicolon.

reetalil *n.* example.

reetalil patz'omq *n.* question mark (?)

reetalil tz'aqob'tz'iib' *n.*
punctuation mark.

reetalilk'utb'ch'oolejil *n.*
asterisk.

reetalsachb'ach'oolej *n.*
exclamation point (!).

rochochilmolam *n.* office.

ruhil *n.* cover, cover page.

sa' tzoltz'iib' *adv.*
alphabetically.

seeraq' *n.* story, tale, chat,
message.

sik'leb' aatin *n.* dictionary,
lexicon.

sik'ok-eetalil *n.* iconography.

tasalhu *n.* book.

teb'tookil hu *n.* cardboard.

tiiqeltz'uq *n.* period.

tuqlaaltz'iib' *n.* orthography.

tuqleb' *n.* correcting fluid,
White Out.

tuqtutz'iib' *n.* orthography.

tusleb' aatin *n.* glossary.

tusleb'aal aatin *n.* vocabulary.

tusleb'hu *n.* paper collator.

tusna'leb' *n.* index.

tzoltz'iib' *n.* alphabet.

tz'iib' *n.* writing, letter.

tz'iib'ak *v.* to write, take notes.

tz'iib'anb'il esil *n.* newspaper.

tz'iib'leb' *n.* pen.

tz'iib'leb' che' *n.* pencil.

tz'iib'leb'aal *n.* office.

tz'iib'leb'aal che' *n.*
blackboard, chalkboard.

tz'iib'leb'aalhu *n.* notebook.

tz'iib'leb'che' *n.* blackboard,
chalkboard.

tz'iib'leb'on *n.* pen.

tz'iib'uuchil *n.* ideograph.

tz'uq *n.* period, apostrophe.

tz'uq aatin *n.* accent mark.

tz'uq kawyaab' *n.* accent
mark.

uq'miltz'iib' *n.* manuscript.

uutz'u'jinb'il aatin *n.* poem.

uutz'u'jinb'ilraq *n.* rhyme.

wech'ok *v.* to describe.

wech'ok *n.* description.

Var: xwech'b'al rix.

xche'elhu *n.* papyrus.

xch'olch'ookilal *n.* legibility.

xch'oolaatin juntaq'eetil *n.* thesaurus.

xhuhul esil *n.* newspaper.

xhuhul uutz'u'jinb'il aatin *n.* poetry collection.

xjolom muluq'util tz'uq *n.* semicolon.

xna'aj tasal hu *n.* library.

xna'leb'il *adj.* thematic.

xokleb' *n.* file.

xokok *v.* to file, save.

xoy *n.* cover page, decoration, adornment.

xpuktasinkil *n.* edition, publication.

xsa' *adj.* area, contents.

xsahob'resinkil *n.* illustration.

xtusulal aatin *n.* dictionary, lexicon. *Var:* xtuslal aatin.

yehom *n.* language, narration.

yeeb'il *adj.* verbal.

yoob'k'a'aq *n.* author, inventor. *Var:* yoob'k'a'aj.

yu'yuukil k'a'uxl *n.* paraphrase.

Wajb'ak / Music

ab'ib'aal *n.* earphones, headphones.

ab'ib'aal aatin *n.* radio (receiver).

ab'ib'aalson *n.* radio (receiver).

ab'inel *n.* audience.

aj aatinanel *n agt.* announcer.

aj b'ichanel *n agt.* singer.

aj iitz'in *n agt.* violinist.

aj jultikahonel *n agt.* prompter, commentator.

aj si'b'ich *n.* serenade.

aj wajb' *n agt.* musician.

aj wajb' *n agt.* band.

ajsi'baalb'ich *n.* serenade.

aatik'uul *n.* microphone.

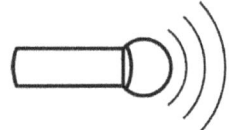

aatinob'aal *n.* microphone.

b'ich *n.* song. *Var:* b'ichk.

b'ich k'uula'al *n.* lullaby.

b'ichank *v.* to sing.

b'ichleb' *n.* songbook, hymnal.

chapleb'aal aatin *n.* tape recorder, tape player.

chapleb'aatin *n.* tape recorder, tape player.

chapok aatin *v phr.* to record.

choqtin *n.* cassette. *Var:* xochtin.

ch'uut aj wajb' *n agt.* musical group.

echb'enink *v.* to accompany.

eetalil hu *n.* play bill, advertising poster.

komon b'ichank *n.* choir.

kuxil *n.* melody.

k'utb'esib'aal *n.* stage.

meexwajb' *n.* speaker.

nimla ramleb'aal t'ikr *n.* curtain.

nimob'resink *v.* to amplify.

ochb'enb'il *adj.* accompanied.

ochb'enej *n.* accompanist.

puktasib'aal *n.* radio (transmitter).

pukyaab' *n.* microphone, speaker.

rab'inkil *v.* to tune in.

ray *n.* radio. *From:* radio 'the radio' (Spanish) (1).

raapal *n.* verse, stanza.

roqil *n.* rhythm.

sahilyaab' *n.* harmony (musical).

son *n.* music. *From:* son 'music' (Spanish) (1).

sur chapleb'aal *n.* CD-ROM, compact disk, disk, CD.

surb'ich *n.* record, album, CD.

surb'ichleb'aal *n.* record player.

surchoch *n.* disk.

taqleb'aal *n.* scaffolding, platform.

taab'leb'aal b'ich *n.* tape player.

toch'ok *v.* to play (instruments).

tusb'ich *n.* score, sheet music.

tzinb'ak *v.* to sound, ring.

tzinb'ank *v.* to sound, toll.

wajb'ak *n.* music, concert.

wajb'ak *v.* to play instruments.

xikelyaab' *n.* earphones, headphones.

xna'aj aj aatinanel *n.* recording studio.

xna'aj xhu b'ich *n.* music stand, easel.

xokleb' *n.* cassette.

xolb'ak *v.* to play the flute.

xolib'k *v.* to play the flute.

xtoonal li ab'ib'aal aatin *n.* radio studio.

xtz'apb'al surb'ich *n.* album cover.

xtz'iib'ul b'ich *n.* verse.

xyaab' b'ich *n.* note, musical note.

yalb'ek *v.* to rehearse.

yalok *v.* to rehearse.

yaab'aal *n.* speaker.

yaab'ich *n.* melody.

yaab'il *n.* resonant, loud.

yu'leb'yaab' *n.* amplifier.

yu'uk ru *v.* to amplify, expand.

Eb' li Wajb' / Instruments

aj wajb'a'apuul *n.* trumpeter.

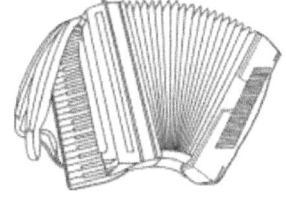

b'aswajb' *n.* accordion, concertina.

che'wajb' *n.* wood drum.

ch'ere'wajb' *n.* saxophone.

ch'ina tun *n.* wood drum.

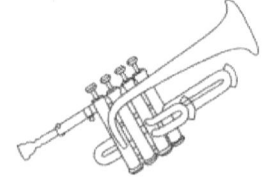

jayaab'wajb' *n.* horn, trumpet.

jitz'jitz' *n.* violin.

job'wajb' *n.* drum.

jook' *n.* maracas.

kampaan *n.* bell. *From:* Spanish 'campana'.

kaxxuxb' *n.* horn, trumpet.

kitaar *n.* guitar. *From:* Spanish 'guitarra'.

kottzuj *n.* tambourine.

luk'luk' che' *n.* rattle.

meexwajb' *n.* piano.

moor *n.* drum.

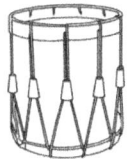

nimla tun *n.* drum, bass drum.

q'anch'iich' *n.* horn, trumpet.

tzilinch'iich' *n.* bell.

rinwajb' *n.* harp.

ruq'wajb' *n.* drumstick, hammer.

suwajb' *n.* guitar.

tzintzin *n.* guitar.

talanch'iich' *n.* bell.

tamb'or *n.* drum. *From:* tambor 'drum' (Spanish) (1).

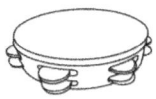

tilin *n.* bell.

tzojtzojch'iich' *n.* tambourine.

trompeet *n.* horn, trumpet. *From:* trompeta 'trumpet' (Spanish) (1).

tzujtzuj *n.* maracas.

tz'uywajb' *n.* organ.

wajb' *n.* musical instrument.

tuntun *n.* drum.

tusb'il che' son *n.* marimba.

tusb'ilche'wajb' *n.* marimba.

tusche'wajb' *n.* marimba.

xolb' *n.* flute. *From:* xool 'stick or flute' (Yucatecan, Ch'olan, possible) (2).

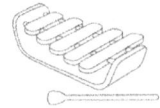

tusch'iich'wajb' *n.* lyre.

xolb'ch'iich' *n.* xylophone.

Xcha'alil li Tz'ejwalej / Human Anatomy

a' *n.* leg.

b'aq *n.* bone.

b'aq xtib'el *adj.* thin.

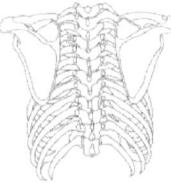

b'aqel *n.* skeleton.

b'aqel xb'een tel *n.* shoulder blade.

b'aq'el'a' *n.* femur.

b'e jolom *n.* hair part.

b'uq' *n.* bun.

b'uq' ja'aj *n.* Adam's apple, goiter. *Var:* **b'uq' ja'j.**

cha'al *n.* organ, body part.

cha'alil *n.* organs.

chi ixkej *n.* bottom.

cho'b'ol *n.* surgical scar.

cholok' *n.* breastbone.

chu' *n.* urine.

chut *n.* mole.

ch'och' *n.* liver.

ch'ool *n.* heart.

ch'oolej *n.* heart.

ch'up *n.* belly button, navel.

ch'utb'aq cha'al *n.* bone tissue.

ch'ut-eek' cha'al *n.* nerve tissue.

ch'utq'ooq cha'al *n.* fat tissue.

ch'uukum *n.* elbow.

e *n.* mouth.

e *n.* tooth.

eek'al uhej *n.* optic nerve.

eetalil xtz'uumal *n.* tattoo.

eetalil yok'ol *n.* scar.

ich'mul *n.* vein, artery.

ich' *n.* sinew, tendon.

ich' *n.* vein, artery.

ich'mej *n.* nerve.

ich'mul *n.* sinew, tendon.

ismal *n.* hair.

it *n.* buttock, anus.

ix *n.* back.

ixi'ij *n.* nail, fingernail.

ixkej *n.* back.

jayiltz'uumal'u *n.* retina.

ja'aj *n.* neck.

jochol *n.* scratch.

jolom *n.* head.

job'nil *n.* stomach. *From:* *job'nel 'entrails, belly' (Yucatecan, Ch'olan, possible) (2).

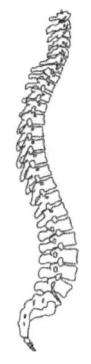

juruch' *n.* spine, backbone, spinal column. *Var:* huruch'ix.

kamenaq *n.* corpse.

kamenaq *adj.* dead.

katz *n.* itch. *Var:* katzil.

katzkatz *n.* itch, tickle.

ka' e *n.* molar.

kenq' *n.* kidney.

kik' *n.* blood.

kik' ru *adj.* bloody.

kik'el *n.* blood.

kik'elej *n.* blood.

ko *n.* cheek. *From:* *ko:h (the cheek) (Western Mayan) (2).

kok' k'amk'ot *n.* small intestine.

kux *n.* neck.

k'a *n.* bile.

k'a'ej *n.* bile.

k'amk'otej *n.* intestines, guts.

k'atq jolom *n.* temples.

k'ehok tiq *n.* fever.

k'inich *n.* freckle.

k'onx a' *n.* hip.

k'ulb'ab'aq *n.* joint (bones).

k'utunel ru'uj uq' *n.* index finger.

k'uub'suutaalkik' *n.* circulatory system.

mach *n.* beard.

mam *n.* rectum.

maqab' *n.* chest, torso, thorax.

maal *n.* pancreas.

maatzab' u *n.* eyebrow.

mich'mo *adj.* naked.

moch' *n.* fist.

moq'mo *adj.* naked.

musiq'ab'aal *n.* respiratory system.

mutz' *adj.* blind.

na' uq'm *n.* thumb.

nim xtib'el *adj.* fat.

numleb' yaab'ej *n.* Eustachian tube.

numleb'yaab' xik *n.* inner ear.

nums *n.* footprint.

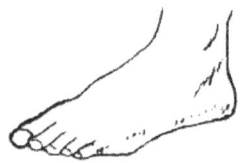

oq *n.* foot, feet.

oq uq' *n.* body parts.

oqej *n.* foot, feet.

oqej *n.* footprint.

oqil *n.* footprint.

peekem *n.* forehead.

polook' *n.* thorax.

pos *n.* lung.

pospo'oy *n.* lung. *Var:* pospoy.

poolok'il *n.* rib.

puchha' *n.* blister.

puj *n.* belly.

q'ol is *n.* body hair, peach fuzz.

q'oyol *n.* scratch.

raxtint *n.* bruise.

re ch'ool *n.* breast, bust, chest.

re maqab' *n.* chest.

reetalil tiq'ilal *n.* scar.

rismal jolom *n.* hair.

rismal u *n.* eyelash.

rit oq *n.* heel.

rit telb' *n.* elbow.

rit uq'b' *n.* elbow.

rix ja'aj *n.* nape of the neck.

rix kux *n.* nape of the neck.

rix u *n.* eyelid. *Var:* rix'uhej.

rix uq'm *n.* back of the hand. *Var:* rix uq'b'.

roq ruq'm *n.* limbs.

ru a' *n.* thigh.

ru oq *n.* instep.

ru sa' *n.* abdomen.

ru tzelek *n.* shin.

ru'uj aq' *n.* tongue.

ru'uj tu' *n.* nipple, teat.

ru'uj tu' *n.* aureola.

ru'uj uq' *n.* finger. *Var:* ru'uj uq'b'.

sa' yi *n.* waist.

sa'ej *n.* bowels.

salb'a *n.* dandruff. *Var:* sakb'a.

sam *n.* nasal mucus.

saqi ismal *n.* gray hairs.

sa' e *n.* gums.

sa' u *n.* eye.

sa' u'uj *n.* nostril.

saaseb' *n.* liver.

sooto'y *n.* digestive system.

sooyom *n.* intestines, guts.

ru'uj uq'b' *n.* fingerprint.

ru'uj xkaalam e *n.* chin.

rub'el e *n.* jaw, chin.

ruuch e *n.* tooth, teeth. *Var:* uuch e.

sa' *n.* stomach.

sa' *n.* belly.

sa' kuxej *n.* throat.

sa' oq *n.* sole.

sa' tel *n.* armpit. *Var:* sa' talb'; sa' telb'.

sa' uq' *n.* palm (of the hand).

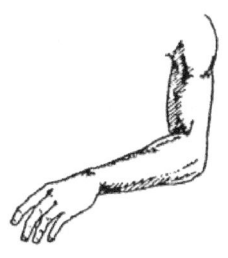

tel *n.* arm. *Var:* telb'.

tib' *n.* flesh.

tib'elej *n.* thigh.

tib'elej *n.* muscles, flesh.

tiqob' *n.* sweat.

toon xik *n.* temples.

tu' *n.* breast, bust.

tu'ej *n.* breast, bust.

t'inis *adj.* fat. *Var:* t'initz.

t'ojoch *adj.* bald.

t'ojt'o *adj.* bald.

t'urt'u *adj.* naked.

t'uru' xjolom *adj.* bald.

t'usam *n.* nakedness.

t'ust'u *adj.* naked.

tzelek *n.* pimple.

tz'apxik *adj.* deaf.

tz'apyaab'il *adj.* deaf.

tz'ej *n.* thigh, flesh.

tz'ejwalej *n.* body. *Var:* tz'ejwal.

tz'uumal *n.* tissue.

tz'uumal e *n.* lips.

tz'uumalej *n.* skin.
Var: tz'uumal.

u *n.* face, forehead.

u'uj *n.* nose.

u'ujej *n.* nose.

uhej *n.* face.

ulul *n.* brain. *From:* ulul 'marrow, brains' (Ch'olti') (5).

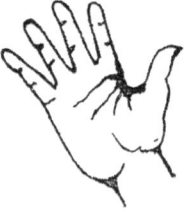

uq'm *n.* hand. *Var:* uq'b'. *From:* uuq' ooq ooq' uuq 'handle' (Ch'olan) (3).

wotz'okil *n.* itch.

wotz'otz' *n.* tickle.

xaqal *n.* posture.

xaal it *n.* back.

xaaqalil *n.* posture.

xb'aqel jolom *n.* skull, cranium.

xb'aqel xukuy *n.* rib.

xb'een aq *n.* knee. *Var:* xb'een oq.

xb'een tel *n.* shoulder.

xcha'alil li tib'elej *n.* body parts.

xchakachil b'aq *n.* rib.

xch'i'pul uq'mej *n.* pinkie finger.

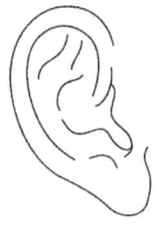

xik *n.* ear.

xjis'ich'mul xikej *n.* auditory nerve.

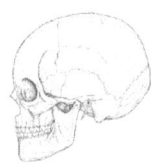

xjolom kamenaq *n.* skull.

xkaalam e *n.* jaw. *Var:* kalam e.

xko it *n.* hip.

xko rit *n.* buttocks, butt.

xko uhej *n.* cheekbones.

xkux oq *n.* ankle. *Var:* xkuxb' oq.

xkux uq'b' *n.* wrist. *Var:* xkux uq'm.

xk'ot xik *n.* earwax.

xk'ot oq' *n.* calf (of the leg).

xlem u *n.* iris (eye).

xlemtz'iil u *n.* cornea.

xmach u *n.* mustache.

xmama'il uq'mej *n.* thumb.

xmap oq *n.* ankle, shin.

xna'aj chu *n.* bladder.

xna'aj tiiq' *n.* scar.

xnaq' u *n.* eye.

xnaq' uhej *n.* eye.

xnaq' telb' *n.* forearm.

xnaq' u *n.* face.

xolol *n.* throat.

xq'ootil xik *n.* cochlea.

xsa' ja'aj *n.* throat.

xsa' oq *n.* sole.

xsa' uq'b' *n.* palm (of the hand). *Var:* xsa' uq'm.

xsu oq *n.* calf (of the leg). *Var:* su oq.

xsulutzil b'aq *n.* marrow.

xtehelal xkux *n.* bust, cleavage.

xtehelem'u *n.* pupil (eye).

xtoon telb' *n.* forearm.

xt'oy oq' *n.* calf (of the leg).

xukuy *n.* rib.

xulel xikej *n.* eardrum, tympanic membrane.

xxaali it *n.* back. *Var:* xxala it.

xxuk e *n.* chin.

xya'al e *n.* dribble, drool.

xya'al tu' *n.* breast milk, mother's milk.

xya'al u *n.* tear.

xyi *n.* retina.

xyihil ru'uj uq' *n.* middle finger.

yach'yo *adj.* naked.

yi *n.* waist.

yiib'ej *n.* waist. *Var:* yihej.

yiitoq *n.* waist, torso.

yoch *n.* wrinkles.

yolojilb'aq *n.* skeleton.

yolojilb'aq *n.* human skeleton.

yotolal *n.* scar.

yotom *n.* scar.

yupus *n.* anus.

Xcha'alil li K'ajolink / Reproductive Parts

ab'aj *n.* testicles, scrotum.

alk'uula'al *n.* fetus.

alob'aal *n.* womb, uterus.

b'irich *n.* penis.

b'irk *n.* clitoris.

b'irk *n.* vulva.

b'o *n.* genitals (female).

b'ub' *n.* semen, ejaculate.

b'uuy *n.* genitals (female).

cha'alil *n.* genitals.

choy *n.* vulva.

kub'sa' *n.* womb, uterus.

kun *n.* penis.

kunutz' *n.* penis.

k'oopopo' *n.* genitals (female).

lal *n.* semen, ejaculate.

mi' *n.* vagina. *From:* mi' 'mother' (Q'anjob'alan) (2).

molb' *n.* testicles.

naq' it *n.* testicles.

naq' kun *n.* testicles.

peekem kun *n.* pubis.

pirich *n.* penis.

pirk' *n.* vulva.

pur *n.* penis.

ralyu'amej *n.* embryo.

ranq' *n.* hymen.

riiqk'uula'al *n.* placenta.

sa' ixq *n.* womb, uterus.

tz'ejwal *n.* penis, genitals (male).

tz'ik *n.* penis.

xche'el ab'aj *n.* penis.

xn'aj alaal *n.* ovary.

xnumleb' iyajiil *n.* fallopian tube.

Xk'anjel li Tz'ejwal / Bodily Functions

ajk *v.* to wake up. *From:* *aj 'wake up' (Yucatecan) (2).

alank *v.* to give birth.

at'isb'ak *v.* to sneeze.

b'oqok chi yaab' *v phr.* to whistle.

chu'uk *v.* to urinate, pee, piss.

chuq'ub'ak *v.* to hiccough, hiccup. *From:* chuq'ub' 'hiccoughs' (Q'anjob'alan) (4).

chuub' *n.* saliva, spit.

chuub'ak *v.* to spit. *Var:* chuub'ank.

eek'asink rix u *v phr.* to blink.

hach'lenk *v.* to bite.

hach'ok *v.* to bite.

isink xya'al tz'ejwal *v phr.* to ejaculate.

jach'ok *v.* to bite.

japink e *v phr.* to yawn.

jilq'ank *v.* to snore.

jochlenk *v.* to scratch.

joq'ank *v.* to snore. *Var:* jok'ank; joq'yank.

kamk *v.* to die.

kanaak sa' yu'am *v phr.* to conceive.

kaqlak *n.* menstruation, menses.

kisik *v.* to fart, pass gas.

k'ajolink *v.* to beget.

k'apok chi e *v phr.* to bite.

k'atzok *v.* to bite.

k'ehok chuq'ub' *v phr.* to hiccough, hiccup.

k'otak *v.* to defecate. *From:* k'ot 'to throw' (Q'anjob'alan) (4).

leeleb'ak *v.* to dribble.

musiq'ak *v.* to breathe, respire. *From:* *mus iik' 'to breathe' (Yucatecan, Ch'olan, possible) (2).

musiq'ank *v.* to breathe. *From:* *mus iik' 'to breathe' (Yucatecan, Ch'olan, possible) (2).

mutz'mutz'ink *v.* to blink.

na'uuchik *v.* to dream.

parok *v.* to scratch.

parpotk *v.* to shiver, tremble.

puch'uk *v.* to menstruate.

qachok *v.* to bite. *Var:* qatzok.

qixb' *n.* burp.

qixb'ak *v.* to burp.

qoorank *v.* to snore.

q'uusank *v.* to snore. *Var:* q'usank.

req'ok *v.* to lick.

rik'ok *v.* to blink.

roq tz'ik *n.* erection.

seeb'al rib' *n.* involuntary reflex.

siksotk *v.* to shiver.

siyaak *v.* to be born. *From:* *sih 'to be born (Yucatecan, Ch'olan, possible) (5).

ti'ok *v.* to bite.

tiqob'ak *v.* to perspire. *Var:* tiqob'ank.

tiwok *v.* to eat, bite.

tu'resink *v.* to nurse.

tu'uk *v.* to breastfeed.

tz'eqok ib' *v phr.* to defecate.

tz'ikib' *n.* coitus.

wara *n.* sleepiness.

wark *v.* to sleep.

xa'wak *v.* to vomit.

xuxb' *n.* whistle (sound).

yo'lajik *n.* birth.

yo'laak *v.* to be born, exist, give birth.

yo'yo *adj.* alive.

yo'yook *v.* to be alive.

yuqyuqink *v.* to blink.

Xk'ihal ut B'islal / Counts and Measures

alab' *n.* pair.

anchal *adj.* all.

aalal *n.* weight.

aalank *v.* to weigh.

aalom *n.* thing to be weighed.

b'isleb' *n.* scale.

b'isok *v.* to weigh, measure.

b'iis'aal *n.* pound.

b'ut' *adj.* full. *From:* b'ut' 'full' (Yucatecan, Ch'olan, possible) (3).

b'uuy *adj.* full.

chamal *n.* depth.

chi junil *adj.* all, everything. *Var:* chi xjunil.

chi ok'aalil *adj.* by the hundred.

chumay *n.* cubit.

ch'ikok *v.* to measure.

ch'inapuum *n.* gallon.

ch'iil *n.* piece.

ch'ol *n.* part.

ch'otolal *n.* piece.

ch'otonel *adj.* last, final.

ch'utub'ank *v.* to join.

ch'uyul *n.* piece.

ela' *n.* remains.

hiil *n.* kilometer.

ho'meet *n.* gallon.

ink'a' tz'aqal *adj.* incomplete.

jachal *n.* piece.

jachok *v.* to separate, divide.

job' *adj.* empty.

jun cheet *n.* a bunch.

jun kuchaar *n.* a spoonful.

jun mooch' *n.* a handful.

jun nub'uk *n.* a mouthful.

jun q'aal *n.* an armful.

jun surul *n.* a slice.

jun suumal *n.* a pair.

jun toseen *n.* a dozen. *From:* Spanish 'docena'.

jun tuub' *n.* a heap.

junaq *adj.* some.

junmay kintal *n.* a ton.

junqalil *n.* unit, unity.

juntuub' *adj.* abundant.

ka' aj wi' *adj.* only, alone. *Var:* ka'j wi'.

kach'in *adj.* few.

kalon *n.* gallon. *From:* from Spanish 'galón'.

kaxon *n.* crate. *From:* from Spanish 'cajón'.

ka'b'ayaq *adj.* some.

kiil *n.* kilo. *From:* from Spanish 'kilo'.

koxtal *n.* sack. *From:* from Spanish 'costal'.

k'a'na *adj.* some.

k'aal *n.* twenty-day period.

k'ihal *adj.* many.

liitr *n.* liter. *From:* Spanish 'litro'.

liiwr *n.* pound. *From:* Spanish 'libra'.

majel *adj.* scarce.

marilb'ej *adj.* last.

mayalok *adj.* many.

maak'a' xsa' *adj.* empty.

meetilsu *n.* liter.

mitz'jisb'ilis *n.* millimeter.

miin *n.* centimeter.

moqoj *n.* fathom.

naab'al *adj.* abundant.

naab'alil *n.* crowd.

nim xteram *n.* height.

nimal *n.* size, quantity.

nimroq *n.* length.

ninqal *n.* size.

nujenaq *adj.* full.

ok'aalil *n.* hundred.

ok'aalil b'isleb' *n.* measure (by one hundred).

ons *n.* ounce. *From:* Spanish 'onza'.

ox ox *adv.* three by three.

oxichal *n.* group of three.

oxjach *adj.* in three parts, in thirds.

parenheitil b'iis *n.* degrees Fahrenheit.

paay *n.* type, class, variety.

paayil *n.* type, class, variety.

peex *n.* scale. *From:* Spanish 'pesa'.

q'aal *n.* fathom.

raqal *n.* part, article.

raqaxink *v.* to separate.

raqik *adj.* last.

rek' *adj.* all.

rela' *n.* rest, remains.

roso'jik *adj.* last.

rosob' *adj.* last.

sa' junesal *adj.* alone.

sero *n.* zero. *From:* cero 'zero' (Spanish) (1).

sumal *n.* pair.

tas *n.* division, level.

teep *n.* part.

teep *n.* batch.

tiqam *n.* continuation.

toj *adj.* more.

tolche' *n.* piece.

tuqb'isleb' *n.* scale.

tzaqal jun *adj.* whole.

tz'ajtz'otk *adj.* full.

tz'aqal *adj.* enough, sufficient, complete.

waqib' *n.* half dozen.

waqib' ru *n.* six-pack.

we'ej *adj.* scarce. *Var:* wi'ej.

wechelal *n.* piece. *Var:* wechel.

xb'een *n.* remains.

xeel *n.* remains.

xiikil *adj.* a lot.

xjachalal *n.* part.

xmajolil *n.* height.

xna'b'iisaalob' *n.* gram.

xraqalil *n.* unit.

xtasalal *n.* division.

xtiqwal *n.* calorie.

xyuwa'ilb'iis *n.* a ton.

yal *adj.* only.

yam *n.* zero.

yamyo *adj.* empty.

yanq *n.* space, interval.

yanqil *n.* intermediate point.

yijach *n.* half.

yijachal *n.* half.

yo'oon ru *adj.* enough.

yok *n.* step.

yook *n.* gallon.

Xtijb'al ut Tzolok / Education and Learning

K'a'uxl ut Seeb'al / Thought and Intelligence

aj k'a'uxl *n agt.* thinker.

aj tz'ilom k'a'uxl *n agt.* philosopher.

aak'ab' *adj.* unknown, dark.

b'atz'il b'aanuhom *n.* artistic expression.

b'aan *n.* cause.

b'ehil *n.* method.

b'orok na'leb' *v phr.* to lose your train of thought.

chanchan aj wi' a'an *adj.* similar.

chankatq ru *n.* type.
Var: chankatqru.

chaab'ilob'resink *n.* paradigm.

chi junaqlil *adv.* individually.

ch'a'aj *adj.* difficult, hard.

ch'a'ajkil *n.* difficulty, problem.

ch'olch'o *adj.* certain.

ch'olk'anjel *n.* process.

ch'olk'anjel tijok *n.* educational process.

ch'uch'ib'k *v.* to joke.

ech ajaatink *v phr.* to imitate.

eek'ank *v.* to guess.

ilok ib' *n.* sustainability.

ink'a' ch'a'aj *adj.* easy.

ink'a' ch'olch'o *adj.* obscure.

jaljookil'aatin *n.* refrain, saying, proverb.

jip *adj.* stupid, foolish, clumsy.

jo'kanil *n.* inference.

jok *adj.* stupid.

jorb'ana'leb' *n.* riddle.

jultikank *v.* to train, remember.

junajink *v.* to globalize, generalize.

junaqlil *n.* individual.

juntaq'eetil *n.* equity, equality.

ka'jultikank *v.* to emphasize, highlight.

ka'yank *v.* to contemplate.

kab'lanb'il na'leb' *n.* constructivism.

kaw rib' *adj.* clever.

kaan ru *adj.* mad.

kiib'ank ch'ool *n.* doubt.

k'a'ux *n.* mind.

k'a'uxl *n.* idea, thought.

k'a'uxlak *v.* to think, suspect.

k'a'uxlanb'il *adj.* hypothetical.

k'a'uxlanb'il *n.* hypothesis.

k'a'uxlanb'ilal *n.* irrealism.

k'a'uxlanb'ilna'leb' *n.* imagination.

k'oxlak *v.* to think.

k'oxlank *v.* to reflect.

k'ub'el *n.* fundamental.

k'ulb'ilal *n.* consequence.

k'ulub'ank *v.* to accept, contemplate.

k'uulank *v.* to save, memorize.

look *adj.* mad. *From:* loco 'crazy' (Spanish) (1).

manawb'il *adj.* unknown.

matk' *n.* dream.

matk'ek *v.* to dream.

minb'ilna'leb' *n.* ideological imposition.

na'leb' *n.* advice.

na'leb' *n.* idea, intelligence, theme.

na'leb'ank *v.* to reason.

na'link *v.* to recognize.

na'ok *v.* to know, be familiar with.

na'ol *n.* he who knows.

na'onel *n.* he who knows.

na'uuchik *v.* to dream.

naqk sa' ch'ool *v phr.* to remember.

naraj *n.* manner.

nawal *n.* alter ego. **Laa'in wan we jun in nawal. Maani naxnaw li xk'ab'a'.** « I have an alter ego. Nobody knows his name.»

nawb'ehil *n.* methodology.

nawink *v.* to know.

nawom *n.* knowledge.

nawtuqch'oolil *adv.* psychologically.

nawyaalal *n.* decipherment.

nawyaalalink *v.* to decipher.

nimajel *adj.* deductive.

ninqi seeb'alil *n.* macro competencies.

numsachk *adj.* absurd.

numseeb' *n.* genius.

numseeb' xch'ool *n.* prodigy.

oksinb'il na'leb' *n.* pragmatism.

q'ehink *v.* to guess, predict.

q'ehink chi ru *v.* to prognosticate.

rajb'al *n.* intention.

raasa *adj.* difficult.

roqel *n.* origin, factor.

rub'elal'aj'ookil *n.* subconscious.

sa' taqb'eet *adv.* inductively.

sachk *v.* to confuse.

sachk sa' ch'ool *v phr.* to forget.

seeb'alil *n.* competence, capability.

sik'mank'a'uxl *n.* ideal.

taqb'eetil *adj.* inductive.

taq'eetil *n.* likeness.

taq'eetink *n.* analogy.

tawilna'leb' *n.* refrain, saying, proverb.

tawok u *v phr.* to understand.

tawok xyaalal *v phr.* to understand.

teeb'il xk'a'uxl *v phr.* to consider.

tuqtuukil *n.* balance, equilibrium.

tuqtuukil k'a'uxl *n.* logic.

tuqub'ank *v.* to balance, reform.

tusb'ehul *n.* methodological steps.

tusnaw *n.* logic.

tzilb'a'ix *n.* analysis.

tz'aqal re ru *adj.* clear.

us'elk *adj.* outstanding.

usaak wakliik *n.* development.

ustaanankil *n.* validation.

wakliik *n.* progress.

wakliik *v.* to progress.

wakliikil *n.* progressivity.

wan xna'leb' *adj.* wise, smart, intelligent.

wankil *adj.* clever.

wax ru *adj.* mad. *From:* wax "mad' (Ch'olti') (2).

xb'ehul *n.* method.

xb'ehul k'osok *n.* synthesis.

xb'ehul k'utuk *n.* teaching methods.

xcha'al seeraq' *n.* moral (to a story).

xk'a'uxlankil *n.* reflection (thought).

xokch'oolej *n.* concentration.

xq'ehinkil *n.* prediction.

xsumenkil *n.* validation.

xtawb'il li manawb'il *v phr.* to work out, make clear.

xtijb'al *n.* education.

xtuqub'ankil *n.* reform.

xtz'aqalil *adj.* complementary.

xtz'aqob'l *n.* complement.

xtz'aqob'l esilal *n.* additional information.

xyaalalil *n.* reality, meaning.

yalok ch'ool *v phr.* to give it a shot.

yu'k *v.* to progress.

Sa' li Tzoleb'aal / At School

ahom *n.* aim, goal, objective. *Var:* ajom.

ajsib'aal'u *n.* recreation, fun, recess.

b'alq'hu *n.* flipchart.

b'orleb' *n.* eraser.

b'orok *v.* to erase, unwind, untie, unroll.

champa *n.* woven shoulder bag.

chapokhu *v.* to staple.

chunleb'aal *n.* desk, bench.

ch'ina al *n.* boy.

ch'inajelool *n.* briefcase.

ch'uutal *n.* section.

eetalhu *n.* diploma.

eetalil *n.* sticker.

hoonalhilaal *n.* recreation, fun, recess.

huraqb'atzolok *n.* diploma, title, credential.

ilok chi us *v phr.* to study.

jayalihom *n.* aim, goal.

jolomilal tzoleb'aal *n.* principal's office.

jolomnib'aal *n.* principal's office.

juch'leb' *n.* ruler.

ka'ch'olob'ank *n.* survey.

kampaan *n.* bell. *From:* Spanish 'campana'.

kanhub'aal *n.* briefcase.

kaxchampa *n.* briefcase.

komon sa' tzoleb'aal *n.* classmate.

kuukil tz'ak *n.* wall.

k'achleb' *n.* stapler.

k'amleb'aal *n.* briefcase.

k'anjel *n.* homework.

k'atz'leb'hu *n.* stapler. *Var:* qatz'leb' hu.

k'axleb'hu *n.* stapler.

k'aytesiil *n.* preschool.

k'utleb'hu *n.* poster, sign.

k'utuk *v.* to teach, show, indicate.

lakaam *n.* flag. *Var:* lakan.

latz-eetal *n.* sticker.

letzelhu *n.* sticker.

letzleb' *n.* glue, tape. *Var:* latz'leb'.

letzok *v.* to glue, tape.

masleb' *n.* eraser.

maa'ani *adj.* absent.

maa'anihilk *n.* absence.

meexil tz'iib' *n.* student desk.

mochiil *n.* backpack. *From:* Spanish 'mochila'.

na'el *n.* product, result.

neb'aal *n.* playground.

nimk'uub'tzolok *n.* curriculum.

ninqiperhu *n.* poster.

q'eqhilk'anjel *n.* schedule.

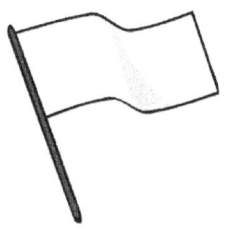

q'uq'il t'ikr *n.* flag.

q'usunel *n.* teacher.

rajlil ketom *n.* grade, score.

raqalyalb'a'ix *n.* survey, questionnaire.

raqaxinkil *n.* diagram.

reetalil *n.* example.

reetalil ch'och' *n.* map.

reetalil ru chi ch'och' *n.* globe.

reetalil tzolom *n.* diploma.

reetalilruuchich'och' *n.* world map.

ro' na'aj *n.* fifth grade.

roqechal q'uq'il t'ikr *n.* flagpole.

roqechal xmukab'l *n.* pillar.

rox na'aj *n.* third grade.

ru meex *n.* desk mat.

ru tzoleb'aal *n.* class.

ru tzolom *n.* course, subject.

ru tz'ak *n.* floor.

ruq'il *n.* branch, extension, outlet. *Var:* **ruq'b'il.**

ruuch *n.* productivity.

sachleb' *n.* eraser.

sachok *v.* to erase.

sachso *adj.* absent.

sukhu *n.* book bag, school bag.

tahu *n.* folder, binder.

tenq' *n.* scholarship.

tijok *v.* to educate.

tijom *n.* pupil, student.

tiikal juch'leb' *n.* ruler.

tusub'ank *v.* to order, arrange.

tusuk *v.* to order, arrange.

tzoleb'aal *n.* school, academy.

tzoleb'aal xb'een na'aj *n.* elementary school.

tzolok *v.* to teach.

tzolok *v.* to learn, study.

tzolom *n.* pupil, student.

tzolom k'anjel *n.* lesson.

tzolomil *n.* assignment, course.

tz'eqok *v.* to fail.

tz'ilb'a'ix *n.* examination, exam, test.

tz'ilok ib' *n.* self-test.

tz'ilok ib'ink *v phr.* to self-test.

tz'ilok-ix *v.* to test, examine, investigate, research.

tz'ilool'ix *n.* examination, exam, test.

tz'iib'leb'meex *n.* desk.

wan *adj.* present.

x'el *n.* product, result.

xb'ehulk'utuk *n.* study guide.

xb'een na'aj *n.* first grade.

xb'eenil tzoleb'aal *n.* principal.

xb'onilkaaxt *n.* ink pad, stamp pad.

xch'uutamil *n.* academy.

xch'uutulal *n.* module.

xhoonal asjsink-u *n.* recreation, fun, recess.

xhoonalil *n.* schedule.

xjayalihom tijok *n.* educational aims.

xjolomil tzoleb'aal *n.* principal.

xjotzb'al ru'uj *v phr.* to sharpen (a point).

xka na'aj *n.* fourth grade.

xkab' na'aj *n.* second grade.

xkab' na'aj tzoleb'aal *n.* high school.

xkaatanal tzolok *n.* university level.

xmolamil aj k'utunel *n.* faculty, teaching staff, educators.

xna'aj hu *n.* folder, binder.

xna'aj k'a re ru *n.* locker, cubby.

xna'aj xb'eenil *n.* principal's office.

xokleb' hu *n.* folder, binder.

xsa' tzoleb'aal *n.* classroom.

xtasalil *n.* module.

xtasalil tzolok *n.* teaching module.

xtasalil xsa' tzoleb'aal *n.* classrooms.

xtij tenamit *n.* pledge of allegiance.

xtzolb'al *n.* learning.

xtz'aq *n.* grade.

xwaq na'aj *n.* sixth grade.

xwaq po *n.* semester.

yalb'a'ix *n.* examination, exam, test.

yalok ix *n.* to test, assess.

yalok ix *n.* quiz.

yiib'anb'il *adj.* arranged.

Xch'uutalil Tzolok / Fields of Study

ab'lil aatinob'aal *n.* foreign language.

amaq'il loq'alil *n.* social studies.

amaq'kab'lk'a'uxl *n.* socio constructivism.

aatinab'aal *n.* media, means of communication, communications.

aatinob'aal *n.* language, tongue.

b'atz'iil *n.* art.

eetalb'irool *n.* algebra.

jaljookil ru ajl *n.* algebra.

jultik uxk *n.* history.

kawilal *n.* health.

k'aj nawcha'al *n.* particle physics.

k'utleb'ruuchich'och' *n.* geography.

maayab' na'leb' *n.* Maya culture, Maya tradition.

muhilb'atijok *n.* virtual education.

naw'ajl *n.* mathematics, math.

naw'amaq'il *n.* social studies, sociology.

naw'amaq'ilchi' *n.* sociolinguistics.

naw'awk *n.* agriculture, agronomy.

naw'q'och *n.* kinesiology.

nawb'anok *n.* medicine.

nawcha'al *n.* physics.

nawha'il *n.* hydrology.

nawhiik *n.* seismology.

nawkab'lank *n.* architecture.

nawkomonil *n.* sociology.

nawkomonyajel *n.* epidemiology.

218

nawk'ajyaab'aatin *n.* morphology.

nawk'anjel *n.* engineering.

nawk'iche' *n.* botany.

nawk'iijikch'ool *n.* evolutionary psychology.

nawk'uhil *n.* volcanology.

nawk'utuk *n.* teaching.

nawk'uub'tzuul *n.* structural geology.

nawom chi rix ajl *n.* math, mathematics.

nawom chi rix k'a re ru *n.* science.

nawom chi rix yu'am *n.* biology.

nawpoyanam *n.* anthropology.

nawpoyaatinob'aal *n.* ethnolinguistics.

nawq'ehil *n.* meteorology.

nawralab'aatinob'aal *n.* dialectology.

nawsutam *n.* science.

nawtijok *n.* pedagogy.

nawtuqch'ool *n.* psychology.

nawtus'aatin *n.* lexicography.

nawtus'aatin *n.* syntax.

nawxokok *n.* obstetrics.

nawxul *n.* zoology.

nawyajel *n.* pathology.

nawyu'am *n.* biology.

nawyu'amilsutaal *n.* ecology.

poyanimil nawyu'am *n.* human biology.

q'ochleb'tzolom *n.* physical education.

resilal b'aanuhom *n.* history.

resilal wank *n.* history.

sachomj *n.* economics.

sachomj junkab'lal *n.* home economics.

seeb'altz'iib' *n.* stenography, shorthand.

suutalnawom *n.* cosmology.

tijb'a'ajsiil *n.* physical education.

tijb'ab'atz'il *n.* art education.

tijb'ab'ich *n.* music education.

tijb'ajunesal *n.* distance education.

tijb'apoyanam *n.* adult education.

tijok chi rix kawilal *n.* health education.

tijok chi rix loq'ok *n.* consumer finance.

tijok sa' ka'aatinob'aal *n.* bilingual education.

tiikalil *n.* ethics, values.

tiikil loq'alil *n.* ethics, values.

tuqtuukil k'a'uxl *n.* logic.

tusnaw *n.* logic.

tzoljalam'uuch'ink *n.* visual arts, plastic arts.

tzolomilchoxach'och' *n.* natural sciences.

tzolomilkomon *n.* social studies.

tzolomilk'uub' *n.* home economics.

tzolyiib'ahom *n.* industrial arts.

uxb'il b'aanunb'il *n.* history.

uutz'u'jinb'iltz'iib' *n.* poetry.

wanjik *n.* ecology.

xcha'alil ruuchich'och' *n.* geography.

xe'k'a'uxl *n.* metaphysics.

xe'nawom *n.* philosophy.

xk'anjelankil li ch'och' *n.* farming.

xk'ub'laltzolok *n.* curriculum.

yehom'uxb'il *n.* history.

Xul ut K'ajxul / Animals and Insects

ahin jukxul *n.* reptile.

b'aqil xuleb' *n.* vertebrate.

chajok e *v phr.* to roar.

ch'uyuk *v.* to scratch.

ch'uutulal *n.* species.

ch'uuxul *n.* fauna.

ha'il ajtu'xul *n.* cetaceans.

ixi'ij *n.* hoof.

ixq *adj.* female.

jukunk *v.* to crawl.

ka'na'jilxul *n.* amphibian.

kamenaq *n.* carcass.

kapun *adj.* castrated.

ketomq *n.* livestock, farm animals. *Var:* ketomj.

koral wakax *n.* pasture. *From:* corral, vacas 'corral, cows' (Spanish) (1).

k'ol *adj.* male (of animals).

nimqi ixi'ij *n.* claw, talon.

pemech *n.* shell.
Var: xpemechul rix.

potreer *n.* pasture, meadow, paddock. *From:* potrero 'pasture' (Spanish) (1).

q'urq'utk *v.* to growl, grunt.

rax ch'och' *n.* pasture.

rix xul *n.* skin, hide.

rochoch aaq *n.* pigpen.

rochoch kab' *n.* beehive, apiary.

roq *n.* paw.

ru'uj *n.* snout.

suk *n.* nest. *From:* sik 'house construction' (Ch'olan) (2).

tikok *v.* to attack.

tu' *n.* teat.

tu'resink *v.* to nurse.

tu'unel *n.* mammal, mammalian.

tzo' *adj.* male (of birds).

tz'aak *n.* beeswax.

tz'uyte'ek *v.* to howl.

tz'uytz'utk *v.* to growl, grunt.

wa'lem *n.* pasture.

wote'ek *v.* to howl. *Var:* wute'ek.

xche'el kab' *n.* beehive.

xeq'el *adj.* gored.

xik' *n.* wing, fin.

xkem aj am *n.* spider web.

xna'aj wakax *n.* stable, stall.

xoob' *n.* gill. *Var:* xob'.

xtu' wakax *n.* udder.

xukub' *n.* horn. *From:* *xukub' 'the horn' (Ch'olan) (2).

xul *n.* animal.

yax *n.* claw, pincer. *From:* *yax 'the crab' (Ch'olan) (2).

yaab'ak *v.* to peep.

ye *n.* tail.

Eb' li Tu'unel / Mammals

aj b'oob' *n.* panther.

aj ixi'jeb' *n.* felines.

aj maxxul *n.* primate.

aj ow *n.* fox.

aj paar *n.* skunk. *Var:* paar xul.

aj tz'uum xik' *n.* bat.

aj uch *n.* opossum.

aj xoj *n.* wolf.

aaq *n.* pig, hog, swine.

aaqha' *n.* hippopotamus.

b'alam *n.* jaguar.

b'alaq xul *n.* zebra.

b'aqlaq xul *n.* opossum.

b'aqxul *n.* armadillo.

b'atz' *n.* monkey.

b'aak *n.* cow. *From:* vaca 'the cow' (Spanish) (1).

b'oreeg *n.* lamb. *From:* borrego 'the lamb' (Spanish) (1).

b'ooyx *n.* ox, yoke (of oxen). *From:* buey 'the ox' (Spanish) (1).

b'uq'ultzimitz *n.* camel.

b'uur *n.* donkey, ass. *From:* burro 'donkey or ass' (Spanish) (1).

chakow *n.* boar.

chib'aat *n.* goat, lamb. *From:* Spanish 'chiva'.

cho'hix *n.* leopard.

cho'k'oj *n.* bat.

ch'em samxul *n.* elephant.

ch'ina kawaay *n.* pony.

ch'ina wakax *n.* calf (of a cow).

elepaant *n.* elephant. *From:* elefante 'the elephant' (Spanish) (1).

222

hix *n.* jaguar, leopard, tiger, panther.

ib'oy *n.* armadillo.

imul *n.* rabbit.

ixqi aaq *n.* sow.

jilix kawaay *n.* zebra.

kameey *n.* camel. *From:* camello 'the camel' (Spanish) (1).

kapuninb'il wakax *n.* ox.

kapunwakax *n.* ox.

kaqkoj *n.* mountain lion. *Var:* **kaqkojl.**

karneer *n.* sheep, ewe, ram. *From:* carnero 'the sheep' (Spanish) (1).

kawaay *n.* horse, stallion. *From:* caballo 'the small horse' (Spanish) (1).

kax aaq *n.* hippopotamus.

kaxchixl *n.* rhinoceros.

kaxwakax *n.* buffalo, bison.

223

kej *n.* deer.

kordeer *n.* lamb. *From:* cordero 'the lamb' (Spanish) (1).

kranyon *n.* stallion. *Var:* **granyon**. *From:* grañón (possible) (Spanish) (1).

kuy *n.* pig.

k'amb'olay *n.* oncilla, tiger cat.

k'iche' aaq *n.* wild boar.

k'ila wakax *n.* herd of cattle.

k'olwakax *n.* bull.

k'unuch imul *n.* kangaroo.

loob' *n.* wolf. *From:* lobo 'the wolf' (Spanish) (1).

mama' max *n.* gorilla.

max *n.* monkey.

mes *n.* cat. *Var:* **mis**. *From:* mis 'call made to a cat' (Spanish) (3).

muul *n.* mule. *From:* mula 'the mule' (Spanish) (1).

na'wakax *n.* cow.

ob'eja *n.* lamb. *From:* oveja 'sheep' (Spanish) (1).

oos *n.* bear. *From:* oso 'the bear' (Spanish) (1).

pakun wakax *n.* ox.

q'olxulkar *n.* dolphin.

ral chib'aat *n.* baby goat, kid.

ral kawaay *n.* foal, colt. *From:*
Spanish 'caballo'.

ral wakax *n.* calf (of a cow),
bull calf.

ral yuk *n.* baby goat, kid.

samxul *n.* elephant.

saq b'alam *n.* tiger cat.

seelxul *n.* armadillo.

sotz' *n.* bat.

tixl *n.* tapir. *Var:* tis.

toor *n.* bull. *From:* from Spanish
'toro'.

t'initz *n.* wild horse.

tzimitz *n.* horse.

tzukxul *n.* sheep.

tz'i' *n.* dog.

tz'i' e *n.* tusk.

tz'i' k'iche' *n.* wolf.

tz'i' pim *n.* coyote.

tz'i' tzuul *n.* coyote.

tz'i'ha' *n.* seal.

tz'uqtz'um *n.* anteater.
Var: tz'uqtz'un; tz'uqtz'uum.

wakax *n.* cow, cattle. *From:*
vaca 'the cow' (Spanish) (1).

wonxul *n.* bear.

xa'n wakax *n.* cow.

xa'an aaq *n.* sow.

xmama' wakax *n.* bull.

xna' kawaay *n.* mare.

xojb' *n.* coyote.

xul iiqanel *n.* donkey, ass, mule, beast of burden.

xyuwa'il xul *n.* lion.

yak *n.* lynx, fox.

yak'achkej *n.* giraffe.

yuk *n.* goat. *Var:* kaxlan yuk. *From:* *yuuk 'brocket deer' (Yucatecan) (2).

Eb' li Xul Aj K'oyoneleb' / Rodents

aj b'oox uch *n.* opossum.

aj k'oyoneleb' *n.* rodents.

aj setoneleb' *n.* rodents.

aaqam *n.* agouti (dasyprocta).

b'a *n.* gopher.

ch'o *n.* rat.

halaw *n.* agouti (dasyprocta).

hot'ok *v.* to gnaw, chew.

kaxmis *n.* marmot.

kaxxul *n.* beaver.

kuk *n.* squirrel.

k'axkuk *n.* chinchilla.

k'iche' ch'o *n.* dormouse.

k'iche' imul *n.* hare.

k'ix uch *n.* porcupine.

ow *n.* raccoon. *Var:* aj ow.

q'an tu'lay aj imul *n.* guinea pig.

rupkuk *n.* flying squirrel.

saqb'in *n.* weasel.

sis *n.* white-nosed coati.

uch ch'o *n.* mouse, rat.

xa'nch'o *n.* mouse.

xa'an imul *n.* hare, rabbit.

Eb' li Tz'ik / Birds

ak'ach *n.* turkey.

chakmut *n.* pheasant.

chocho' *n.* parrot.

ch'ejej *n.* crow.

ch'ina kaxlan *n.* chick.

ch'onpatz *n.* goose.

ixi'ij *n.* claw.

jotz *n.* heron.

joob'aq *n.* owl.

kaxjukin *n.* flamingo.

kaxkatras *n.* swan.

kaxlan *n.* chicken. *From:* Spanish 'Castellano'.

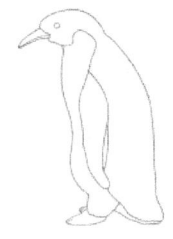

kaxpatz xul *n.* penguin.

kaxsaq eknil *n.* flamingo.

kaans *n.* goose. *From:* ganso (Spanish) (1).

kokech *n.* guinea hen.

kok' kaxlan *n.* chick.

kok' q'an tz'ik *n.* canary.

kok' xul *n.* bird.

kormaach *n.* partridge.

k'ochlaak *v.* to land, alight.
Var: **k'ojlaak.**

k'uch *n.* hawk.

k'uuk'um *n.* feather.

liklik *n.* hawk.

loor *n.* parrot. *From:* loro 'the parrot' (Spanish) (1).

mayta' *n.* bird guano.

mo' *n.* macaw.

mukuy *n.* pigeon, dove. *From:* *mukuy 'dove' (Yucatecan, Ch'olan , ?) (2).

najtil t'uru' ak'ach *n.* ostrich.

pap tz'unun *n.* large hummingbird.

patux *n.* duck. *From:* pato 'duck' (Spanish) (1).

patux ha' *n.* heron.

pich' *n.* woodpecker.

puyuch' *n.* parakeet.

qoch *n.* crow.

q'eq'i ch'ejej *n.* black crow.

q'uq' *n.* quetzal.

rak'ach tzuul *n.* roadrunner.

ral kaxlan *n.* chick.

raxpan *n.* toucan.

rismal xul *n.* feather.

rismal xxik' *n.* feather.

rochochil tz'ik *n.* birdhouse.

ruuch e *n.* beak.

saqikil *n.* heron.

seelapan *n.* toucan.
Var: selepan; seleepan.

sok xul *n.* nest.

sokink *v.* to nest.

so'sol *n.* vulture. *Var:* so'sool.
From: sosool 'vulture' (Yucatecan,
Ch'olan, possible) (2).

tonq' *n.* quail.

tuntz'oq *n.* raven.

turunhut tz'ik *n.* quail.

tux kaxlan *n.* hen.

t'int'ookil patux *n.* goose.

t'iw *n.* eagle.

tzentzejer *n.* woodpecker.

tzo' pu' *n.* peacock.

tzo' kaxlan *n.* cock, rooster.

tzo'xul *n.* cock, rooster.

tz'alam *n.* cage.

tz'ik *n.* bird, fowl.

tz'unun *n.* sparrow.

tz'unun *n.* hummingbird.

uut *n.* wild dove.

warom *n.* owl.

wilix *n.* sparrow.

xa'an kaxlan *n.* hen.

xik' *n.* feather.

xmama' t'iw *n.* condor.

xtz'ik ha' *n.* seagull.

yenyookil patux *n.* swan.

Eb' li Kar ut Jukxul / Fish and Reptiles

amoch *n.* frog, toad. *From:* *amuch 'frog' (Yucatecan, Ch'olan, possible) (4).

ayin *n.* alligator. *Var:* ahin.

ayin kar *n.* shark.

ayin kaaq *n.* dinosaur.

b'ayeen *n.* whale. *From:* ballena 'the whale' (Spanish) (1).

chakti' *n.* mojarra.

ch'ina perk'anti' *n.* cobra.

iwaan *n.* iguana. *From:* Spanish 'iguana'.

jit *n.* prawns, shrimp. *From:* jit 'large shrimp' (Tzeltal) (3).

jukxul *n.* reptile.

jutz' kar *n.* swordfish.

kaq ra' *n.* frog.

kar *n.* fish.

karil *n.* fish.

kok *n.* tortoise, turtle.

k'anti' *n.* snake. *From:* *k'anti' 'yellow bearded snake' (Ch'olan) (4).

k'anti' kar *n.* eel.

k'anti' ra xmay re *n.* viper.

k'ox *n.* prawns, shrimp.

k'oxib'k *v.* to shrimp, fish for shrimp.

k'oopopo' *n.* toad.

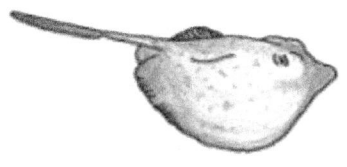

mama' ayin *n.* crocodile.

Var: **ahin.**

mama' kar *n.* shark.

perkar *n.* ray, stingray.

pospo'ykar *n.* gills.

rax k'aj *n.* flying serpent.

rep'ix *n.* scale.

resil yu'amej *n.* biography.

rix kok *n.* turtle shell.

saqi kar *n.* sardines.

soch *n.* shell, sea snail.

solel *n.* scale.

moch'kar *n.* octopus.

paqmaal *n.* salamander.

pat *n.* scale (reptilian).

pati kar *n.* fish scale.

tap *n.* crab.

tap re nima' *n.* crayfish.

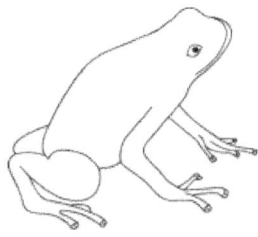

pelpel *n.* frog.

pere'maal *n.* chameleon.

tiburon *n.* shark. *From:* tiburón 'the shark' (Spanish) (1).

tolokok *n.* lizard. *Var:* **toolok**; **tookok**. *From:* *to:loki, *tohloki 'izard' (Nahuatl) (2).

xch'ina kawaay palaw *n.* seahorse.

xna' kar *n.* whale.

xna' k'anti' *n.* viper.

xsol rix *n.* scale.

xtap palaw *n.* crab.

xyuwa'il ayin *n.* crocodile.

xyuwa'il paqmaal *n.* chameleon.

Eb' li K'ajxul / Insects

aj am *n.* spider.

aj pitz' *n.* grasshopper.

aaq kab' *n.* wild bee.

b'itonk'ot *n.* beetle.

b'itzkiri' *n.* worm.

b'ujl *n.* fly (insect).

chajal *n.* worm.

chawinik *n.* bee.

chikiriin *n.* cicada.

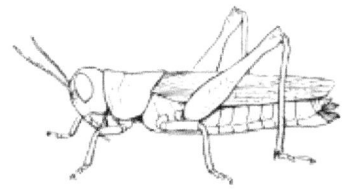

chili' *n.* grasshopper, cricket.

chupil *n.* worm.

ch'een *n.* mosquito. *Var:* **ch'en**.

ch'ub' *n.* wasp, hornet.

hay *n.* worm.

inseekt *n.* insect. *From:* insecto 'the insect' (Spanish) (1).

kojoj *n.* centipede.

kokxul *n.* ladybug.

kok' utz' *n.* mosquito.

kok' xul *n.* insect.

koton is *n.* worm.

kuluk *n.* worm, caterpillar. *From:* *kuluk 'hairy worm' (Yucatecan, Ch'olan, possible) (2).

k'ajxul *n.* insect, bug.

k'ams *n.* termites. *From:* *k'amas 'termite' (Yucatecan, Ch'olan, possible) (2).

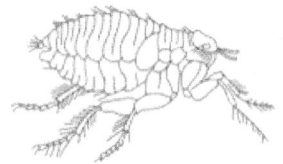

k'aq *n.* flea.

k'ixix *n.* worm.

k'ot uk' *n.* nit.

k'ulim *n.* bedbug. *Var:* k'ulin.

k'utub' *n.* worm.

k'uxuk *n.* sandfly, midge, gnat.

lukum *n.* worm, earthworm.

mams *n.* firefly, lightning bug. *Var:* mans.

max *n.* moth, weevil.

maxel hal *n.* weevil.

misik *n.* antenna (insect).

motzo' *n.* worm. *From:* motzo' 'worm' (Ch'olan) (2).

mutzuy *n.* centipede.

pachi' *n.* beetle.

pataal *n.* centipede.

paachach *n.* cockroach, roach. *From:* pachajk 'insect said to resemble the cockroach' (Ch'orti') (2).

pemech *n.* snail.

peepem *n.* butterfly.

pirik' *n.* worm.

pumpuri' *n.* beetle.

pur *n.* snail.

q'anch'ub' *n.* yellow hornet.

q'eq aj am *n.* tarantula.

raxq'een *n.* grasshopper.

sank *n.* ant.

saqxul *n.* fly (insect).

saak' *n.* grasshopper.

seer *n.* bee. *From:* cera 'bee's wax' (Spanish) (1).

sij *n.* cricket.

sip *n.* tick.

suq *n.* fly (insect), sandfly, midge, gnat.

suq *n.* mosquito.

tin *n.* worm.

tuulux *n.* dragonfly.

t'ot' *n.* snail.

tziitzib' *n.* snail.

tzonok' *n.* worm.

tz'iray *n.* cricket.

tz'upq'een *n.* praying mantis.

uk' *n.* flea.

uk' *n.* louse.

utz' *n.* fly (insect).

utz' *n.* mosquito.

x'am *n.* spider.

xamxul *n.* firefly.

xna' k'anti' *n.* salamander.

xna'aj kab' *n.* beehive.

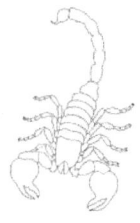

xook' *n.* scorpion.

xulkab' *n.* bee.

xulk'aq *n.* chigger.

Yohob'k ut Karib'k / Hunting and Fishing

aj kar *n agt.* fisherman.

aj yo *n agt.* hunter.

b'itzilch'iich' *n.* knife.

chapleb' kar *n.* fishhook.

chapok kar *v phr.* to fish.

ch'antun *n.* fish net. *From:*
*ch'antun 'fishnet' (Yucatecan, Ch'olan, possible) (4).

ch'imb' *n.* trap.

ch'imb'ul *n.* trap.

ch'imb'unk *v.* to trap.

jok' *n.* sling.

jok'ib'k *v.* to sling.

jusk'aam *n.* cord, line.

jutz'che' *n.* spear.

jutz'leb' *n.* spear.

kamsink *v.* to kill.

karib'k *v.* to fish. *Var:* karab'k.

karink *v.* to fish.

kordel *n.* fishing line. *From:*
cordel 'the string' (Spanish) (1).

kutuk *v.* to shoot, throw.

kuux re karab'k *n.* fishhook.

k'aam *n.* fishing line.

lokoch *n.* hook.

oont *n.* sling. *From:* honda 'sling' (Spanish) (1).

puub' che' *n.* blowgun.

ra'al *n.* trap.

ra'alenk *v.* to trap.

ra'leb'kar *n.* fishhook.

rant'in *n.* sling.

ra'l kar *n.* fish trap.

sekch'iich' *n.* knife.

sijb' *n.* arrow.

soq' *n.* net bag, rope net.

soq' re karab'k *n.* fish net.

topleb' *n.* spear.

toqb'ilpuub' *n.* shotgun.

traamp *n.* fish trap. *From:* trampa 'the trap' (Spanish) (1).

tzak *n.* prey. *From:* tzak 'to take or look for' (Ch'olan) (5).

tzakib'k *v.* to hunt.

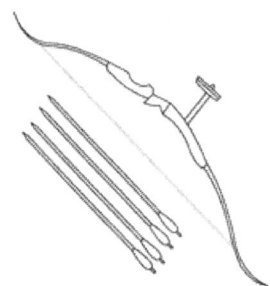

tzimaj *n.* bow and arrow. *Var:* simaj.

xna' sijb' *n.* bow.

xsokilkar *n.* fish net.

xuq'l *n.* club, billy club.

xwah kar *n.* bait.

yohob'k *v.* to hunt.

yooy *n.* fish net, fishing net. *From:* yoyo (Spanish) (2).

Kok' Raqal Aatin / Basic Phrases

a' yaal aawe *phr.* it's up to you.

aj b'arat *phr.* where are you from?

ay xkux na' *phr.* damn it.

b'antyox *phr.* thank you, thanks.

b'ar nakatchal *phr.* where do you come from?

b'ar rajlil laab'oqleb' *phr.* what's your phone number?

b'ar wan aatenamit *phr.* where are you from?

b'ar wan aawochoch *phr.* where do you live?

b'ar wan li tz'eqleb'aal *phr.* where is the toilet?

b'ar wankat *phr.* where are you?

b'aanu sa' xyaalal *phr.* take your time.

b'aanu usilal *phr.* please.

b'aanu usilal aatinan chi timil *phr.* please speak slowly.

b'aanu usilal tz'iib'a *phr.* please write it down.

b'aanu ye jun sutaq chik *phr.* please say that again.

chan ru la weetalil sa' internet *phr.* what's your email?

chan ru li kutan *phr.* how's the weather?

chan ru nakaayaab'asi [   ] *phr.* how do you pronounce [   ]?

chan ru nayehman [   ] *phr.* how do you say [   ]?

chan ru wankat *phr.* how are you?

chan xaawil *phr.* hello, hi.

chap aawe *phr.* help yourself.

chaqiq we *phr.* I'm thirsty.

chatwarq chi us *phr.* sleep well (singular).

chaaab'il *phr.* great!

chaab'aanu went *phr.* be careful.

chaab'il xaab'anu *phr.* well done!

chaakuy inmaak *phr.* I'm sorry, forgive me.

chaanumsi chi us li kutan *phr.* have a nice day.

chaanumsi chi us li xamaan *phr.* have a nice week.

chaayehaq we *phr.* let me know.

chexwarq *phr.* sleep well, good night (plural).

chi qilaq qib' *phr.* see you later.

chinaakuy *phr.* excuse me, pardon me.

chinaakuy xatink'e chi oyb'enink *phr.* sorry to keep you waiting.

chinaakuy xib'ayon chaq *phr.* sorry I'm late.

chinaawoyb'en b'ayaq *phr.* hang on a second, wait a minute.

chineetenq'aaaq *phr.* help!

chunlan *phr.* have a seat.

ch'ich'i' we *phr.* I'm in a bad mood.

ch'olch'o b'i'an *adv phr.* certainly.

enhe' *adv.* yes.

heehe' *adv.* yes.

i' *adv.* no.

iliii *phr.* look!

ink'a' *adv.* no.

ink'a' b'i' *phr.* of course not.

ink'a' ch'olch'o *phr.* I'm not sure.

ink'a' jwal sa naweek'a *phr.* I don't feel very well.

ink'a' jwal us *phr.* not so well.

ink'a' nahulak chi wu [ ] *phr.* I don't like [ ].

ink'a' naxk'ul inch'ool *phr.* I disagree.

ink'a' nin'aatinak sa' inkles *phr.* I don't speak English.

ink'a' nin'aatinak sa' q'eqchi' *phr.* I don't speak Q'eqchi'.

ink'a' ninnaw *phr.* I don't know.

ink'a' us xat-elq *phr.* too bad (for you)!

inwan b'i' *phr.* goodbye, bye.

jarub' chihab' wan aawe *phr.* how old are you?

jo' junelik *phr.* same as usual.

jo' wan chik *phr.* see you soon.

jo'kan ajwi' tinye aawe *phr.* same to you.

jo'kan b'i'an *adv phr.* definitely, absolutely.

jo'kan li wank *phr.* that's life.

jo'kan tz'aqal *phr.* sure.

jwal aajel *phr.* very important.

jwal laatz' wu *phr.* I've been busy.

ka'aj wi a'an *phr.* nothing more, that's it, that's all.

kelo *phr.* pull.

k'a' ru a'an *phr.* what is that?

k'a' ru a'in *phr.* what is this?

k'a' xja'lenkil *phr.* what a pity, what a shame.

k'a'ru naraj naxye [ ] *phr.* what does [ ] mean?

k'a'ru xaaye *phr.* what did you say?

k'a'ru xk'ulman *phr.* what's the matter?, what happened?

k'a'ru yo *phr.* what is happening?

k'a'ru yookat *phr.* what are you doing? (singular).

k'a'ut naq ink'a' *phr.* why not?

k'e reetal li taab'aanu *phr.* watch out, look out.

k'ojob' aach'ool *phr.* calm down.

laa'in ajwi' *phr.* me too.

loq' jun ut yal siib'il li xkab' *phr.* buy one get one free.

lub'luukin *phr.* I'm exhausted.

ma ak nakenaw eeru *phr.* do you know each other?

ma nakat-aatinak sa' inkles *phr.* do you speak English?

ma nakat-aatinak sa' q'eqchi' *phr.* do you speak Q'eqchi'?

ma ra xk'ul *phr.* is anything wrong?

ma relik chi yaal *phr.* are you sure?

ma sa laach'ool *phr.* how are you?

ma tawaj uk'ak *phr.* would you like a drink?

ma us wankat *phr.* are you OK?

ma wan b'ayaq aahoonal *phr.* have you got a minute?

ma yaal *phr.* really?

ma'laq *adv.* a while ago.

matchoqin *phr.* shut up! (singular).

matk'a'uxlak *phr.* think nothing of it, don't mention it, don't worry about it.

maak'a' *phr.* not at all.

maak'a' chik *phr.* there is no more.

maak'a' ink'as chi rix *phr.* I don't mind.

maak'a' naxye *phr.* you're welcome, it doesn't matter.

maak'a' nume'k *phr.* no entry.

maak'e xloq'al *phr.* it's not worth it.

maare jo'kan *phr.* I hope so.

maawa' *phr.* it is not.

mi naach'ich'i *phr.* leave me alone.

mi sach sa' laach'ool *phr.* don't forget.

mixk *adv.* a while ago.

moko us ta *phr.* out of order.

moko wan ta xloq'al *phr.* it doesn't matter, it's not important.

moko yaal ta laak'a'uxl *phr.* you're wrong.

moko [ ] ta *adv phr.* not, no. *Note:* That which is inserted between 'moko' and 'ta' is negated. **A' kok' kab' a'an moko sa ta.** « That candy does not taste good. »

nahulak chi wu [ ] *phr.* I like [ ].

nakatinjultika *phr.* I miss you.

nasaho inch'ool xnawb'al aawu *phr.* nice to meet you.

naab'alwa b'antyox *phr.* thank you very much.

ninb'anyoxi laa tenq' *phr.* thanks for your help.

ninnaw *phr.* I know.

nujenakin *phr.* I'm full.

numen laat xb'een wa *phr.* after you.

ojob'an b'aanu usilal *phr.* cough please.

ok we chi elk *phr.* I'm going out.

okan *phr.* come in (singular).

okanqex *phr.* come in (plural).

sa inch'ool chi rab'inkil *phr.* happy to hear it.

sa naxye *phr.* sounds good.

sa' junpaat jo'naxk'e rib' *phr.* as soon as possible.

sachsookin *phr.* I am lost.

sahil ch'oolejil choq' aawe *phr.* congratulations!

sahil ch'oolejil choq' aawe sa' laakutan *phr.* happy birthday.

sahil ch'oolejil choq' aawe sa' ralankil *phr.* Merry Christmas.

tawajenaqin *phr.* I'm tired.

tento tinxik *phr.* I've got to go.

tiikis *phr.* push.

toj ruch... *phr.* there still are...

toj wan... *phr.* there still are...

toja' yaal *phr.* that depends.

twaj ru *phr.* I'm in a hurry.

tz'aqal *phr.* that's enough.

us *adv.* yes.

us chat-elq *phr.* good luck!

us maak'a naxye *phr.* it's OK.

us naq nawil *phr.* it's OK.

us raj *phr.* that's interesting, I'd love to.

us wankin b'antyox *phr.* I'm fine thanks.

usaq b'i' *phr.* of course.

usilk'ulunk *adj.* welcome.

usilk'ulunk cho'q eere *phr.* welcome to all of you.

wahi' *phr.* here it is.

wan b'ayaq rusilal *phr.* not bad.

wankin sa' wochoch *phr.* I'm at home.

xintaw ru *phr.* I understand.

xintitz' *phr.* I'm bored.

xxaqlin *phr.* stop it!

yal b'ayaq nin'aatinak sa' kastiiy *phr.* I only speak a little Spanish.

yal b'ayaq nin'aatinak sa' q'eqchi' *phr.* I only speak a little Q'eqchi'.

yal ch'uch'ib'k we *phr.* just kidding, just joking.

yaal *phr.* that's true.

yaal laak'a'uxl *phr.* you're right.

ye chi timil *phr.* speak slowly.

ye wi'chik *phr.* say again, repeat that.

yo inch'ool chi royb'eninkil *phr.* I'm looking forward to it.

yo ink'a'uxl *phr.* I'm worried.

yo inyajel *phr.* I feel sick.

yo wix *phr.* I'm in a bad mood.

yo'o *phr.* let's go, come on.
Var: yo'qeb'.

yo'ooo *phr.* come on!

Nawchi' Aatin / Linguistic Terms

aj ka'aatin *n agt.* bilingual, polyglot.

aj k'ila'aatin *n agt.* polyglot.

ak'aatin *n.* neologism.

anaqwankil'uxk *n.* present tense.

aatin *n.* word.

aatinob'aalil *adj.* idiomatic.

b'aanunel *n.* subject.

cholob'anel *n.* adjective.

ch'olob'ihom *n.* predicate.

ch'otonel *adj.* last, final.

ch'oolyaab' *n.* phoneme.

eechaninb'il *n.* possessive.

jalb'esiil'aatin *n.* dialect.

jalch'ool'aatin *n.* adverb.

jalch'ool'aatin kok'raq aatin *n.* adverbial phrase.

jalok-aatin *n.* translation, interpretation.

jap yahiil *n.* open syllable.

jayaab' na'tz'iib' *n.* relaxed vowel.

jilb'il yaab' *n.* fricative.

junaatalil *adj.* singular.

junesal'uxk *n.* intransitive (verb).

juneetil'aatin *n.* synonym.

juneetilk'ab'a' *n.* homonym.

junil na'tz'iib' *n.* short vowel.

juntaq'eetil'aatin *n.* synonym.

juntaq'eetyaalalil *n.* synonym.

ka' paay ru k'ab'a'ej *n.* composite noun.

ka'kab'iluxk *n.* transitive (verb).

ka'pak'alil ru aatin *n.* antonyms.

ka'sutink *n.* repetition.

ka'wahink *n.* repetition.

kajunajink xna'tz'iib' *n.* diphthong.

kawyaab' na'tz'iib' *n.* stressed vowel.

kawyaab'ink *v.* to stress.

kaayehiil *n.* tetrasyllable.

kok'raq aatin *n.* phrase.

k'ab'a'atq *n.* noun.

k'ab'a'ej *n.* noun.

k'ab'a'ej k'a'aqru *n.* common noun.

k'ab'a'na'jej *n.* toponym.

k'aj'aatin *n.* particle.

k'ajtz'iib' *n.* particle.

k'ajyaab'aatin *n.* morpheme.

k'ihalatq *adj.* plural.
Var: **k'ihalatqil.**

k'ila'aatinob'aal *adj.* multilingual.

k'ilayehiil *n.* polysyllable.

k'ulb'atz'iib' *n.* synaleph, linkage of syllables.

k'ulb'ayaab' *n.* articulation.

k'ultiq *n.* connection.

moqonil'uxk *n.* future tense.

murink *v.* to separate, segregate, break down, fragment. *Var:* **xmurb'al.**

najunajin aatin *n.* conjunction.

nat'yaab' *n.* glottal, glottalization.

naw'amaq'ilchi' *n.* sociolinguistics.

naw'aatinob'aal *n.* linguistics.

nawchi' *n.* linguistics.

nawk'ajyaab'aatin *n.* morphology.

nawralab'aatinob'aal *n.* dialectology.

nawtus'aatin *n.* syntax.

nawtzoltz'iib' *n.* literacy.

nawtz'iib'ak *n.* orthography.

nume'k'uluk *n.* passive voice.

nume'uxkb'il *n.* antipassive voice. *Note:* Antipassive voice refers to intransitive verb forms that have an active sense but no direct object.

numenaqil'uxk *n.* past tense.

nut'b'il yaab' *n.* fricative.

oxjunajink xna'tz'iib' *n.* triphthong.

oxraqyehok *n.* trisyllable.

oxtz'uq *n.* suspension points, ellipsis.

patz'leb' aatin *n.* interrogative.

q'inolaatin *n.* preposition.

ralab'aatinob'aal *n.* dialect.

raqal'aatin *n.* phrase.

raqtz'aqob'l *n.* suffix, ending.

raatinul *n.* idiolect.

raatinxcha'alil aatinib'aal *n.* variant form.

roksinkil naw'aatinob'aal *n.* applied linguistics.

rox kawil yaab' *n.* stress on third to last syllable.

roxch'otonel *adj.* antepenultimate, third to last. *Var:* **roxch'otol.**

ru'uj'aq' yaab' *n.* alveopalatal.

rub'elal xraqik *adj.* penultimate, second to last.

ruuchik'ab'a'ej *n.* pronoun. *Var:* **ruuchil k'ab'a'ej.**

sa'iltz'aqob'l *n.* infix.

sum na'tz'iib' *n.* long vowel.

tiktz'aqob'l *n.* prefix.

to'aatin *n.* borrowed word.

to'chi' *n.* linguistic borrowing, borrowed word.

tuqlaaltz'iib' *n.* orthography.

tuqtutz'iib' *n.* orthography.

tzoltz'iib'ak *v.* to become literate.

tzoltz'iib'ank *n.* literacy.

tz'ap yehiil *n.* closed syllable.

tz'apyaab' *n.* occlusive.

tz'uqux *n.* suspension points, ellipsis.

ujinb'ilyaab' *n.* nasal, nasalization.

uuchilk'ab'a'ej *n.* pronoun.

waklesink naw'aatinob'aal *n.* linguistic development.

xb'ehul k'utuk xkab'aatinob'aal *n.* second language acquisition.

xb'een aatinob'aal *n.* mother tongue.

xb'een'e *n.* palate, soft palate.

xb'een'e yaab' *n.* palatal.

xb'een'e yaab' *n.* velar.

xcha'alil aatinob'aal *n.* dialectal variety.

xch'oolaatin *n.* verb.

xhuhul raq *n.* syllabary.

xjalob'aatinob'aal *n.* variant form.

xjalpaq'il *n.* antonym.

xkab' kawil yaab' *n.* stress on second to last syllable.

xkab'aatinob'aal *n.* second language.

xk'ab'a'il *n.* proper noun.

xk'aj aatin *n.* article.

xmaril kawil yaab' *n.* stress on last syllable.

xmolamil aatinob'aal *n.* linguistic community.

xna'leb'il *n.* policy, theme.

xna'leb'il nawaatinob'aal *n.* language policy.

xna'tz'iib' *n.* vowel.

xna'tz'iib'eb' *n.* vowels.

xraqilal li aatinob'aal *n.* parts of speech.

xsumalil *n.* minimal pair.

xtiqb'al aatin *n.* preposition.

xtuqlal'aatinob'aal *n.* grammar.

xtz'iib'ul *n.* rule, norm.

xtz'iib'ul aatinob'aal *n.* linguistic norms.

xxe'ilal *n.* etymology.

xyaab'kuxil *n.* intonation.

xyaab'tz'iib' *n.* consonant.

xyikutb'il aatin *n.* interjection.

yaab' aatin *n.* stress.

yaab' kux *n.* phonetics.

yaab'ank *v.* to vocalize.

yaab'aatin *n.* phonetics.

yaab'il *n.* resonant, loud.

yaab'kuxink *n.* to sound, intone.

yaab'k'ab'a'il *n.* onomatopoeia.

yehiil *n.* syllable.

yehiileb' *n.* syllabary.

yehom *n.* language, narration.

yeeb'il *adj.* verbal.

yoob'aal aatin *n.* neologism.

Xraqtz'aqob'leb' Xch'ool Aatin / Verb Endings

-ak raqtz'aqob'l / -ak ending

ab'enak *v.* to ask for a favor.

at'isb'ak *v.* to sneeze.

atz'umak *v.* to flower.

aakanak *v.* to have difficulty breathing at night.

aakanak *v.* to have nightmares.

aanilak *v.* to run. *Var:* alinak.

aatinak *v.* to speak, talk, chat.

chuq'ub'ak *v.* to hiccough, hiccup. *From:* chuq'ub' 'hiccoughs' (Q'anjob'alan) (4).

chuub'ak *v.* to spit. *Var:* chuub'ank.

elq'ak *v.* to steal.

hasb'ak *v.* to whisper, mumble.

hulak *v.* to arrive, become. *Var:* wulak.

k'aamak *v.* to spin.

k'otak *v.* to defecate. *From:* k'ot 'to throw' (Q'anjob'alan) (4).

k'oxlak *v.* to think.

leeleb'ak *v.* to dribble.

mayejak *v.* to make an offering.

musiq'ak *v.* to breathe, respire. *From:* *mus iik' 'to breathe' (Yucatecan, Ch'olan, possible) (2).

ojb'ak *v.* to cough.

pamamnak *v.* to float.

puub'ak *v.* to shoot.

qixb'ak *v.* to burp.

q'alnak *v.* to carry (under the arm).

telnak *v.* to carry (in hand).

tiqob'ak *v.* to perspire. *Var:* **tiqob'ank.**

tob'b'ak *v.* to fall.

tzinb'ak *v.* to sound, ring.

tzoltz'iib'ak *v.* to become literate.

tz'iib'ak *v.* to write, take notes.

uk'ak *v.* to drink.

ula'ak *v.* to visit.

wa'ak *v.* to eat.

wajb'ak *v.* to play instruments.

xa'wak *v.* to vomit.

xolb'ak *v.* to play the flute.

xuxb'ak *v.* to whistle. *Var:* **xuxb'ank.** *From:* xuxub' 'to whistle' (Yucatecan, Ch'olan, possible) (2).

yaab'ak *v.* to cry, shriek.

yaab'ak *v.* to peep.

yumb'eetak *v.* to fornicate.

-ek raqtz'aqob'l / -ek ending

juylek *v.* to beat, whip.

ke'ek *v.* to grind.

lochte'ek *v.* to climb.

matk'ek *v.* to dream.

se'ek *v.* to laugh, smile.

tz'uyte'ek *v.* to howl.

wote'ek *v.* to howl. *Var:* **wute'ek.**

yalb'ek *v.* to rehearse.

-ik raqtz'aqob'l / -ik ending

b'alaq'ik *v.* to lie (tell falsehoods).

eelelik *v.* to retreat, flee.

kisik *v.* to fart, pass gas.

lemtz'b'onik *v.* to varnish.

na'uuchik *v.* to dream.

numxik *v.* to swim.

purik *v.* to fly.

rupik *v.* to fly. *Var:* rupupik.

ruujik *v.* to cease.

sachik *v.* to use up.

seeraq'ik *v.* to speak, talk, tell stories, narrate. *Var:* saaraq'ik; saraq'ik; seraq'ik.

sik'lik *v.* to smoke.

xik *v.* to go.

-ok raqtz'aqob'l / -ok ending

b'ak'ok *v.* to tie.

b'alok *v.* to slide, slip.

b'asok *v.* to fold.

b'atok *v.* to pack, wrap.

b'ayok *v.* to delay, hold up, put off.

b'ekok *v.* to dig.

b'ich'ok *v.* to peel, skin.

b'iqok *v.* to rub, handle.

b'isok *v.* to weigh, measure.

b'onok *v.* to dye, paint, stain.

b'oqok *v.* to summon, call, invite.

b'orok *v.* to erase, unwind, untie, unroll.

chapok *v.* to take, grasp, hold.

chapok b'e *v phr.* to leave, hit the road.

chaq'ok *v.* to answer, respond, reply.

chiqok *v.* to cook.

chiqok tz'uum *v phr.* to tan.

chiq'ok *v.* to shake.

chirok *v.* to spread out.

choyok *v.* to end, finish.

ch'ajok *v.* to wash.

ch'e'ok *v.* to touch, feel.

ch'e'ok *v.* to fight.

ch'epok *v.* to thresh.

ch'epok *v.* to pinch.

hab'ok *v.* to chew.

hach'ok *v.* to bite.

helok *v.* to spread out, roll out.

helok *v.* to hang out (clothing).

hirok *v.* to sow.

hirok *v.* to untangle.

hitok *v.* to untie, untangle, unravel. *From:* *hit 'to untie' (Ch'olan) (3).

hopok *v.* to bore, drill.

hot'ok *v.* to gnaw, chew.

hoyok *v.* to pour, water, irrigate. *From:* *hoy 'to irrigate' (Yucatecan) (2).

ilok *v.* to see.

jachok *v.* to cut down.

jachok *v.* to halve, split.

jahok u *v phr.* to entertain, amuse, distract.

jalok *v.* to change.

jaqok *v.* to open.

jeb'ok *v.* to subtract.

jesok *v.* to chop.

ji'ok *v.* to iron (clothing).

ji'ok *v.* to sand, file, smooth, plane, shave (wood).

jichok *v.* to grate, scrape.

jilok *v.* to rub, handle.

jiqok *v.* to advance.

jisok *v.* to cut in strips.

jitok *v.* to accuse.

jit'ok *v.* to tie.

jit'ok kotox ch'iich' *v phr.* to screw.

jochok *v.* to scratch.

johok *v.* to shave.

jokok *v.* to scrape, scoop.

jorok *v.* to break.

jot'ok *v.* to injure.

jot'ok *v.* to scrape.

jot'ok *v.* to interrupt.

jotzok *v.* to peel.

jotzok ru'uj *v phr.* to sharpen.

kaq'ok *v.* to blush, turn red.

ke'ok *v.* to grind.

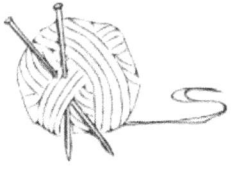

kemok *v.* to weave, braid, plait, knit.

ketok *v.* to beat, hit, strike.

kolok *v.* to rescue, save.

kolok *v.* to dodge, avoid.

kolok *v.* to defend, protect.

koq'ok *v.* to drop.

kotzok *v.* to loosen.

k'amok *v.* to bring.

k'amok b'e *v phr.* to lead.

k'amok chaq *v.* to bring.

k'asok *v.* to owe.

k'atok *v.* to burn.

k'atzok *v.* to bite.

k'ehok *v.* to put, place.

k'ehok *v.* to serve.

k'ehok chi ru saq'e *v phr.* to sun dry.

k'ehok eetal *v phr.* to control.

k'ehok numik *v phr.* to let through, cede way, give way.

k'ehok q'esnal *v phr.* to sharpen.

k'ehok xtz'aqob' *v phr.* to add.

k'ixok *v.* to untie.

k'ob'ok *v.* to bore.

k'okok *v.* to slice.

k'olok *v.* to shorten. *Var:* k'osok.

k'onok *v.* to twist, bend. *From:* *k'ong 'to bend' (Ch'olan) (1).

k'osok *v.* to reduce, shrink, trim.

lanok *v.* to wrap.

lapok *v.* to kick.

latzok *v.* to seal.

lekok *v.* to draw water.

lepok *v.* to cover.

let'ok *v.* to carve.

letzok *v.* to glue, tape.

liq'ok *v.* to bend.

lochok *v.* to light. *Var:* lechok.

lokok *v.* to bend.

loq'ok *v.* to buy, purchase.

mesok *v.* to shine, polish, wipe.

mich'ok *v.* to skin.

mich'ok ix *v phr.* to peel.

minok *v.* to push.

mochok *v.* to fold.

molok *v.* to gather.

molok *v.* to choose.

na'ok *v.* to know, be familiar with.

nat'ok *v.* to press, tighten.

ok *v.* to begin, enter.

oq'lok *v.* to howl.

pach'ok *v.* to splash.

pak'ok *v.* to mold, form, shape. *From:* pak' 'to shape' (Yucatecan, Ch'olan, possible) (2).

parok *v.* to scratch.

patz'ok *v.* to interrogate.

patz'ok *v.* to ask, beg, plead, survey, inquire.

payok *v.* to whisper sweetly.

payok *v.* to fall in love, entrust.

pech'ok *v.* to carve. *From:* pech' 'to carve in wood' (Ch'olan) (2).

pejok *v.* to tear.

pikok *v.* to dig. *From:* *pik 'to dig' (Ch'olan) (2).

pisk'ok *v.* to jump, leap.

pitzok *v.* to jump, leap.

pitz'ok *v.* to squeeze, press.

po'ok *v.* to undo, break down.

pomok *v.* to broil, grill, roast, fry.

potz'ok *v.* to strike, hit, beat.

po'ok *v.* to destroy.

qachok *v.* to bite. *Var:* qatzok.

qapok *v.* to chop.

qirok *v.* to scrape.

q'axok *v.* to cross.

q'ichok *v.* to tear.

q'irok *v.* to tear.

q'ochok *v.* to wrap.

q'olok *v.* to harvest.

q'otok *v.* to turn.

q'oyok *v.* to scratch, scrape.

rachok *v.* to splash.

rahok *v.* to love.

ramok *v.* to catch, block, prevent.

raqok *v.* to finish, end.

raqok *v.* to cross.

re'ok *v.* to tear.

repok *v.* to splash.

req'ok *v.* to lick.

rik'ok *v.* to blink.

rinok *v.* to stretch.

romok *v.* to prevent.

sachok *v.* to erase.

sachok *v.* to spend.

sachok *v.* to destroy.

sachok *v.* to lose.

setok *v.* to mow.

setok *v.* to trim, cut.

setok *v.* to saw.

setok chi kaaxukut *v phr.* to dice.

setok chi kok' *v phr.* to chop.

setok tib' *v phr.* to mince.

sik'ok *v.* to look for, seek.

siq'ok *v.* to twist.

sob'ok *v.* to crush, grind, dent.

tawok *v.* to get, find.

tawok *v.* to appear.

tehok *v.* to open.

tenok *v.* to beat, hit, strike. *From:* *ten 'to hammer, flatten' (Ch'olan) (2).

tenok *v.* to crush, grind. *From:* *ten 'to hammer, flatten' (Ch'olan) (2).

ti'ok *v.* to bite.

tichk'ok *v.* to trip.

tijok *v.* to pray.

tijok *v.* to educate.

tijok *v.* to indoctrinate.

tikok *v.* to attack.

tikok *v.* to challenge.

tiqok *v.* to add.

tiwok *v.* to eat, bite.

tob'ok *v.* to let go.

toch'ok *v.* to play (instruments).

toch'ok *n.* hurt, harm.

toch'ok *v.* to assault.

tojok *v.* to pay.

toqok *v.* to break, split.

t'i'ok *v.* to kick.

t'i'ok *v.* to pound.

t'ojok *v.* to hammer.

tzemok *v.* to covet.

tzolok *v.* to teach.

tzolok *v.* to learn, study.

tz'ab'ok *v.* to light.

tz'ahok *v.* to soak.

tz'apok *v.* to shut, close, cover.

tz'apok *v.* to lock up.

tz'eqok *v.* to throw.

tz'eqok *v.* to fail.

tz'eqok *v.* to lose (a game).

tz'ilok *v.* to sieve, strain. *From:* tz'iil 'to sieve or strain' (Mopan) (4).

wa'ok *v.* to eat.

wech'ok *v.* to describe.

wohok *v.* to bark.

wojok *v.* to beat, strike, hit.

wotzok *v.* to share.

xajok *v.* to dance.

xeb'ok *v.* to pinch. *From:* *xeb' 'to pinch' (Yucatecan, Ch'olan, possible) (2).

xeq'ok *v.* to stab. *From:* *xeq', xek' 'to stab or pierce' (Ch'olan) (2).

xerok *v.* to split.

xokok *v.* to pick up.

xokok *v.* to keep.

xokok *v.* to file, save.

xolk'ok *v.* to drown.

xorok *v.* to make tortillas.

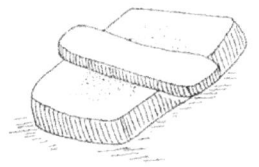

yab'ok *v.* to crush, grind.

yalok *v.* to try, taste, savor.

yalok *v.* to rehearse.

yalok *v.* to fight.

yatz'ok *v.* to milk.

yatz'ok *v.* to squeeze, wring.

yehok *v.* to say, communicate.

yeq'ok *v.* to kick.

yo'yook *v.* to be alive.

yok'ok *v.* to cut, chop.

yok'ok si' *v phr.* to chop wood.

yolk'ok *v.* to slide, slip.

yoq'ok *v.* to knead.

-uk raqtz'aqob'l / -uk ending

b'ujuk *v.* to beat, hit, strike.

b'utuk *v.* to fill.

b'ut'uk *v.* to stuff.

chu'uk *v.* to urinate, pee, piss.

chupuk *v.* to extinguish, blow out.

ch'uyuk *v.* to pinch.

ch'uyuk *v.* to scratch.

humuk *v.* to burn.

hutzuk *v.* to bend.

juch'uk *v.* to trace.

juch'uk *v.* to vote.

juk'uk *v.* to destroy, undo.

juyuk *v.* to row. *From:* *juy 'to move' (Ch'olan) (2).

kuruk *v.* to split, cut.

kutuk *v.* to shoot, throw.

kutuk *v.* to inject.

kuyuk *v.* to tolerate.

k'uluk *v.* to assist.

k'unuk *v.* to bend.

k'utuk *v.* to teach, show, indicate.

k'utuk b'e *v phr.* to lead.

k'uxuk *v.* to chew.

much'uk *v.* to break.

muquk *v.* to bury, hide.

muxuk *v.* to rape, violate.

nuq'uk *v.* to swallow. *From:* *nuq' 'throat' (Western Mayan) (4).

puch'uk *v.* to wash.

pumuk *v.* to throw.

q'unuk *v.* to hold.

q'usuk *v.* to scold, warn, reprimand.

rumuk *v.* to throw.

tu'uk *v.* to breastfeed.

tusuk *v.* to order, arrange.

tz'ub'uk *v.* to suck, absorb.

tz'uqluk *v.* to drip.

251

utz'uk *v.* to smell, sniff.

xut'uk *v.* to wrap.

yu'uk *v.* to stretch.

yu'uk ru *v.* to amplify, expand.

yutuk *v.* to wrap.

-ank raqtz'aqob'l / -ank ending

ab'enank *v.* to commission, entrust.

ach'ab'ank *v.* to liberate, free, let go.

ach'ab'ank *v.* to cease.

ajlank *v.* to count.

alank *v.* to give birth.

aq'ab'ank *v.* to brake.

atawank *v.* to want.

aalank *v.* to weigh.

aatinamank *v.* to speak, talk.

aatinank *v.* to have sexual relations.

aatinank *v.* to consult.

b'ichank *v.* to sing.

chok'ob'ank *v.* to crouch.

ch'anab'ank *v.* to cease.

ch'iilank *v.* to scold.

ch'olob'ank *v.* to swear (an oath), inform.

ch'utub'ank *v.* to join.

esilank *v.* to announce.

eechank *v.* to take possession of.

eek'ank *v.* to guess.

heleb'ank *v.* to hang out (clothing).

hilank *v.* to rest.

iiqank *v.* to carry.

jalmuqank *v.* to deny, hide.
  Var: jalmuqink.

jilq'ank *v.* to snore.

joq'ank *v.* to snore.
  Var: jok'ank; joq'yank.

jorank *v.* to bake.

jorank *v.* to bake, toast.

jultikank *v.* to train, remember.

ka'jultikank *v.* to emphasize, highlight.

ka'tz'iib'ank *v.* to rewrite.

ka'yank *v.* to contemplate.

kab'lank *v.* to build.

kanab'ank *v.* to put, place.

ka'yank *v.* to look, observe.

kiib'ank *v.* to split.

kolb'eetank *v.* to preserve.

k'anjelank *v.* to cultivate.

k'oxlank *v.* to reflect.

k'ukub'ank *v.* to crouch.

k'ulub'ank *v.* to accept, contemplate.

k'uub'ank *v.* to arm, set up, assemble.

k'uub'ank *v.* to fix.

k'uulank *v.* to save, memorize.

k'uulank *v.* to watch over.

laq'ab'ank *v.* to join.

lukub'ank *v.* to hang.

molob'ank *v.* to gather, collect.

musiq'ank *v.* to breathe. *From:* *mus iik' 'to breathe' (Yucatecan, Ch'olan, possible) (2).

na'leb'ank *v.* to reason.

na'leb'ank tz'iib' *v phr.* to edit, redact, write up.

nimank *v.* to grow.

ninqank *v.* to grow.

paab'ank *v.* to obey, believe.

puub'ank *v.* to shoot.

qoorank *v.* to snore.

q'ab'ank *v.* to accuse.

salab'ank *v.* to recline.

seeb'ank *v.* to hurry.

sisank *v.* to roast, fry.

taqlank *v.* to send.

taqlank *v.* to rule, govern.

taqlank *v.* to command, order.

tenq'ank *v.* to help, protect.

tikib'ank *v.* to begin.

tuqub'ank *v.* to balance, reform.

tusk'anjelank *v.* to plan.

tusub'ank *v.* to order, arrange.

tuub'ank *v.* to memorize.

t'uyub'ank *v.* to hang up.

tzakank *v.* to eat, feed. *Var:* tzekank.

tzinb'ank *v.* to sound, toll.

tz'aqtaanank *v.* to condemn.

tz'eqtaanank *v.* to reject. *Var:* tz'eqtanank.

ula'ank *v.* to visit.

wank *v.* to live, reside, be.

xaqab'ank *v.* to assemble.

xaqab'ank *v.* to elect, vote, name, propose, nominate.

xaqab'ank *v.* to raise.

xaq'ab'ank *v.* to detain, stop.

xaab'ank *v.* to kick.

xiiqank *v.* to nod off.

xulub'ank *v.* pour.

yaab'ank *v.* to vocalize.

yiib'ank *v.* to make, fix, build, construct.

yokob'ank *v.* to lie down.

yoob'ank *v.* to begin, invent.

-enk raqtz'aqob'l / -enk ending

aalenk *v.* to induce, tempt.

ji'lenk *v.* to scrub.

job'enk *v.* to hollow out.

jochlenk *v.* to scratch.

kojlenk *v.* to row.

k'aak'alenk *v.* to keep.

k'eelenk *v.* to preach.

k'oylenk *v.* to chew.

pach'lenk *v.* to splash.

pixlenk *v.* to tangle.

poqlenk *v.* to register.

ra'alenk *v.* to trap.

sib'tehenk *v.* to smoke.

sumenk *v.* to assist.

sumenk *v.* to answer, respond, reply.

taaqenk *v.* to follow, pursue.

tzuklenk *v.* to tangle.

wenb'enk ib' *v.* to brag, boast, show off.

xib'enk *v.* to threaten.

yulenk *v.* to whisk.

-ink raqtz'aqob'l / -ink ending

ab'ink *v.* to listen, hear.

ab'lilk'ayink *v.* to export.

ajsink u *v phr.* to entertain, enjoy.

ak'ob'resink *v.* to renew.

alab'tesink *v.* to reproduce.

apusink *v.* to inflate, blow up.

aq'ink *v.* to dig.

atink *v.* to bathe. *Var:* achink.

awab'ejink *v.* to rule, govern.

b'alaq'ink *v.* to betray.

b'alq'usink *v.* to wring.

b'alq'usink *v.* to turn, turn around.

b'alq'usink *v.* to drop.

b'antyoxink *v.* to thank.

b'arb'arink *v.* to roll.

b'eenink *v.* to travel around, travel.

b'eeresink *v.* to drive.

b'ihomink *v.* to be rich.

b'uyuxink *v.* to pile up.

b'uulink *v.* to raffle.

chajb'a'esink *v.* to alarm.

chaqob'resink *v.* to dry.
Var: chaqhiob'resink.

chaq'rab'ink *v.* to say goodbye, bid farewell.

chiq'chiq'ink *v.* to shake.

ch'i'ch'i'ink *v.* to bother.

echanink *v.* to earn.

echb'enink *v.* to accompany.

etalink *v.* to copy.

eechanink *v.* to own, possess.

eek'asink *v.* to move.

eeqaj *n.* substitute, retribution.

eeqajink *v.* to represent.

eetalink *v.* to mark.

ha'ob'resink *v.* to melt, dissolve.

isink *v.* to take out, remove.

isink b'aq *v phr.* to debone.

isink sa' re che' *v phr.* to notch.

ixi'jink *v.* to steal.

jalam'uuchink *v.* to sketch, draw.

jalb'eetink *v.* to lend.

jaltesink *n.* to change, transform, convert.

jatz'uuchink *v.* to hate.

jayalink *v.* to point, aim.

jech'exink *v.* to carry (in hand).

jek'ink *v.* to divide.

jilosink *v.* to separate.

jiq'jiq'ink ib' *v phr.* to whisper.

jolomink *v.* to lead, direct.

junajink *v.* to globalize, generalize.

junajink *v.* to stir, mix.

ka'oksink *v.* to recycle, reuse.

ka'sutink *v.* to reproduce.

kaltesink *v.* to get drunk.

kamsink *v.* to murder.

kamsink *v.* to kill.

karink *v.* to fish.

katunink *v.* to make war.

kawaayink *v.* to ride (a horse).

kawresink *v.* to exercise, get ready, prepare.

kawresink ch'ool *v.* to stimulate.

kaaxtink *v.* to seal, stamp.

keresink *v.* to chill.

kiib'ch'oolink *v.* to regret, be sorry.

kutanob'resink *v.* to develop photos.

kuuxink *v.* to sew.

k'ab'a'ink *v.* to call (a name), name.

k'ajolink *v.* to beget.

k'ajtesink *v.* to punish.

k'atink *v.* to burn.

k'ayink *v.* to sell.

k'ilink *v.* to fry.

k'irtesink *v.* to cure. *Var:* **k'irtasink**.

k'utb'esink *v.* to perform, present.

k'utb'esink *v.* to demonstrate, motivate, signal.

loq'onink *v.* to worship.

min'isink *v.* to loot, sack, plunder.

minyamtesink *v.* to loot, sack, plunder.

miikisink *v.* to push.

murink *v.* to separate, segregate, break down, fragment. *Var:* **xmurb'al**.

mutz'mutz'ink *v.* to blink.

na'ajink *v.* to live.

na'link *v.* to recognize.

nawink *v.* to know.

nawrub'elalink *v.* to diagnose.

nawyaalal *n.* decipherment.

nawyaalalink *v.* to decipher.

nimob'resink *v.* to amplify.

nimq'ehink *v.* to party.

nub'resink *v.* to rinse.

nujab'resink *v.* to fill.

numsink *v.* to transmit.

okesink *v.* to drip.

oxloq'ink *v.* to love, appreciate, respect.

oyb'enink *v.* to wait.

pajink *v.* to pour.

perperink *v.* to pedal.

pu'akink *v.* to work metal.

puktasink *v.* to edit.

puktasink *v.* to multiply.

putz'ink *v.* to liquify.

puxink *v.* to shake.

puulesink *v.* to throw.

puutzink *v.* to spray.

q'ajsink *v.* to give back.

q'axtesink *v.* to return.

q'axtesink *v.* to present, give.

q'ehink *v.* to guess, predict.

q'emrasink *v.* to knead.

q'unb'esink *v.* to campaign.

rahink *v.* to want.

raqaxink *v.* to separate.

raqink *v.* to chop.

rininink *v.* to carry (in hand).

sab'esink *v.* to clean up.

sasob'resink *v.* to thicken.

seb'esink *v.* to threaten.

sihink *v.* to share.

sokink *v.* to nest.

sumsihink *v.* to exchange (gifts).

sutisink *v.* to spin.

sutuxink *v.* to surround.

suurisink *v.* to flip.

taqsink *v.* to rise, raise.

tawasink *v.* to injure.

tik'ti'ink *v.* to lie (tell falsehoods).

tiqwasink *v.* to heat.

tiikink *v.* to push. *Var:* tiikisink.

tiikob'resink *v.* to season.

to'nink *v.* to lend, loan.
Var: to'onink.

to'nink *v.* to borrow.
Var: to'onink.

tu'resink *v.* to nurse.

t'aqresink *v.* to wet, irrigate.

tzakink *v.* to earn.

tz'eqink *v.* to waste.

tz'uyink *v.* to groan.

ula'anink *v.* to receive visitors.

uq'mink *v.* to steal.

uq'unink *v.* to liquify.

uuchilink *v.* to represent.

uutz'u'ujink *v.* to decorate.

wa'tesink *v.* to perform rituals.

waklesink *v.* to raise, lift.

waalesink *v.* to fan.

we'ejink *v.* to go hungry.

woqxink *v.* to boil.

wotz'otz'ink *v.* to tickle.

xab'onink *v.* to wash with soap.

xik'uchink *v.* to hate.

xiitink *v.* to mend, darn.

xootonink *v.* to confess.

yamresink *v.* to empty.

yaab'asink *v.* to recite, dictate, pronounce.

yeechi'ink *v.* to offer.

yik'ti'ink *v.* to lie (tell falsehoods).

yokosink *v.* to twist.

yo'nink *v.* to hope.

yuqyuqink *v.* to blink.

yuuk'ink *v.* to stir.

yuulink *v.* to dilute, blend.

-onk raqtz'aqob'l / -onk ending

b'itonk *v.* to carry (on head).
From: *b'it 'to carry on head or shoulder' (Ch'olan) (2).

ch'ilonk *v.* to carry (in hand).

jelonk *v.* to carry (on shoulder).

jeqonk *v.* to approach.

jilonk *v.* to approach.

kelonk *v.* to pull. *From:* *kehl 'to pull' (Ch'olan) (2).

kelonk *v.* to absorb.

mek'onk *v.* to embrace, hug.
From: mek' 'to embrace' (Yucatecan, Ch'olan, possible) (1).

paqonk *v.* to carry.

paqonk *v.* to raise, lift.

q'otonk *v.* to turn around.

telonk *v.* to carry (on shoulder).

xotonk *v.* to confess.
Var: xootonk.

-unk raqtz'aqob'l / -unk ending

apuunk *v.* to blow.

b'aanunk *v.* to practice.

b'aanunk *v.* to make, do.

b'aanunk ib' *v phr.* to fake.

ch'imb'unk *v.* to trap.

jukunk *v.* to crawl.

jukunk *v.* to pull.

kuutunk *v.* to lean.

k'ajk'amunk *v.* to reward.

k'ulunk *v.* to come, arrive.

k'utunk *v.* to appear.

mesunk *v.* to sweep.

muqunk *v.* to sink, disappear.

nuq'unk *v.* to sink.

q'alunk *v.* to embrace, hug.

saapunk *v.* to catch.

waalunk *v.* to blow, fly.

Jalaneb' Raqtz'aqob'l / Other Endings

ak'o'k *v.* to renew.

b'ayk *v.* to last.

b'aayk *v.* to take (an amount of time).

b'iq'e'k *v.* to choke.

chak'chotk *v.* to run.

chalk *v.* to come. *Var:* chaalk.

chok'laak *v.* to crouch.

chunlaak *v.* to sit. *From:* chum 'to sit' (Yucatecan, Ch'olan, possible) (4).

ch'amok' *v.* to ferment.

ch'uch'ib'k *v.* to joke.

ch'ume'k *v.* to be hungry.

elk *v.* to go out, leave.

eek'aj ib' *v phr.* to know how to act.

haye'k *v.* to approach.

hech'hotk *v.* to carry (in hand).

iximaak *v.* to thresh. *Var:* iximak.

jalam'uuchib'k *v.* to mark, trace.

jiqe'k *v.* to approach.

jiq'e'k *v.* to choke.

jok'ib'k *v.* to sling.

jole'k *v.* to slip, slide.

ju'e'k *v.* to erode.

ka'k'a'b'aink *v.* to rename.

kamab'k *v.* to help.

kamk *v.* to die.

kanaak *v.* to remain.

karib'k *v.* to fish. *Var:* karab'k.

kub'eek *v.* to go down.

k'achiik *v.* to crawl.

k'atk *v.* to burn.

k'iche'b'aalik *v.* to travel through the mountains.

k'iche'b'aalik *v.* to travel through the forest.

k'iik *v.* to grow.

k'ochlaak *v.* to land, alight. *Var:* k'ojlaak.

k'oxib'k *v.* to shrimp, fish for shrimp.

lemlotk *v.* to shine.

loqlotk *v.* to boil.

loq'oniik *v.* to take communion.

lub'k *v.* to tire, get tired.

mayib'k *v.* to smoke.

muqa'lik *v.* to dive, scuba dive. *Var:* muqa'alik.

nach'o'k *v.* to approach.

najto'k *v.* to be late.

naqk *v.* to begin.

neb'a'irk *v.* to slowly go broke.

neb'a'o'k *v.* to go broke.

nume'k *v.* to pass, cross.

oso'k *v.* to run out, end.

paq'e'k *v.* to drown.

parpotk *v.* to shiver, tremble.

pekark *v.* to harden, become hard.

poyte'ib'k *v.* to raft.

poopirk *v.* to rule, govern, reign.

q'ajk *v.* to return, come back, go home.

rachrotk *v.* to drip.

raho'k *v.* to hurt, suffer.

rajikru *v.* to be reborn.

raqe'k *v.* to cease.

sachk *v.* to get lost, go astray, disappear.

saqb'yino'k *v.* to fainting.

siksotk *v.* to shiver.

siyaak *v.* to be born. *From:* *sih 'to be born (Yucatecan, Ch'olan, possible) (5).

sob'e'k *v.* to sink, fall.

sote'k *v.* to remove.

sotlaak *v.* to lie down.

sub'e'k *v.* to sink. *From:* *suhp' 'to sink' (Ch'olan) (2).

sumchi'ib'k *v.* to exchange (words).

sumlaak *v.* to marry.

suq'iik *v.* to come back.

sutq'iik *v.* to repatriate, revert, return.

taqe'k *v.* to go up, climb, mount.

tiklaak *v.* to begin.

titz'k *v.* to bore.

tixk *v.* to grow old.

t'ane'k *v.* to fall.

t'anliik *v.* to fall sick.

tzakib'k *v.* to hunt.

tzakib'k *v.* to win.

tz'iltz'otk *v.* to drip.

tz'okaak *v.* to be hungry.

tz'uytz'utk *v.* to growl, grunt.

uq'e'k *v.* to erode.

usaak *v.* to improve, get better.

uxk *v.* to become, happen.

wa'tesiik *v.* to receive rites.

wakliik *v.* to rise, get up.

wakliik *v.* to progress.

wark *v.* to sleep.

wiq'laak *v.* to kneel.

woq'laak *v.* to sit.

xaqliik *v.* to rise, stand.

xolib'k *v.* to play the flute.

yajerk *v.* to get sick, sicken.

yeqo'k *v.* to limp.

yo i roq *v phr.* to flow.

yo'laak *v.* to be born, exist, give birth.

yo'laak xka'wa *v phr.* to be reborn.

yohob'k *v.* to hunt.

yoklaak *v.* to lie down.

yole'k *v.* to slide, slip.

yot'o'k *v.* to repent.

yu'k *v.* to progress.

Xraqilal li Aatinob'aal / Parts of Speech

Ch'olob'anel / Adjectives

an'o *adj.* leaning, sloping, inclining, at an angle.

aajel *adj.* important, useful.

aal *adj.* heavy.

b'aq' *adj.* oval.

b'aq'b'o *adj.* oval.

b'arich' *adj.* thin.

b'ayk *adj.* extensive.

b'orb'il *adj.* erased.

b'ulux *adj.* dirty. *Var:* b'alux.

b'urux b'urux *adj.* thick.

cham *adj.* deep.

chanchan *adj.* like, similar.

chaq re ru *adj.* ordinary, rough, crude.

chaab'il *adj.* good.

chek' *adj.* stiff.

chek'chek' *adj.* very stiff.

chi rix *adj.* exterior.

chi rub'el *adj.* down.

ch'a'ch'o *adj.* wide open.

ch'anaak *adj.* calm. *From:* *ch'an 'to become calm' (Ch'olan) (2).

ch'ina *adj.* small. *Var:* ch'in; ch'inaj.

ch'iqch'o xch'ool *adj.* unsatisfied.

ch'ot *adj.* short.

elajik *adj.* slow.

ink'a' cham *adj.* shallow.

jalan *adj.* other.

jaqam *adj.* permanently open.

jay *adj.* thin. *From:* *jaay 'thin' (Yucatecan, Ch'olan, possible) (2).

jo' *adj.* like, similar.

jorol *adj.* broken.

jukuch *adj.* long.

jumpaat *adj.* brief. *Var:* junpaat.

jun *adj.* unique.

junaj *adj.* same.

juneet *adj.* same.

junrib' *adj.* unique.

juntaq'eet *adj.* same.

jwal *adj.* much.

ka'ch'in roq *adj.* short.

ka'ch'in xteram *adj.* short.

kach'in *adj.* small.

kach'in ru *adj.* narrow.

kach'in xteram *adj.* low.

kelonb'il *adj.* absorbed.

ko'xib' *adj.* brief.

kok' *adj.* small.

kok' ru *adj.* narrow.

kotko *adj.* round.

koxib' *adj.* a little.

k'ojkookilch'ool *adj.* satisfied.

k'ooq *adj.* slow.

k'ub'k'u *adj.* ready.

laatz' *adj.* narrow.

laatz' ru *adj.* busy.

leb'lo *adj.* thick.

lil *adj.* used.

lujuch *adj.* long.

makach'in *adj.* extensive.

met *adj.* dwarf.

mitz *adj.* small.

mochmo *adj.* wrinkled.

mochox *adj.* wrinkled.

moko ch'a'aj ta *adj.* easy.

much'ul *adj.* broken.

na'ajil *adj.* same.

na'no ru *adj.* familiar.

nach' *adj.* near.

najt *adj.* far.

najt roq *adj.* long, tall.

najt xteram *adj.* tall, high.

nim *adj.* big.

nim roq *adj.* long, tall.

nim ru *adj.* wide.

nim xkelam *adj.* long.

nim xsa' *adj.* thick.

nim xteram *adj.* high, tall.

nimnim *adj.* giant, tall.

ok eechej *adj.* typical.

oxloq'inb'il *adj.* respected.

pahpo *adj.* open.

paq'al *adj.* broken.

pim *adj.* thick.

poy *adj.* light (in weight).

qeel *adj.* used, old.

q'anq'an *adj.* brilliant.

q'ochq'och *adj.* elastic.

q'unq'un ru *adj.* fine.

rek' *adj.* well done.

rik'in *adj.* near.

rinrin *adj.* elastic.

ru *adj.* similar.

sa *adj.* comfortable.

sa' jun chik *adj.* next.

sa' nim *adj.* right (spatial).

sa' tz'e *adj.* left. *From:* *tz'eh 'left' (Ch'olan) (2).

salso *adj.* reclined.

sas *adj.* thick.

saasa xch'ool *adj.* satisfied.

seeb' *adj.* light (in weight).

teb'es *adj.* thick.

tehto *adj.* open. *Var:* teeto.

tun is *adj.* hairy.

tupus roq *adj.* short.

tutz'tu *adj.* giant, tall.

t'ikt'o *adj.* thick.

tz'aj ru *adj.* dirty. *Var:* tz'ajn; tz'aj.

tz'aptz'o *adj.* closed.

tz'e *adj.* left. *From:* tz'eh 'left, left hand' (Ch'olan) (2).

tz'eeqel *adj.* disposable.

tz'ub'il *adj.* absorbed.

waa *adj.* viscous.

xa'wil ru *adj.* disgusting.

xaqam *adj.* standing.

xb'atz'iilal *adj.* artistic.

xchaq' *adj.* like.

yak'ach *adj.* giant.

yak'ach *adj.* high, tall.

yamyo ru *adj.* unoccupied.

yolyol *adj.* slippery, slick.

yotzotznak *adj.* loose.

yootzan *adj.* loose.

Jalch'ool'aatin / Adverbs

aka' *adv.* immediately.

ake' *adv.* shortly, soon. *Var:* a'ke.

anaqwan *adv.* now.

anaqwan tz'aqal *adv phr.* immediately.

aran *adv.* there.

arin *adv.* here.

ayi' *adv.* here.

chalen *adv.* since.

chalen *adv.* always.

chalen anaqwan *adv.* starting today, from now on.

chalen chaq *adv.* since then.

chaab'il *adv.* well.

chi rix *adv.* backwards.

chi ru *adv.* onwards.

chi seeb' *adv phr.* soon.

chi timil *adv.* slowly.

chi xjunil *adv.* rather, quite.

chik *adv.* again, already.

chik *adv.* more.

choq' re *adv.* for, to, in order to. *Var:* cho'q' re; chioq re.

ch'in *adv.* little.

ch'inqal *adv.* little by little.

ch'utch'u *adv.* together.

hoon *adv.* today. *Var:* hooni hoon.

ink'a' *adv.* not.

jach'bil *adv.* separate, separated.

jo' *adv.* according to.

jo' chanru *adv.* naturally.

jo' wanaq *adv.* later.

jo'kan *adv.* naturally.

jo'kan *adv.* so.

jun chik *adv.* another, one more.

junelik *adv.* always.

junwa *adv.* one time, once.

junxil *adv.* before.

junxil chik *adv.* a long time ago.

jwal *adv.* very.

ka'wa *adv.* twice, two times.

kama'an *adv.* like that.

kama'in *adv.* like this.

ka'ta *adv.* twice, two times.

koko *adv.* immediately.

kok'sa' *adv.* often.

laq'lo *adv.* together.

le' *adv.* there.

mayer *adv.* a long time ago.

maab'ar *adv.* nowhere.

maajaruj *adv.* never.

maaji' *adv.* not yet.

maajoq'e *adv.* never.

maare *adv.* suddenly.

maare *adv.* probably.

maare *adv.* maybe, perhaps. *Var:* mare.

moqon *adv.* after, afterwards, later.

najter *adv.* a long time ago.

numtajenaq *adv.* too much.

oxsut *adv.* three times.

oxwa *adv.* three times.

q'ajel ix *adv phr.* backwards.

q'axal *adv.* more.

q'emalk'uub' *adv.* artistically.

rajlal *adv.* always.

ramro' *adv.* sometimes.

re *adv.* for.

retal *adv.* finally, always.

rub'elaj *adv.* before.

sa' a'an *adv phr.* there, over there.

sa' xsal *adv phr.* backwards.

sa'in *adv.* here.

tana *adv.* maybe, perhaps.

taqe'q *adv.* above.

taq'a *adv.* below.

tikto *adv.* soon, immediately.

toj eq'la *adv.* earlier.

tojaq *adv.* since.

us *adv.* quite, rather, well.

utwchx *adv.* etcetera, etc., and so forth, and on and on. *Note:* Derived from 'ut' (and), 'w' (first letter of 'wank', to exist or be), 'ch' (first letters of 'chik', more), and 'x' (first letter of 'xcomon', all other companions).

xe'nawomil *adv.* philosophically.

K'ajtz'iib' / Particles

a' *part.* [emphasis particle]. *Note:* Occasionally used with a noun in place of a definite article to provide emphasis or indicate one among many. **A' che' wan aran.** « That tree over there. »

aj *part.* [origin particle], from. *Note:* Used before place names when speaking about where an individual is from. **Aj kob'an inna' inyuwa'.** « My parents are from Coban. »

aj *part.* [masculine particle]. *Note:* Used before masculine names when speaking about an individual (not to them). **Aj Mek xk'ulun mixk.** « Mike arrived a little while ago. » *Var:* **laj.**

aj *part.* [adjectival particle]. *Note:* Used before some nouns to create an adjective which highlights a particular quality in the subject of a sentence. **Moko josq' ta li winq aran. A'an aj kuyanel.** « That man is not angry. He is calm. »

265

aj *part.* [agentive particle]. *Note:* Used before nouns that imply an action to indicate the doer of the action or the profession or occupation of the doer. **Ma laa'at aj isihom ruuch e?** « Are you a dentist? »

aq *part.* [indefinite or future particle]. *Note:* Used as a suffix on words to indicate a hypothetical, indefinite, desired or future state. **Usaq choq' qe xsik'b'al li yaal.** « It would be good for us to seek the truth. » **Ma wan junaq aapatz'om?** « Do you have any questions? »

at *part.* [address particle, singular]. **At in qaawa', chinaatenq'a.** « Oh god, please help me. » *Note:* Used as a modifier to address an individual or being. It is used as a prefix and can modify a variety of singular nouns.

chan *part.* [citation particle, singular]. *Note:* Used when referring to what someone has said. **Tachalq li hab' wuulaj, chankin.** « It will rain tomorrow, I say. »

chankeb' *part.* [citation particle, plural]. *Note:* Used when referring to what someone has said. **"Ayuqex ut k'ehomaq chaq reetal chanru li na'ajej", chankeb'.** « And they said to them, "Go, search the land." »

chaq *part.* [distance or motion particle]. *Note:* Used when referring to motion from there to here. **Kim chaq arin.** « Come over here. »

chaq *part.* [time particle]. *Note:* Used when referring to things that happened in the past. **Numenaq chaq junmay chihab' naq ink'a ninchal kob'an.** « Twenty years have passed since I came to Coban. »

eb' *part.* [pluralization particle]. *Note:* Used preceding the definite article [li] to form plural; also as a suffix to pluralize nouns. **Ma xat-aatinak rik'in jun winq? Ink'a, xin'aatinak rik'in wiibeb'.** « Did you speak with one man? No, I spoke with two of them. »

ex *part.* [address particle, plural]. *Note:* Used as a modifier to address a group of people. It is used as a prefix and can modify a variety of plural nouns. **Ex was wiitz'in, ink'a' nink'oxla naq ak ta xweechani.** « Brothers and sisters, I do not consider myself yet to have taken hold of it. »

ib' *part.* [reflexive particle]. *Note:* Used with verbs to indicate a reflexive action or one where the subject and the object are the same. **Chi qilaq qib'!** « See you soon! »

kax *part.* [foreign particle]. *Note:* [kax] or [kaxlan] is said of many things foreign, artificial or imported. **Ch'ina us li kaxpo'ot re li xMar.** « Maria's blouse is nice. » **Ma nakanaw aatinak sa' kaxlan aatin?** « Do you know how to speak Spanish? »

len *part.* [citation particle, plural]. *Note:* Used when referring to what someone has said. **Laa'in aj q'an'isul len.** « I'm an American, they say. »

ma *part.* [interrogative particle]. **Ma yaal a'an?** « Is that true? »

ma *part.* [negation particle]. **Makach'in naktinra.** « I love you a lot ('not a little'). »

na *part.* [equivocal particle]. *Note:* Used to express doubt or uncertainty about a preceding idea or notion. **Tinxik na sa' k'ayiil.** « Maybe I'll go to the market. »

pe' *part.* [insistence particle]. *Note:* Used to supply additional emphasis to a declartive or interrogative. **Jo'kan pe'.** « That's the way it is. » **Pe' yaal?** « Is that really true? »

raj *part.* [conditional particle]. *Note:* Used to indicate a desired, hypothetical, or probable action **Laa'in raj aj b'anonel, a'ut xinkanab' li tzolok naq xkam inyuwa'.** « I would have been a doctor, but when my father died I stopped studying. »

ta *part.* [doubt particle]. *Note:* Used to indicate doubt or rhetorical nature of a question. **Ma ink'a' ta a'in li b'e sik'b'il ru inb'aan?** « Is this not the path that I have chosen? » *Var:* ta b'i'.

taxaq *part.* [utterance indicating hope or a wish]. **Us taxaq wi yaal a'an.** « I hope that's true. »

yo *part.* [progressive particle]. *Note:* Used like a verb to indicate that something is alive, happening, or ongoing in nature. **Ma yo li hab' chi kaw?** « Is it raining hard? »

Jalch'ool'aatin Kok'raq Aatin / Adverbial Phrases

ak anaqwan *adv phr.* right away.

ak xnume' chik *adv phr.* after.

ake' hoon *adv phr.* in a moment.

aran tz'aqal *adv phr.* right there.

arin tz'aqal *adv phr.* right here.

chi ch'inqil *adv phr.* little by little.

chi kama'an *adv phr.* like that, thus.

chi kama'in *adv phr.* like this, thus.

chi sa xch'oolil *adv phr.* with pleasure.

elik chi yaal *adv phr.* really.

jo' chan ru *adv phr.* in accordance with.

jo'kan aj wi' *adv phr.* also, too.

jo'kan b'i' *adv phr.* then.

jo'kan tz'aqal *adv phr.* exactly.

jun sut chik *adv phr.* again, once more.

junes yo *adv phr.* frequently.

junsut *adv.* once.

jwal ink'a us *adv phr.* worse.

jwal us *adv phr.* better.

ka'ch'in chi ru *adv phr.* smaller than, younger than.

kab' rix ch'ool *adv phr.* reluctantly.

kach'in chik (ma) *adv phr.* nearly, almost.

kok'atq xsa' *adv phr.* often.

ma chan naxye *adv phr.* not even.

ma jun wa *adv phr.* never.

maak'a' chi junwaakaj *adv phr.* nothing at all.

moko a'an ta *adv phr.* nothing of the kind.

moko chaab'il ta *adv phr.* badly, poorly.

nach' xk'atq *adv phr.* near.

naj xyanq *adv phr.* seldom.

najt xk'atq *adv phr.* far from.

nim chi ru *adv phr.* bigger than.

rajlal naab'al *adv phr.* more and more.

rajlal rajlal *adv phr.* frequently.

sa' jumpaat *adv phr.* immediately, quickly.

sa' jun sut *adv phr.* ever.

sa' junq sut *adv phr.* sometimes.

sa' laanim *adv phr.* to your right.

sa' laatz'e *adv phr.* to your left.

toj le' *adv phr.* over there.

toj reetal *adv phr.* at last, finally.

wan naq *adv phr.* sometimes.

wi' chik *adv phr.* again.

xb'een wa *adv phr.* first of all, in the first place.

Najunajin Aatin / Conjunctions

a' ajb'an *conj.* that's why.

a' chik ut *conj.* however.

a' ut *conj.* but.

ab'an *conj.* but.

ab'anan *conj.* however, nevertheless.

b'i' *conj.* well.

chi moko *conj.* neither.

jo'kan *conj.* that's why.

jo'kan naq *conj.* that's why.

malaj *conj.* or.

malaj ut *conj.* or. *Var:* maraj ut.

retal *conj.* until.

tixto toj *conj.* until.

toj *conj.* until, still.

toja' *conj.* until now, just now.

us ta *conj.* although, though.

ut *conj.* and.

wi *conj.* if.

xb'aan naq *conj.* because.

xmaak naq *conj.* because.

yalaq *conj.* whichever.

yalaq b'ar *conj.* wherever.

yalaq b'ar wan *conj.* whatever.

yalaq chan ru *conj.* however.

yalaq joq'e *conj.* whenever.

yalaq k'a'ru *conj.* whatever.

Patz'leb' Aatin / Interrogatives

ani *interr.* who?

ani aj e *interr.* whose? (singular).

ani aj ik'in *interr.* with whom?

aniheb' aj e *interr.* whose? (plural).

b'ar *interr.* where?

b'ar wan re *interr.* which?

b'ar wank *interr.* which? (singular). *Var:* b'ar wan.

b'ar wankeb' *interr.* which? (plural).

chan ru *interr.* how?

jar *interr.* how much?

jarjar *interr.* how much for each?

jarjartk *interr.* how much each time?

jarmayer *interr.* how long ago?

jarsut *interr.* how many times?

jarub' *interr.* how many?

jarwa *interr.* how many times?

jo' ch'inal *interr.* what size?

jo' k'ihal *interr.* how much?

jo' najtil *interr.* how far?

jo' nimal *interr.* how much?

joq'e *interr.* when?

k'a' *interr.* what?

k'a'ru *interr.* which?

k'a'ru *interr.* what?

k'a'ru aj e *interr.* for what?

k'a'ru aj ik'in *interr.* with what?

k'a'ut *interr.* why?

Ruuchil K'ab'a'ej / Pronouns

a'an *pron.* he, she, that, it. *Var:* ha'an.

a'an *pron.* her, him. *Var:* ha'an.

a'an a'an *pron.* that one.

a'an a'in *pron.* this one.

a'anaq *pron.* it will be that (him, her, it).

a'aneb' *pron.* they.

a'aq *pron.* it will be this.

a'in *pron.* this, this one. *Var:* ha'in.

a'ineb' *pron.* these.

a'wa'ran *pron.* that one. *Var:* a' wan aran.

a'wanle' *pron.* that one (over there). *Var:* a'wa'le'; a'wa'li'; a'wi'le'.

b'ab'ay *pron.* a few, a little. *Var:* b'ayb'ay.

b'ayaq *pron.* some.

eb' a'an *pron.* them, they.

Var: **teb' a'an.**

eb' a'in *pron.* these.

ink'a' k'i *pron.* few.

jalan chik *pron.* another.

kach'in *pron.* a few, a little.

kiib' oxib' *pron.* a few.

k'i *pron.* a lot.

k'ila *pron.* a lot, many.

laa'at *pron.* you (singular).

Var: **at.**

laa'ex *pron.* you (plural).

laa'in *pron.* I.

laa'o *pron.* we, us. *Var:* **aa'o;**
ha'o.

maajun *pron.* nothing.

maak'a' *pron.* nothing.

maalay *pron.* nothing.

maani *pron.* no one.

naq *pron.* when, that.

naab'al *pron.* much, a lot.

naab'al *pron.* enough.

wan le' *pron.* that, that one
(over there).

wotz *pron.* both.

xiikil *pron.* much.

yal ta k'a' *pron.* nothing.

yalaq ani *pron.* whoever.

Xk'aj Aatin / Articles

eb' li *art.* the (plural).

jun *art.* a, an.

junaq *art.* a, an. *Note:* Indicates
an indefinite, desired or future
state of a modified noun. **Junaq
kutan taanaw laa maayil k'ab'a'ej.**
« Someday you will know
your Mayan name. »

li *art.* the (singular).

Xtiqb'al Aatin / Prepositions

chalen *prep.* from.

chi *prep.* to.

chi rix *prep.* outside, behind,
around.

chi ru *prep.* in front of, facing.

chi ru chi xjunil *prep.* above
all.

chi rub'elaj *prep.* before.

Var: **chi ru.**

chi rub'el *prep.* under.

chi sa' *prep.* inside, between.

chi xk'atq *prep.* toward, next
to.

maawa' rik'in *prep.* without.

nach' rik'in *prep.* next to.

pak'po *prep.* facing up.

re *prep.* of, from.

rexb'een *prep.* with.

rik'in *prep.* with, through.
Var: ruk'in.

rub'el *prep.* under.

sa' *prep.* to, through, in, inside, at, by. *Var:* se'.

sa' xb'een *prep.* over, above, on top.

sa' xka'yab'aal *prep.* in front of.

sa' xk'ab'a' *prep.* through.

sa' xmaak *prep.* through.

sa' xyanq *prep.* between.

sa' xk'atq *prep.* beside.

taqe'q *prep.* up.

taq'a *prep.* down.

u *prep.* in front.

xb'aan *prep.* through.

xjunpak'alil (li...) *prep.* opposite.

yalaq chi b'ar *prep.* everywhere.

Xyikutb'il Aatin / Interjections

ah *interj.* [utterance of understanding].

ay *interj.* [utterance of pain].

aaa *interj.* [utterance of pain or pity].

chix *interj.* [utterance of disgust].

eh *interj.* [utterance of doubt or disagreement].

eh! *interj.* [utterance of surprise].

i' *interj.* [utterance indicating lack of interest].

ih *interj.* [utterance of understanding].

sht *interj.* [utterance seeking recognition].

sht! *interj.* [utterance of disapproval].

t' *interj.* [utterance indicating a minor failure].

uy *interj.* [utterance indicating a close call].

uyaluy *interj.* [utterance indicating danger].

III

ENGLISH ~ Q'EQCHI' WORD INDEX

Tusna'leb' Aatin Inkles ~ Q'eqchi'

●●●

A - a

a   *art.* **jun**
        art. **junaq**

a day ago   *n.* **eweraq**

a few   *pron.* **b'ab'ay**
        pron. **kach'in**
        pron. **kiib' oxib'**

a little   *pron.* **b'ab'ay**
           pron. **kach'in**
           adj. **koxib'**

a long time ago   *adv.* **junxil chik**
        adv. **mayer**
        adv. **najter**

a lot   *pron.* **k'i**
        pron. **k'ila**
        pron. **naab'al**
        adj. **xiikil**

a moment ago, recently
        adv. **toje'**

a while ago   *adv.* **ma'laq**
        adv. **mixk**

abandoned house   *n.* **po'lem**

abdomen   *n.* **ru sa'**

abject   *adj.* **tz'i'b'eetal**

above   *prep.* **sa' xb'een**
        adv. **taqe'q**

above all   *prep.* **chi ru chi xjunil**

abscissa   *n.* **xna'ajtz'uq**

absence   *n.* **maa'anihilk**

absent   *adj.* **maa'ani**
         adj. **sachso**

absent-minded   *adj.* **naxik**
        xch'ool

absolutely   *adv phr.* **jo'kan b'i'an**

absorb   *v.* **kelonk**
         v. **tz'ub'uk**

absorbed   *adj.* **kelonb'il**
           adj. **tz'ub'il**

absurd   *adj.* **numsachk**

abundance   *n.* **k'iham**

abundant   *adj.* **juntuub'**
           adj. **naab'al**

abyss   *n.* **siwan**
        n. **xchamal taq'a**
        n. **xjul taq'a**

academy   *n.* **tzoleb'aal**
          n. **xch'uutamil**

accent   *n.* **yaab'aatin**

accent mark   *n.* **eetalkawyaab'**
        n. **tz'uq aatin**
        n. **tz'uq kawyaab'**

accentuation   *n.* **yaab'aatin**

accept   *v.* **k'ulub'ank**

accessory   *n.* **ruutz'u'ujil aq'**
        n. **xkomon rib'**

accident   *n.* **tiq'eek**

accompanied   *adj.* **ochb'enb'il**

accompanist   *n.* **ochb'enej**

accompany   *v.* **echb'enink**

accomplice   *n.* **xkomon rib'**
     n. **xsum**

according to   *adv.* **jo'**

accordion   *n.* **b'aswajb'**

account   *n.* **k'as**
     n. **xna' tumin**

accountant   *n agt.* **aj ajlanel**
     n agt. **aj b'irom tumin**

accumulator   *n.* **k'uulmetz'ew**

accusation   *n.* **q'ab'ankil**

accuse   *v.* **jitok**
     v. **q'ab'ank**

Achi   *lang.* **achi**

acidic   *adj.* **ra re**

acne   *n.* **wa**

acorn   *n.* **ru ji**

acquit   *v phr.* **kuyuk maak**

acquittal   *n.* **ach'abaak**

acrobat   *n agt.* **aj seeb'alk'utb'esink**

acrobatics   *n.* **seeb'ch'oolil**

action   *n.* **xb'aanunkil**

ad   *n.* **yeechi'ink**

Adam's apple   *n.* **b'uq' ja'aj**

adapter   *n.* **jalb'ametz'ew**

add   *v phr.* **k'ehok xtz'aqob'**
     v. **tiqok**

addition   *n.* **molob'ank**
     n. **tamok-ajl**

addition symbol (+)
     n. **reetaltamok-ajl**
     n. **reetal molam ajl**

additional information
     n. **xtz'aqob'l esilal**

address   *n.* **ochochib'aal**
     n. **reetalil ochoch**
     n. **xjayalil**

address of recipient   *n.* **xna'aj b'ar wi' wan li taak'ulu'q re**

address particle (plural)   *part.* **ex**

address particle (singular)
     part. **at**

addressee   *n.* **xk'ab'a' li taak'ulu'q re**

adherent   *n agt.* **aj paab'anel**

adjectival particle   *part.* **aj**

adjective   *n.* **cholob'anel**

adjudicate   *v phr.* **raqok aatin**

adjudicator   *n agt.* **aj raqol'aatin**

administration   *n.* **jolomilal**
     n. **k'amolb'e**

adobe   *n.* **q'ut**
     n. **xan**

adoration   *n.* **loq'onink**

adornment   *n.* **ruutz'u'ujil aq'**
     n. **xoy**
     n. **xsahob' ru**

adrenaline   *n.* **xwaxil rumetz'ew**

adult education
　　n. **tijb'apoyanam**

adultery　*n.* **muxuk**
　　n. **muxuk sumlajik**

advance　*v.* **jiqok**

adventure　*n.* **yaljot'ok**

adventurer　*n.* **yal'ajot'onel**

adventurous　*adj.* **aj b'e**

adverb　*n.* **jalch'ool'aatin**

adverbial phrase
　　n. **jalch'ool'aatin
　　kok'raq aatin**

advertisement　*n.* **yeechi'ink**

advertising poster　*n.* **eetalil hu**

advice　*n.* **na'leb'**

adviser　*n agt.* **aj chi'resilnel**

affection　*n.* **sahilal**

afraid　　*adj.* **xiwajenaq**
　　　　adj. **yo xiw**

after　　*adv phr.* **ak xnume'
　　　　chik**
　　　　adv. **moqon**

after you　*phr.* **numen laat
　　　　xb'een wa**

afternoon　*n.* **ewu**
　　　　n. **najkutan**
　　　　n. **xb'een waleb'**

afterwards　*adv.* **moqon**

again　　*adv.* **chik**
　　　　adv phr. **jun sut chik**
　　　　adv phr. **wi' chik**

age　　　*n.* **xchi hab'**

agenda　*n.* **jultikob'lhu**
　　　　n. **jultik'anjel**
　　　　n. **xb'ehil ru k'anjel**

agentive particle　*part.* **aj**

aggressive　*adj.* **josq'**

agitation　*n.* **ch'i'ch'i'**

agony　*n.* **aakan**

agouti (dasyprocta)　*n.* **aaqam**
　　　　n. **halaw**

agriculture　*n.* **naw'awk**

agronomy　*n.* **naw'awk**

AIDS　　*n.* **kaqyajel**
　　　　n. **maxelyu'am**

aim　　　*n.* **ahom**
　　　　n. **jayalihom**
　　　　v. **jayalink**

air　　　*n.* **iq'**

air compressor　*n.* **xna'aj iq'**

air conditioner　*n.* **keresiil iq'**

air freshener　*n.* **jaq'ilb'an**

air gauge　*n.* **b'isleb' iq'**

air pump　*n.* **k'ehob'a iq'**
　　　　n. **k'eleb' iq'**

airfare　*n.* **xhuhil purik**

airline　　*n.* **aj k'ehol purik**
　　　　n. **xjayal xb'e**

airplane　*n.* **so'sol ch'iich'**

airplane pilot　*n agt.* **aj ch'e'ol
　　　　so'sol ch'iich'**

airplane tail　*n.* **xye so'sol
　　　　ch'iich'**

airplane wing　*n.* **xik so'sol
　　　　ch'iich'**

airport   *n.* **k'ochleb'aal**
      n. **xna'aj so'sol ch'iich'**

Akatek   *lang.* **akateko**

alarm   *n.* **chajb'a'esil**
      v. **chajb'a'esink**

alarm clock   *n.* **ajsib'aal hoonal**
      n. **ajsinel**

alarmed   *adj.* **xiwajenaq**

album cover   *n.* **xtz'apb'al surb'ich**

album, CD   *n.* **surb'ich**

alcohol   *n.* **kaxlan b'oj**

alcohol (isopropyl)   *n.* **alkohol**

alcoholic   *n agt.* **aj kalajel**

alcoholic drink   *n.* **kalha'**

Alejandro   *nick.* **Laj**

alert   *adj.* **aj'aj ru**

algebra   *n.* **eetalb'irool**
      n. **jaljookil ru ajl**

algebraic   *adj.* **eetalb'irok**

alight   *v.* **k'ochlaak**

alive   *adj.* **yo'yo**

all   *adj.* **anchal**
      adj. **chi junil**
      adj. **rek'**

allergy   *n.* **chak'aanil**

alligator   *n.* **ayin**

alluvial erosion   *n.* **xch'ajom hab'**

almonds   *n.* **ru almeentr**

almost   *adv phr.* **kach'in chik (ma)**

aloe vera   *n.* **q'ooqil ik'e**

alone   *adj.* **junes**
      adj. **junesal**
      adj. **ka' aj wi'**
      adj. **sa' junesal**

alphabet   *n.* **ch'oltz'iib'**
      n. **tzoltz'iib'**

alphabetically   *adv.* **sa' tzoltz'iib'**

already   *adv.* **chik**

also   *adv phr.* **jo'kan aj wi'**

altar   *n.* **artal**
      n. **oxloq'il na'aj**
      n. **xna'aj qaawa'**

alter ego   *n.* **nawal**

although   *conj.* **us ta**

aluminum   *n.* **lemtz'ch'iich'**
      n. **saqch'iich'**
      n. **seeb'ajch'iich'**

alveopalatal   *n.* **ru'uj'aq' yaab'**

always   *adv.* **chalen**
      adv. **junelik**
      adv. **rajlal**
      adv. **retal**

amazed   *adj.* **sachenaq xch'ool**

amazement
      n. **sachb'ach'oolej**

ambassador   *n.* **ruuchil ab'l tenamit**

ambitious   *adj.* **atawal**
      adj. **ch'iq**
      adj. **narataw**

ambulance   *n.* **amb'ulaans**
      n. **b'eleb'aal yaj**

American   *n.* **aj q'an'isul**

amp meter   *n.* **b'iismetz'ew**

amphetamine   *n.* **chiq'ch'ool**

amphibian   *n.* **ka'na'jilxul**

amplifier   *n.* **yu'leb'yaab'**

amplify   *v.* **nimob'resink**
   v. **yu'uk ru**

amuse   *v phr.* **jahok u**

amusement   *n.* **k'ehom uhej**

amusing   *adj.* **aj se'**

an   *art.* **jun**
   art. **junaq**

analgesic   *n.* **re kotzok xrahil**

analogy   *n.* **taq'eetink**

analysis   *n.* **tzilb'a'ix**

ancestors   *n.* **xe'toon**

anchor   *n.* **t'ilob'aal**
   n. **xookilch'iich'**

ancient   *adj.* **junxil**
   adj. **najter**

anciently   *adv phr.* **sa' najter q'e
   kutan**

and   *conj.* **ut**

and on and on   *adv.* **utwchx**

and so forth   *adv.* **utwchx**

Andrés   *nick.* **Lex**

anemia   *n.* **puchil**
   n. **saqkirin**

anesthesia   *n.* **re wartesink**
   n. **wartesiilb'an**

anger   *n.* **josq'il**
   n. **po'jik**
   n. **waxerk**

angle   *n.* **jech'xuk**
   n. **xjech'lal**
   n. **xtehelal**
   n. **xxuk**
   n. **yanqxuk**

angry   *adj.* **josq'**

anguish   *n.* **k'a'uxlak**

animal   *n.* **xul**

animal cage   *n.* **xtz'alam xul**

animal trainer   *n agt.* **aj
   q'unb'esihonel xul**

aniseed   *n.* **anis**

ankle   *n.* **xkux oq**
   n. **xmap oq**

ankle boot   *n.* **kok' tzelek xaab'**

annatto   *n.* **xayaw**

announce   *v.* **esilank**

announcement   *n.* **aatin**
   n. **esil**

announcer   *n agt.* **aj aatinanel**

annoyance   *n.* **ch'a'ajkilal**

annoyed   *adj.* **ch'a'aj ru**

annoying   *adj.* **nach'a'ajko'**

annular eclipse   *n.* **jiskotko
   tiwok**

another   *pron.* **jalan chik**
   adv. **jun chik**

answer   *v.* **chaq'b'enk**
   v. **chaq'ok**
   n. **chaq'om**
   v. **sumenk**

ant   *n.* **sank**

antacid   *n.* **aj tuqub'anel sa'**

anteater   *n.* **tz'uqtz'um**

antenna   *n.* **misik'ch'iich'**

antenna (insect)   *n.* **misik**

antepenultimate
        adj. **roxch'otonel**

Anthropocene   *n.* **xwaq
        q'ekutan**

anthropologist   *n agt.* **aj
        nawpoyanam**

anthropology   *n.* **nawpoyanam**

Anthropozoic era   *n.* **xwaq
        q'ekutan**

antibacterial   *n.* **b'anxxulelyajel**

antibiotic   *n.* **chunilb'an
        n. **re xmay**

anti-inflammatory   *n.* **re kotzok
        siip**

anti-itch cream   *n.* **re wotz'ok**

antipassive voice
        n. **nume'uxkb'il**

antivirus   *n.* **xramb'al xxulel
        yajel**

antonym   *n.* **xjalpaq'il**

antonyms   *n.* **ka'pak'alil ru
        aatin**

anus   *n.* **it**
        n. **yupus**

anxiety   *n.* **yot'ik**

apiary   *n.* **rochoch kab'**

apostle   *n.* **apoostl**

apostrophe   *n.* **tz'uq**

appeal   *n.* **titz'e'k**

appear   *v.* **k'utunk**
        v. **tawok**

apple   *n.* **mansaan**

apple cider   *n.* **xya'al mansaan**

apple juice   *n.* **xya'al mansaan**

apple tree   *n.* **mansaan**

application   *n.* **hupatz'om**
        n. **hutz'aam**

applied linguistics   *n.* **roksinkil
        naw'aatinob'aal**

appointment book   *n.* **tasal hu
        re ula'**

appreciate   *v.* **oxloq'ink**

apprehension   *n.* **nawok chi
        yaal**

approach   *v.* **haye'k**
        v. **jeqonk**
        v. **jilonk**
        v. **jiqe'k**
        v. **nach'o'k**

April   *n.* **awril**
        n. **xkaapo**

apron   *n.* **k'ulb'a tz'aj**
        n. **ramb'atz'aj**
        n. **xta ru sa'ej**

Arabic numeral   *n.* **araaw**
        n. **kaxajl**

arch   *n.* **arko**

archaeologist   *n agt.* **aj ilol
        mayer kab'k**

Archaeozoic era   *n.* **mayer q'e**

archbishop   *n.* **arsob'iisp**

Archean era   *n.* **mayer q'e**

architect *n agt.* **aj k'uub'anel kab'l**

architecture *n.* **nawkab'lank**

archive *n.* **k'uulhu**

arctic circle *n.* **xsiraal taq'eq**

ardent desire *n.* **ch'um ch'ool**

are you OK? *phr.* **ma us wankat**

are you sure? *phr.* **ma relik chi yaal**

area *n.* **sutam**
  adj. **xsa'**

arm *v.* **k'uub'ank**
  n. **tel**

armadillo *n.* **b'aqxul**
  n. **ib'oy**
  n. **seelxul**

armed guard *n agt.* **aj puub'**

armful *n.* **jun q'aal**

armour *n.* **ch'iich'**

armpit *n.* **sa' tel**

army *n.* **eb' aj puub'**

around *prep.* **chi rix**

arousal *n.* **tiqwok'**

arrange *v.* **tusub'ank**
  v. **tusuk**

arranged *adj.* **yiib'anb'il**

arrest *v.* **chapok**

arrival *n.* **chalik**

arrivals *n.* **nak'ulun**

arrive *v.* **hulak**
  v. **k'ulunk**

arrogant *adj.* **namunta**

arrow *n.* **sijb'**
  n. **tzimaj**

arson *n.* **k'a'uxlanb'il k'atok**

art *n.* **b'atz'iil**

art education *n.* **tijb'ab'atz'il**

art gallery *n.* **xna'aj k'utleb'aal**

artery *n.* **ich'**
  n. **ich'mul**

artichoke *n.* **kaxch'i'kay**

article *n.* **raqal**
  n. **xk'aj aatin**

article of faith *n.* **raqalil li paab'aal**

articulation *n.* **k'ulb'ayaab'**

artisan *n.* **yiib'anel**

artist *n agt.* **aj b'atz'iil**
  n. **yiib'anel**

artistic *adj.* **xb'atz'iilal**

artistic expression *n.* **b'atz'il b'aanuhom**

artistically *adv.* **q'emalk'uub'**

arts center *n.* **rochochil k'utb'esink**

as soon as possible *phr.* **sa' junpaat jo'naxk'e rib'**

ash *n.* **cha**

ashamed *adj.* **xutaanal**
  adj. **xutaanaq**

ashtray *n.* **xn'aj xchahil may**
  n. **xna'aj cha**

ask *v.* **patz'ok**

ask for a favor *v.* **ab'enak**

ask for alms *v phr.* **patz'ok limoox**

　　　　　v phr. **tz'aamank limoox**

asphalt *n.* **q'eqitz'aakalb'e**

ass *n.* **b'uur**

ass, mule *n.* **xul iiqanel**

assailant *n agt.* **aj tochonel**

assassin *n agt.* **aj kamsinel**

assault *n.* **elq'ak sa' josq'il**
　　　　　n. **toch'ok**
　　　　　v. **toch'ok**

assemble *v.* **k'uub'ank**
　　　　　v. **xaqab'ank**

assess *n.* **yalok ix**

assignment *n.* **taqlil**
　　　　　n. **tzolomil**

assist *v.* **k'uluk**
　　　　v. **sumenk**

assistance *n.* **kamab'k**
　　　　　n. **tenq'aal**
　　　　　n. **xtenq'ankil**

assistant *n agt.* **aj tenq'anel**

associate *n.* **komon**

association *n.* **molam**

asterisk *n.* **chahim'eetalil**
　　　　　n. **reetalilk'utb'ch'ool ejil**

asteroid *n.* **puukchahim**

asthma *n.* **x'am ja'aj**

astonished *adj.* **sachaamil xch'ool**

astonishment
　　　　　n. **sachb'ach'oolej**

astronaut *n agt.* **aj b'e choxa**
　　　　　n agt. **aj b'eenel sa' po**
　　　　　n agt. **aj ch'e'ol b'oq'ch'iich' iq'**

astronomer *n agt.* **aj ilol chahim**
　　　　　n agt. **aj nawchahim**

astronomy *n.* **nawchahim**

asymmetry *n.* **jech'-uhil**

at *prep.* **sa'**

at an angle *adj.* **an'o**

at dawn *adv phr.* **naq ta saqewq**

at dusk *adv phr.* **naq ta ewuuq**

at last *adv phr.* **toj reetal**

at midnight *adv phr.* **naq tk'e tuktu q'oqyin**

at night *adv phr.* **chi ru q'oqyin**

at noon *adv phr.* **naq tk'e waleb'**

at symbol (@) *n.* **aroow**

atheism *n.* **maak'a' xyos**

atheist *n agt.* **aj ateey**

athlete *n agt.* **aj aanilanel**
　　　　　n agt. **aj b'atz'unel**

athleticism *n.* **k'ilab'atz'unk**

Atlantic Ocean *n.* **eetaj palaw**

atmosphere *n.* **ru choxa**
　　　　　n. **xb'een tasal iq'**

atmospheric pressure
　　　　　n. **metz'ewil iq'**

atrium   *n.* **neb'aal**

attack   *n.* **k'uluk**
      v. **tikok**

attentive *adj.* **q'un xch'ool**

attic   *n.* **xb'een che'**

attitude   *n.* **xaqalch'ool**

attorney   *n agt.* **aj na'onel
chaq'rab'**

attraction *n.* **ajok**

audacious *adj.* **seeb'**

audience   *n.* **ab'inel**

auditory nerve *n.* **xjis'ich'mul
xikej**

August   *n.* **akoost**
      n. **xwaqxaqpo**

aunt   *n.* **ikan na'**
      n. **na' eechej**

aureola   *n.* **ru'uj tu'**

author   *n agt.* **aj e re**
      n agt. **aj tz'iib'ahom**
      n. **yoob'k'a'aq**

authority *n agt.* **aj jolominel**

autonomic nervous system
      n. **xk'ub'lal ich'mulej
xtaq rib'**
      n. **xk'ub'lal ich'mul
yal jo'**

autumn   *n.* **otoony**
      n. **xraqik hab'alq'e**

avenue   *n.* **ruq'b'e**

aviary   *n.* **rochoch tz'ik**

aviation   *n.* **nawso'solch'iich'**

aviator   *n agt.* **aj ch'e'ol so'sol
ch'iich'**

avocado   *n.* **o**

avoid   *v.* **kolok**

award   *n.* **raltoj**

awl   *n.* **jotzleb'**
      n. **k'ob'leb'**
      n. **pormon**

axe   *n.* **maal**

axis   *n.* **xch'oolil**

axle   *n.* **xb'aalil**

axon   *n.* **b'olsutaal'eek'**

B - b

baby   *n.* **b'ab'ay**
      n. **kach'in**

baby bib   *n.* **t'ikr re maqab'**

baby bottle *n.* **paach**
      n. **tu'unil**

baby goat *n.* **ral chib'aat**
      n. **ral yuk**

baby rattle *n.* **tzojtzoj**

baby room *n.* **xna'aj k'ula'al**

baby walker *n.* **xb'eeresib'aal
k'ula'al**

babysitter *n agt.* **aj ilol k'ula'al**

back   *n.* **ix**
      n. **ixkej**

n. **xaal it**

n. **xxaali it**

back of the hand *n.* **rix uq'm**

back yard *n.* **xneb'a' rix kab'l**

backache *n.* **rahil xalaa'it**

backbone *n.* **juruch'**

backpack *n.* **iiqaal**

n. **kaxsoq'**

n. **letzool**

n. **mochiil**

backup copy *n.* **eeqajil**

backwards *adv.* **chi rix**

adv phr. **q'ajel ix**

adv phr. **sa' xsal**

bacteria *n.* **xxulel yajel**

bad   *adj.* **ink'a us**

adj. **lab'**

adj. **maa'us**

adj. **yib' ru**

bad advice *n.* **takchi'**

bad guy *n.* **yib' aj poyanam**

bad luck *n.* **awas**

bad odor *n.* **k'isk'is**

bad omen *n.* **ch'i'**

bad words *n.* **lolob' aatin**

badly   *adv phr.* **moko chaab'il ta**

bag   *n.* **b'ools**

bail   *n.* **tojleb' re maak**

bait   *n.* **xwah kar**

bake   *v.* **jorank**

v. **jorank**

baked   *adj.* **jorinb'il**

baked potatoes *n.* **pomb'il paaps**

baker   *n agt.* **aj kaxlanwahinel**

bakery   *n.* **kaxlan wahib'aal**

n. **k'ayib'aal kaxlan wa**

balance   *n.* **tuqtuukil**

v. **tuqub'ank**

balcony   *n.* **kuukch'iich'**

n. **ramleb'ch'iich'**

n. **xramleb' ilob'aal**

bald   *adj.* **t'ojoch**

adj. **t'ojt'o**

adj. **t'uru' xjolom**

ball   *n.* **b'olotz**

ballerina *n agt.* **aj xajonel**

balloon   *n.* **pam'iq'**

ballot   *n.* **b'ootib'k**

ballplayer *n agt.* **aj b'olotz**

bamboo   *n.* **simb'**

banana   *n.* **tul**

banana tree *n.* **tul**

band   *n agt.* **aj wajb'**

bandage   *n.* **b'ir**

n. **b'ot'leb'**

n. **re lanok tiq'il**

n. **xiitleb' b'an**

bandaged   *adj.* **b'irb'o**

Band-Aid *n.* **kuriit**

n. **xiitleb' b'an**

bank   *n.* **k'uuleb'aaltumin**

n. **rochochil tumin**

bank account *n.* **ajlilk'uultumin**
  n. **k'uul tumin**

bank teller *n agt.* **aj xokol tumin**

banker *n agt.* **aj eechal k'uuleb'aal tumin**

banknotes *n.* **huhiltumin**

baptism *n.* **kub'iha'**

baptismal certificate
  n. **huhilkub'ha'**

bar (metal) *n.* **koral ch'iich'**

bar soap *n.* **b'arxab'on**

barbed wire *n.* **k'ix k'ahamch'iich'**

barbeque stall *n.* **sisib'aaltib'**

barbershop *n.* **b'esleb'aal**

bargain *n.* **kotzko xtz'aq**
  n. **kub'enaq xtz'aq**
  v phr. **xwech'b'al xtz'aq**

bark *n.* **rix**
  n. **rix che**
  v. **wohok**

barley *n.* **seb'aad**

barman *n agt.* **aj tenq'**

barometer *n.* **b'isleb'hab'**

barracks *n.* **rochochil aj puub'**

barrel *n.* **kumb'**
  n. **tamleb'aalha'**

barren woman *n.* **xma'al ixq**

barrier *n.* **lit'leb'aal**

barter *v.* **jalok**

basement *n.* **rub'el kab'l**

base-ten *adj.* **lajetqil**

base-twenty *n.* **junqmayil**
  n. **k'aalil**

basil *n.* **alb'aak**

basin *n.* **joom**
  n. **roqtaq'a**

basket *n.* **almul**
  n. **chakach**

basketball *n.* **b'olotz-uq'**
  n. **b'olotz chakach**

basketball player *n agt.* **aj b'olotz chakach**

bass drum *n.* **nimla tun**

bat *n.* **aj tz'uum xik'**
  n. **cho'k'oj**
  n. **sotz'**

batch *n.* **teep**

bath salts *n.* **k'aj atz'am b'an**

bathe *v.* **atink**

bathing suit *n.* **aq' re atink**
  n. **atiyach'**

bathroom *n.* **atib'aal**

bathtub *n.* **xna'aj ha' re atink**

battery *n.* **b'ateriiy**
  n. **kaxmetz'ew**
  n. **tamleb'aal metz'ew**

battle *n.* **pleet**
  n. **raaxiik'**
  n. **yalok**

battle-axe *n.* **maal**

battleship *n.* **jukub' re pleetik**

bay *n.* **rokeb' palaw**

bayleaf   *n.* **xaxaq lawrel**

be   *v.* **wank**

be alive   *v.* **yo'yook**

be born   *v.* **siyaak**
          v. **yo'laak**

be careful   *phr.* **chaab'aanu**
             went

be disgusted   *v.* **yib'ok**

be familiar with   *v.* **na'ok**

be hungry   *v.* **ch'ume'k**
            v. **tz'okaak**

be indoctrinated   *v.* **tije'k**

be late   *v.* **najto'k**

be rich   *v.* **b'ihomink**

be sorry   *v phr.* **ch'inank ch'ool**
           v. **kiib'ch'oolink**
           v phr. **yot'ok ch'ool**

be syphilitic   *v.* **b'uxo'k**

be thirsty   *v.* **chaqi'eel**

beach   *n.* **re ha'**

bead   *n.* **q'ol**

beak   *n.* **ruuch e**

beam   *n.* **oqech**
         n. **tz'amb'a**

bean   *n.* **kenq'**

bear   *n.* **oos**
         n. **wonxul**

beard   *n.* **mach**

beast of burden   *n.* **xul iiqanel**

beat   *v.* **b'ujuk**
         v. **juylek**
         v. **ketok**
         v. **potz'ok**

v. **tenok**

v. **wojok**

beat up   *v phr.* **tenok chi che'**

beater   *n.* **yuuleb'**

beautiful   *adj.* **ch'ina us**
            adj. **chaq'al ru**

beauty   *n.* **xchaq'al u**

beauty salon   *n.* **b'it'b'it'leb'aal**
               n. **t'ujleb'aal**

beaver   *n.* **kaxxul**

because   *conj.* **xb'aan naq**
          conj. **xmaak naq**

become   *v.* **hulak**
         v. **uxk**

become anemic   *v.* **puchirk**

become hard   *v.* **pekark**

become literate   *v.* **tzoltz'iib'ak**

bed   *n.* **ch'aat**
         n. **warib'**

bed crank   *n.* **ruq' ch'aat**

bedbug   *n.* **k'ulim**

bedding   *n.* **aq ru ch'aat**
          n. **ru ch'aat**

bedpan   *n.* **q'otq'ookil sek'**
         n. **xsek'ul tz'aj**

bedrail   *n.* **ramleb'**

bedroom   *n.* **warib'aal**

bedspread   *n.* **ru warib'aal**

bee   *n.* **chawinik**
         n. **seer**
         n. **xulkab'**

beef   *n.* **xtib'el wakax**

beefsteak   *n.* **kilinb'il tib'**

beehive   *n.* **rochoch kab'**
           n. **xche'el kab'**
           n. **xna'aj kab'**
beeper   *n.* **k'ul'esilal**
           n. **tz'uy tz'iib'esil**
beer   *n.* **serwees**
           n. **tzo'xul ha'**
beeswax   *n.* **tz'aak**
beet   *n.* **kik'xe'**
           n. **remolaach**
beetle   *n.* **b'itonk'ot**
           n. **pachi'**
           n. **pumpuri'**
before   *prep.* **chi rub'elaj**
           adv. **junxil**
           adv. **rub'elaj**
beg   *v.* **patz'ok**
beget   *v.* **k'ajolink**
beggar   *n agt.* **aj limoox**
           n. **kok' neb'a'**
           n. **neb'a'**
begin   *v.* **naqk**
           v. **ok**
           v. **tikib'ank**
           v. **tiklaak**
           v. **yoob'ank**
beginning *n.* **k'ojlajik**
           n. **tiklajik**
           n. **xtiklajik**
behind   *prep.* **chi rix**
believe   *v.* **paab'ank**
believer   *n agt.* **aj paab'anel**
believing *adj.* **aj paab'anel**
bell   *n.* **kampaan**
           n. **talanch'iich'**

           n. **tilin**
           n. **tzilinch'iich'**
bell tower *n.* **xna'aj kampaan**
           n. **xna'aj punitch'iich'**
bellboy   *n agt.* **aj k'amol iiq**
belly   *n.* **puj**
           n. **sa'**
belly button *n.* **ch'up**
beloved   *adj.* **rahro**
below   *adv.* **taq'a**
belt   *n.* **jit'leb'wex**
           n. **nimla siinch**
           n. **xb'ak'b'al wex**
           n. **xk'aamal**
           n. **xtaab'il**
           n. **xyi aq'**
bench   *n.* **ch'ina chunleb'**
           n. **chunleb'aal**
           n. **hilaal**
           n. **kelkookil tem**
           n. **tem**
bend   *v.* **hutzuk**
           v. **k'onok**
           v. **k'unuk**
           v. **liq'ok**
           v. **lokok**
benefit   *n.* **rusilal**
beret   *n.* **soq'keep**
           n. **soq'punit**
beside   *prep.* **sa' xk'atq**
bet   *v phr.* **yalok hu**
betray   *v.* **b'alaq'ink**
better   *adv phr.* **jwal us**
between   *prep.* **chi sa'**
           prep. **sa' xyanq**

bible   *n.* **loq'tasalhu**
            n. **santil hu**

bibliography   *n.* **esilalil**

bicycle   *n.* **b'aqlaq ch'iich'**
            n. **b'isikleet**

bid farewell   *v.* **chaq'rab'ink**

big   *adj.* **nim**

bigger than   *adv phr.* **nim chi ru**

bile   *n.* **k'a**
            n. **k'a'ej**

bilingual   *adj.* **ka'aatin**
            n agt. **aj ka'aatin**

bilingual education   *n.* **tijok sa' ka'aatinob'aal**

bill   *n.* **kweent**
            n. **sachom**

bill (legislative)   *n.* **xk'ub'ankil ru chaq'rab'**

billboard   *n.* **xna'aj esil**

bills   *n.* **huhiltumin**

billy club   *n.* **xuq'l**

binary system   *n.* **sum ajlil**

binder   *n.* **tahu**
            n. **xna'aj hu**
            n. **xokleb' hu**

binomial   *n.* **ka'eetalb'irok**

biography   *n.* **resil yu'amej**

biologist   *n agt.* **aj nawyu'amilal**

biology   *n.* **nawom chi rix yu'am**
            n. **nawyu'am**

biotope   *n.* **siyab'aal**

bird   *n.* **kok' xul**
            n. **tz'ik**

bird guano   *n.* **mayta'**

birdhouse   *n.* **rochochil tz'ik**

birth   *n.* **yo'lajik**

birth certificate   *n.* **hab'ilhu**
            n. **papelseya**
            n. **pereera**
            n. **reetalil xyo'lajik**
            n. **yo'lhu**

birth registry   *n.* **xtz'iib'ankil li yo'lajik**

birthday   *n.* **xkutankil yo'lajik**

bishop   *n.* **ob'iisp**

bison   *n.* **kaxwakax**

bite   *v.* **hach'lenk**
            v. **hach'ok**
            v. **jach'ok**
            v phr. **k'apok chi e**
            v. **k'atzok**
            v. **qachok**
            v. **ti'ok**
            n. **tiwb'il**
            v. **tiwok**

bitter   *adj.* **k'a**

bitterness   *n.* **q'etq'etil**

black   *adj.* **q'eq**

black crow   *n.* **q'eq'i ch'ejej**

black hole   *n.* **xhoplalil**

blackberry   *n.* **tokan**

blackboard   *n.* **tz'iib'leb'aal che'**
            n. **tz'iib'leb'che'**

blackmail   *n.* **takchi'**

blackmailer *n agt.* **aj takchi'**

blacksmith *n agt.* **aj tenol ch'iich'**

bladder *n.* **xna'aj chu**

blanket *n.* **isb'**
        n. **ru ch'aat**

bleach *n.* **b'anha'**

bleachers *n.* **tusb'il chunleb'al**

bleeding *n.* **tz'eqok kik'**

blemish *n.* **xox**

blend *v.* **yuulink**

blender *n.* **kaxka'**
        n. **puq'leb'**
        n. **uq'unleb'aal**

bless *v.* **osob'tesink**

blessed *adj.* **osob'tesinb'il**

blimp *n.* **pamb'eeresinb'il**

blind *adj.* **mutz'**
       n. **ramleb' saqen**
       adj. **xo't'**

blink *v phr.* **eek'asink rix u**
       v. **mutz'mutz'ink**
       v. **rik'ok**
       v. **yuqyuqink**

blister *n.* **porha'**
         n. **poxe'k**
         n. **puchha'**

block *v.* **ramok**

blood *n.* **kik'**
       n. **kik'el**
       n. **kik'elej**

blood loss *n.* **tz'eqok kik'**

blood pressure *n.* **nat'ich'mul**

blood pressure meter
        n. **ich'leb'ch'iich'**

blood sausage *n.* **moronk**

blood test *n.* **reetalil kik'**

bloody *adj.* **kik' ru**

blouse *n.* **kamiis ixq**
        n. **kaxpo'ot**

blouse (typical Mayan) *n.* **po'ot**

blow *v.* **apuunk**
      n. **temb'il**
      v. **waalunk**

blow out *v.* **chupuk**

blow up *v.* **apusink**

blowgun *n.* **puub' che'**

blowtorch *n.* **puub'xaml**

blue *adj.* **raxtz'o'in**
      adj. **rax ju'in**
      adj. **rax q'u'in**

blue galaxy *n.* **raxmoyinil tzoqchahim**

blue jeans *n.* **loonil wex**
        n. **wex re loon**

bluish *adj.* **raxmo'in**

blunt *adj.* **room**

blush *v.* **kaq'ok**

boar *n.* **chakow**

board *n.* **tz'alamche'**

board of directors *n.* **jolomilal**
        n. **k'amolb'e**

boarding house *n.* **warb'etaal**

boarding pass *n.* **xhuhil purik**

boardwalk *n.* **b'eeche'**

boast   *v phr.* **k'anasink rix**
           v phr. **nimob'eresink**
           ib'
           v. **wenb'enk ib'**

boastful   *adj.* **aj yoob'anel**
           aatin

boat   *n.* **b'aark**
           n. **jukub'**

bobbin   *n.* **xche'el noq'**

body   *n.* **tz'ejwalej**

body hair *n.* **q'ol is**

body part *n.* **cha'al**

body parts *n.* **oq uq'**
           n. **xcha'alil li tib'elej**

body text *n.* **esil tz'iib'anb'il**
           sa' li hu

body work
           n. **kuukb'eleb'ch'iich'**

boil   *v.* **loqlotk**
           v. **woqxink**

boiling point *n.* **woqxeel**

bolt of lightning *n.* **lemskaaq**
           n. **xrepom kaaq**

bomb   *n.* **b'oom**

bond paper *n.* **kaaxtinb'il hu**

bone   *n.* **b'aq**

bone tissue *n.* **ch'utb'aq cha'al**

boneless   *adj.* **xjunes tz'ej**

bonus   *n.* **raltoj**

book   *n.* **hu**
           n. **liib'r**
           n. **tasalhu**

book bag   *n.* **sukhu**

bookcase   *n.* **rochochil tasal**
           hu
           n. **xna'ajtasalhu**
           n. **xna'aj hu**

bookstore *n.* **k'ayib'aalhu**
           n. **k'ayib'aal tasal hu**

boot   *n.* **b'oot**
           n. **jurxaab'**
           n. **tzelek xaab'**

boots   *n.* **b'ootaxaab'**

border   *n.* **nub'aal**

bore   *v.* **hopok**
           v. **k'ob'ok**
           v. **titz'k**

bored   *adj.* **titz'jenaq**

borrow   *v.* **to'nink**

borrowed word *n.* **to'aatin**
           n. **to'chi'**

bossy   *adj.* **aj taqlanel**

botany   *n.* **nawk'iche'**

both   *pron.* **wotz**

bother   *v.* **ch'i'ch'i'ink**

bottle   *n.* **meet**

bottle cap *n.* **nat'b'iltz'ap**

bottle opener *n.* **teeleb' meet**

bottlerocket *n.* **jutzutzu**

bottom   *n.* **chi ixkej**
           n. **sa'**

boundary   *n.* **nub'aal**

bouquet   *n.* **junq'aal uutz'u'uj**

bow   *n.* **tzimaj**
           n. **xna' sijb'**

bowels   *n.* **sa'ej**

bowl   *n.* **sek'**

box   *n.* **ka'suut**
       n. **kaax**

box office *n.* **tojleb'aal**

box truck *n.* **motzo'ch'iich'**
      n. **nimla iiqob'aal ch'iich'**

boxing *n.* **potz'b'aqib'k**

boy   *n.* **ch'ajom**
      n. **ch'ina al**
      n. **ch'ina teelom**
      n. **saaj al**

boyfriend *n.* **suunal**
      n. **suunuhom**
      n. **xsum aam**
      n. **xsum ch'ool**

bra   *n.* **lamb'a tu'**
      n. **lantu'**

bracelet *n.* **pulseer**
      n. **q'ol'uq'**

braces *n.* **lit'ob'l uuch e**

brackets *n.* **k'ontz'uq**
      n. **nimaljuch'**

brackish *adj.* **remrem**

brag   *v.* **wenb'enk ib'**

braid   *v.* **kemok**
      n. **tz'uluk**

brain   *n.* **ulul**

brake   *v.* **aq'ab'ank**

brake fluid *n.* **olb'lit'b'e**
      n. **olb'xaqleb'**
      n. **ruk'a'il lit'olb'**

brakes *n.* **lit'b'e**
      n. **xaqleb'**

branch *n.* **ruq'**
      n. **ruq'il**
      n. **ruq' che'**

brassiere *n.* **lamb'a tu'**
      n. **lantu'**

brave   *adj.* **kaw rib'**
      adj. **wankil**

bravery *n.* **winqilal**

bread   *n.* **kaxlan wa**

bread pan *n.* **xk'ilul kaxlan wa**

break   *n.* **hilaal**
      v. **jorok**
      v. **much'uk**
      v. **toqok**

break down *v.* **murink**
      v. **po'ok**

breaker switch *n.* **chuplech**

breakfast *n.* **wa re eq'la**

breast   *n.* **re ch'ool**
      n. **tu'**
      n. **tu'ej**

breast milk *n.* **xya'al tu'**

breastbone *n.* **cholok'**

breastfeed *v.* **tu'uk**

breath deeply *v phr.* **jiq'ok ch'ool**

breathe *v.* **musiq'ak**
      v. **musiq'ank**

breathe rapidly *v phr.* **jiq'ok iq'**

briber *n agt.* **aj b'alaq'**

bribery *n.* **b'alaq'ik**

brick   *n.* **xan**

bricklayer *n agt.* **aj tz'ak**

bridge   *n.* **q'a**

brief   *adj.* **jumpaat**
            adj. **ko'xib'**
            n. **xyach'winq**
            n. **yach'**

briefcase   *n.* **ch'inajelool**
            n. **kanhub'aal**
            n. **kaxchampa**
            n. **k'amleb'aal**

briefs   *n.* **ch'otwex**

bright   *adj.* **lemtz'**

bright red *adj.* **kaqjorin**

brilliant   *adj.* **q'anq'an**

bring   *v.* **k'amok**
            v. **k'amok chaq**

broadcaster *n.* **aj pukaatin**

broad-minded *adj.* **nakuyuk**

broccoli   *n.* **b'rookl**
            n. **raxwak'**

broil   *v.* **pomok**

broken   *adj.* **jorol**
            adj. **much'ul**
            adj. **paq'al**
            adj. **toqolal**

broken leg *n.* **toqol a'**

broken tooth *n.* **xulum**

bronchitis *n.* **xyajelpospo'oy**

bronze   *n.* **q'an ch'iich'**

brook   *n.* **roq ha'**

broom   *n.* **mesleb'**

broth   *n.* **kaalt**
            n. **xya'al ik**

brother (generic) *n.* **asb'ej**

brother (older) *n.* **as**

brother (younger) *n.* **itz'in**

brother-in-law *n.* **b'alk winq**

brown   *adj.* **kaqyojin**
            adj. **q'eqmoyin**

bruise   *n.* **raxtint**

brush   *n.* **b'onleb'**
            n. **ji'b'al e**
            n. **kok' pim**
            n. **k'atk'al**
            n. **machb'onleb'**
            n. **sepiiy**

bubble   *n.* **woqx**

bucket   *n.* **b'oot**
            n. **kub'eet**
            n. **kumb'i'uk'al**

buckle   *n.* **jit'aal**
            n. **xch'ina ch'iich'ul**

bud   *n.* **xtorol ru uutz'u'uj**

budget   *n.* **sachom**

buffalo   *n.* **kaxwakax**

bug   *n.* **k'ajxul**

bug spray   *n.* **xb'anol suq**

build   *v.* **kab'lank**
            v. **yiib'ank**

building   *n.* **nimla kab'l**
            n. **nimla ochoch**
            n. **ninqi'ochoch**

buildings   *n.* **nimqi kab'l**

bulb   *n.* **xe'**

bull   *n.* **k'olwakax**
            n. **toor**
            n. **xmama' wakax**

bull calf   *n.* **ral wakax**

bullet   *n.* **xnaq'puub'**

bullet casing   *n.* **rixnaq'puub'**

bullet shell   *n.* **rixxnaq'puub'**

bulletin   *n.* **yehol'esilal**

bump   *n.* **b'uqux**

bumper   *n.* **kolten**

bun   *n.* **b'uq'**

bunch   *n.* **jun cheet**
          n. **kuut**

bureaucracy   *n.* **xb'ehil ru
          k'anjel**

burglar   *n agt.* **aj elq'**

burglary   *n.* **elq'**

burial notice   *n.* **xhuhil resil
          kamk**

burn   *v.* **choqlenk**
          v. **humuk**
          n. **k'atal**
          v. **k'atink**
          v. **k'atk**
          v. **k'atok**
          n. **k'atom**

burp   *n.* **qixb'**
          v. **qixb'ak**

bury   *v.* **muquk**

bus   *n.* **b'eleb'aalch'iich'**
          n. **b'eleb'poyanam**
          n. **kamyoneet**
          n. **poy ch'iich'**

bus station   *n.* **hilob'eleb'aal
          ch'iich'**
          n. **xna'aj b'eleb'aal
          ch'iich'**

bus stop   *n.* **xaqleb'aal ch'iich'**

bush   *n.* **chik che'**
          n. **kok' pim**
          n. **pim**

bust   *n.* **re ch'ool**
          n. **tu'**
          n. **tu'ej**
          n. **xtehelal xkux**

busy   *adj.* **laatz' ru**

but   *conj.* **a' ut**
          conj. **ab'an**

butcher   *n agt.* **aj k'ay tib'**

butcher shop   *n.* **k'ayib'aal tib'**

butt   *n.* **xko rit**

butter   *n.* **k'uub'anb'il olb'**
          n. **manteek**

butterfly   *n.* **peepem**

buttock   *n.* **it**

buttocks   *n.* **xko rit**

button   *n.* **b'otonx**
          n. **chapleb't'ikr**
          n. **kotchapleb'**

buy   *v.* **loq'ok**

buy one get one free   *phr.* **loq'
          jun ut yal siib'il li
          xkab'**

buzzer   *n.* **jultikleb'**
          n. **tz'iraych'iich'**

by   *prep.* **sa'**

by fraction   *adv.* **chi jachal**

by tens   *adv phr.* **chi lajetqil**

by the hundred   *adj.* **chi ok'aalil**

bye   *phr.* **inwan b'i'**

C - c

cabbage *n.* **repooy**
    n. **torol'ichaj**
cabin *n.* **po'lem kab'l**
cabinet (presidential)
    n. **xjolomil**
    awab'ejilal
cable *n.* **roopilch'iich'**
cable television *n.* **xk'aamal**
    kaxmu
cactus *n.* **peetaq**
cafe *n.* **k'ayib'aal kape**
    n. **uk'leb'aal kape**
cafeteria *n.* **k'ayib'aal kape**
    n. **uk'leb'aal kape**
cage *n.* **koral ch'iich'**
    n. **tz'alam**
cake *n.* **kaxlank'uluj**
    n. **uutz'u'jinb'ilkaxlan**
    wa
    n. **xoyk'uluj**
calcium *n.* **kawb'aqel**
calculator *n.* **ajleb'aal**
    n. **aj b'ironel**
    n. **b'irleb'aal**
calendar *n.* **ajleb'aal kutan**
    n. **ch'olq'e**
    n. **xq'ehil kutan**
calf (of a cow) *n.* **ch'ina wakax**
    n. **ral wakax**

calf (of the leg) *n.* **xk'ot oq'**
    n. **xsu oq**
    n. **xt'oy oq'**
call *v.* **b'oqok**
call (a name) *v.* **k'ab'a'ink**
call button *n.* **jultikleb'**
    n. **tz'iraych'iich'**
call center *n.* **rochochil**
    b'oqleb'
calligraphy *n.* **chaq'aliltz'iib'**
    n. **chaab'iltz'iib'**
calm *adj.* **aj kuyunel**
    adj. **ch'anaak**
calm down *phr.* **k'ojob'**
    aach'ool
calorie *n.* **xtiqwal**
camel *n.* **b'uq'ultzimitz**
    n. **kameey**
camera *n.* **isihob'aal**
    jalam'uuch
    n. **jalam'uuchib'aal**
    n. **jalam'uuleb'**
camera (television) *n.* **k'utleb'**
    mu
cameraman *n agt.* **aj**
    chapol'esil
camisole *n.* **b'atz'unk b'aatal**
camp *n.* **kampameent**
campaign *v.* **q'unb'esink**
    n. **yehokb'aanunk**

can   *n.* **laat**

can opener   *n.* **teeleb' laat**

canal   *n.* **numleb'ha'**

canary   *n.* **kok' q'an tz'ik**

cancelled   *adj.* **xraqman ru**

cancer   *n.* **kanser**
           n. **q'aayajel**
           n. **sob'yajel**

candidate   *n agt.* **aj okenel chi**
           awab'ejink

candle   *n.* **kanteel**
           n. **uutz'u'uj**

candlestick *n.* **xna'aj kanteel**

candy   *n.* **kab'**
           n. **saa'us**

candy store   *n.* **k'ayib'aal**
           k'areru

canister   *n.* **laat**

cannon   *n.* **ru'uj puub'**
           n. **xb'oolpuub'**

canoe   *n.* **jukub'**

canton   *n.* **teep**
           n. **xteepal tenamit**

canvas   *n.* **loon**

canyon   *n.* **xyanq tzuul**

cap   *n.* **punit**
           n. **soq'keep**
           n. **tz'apb'al re**
           n. **tz'apil**
           n. **xta jolom**

capability *n.* **seeb'alil**

cape   *n.* **kopmokooch**

capital   *n.* **xjolomiltenamit**

capital letter *n.* **astz'iib'**

caplet   *n.* **b'otb'an**
           n. **b'otb'il b'an**

capsule   *n.* **b'otb'an**
           n. **b'otb'il b'an**

captain   *n agt.* **aj jolominel**
           b'eeleb'

captive   *n agt.* **aj tz'alam**
           n. **preex**

car   *n.* **ch'ina b'eleb'aal**
           ch'iich'
           n. **ch'iich'**

car accident *n.* **xtoch'ol**
           b'eleeb'aal ch'iich'

car parts   *n.* **xcha'aleb'**
           b'eleb'aal ch'iich'

caramel   *n.* **kab'**

carbohydrates *n.* **sib'ha'**
           n. **xtz'aqob'l ajsiil**

carbon   *n.* **sib'eel**

carbon paper *n.* **ab'aqhu**

carbonated drink *n.* **kaxlanha'**

carburetor *n.* **yuuk'isib'aal**

carcass   *n.* **kamenaq**

card   *n.* **perhu**

cardboard   *n.* **karton**
           n. **pimilhu**
           n. **teb'tookil hu**

cardholder *n.* **perhub'aal**

cardinal directions *n.* **xtz'uq**
           junajroqil

cardiologist *n agt.* **aj**
           nawch'oolej

cardiology *n.* **nawch'oolej**

career *n.* **xb'ehil k'anjel**

caring *n.* **xik aak'a'uxl**

carnation *n.* **kalawx**

carpenter *n agt.* **aj pech'ol che'**
  n agt. **aj peech'**

carpentry *n.* **peech'ab'k**

carpet *n.* **alfoombr**
  n. **ruhiltz'ak**
  n. **xsok oq**

Carribean sea *n.* **palaw kariiw**

carrier *n agt.* **aj kelonel**

carrot *n.* **q'anxe'**
  n. **sanahoor**

carry *v.* **iiqank**
  v. **paqonk**

carry (in hand) *v.* **ch'ilonk**
  v. **hech'hotk**
  v. **jech'exink**
  v. **rininink**
  v. **telnak**

carry (on head) *v.* **b'itonk**

carry (on shoulder) *v.* **jelonk**
  v. **telonk**

carry (under the arm) *v.* **q'alnak**

cart *n.* **iiqaal**
  n. **kareton**
  n. **kareet**
  n. **toltol**

cartridge *n.* **xnaq' puub'**

carve *v.* **let'ok**
  v. **pech'ok**

case *n.* **rix**
  n. **rixch'iich'**

cask *n.* **kumb'**
  n. **tamleb'aalha'**

cassava *n.* **tz'in**

cassette *n.* **choqtin**
  n. **xokleb'**

cast *n.* **chunt'ikr**
  v phr. **xb'otb'al chi chunt'ikr**

Castilian *lang.* **kastiiy**
  lang. **kaxlanchi'**
  lang. **kaxlan aatin**

castrated *adj.* **kapun**

cat *n.* **mes**

catalysis *n.* **xjalalik ru**

catalytic *adj.* **metz'ewanb'il**

catalytic converter
  n. **k'atolch'iich'**

catch *v.* **ramok**
  v. **saapunk**

catchment area *n.* **roqtaq'a**

caterpillar *n.* **kuluk**

cathedral *n.* **nimla tijob'aal**

Catholic *n.* **katoolk**

cattle *n.* **wakax**

cattleman *n agt.* **aj ilol wakax**

catwalk *n.* **q'axleb'aal**

cauliflower *n.* **koliplor**
  n. **saqmot**
  n. **saqwak'**

cause *n.* **b'aan**

cave *n.* **julpek**
  n. **ochoch pek**

n. **saqoonak**
n. **siwan**
caveman   *n.* **ch'olwinq**
cavity   *n.* **xul e**
CD   *n.* **sur chapleb'aal**
CD-ROM   *n.* **sur chapleb'aal**
cease   *v.* **ach'ab'ank**
　　　v. **ch'anab'ank**
　　　v. **raqe'k**
　　　v. **ruujik**
cedar   *n.* **chakalte'**
　　　n. **muy che'**
　　　n. **sutz'uj**
cede way   *v phr.* **k'ehok numik**
ceiba   *n.* **inup**
ceiling   *n.* **ru tz'amb'a**
ceiling fan   *n.* **xwalub'aal kab'l**
ceiling light   *n.* **saqenk'im**
celery   *n.* **aapy**
　　　n. **kax'isk'i'ij**
celery salt   *n.* **atz'am aapy**
cell (biological)   *n.* **xna'yu'am**
cell (jail)   *n.* **ch'ilb'oqleb'**
　　　n. **xraqlil xsa' tz'alam**
cell (phone)   *n.* **b'oqleb'**
　　　n. **ch'ilb'oqleb'**
cell membrane   *n.* **xtzuumal xna'yu'am**
cell nucleus   *n.* **xyich'ool xna'yu'am**
cell phone   *n.* **b'oqleb'**
　　　n. **ch'ilb'oqleb'**

cell phone signal   *n.* **xkutum b'oqleb'**
cellar   *n.* **xna'aj k'uleb'aal**
cellphone   *n.* **ch'ilb'oqleb'**
cells   *n.* **na'yu'am**
cellular (phone)   *n.* **b'oqleb'**
　　　n. **ch'ilb'oqleb'**
cement   *n.* **poq re tz'akab'ak**
cemetery   *n.* **muqleb'aal**
Cenozoic era   *n.* **ro' q'ekutan**
census   *n.* **tz'ilpoyanam**
census taker   *n agt.* **aj tz'ilpoyanam**
center   *n.* **xyi**
centimeter   *n.* **miin**
centipede   *n.* **kojoj**
　　　n. **mutzuy**
　　　n. **pataal**
Central America   *n.* **xyi ab'yayala**
　　　n. **yiib'ejilch'och'**
central nervous system
　　　n. **xtuslal'ich**
　　　n. **xyihil xk'ub'lal ich'mulej**
central processing unit
　　　n. **ch'olk'anjelob'aal**
century   *n.* **ok'aal hab'**
certain   *adj.* **ch'olch'o**
certainly   *adv phr.* **ch'olch'o b'i'an**
cerulean   *adj.* **raxpotz'in**
　　　adj. **saqirax**

cetaceans *n.* **ha'il ajtu'xul**

chain *n.* **b'aqb'il k'aham ch'iich'**
n. **kareen**
n. **q'ol**

chainsaw *n.* **jachleb'aal che'**

chair *n.* **chunleb'aal**
n. **k'ojarib'**
n. **tem**

Chalchitek *lang.* **chalchitan**

chalk *n.* **chuntz'iib'l**

chalkboard *n.* **tz'iib'leb'aal che'**
n. **tz'iib'leb'che'**

challenge *n.* **tikb'il**
v. **tikok**

challenger *n.* **tikonel**

chamber pot *n.* **xsek'ul tz'aj**

chameleon *n.* **pere'maal**
n. **xyuwa'il paqmaal**

champagne *n.* **champan**

change *v.* **jalok**
n. **jaltesink**

change of clothes *n.* **sumal'aq'**

channel *n.* **xb'e ha'**

chapel *n.* **kapiiy**
n. **tijob'aal**

chapter *n.* **ch'ol**

charcoal *n.* **ru xaml**
n. **ruuxam**
n. **sib'j**

chard *n.* **aselk**
n. **jur'ichaj**

charge *v phr.* **xk'ulb'al xtz'aq**

charger *n.* **metz'ewib'aalb'oql eb'**

charity *n.* **uxtanank**

charming *adj.* **tk'ul ach'ool**

chassis *n.* **tz'amb'ahilch'iich'**

chat *v.* **aatinak**
n. **seeraq'**

chauffeur *n agt.* **aj b'eresinelch'iich'**
n agt. **aj ch'e'ol ch'iich'**

cheap *adj.* **kotzko**
adj. **kub'enaq xtz'aq**

check *v.* **ilok**
n. **tojleb'hu**
n. **xhuhiltumin**

checkbook *n.* **xtasal xhuhil tumin**

check-up *n.* **rilom aj b'anonel**

cheek *n.* **ko**

cheekbones *n.* **xko uhej**

cheeky *adj.* **naxkuj rib'**

cheese *n.* **kees**
n. **q'emtu'**
n. **q'emya'altu'**

chef *n agt.* **aj k'uub'anel tzakahemq**

chemist *n agt.* **aj k'ayinel b'an**
n. **k'ayib'aal b'an**

cherry *n.* **ab'aal**
n. **serees**

chest   *n.* **maqab'**
     n. **re ch'ool**
     n. **re maqab'**

chest of drawers   *n.* **xna'aj aq'**

chew   *v.* **hab'ok**
     v. **hot'ok**
     v. **k'oylenk**
     v. **k'uxuk**

chick   *n.* **ch'ina kaxlan**
     n. **kok' kaxlan**
     n. **ral kaxlan**

chick peas   *n.* **karwans**

chicken   *n.* **kaxlan**
     n. **xtib'el kaxlan**

chicken breast   *n.* **xsaqal kaxlan**

chicken wire   *n.* **soq'ch'iich'**

chickenpox   *n.* **atz'umxox**
     n. **ninqixox**

chieftain   *n.* **awab'ej**
     n. **jolomil**

chigger   *n.* **xulk'aq**

child   *n.* **al**
     n. **k'ajol**

childhood   *n.* **kok'alil**

children   *n.* **alaleb'**
     n. **kok'al**

chili pepper   *n.* **ik**
     n. **ki'il ik**

chill   *v.* **keresink**
     n. **wosol**
     n. **xsik ke**

chilly   *adj.* **ke**

chimney   *n.* **releb'aal sib'**
     n. **releb'sib'**
     n. **xb'ehil sib'**

chin   *n.* **ru'uj xkaalam e**
     n. **rub'el e**
     n. **xxuk e**

chinchilla   *n.* **k'axkuk**

Chinese   *n.* **aj mitz-u**

chisel   *n.* **jotzleb'**
     n. **pikleb'**
     n. **pormon**

chlorine   *n.* **b'anha'**

choice   *n.* **sik'ok-u**

choir   *n.* **komon b'ichank**
     n. **xch'uut aj b'ichk**

choke   *v.* **b'iq'e'k**
     v. **jiq'e'k**

choking   *n.* **paq'ek**

cholera   *n.* **nume'sa'xa'aw**

choose   *v.* **molok**
     v phr. **sik'ok u**
     v phr. **tihok u**

chop   *v.* **jesok**
     v. **qapok**
     v. **raqink**
     v phr. **setok chi kok'**
     v. **yok'ok**

chop wood   *v phr.* **yok'ok si'**

chore   *n.* **kok'anjel**
     n. **kub'siil**
     n. **tenq'**

chorizo   **b'utb'iltib'**
     n. **b'utb'iltib'aaq**

Chorti   *lang.* **ch'orti'**

Christian *n.* **kristyaan**

Christian faith *n.* **kristyaanil paab'aal**

chromosome *n.* **iyajib'aal**

chronometer *n.* **b'isleb'hoonal**

Chuj *lang.* **chuj**

church *n.* **iklees**
n. **tijob'aal**

church services *n.* **kuult**

churro *n.* **k'ilimb'il saa'us**

chute *n.* **jolool**

cicada *n.* **chikiriin**

cider *n.* **xya'al mansaan**

cigar *n.* **may**
n. **sik'l**

cigarette *n.* **may**
n. **sik'l**
n. **xaqmay**

cilantro *n.* **kok' samat**

cinder block *n.* **pak'b'il tzak**

cinema *n.* **eetalmu**
n. **ileb'aalmu**
n. **rochochil ilob'aal mu**

cinnamon *n.* **kaneel**

circle *n.* **kotko**
n. **siril**
n. **sirso**

circuit board *n.* **jekb'ametz'ew**

circuit breaker
n. **nimlaraqalmetz'ew**

circular *adj.* **q'otq'o**
adj. **sursu**

circulatory system
n. **k'uub'suutaalkik'**

circus *n.* **ch'uch'ib'leb'aal**
n. **xna'aj payas**

circus tent *n.* **kaxmuheb'aal ch'uch'ib'leb'aal**

citation particle, plural
part. **chankeb'**
part. **len**

citation particle, singular
part. **chan**

citizen *n.* **aj tenamit**

citrus fruit *n.* **lamuunx**

city *n.* **mama' tenamit**
n. **nimla tenamit**

city hall *n.* **poopol kab'l**

city improvement tax
n. **hutojxoyiil**

civic *adj.* **loq'altenamit**

civic leadership committee
n. **jolomilk'aleb'aal**

civil marriage *n.* **sumlaak chi ru chaq'rab'**

civil registry *n.* **xna'ajil tz'iib'ahom k'ab'a'ej**

civil rights *n.* **xk'ulub'poyanam**

civil servant *n agt.* **aj k'anjel sa' chaq'rab'**

civilization *n.* **tawloq'aal**

clamorous *adj.* **t'ont'on xyaab'**

clamp *n.* **yutleb'ch'iich'**

clan *n.* **amaq'**
n. **triiw**

class   *n.* **paay**
           n. **paayil**
           n. **ru tzoleb'aal**
classmate *n.* **komon sa'**
           tzoleb'aal
classroom *n.* **xsa' tzoleb'aal**
classrooms *n.* **xtasalil xsa'**
           tzoleb'aal
claw   *n.* **ixi'ij**
           n. **nimqi ixi'ij**
           n. **yax**
clay   *n.* **seb'**
           n. **wa**
clay brick *n.* **pak'b'il tzak**
clay frying pan *n.* **konxik'**
clay pot   *n.* **ch'och' uk'al**
clean   *adj.* **ch'aj**
           adj. **ch'ajmich'aj**
           adj. **saq ru**
clean laundry *n.* **saqi aq'**
clean up   *v.* **sab'esink**
clear   *adj.* **kutan**
           adj. **saqen**
           adj. **tz'aqal re ru**
           adj. **yamyo ruhil**
           kutan
clearance sale *n.* **rosojik k'ay**
cleavage   *n.* **xtehelal xkux**
cleaver   *n.* **ch'ina maal**
           n. **ch'iich' re setok**
clever   *adj.* **kaw rib'**
           adj. **wankil**
client   *n.* **nuumel ula'**

cliff   *n.* **uul**
           n. **uul ch'och'**
           n. **uul pek**
climate   *n.* **xch'och'il**
climb   *v.* **lochte'ek**
           v. **taqe'k**
clinic   *n.* **b'anleb'aal**
clip   *n.* **ch'ina yax ch'iich'**
clitoris   *n.* **b'irk**
cloak   *n.* **nimla t'ikr**
           n. **raq' qaawa'**
clock   *n.* **ilb'ahoonal**
           n. **reloj**
close   *v.* **tz'apok**
close friend *n.* **ech-aatin**
closed   *adj.* **tz'aptz'o**
closed syllable *n.* **tz'ap yehiil**
cloth   *n.* **kem**
           n. **t'ikr**
clothes   *n.* **tiqb'al**
clothes rack *n.* **lukleb'aal**
clothesline *n.* **heleb' puch'um**
           n. **helleb'aal**
clothing   *n.* **aq'ej**
           n. **b'aatal**
           n. **tiqb'al**
           n. **t'ikr**
clothing designer *n agt.* **aj**
           yib'anel eetalil aq'
cloud   *n.* **choq**
cloudless *adj.* **yamyo ruhil**
           kutan

cloudy   *adj.* **muqb'il**
          adj. **nub'un**

clove spice   *n.* **kalawx q'een**

clown   *n agt.* **aj ch'uch'**
         n. **se'eel winq**

club   *n.* **patb'**
        n. **xuq'l**

clumsy   *adj.* **jip**

coach   *n agt.* **aj jolominel
         b'atz'unk**

coagulation (blood)   *n.* **patkik'**

coals   *n.* **ruuxam**

coast   *n.* **re palaw**

coat   *n.* **b'atb'a ib'**
        n. **mama' pimil t'ikr**

cobbler   *n agt.* **aj yiib'om xaab'**

cobblery   *n.* **rochochil li
            yiib'leb'aal xaab'**

cobblestone   *n.* **ruhib'e**

cobblestone street   *n.* **xxanil b'e**

cobra   *n.* **ch'ina perk'anti'**

Coca Cola   *n.* **kokakool**

cochlea   *n.* **xq'ootil xik**

cock   *n.* **tzo'xul**
        n. **tzo' kaxlan**

cockroach   *n.* **paachach**

cocktail   *n.* **yuki'q'een**

cocoa   *n.* **kakaw**

cocoa bean   *n.* **xnaq' kakaw**

coconut   *n.* **kook**

coefficient   *n.* **aj k'ihanel ajl**

coffee   *n.* **kape**

coffee cup   *n.* **sek' re kape**

coffee maker   *n.* **xna'aj kape**

coffee pot   *n.* **xna'aj kape**
             n. **xxaaril kape**

coil   *n.* **q'ochb'il noq'
        ch'iich'**

coin   *n.* **ch'iich'tumin**
        n. **kok' tumin**

coitus   *n.* **tz'ikib'**

Coke   *n.* **kokakool**

colander   *n.* **tz'ileb'**

cold   *n.* **jolomb'ej**
        n. **ke**
        adj. **ke**

cold climate   *n.* **kehilch'och'**

cold cuts   *n.* **b'utb'iltib'**
            n. **pihamb'r**

cold tablets   *n.* **re raxkehob'**

cold water   *n.* **kehil ha'**

colic   *n.* **xtib'l sa'ej**

collar   *n.* **xkux aq'**

collect   *v.* **molob'ank**

collection (of donations)
              n. **ch'uttenq'**

collection of country houses
              n. **kok'k'aleb'aal**

college professor   *n agt.* **aj
              k'utunel re xnimal
              tzoleb'aal**

colloquial   *adj.* **tiikil'aatin**

colon   *n.* **ka'tz'uq**
         n. **luttz'uq**

color   *n.* **b'on**
           n. **b'onol**
color tone *n.* **xchamal xb'onol**
colorless *adj.* **saqmoy**
colt   *n.* **ral kawaay**
column   *n.* **oqech**
comb   *n.* **xiyab'**
combat   *n.* **pleetik**
combed   *adj.* **jot'b'il**
           adj. **t'e'b'il**
come   *v.* **chalk**
           v. **k'ulunk**
come back *v.* **q'ajk**
           v. **suq'iik**
come in (plural) *phr.* **okanqex**
come in (singular) *phr.* **okan**
come on   *phr.* **yo'o**
come on!   *phr.* **yo'ooo**
comet   *n.* **b'utzchahim**
           n. **muluq'utchahim**
comfortable *adj.* **sa**
comforter *n.* **ru warib'aal**
comma   *n.* **k'onk'okiltz'uq**
           n. **k'ontz'uq**
command   *v.* **taqlank**
commandment *n.* **chaq'rab'**
comment   *n.* **k'a'uxlal**
commentator *n agt.* **aj
           jultikahonel**
           n agt. **aj yehonel'uxk**
commercial *n.* **yeechi'ink**

commission *v.* **ab'enank**
           n. **taqlil**
commit adultery *v phr.* **k'atok oq**
commitment *n.* **laatz'al**
common noun *n.* **k'ab'a'ej
           k'a'aqru**
communicate *v.* **yehok**
communication *n.* **xyeb'al**
communications *n.* **aatinab'aal**
communications satellite
           n. **chahimch'iich' re
           puktesink esil**
community *n.* **komonil**
community beautification tax
           n. **hutojxoyiil**
community projects
           n. **tusk'anjel komonil**
compact disk *n.* **sur
           chapleb'aal**
compact galaxy *n.* **junaj
           tzoqchahim**
companion *n.* **ochb'een**
compass   *n.* **junajroqil**
           n. **k'ixkoot**
compassion *n.* **rilb'al
           xtoq'ob'al**
           n. **toq'ob'al u**
competence *n.* **seeb'alil**
complement *n.* **xtz'aqob'l**
complementary *adj.* **xtz'aqalil**
complete   *adj.* **tz'aqal**
composite noun *n.* **ka' paay ru
           k'ab'a'ej**

compound *n.* **ka' paay ru**

compressor *n.* **xna'aj iq'**

computer *n.* **ulul ch'iich'**

computer disk *n.* **ululil xokleb'**
n. **xna'aj xokleb'**

computer programmer *n agt.* **aj yiib'om ulul ch'iich'**

computer science *n.* **tzolom chi rix ululch'iich'**

computer screen
n. **kaxmu'eetalil**

conceive *v phr.* **kanaak sa' yu'am**

concentrated
adj. **xokxoxch'ool**

concentration *n.* **xokch'oolej**

concentric *adj.* **xyirib'**

Concepción *nick.* **Konsep**

concert *n.* **wajb'ak**

concertina *n.* **b'aswajb'**

condemn *v phr.* **raqok aatin chi rix**
v. **tz'aqtaanank**

condiment *n.* **xb'anol tzakahemq**

conditional particle *part.* **raj**

condor *n.* **xmama' t'iw**

conductor *n.* **numsinel**

cone *n.* **jutz'ju**
n. **juutz'**
n. **ru chaj**

conference *n.* **xyeeb'al**

confess *v.* **xotonk**
v. **xootonink**

confession *n.* **xyehok maak**

confessional *n.* **xootonib'aal maak**

confetti *n.* **xk'aj hu**

confidant *n.* **paab'ajel**

confirmed bachelor *n.* **tiixil ch'ajom**

confuse *v.* **sachk**

confused *adj.* **sachenaq ru**

congratulations! *phr.* **sahil ch'oolejil choq' aawe**

congress
n. **k'uub'leb'chaq'rab'**
n. **rochochil aj k'uub'anel chaq'rab'**

congruent triangle *n.* **tawrib' oxxukuut**

conjoined twins *n.* **latzlut**

conjunction *n.* **najunajin aatin**

conjunctivitis *n.* **rahil u**

connection *n.* **k'ultiq**

consequence *n.* **k'ulb'ilal**

consider *v phr.* **teeb'il xk'a'uxl**

considerate *adj.* **teeto xk'a'uxl**

consonant *n.* **xyaab'tz'iib'**

constellation *n.* **ch'uut chahim**
n. **tzoqtzokilchahim**
n. **xch'uutulal chahim**

constipation *n.* **yot'e'k sa'ej**

constitution *n.* **xchaq'rab' li tenamit**

construct *v.* **yiib'ank**

construction *n.* **yiib'ank xaqab'ank**

construction site *n.* **kab'lak**
n. **xna'aj yiib'ank xaqab'ank**

construction worker *n.* **aj yiib'ank xaqab'ank**

constructivism *n.* **kab'lanb'il na'leb'**

consult *v.* **aatinank**

consumer finance *n.* **tijok chi rix loq'ok**

contact lenses *n.* **ch'ik ileb'**

container *n.* **meet**

contemplate *v.* **ka'yank**
v. **k'ulub'ank**

contempt *n.* **tz'eqtanank**

content *adj.* **k'ojk'o xch'ool**
adj. **sa xch'ool**
adj. **tuqtu xch'ool**

contentment *n.* **sahil ch'oolejil**

contents *adj.* **xsa'**

continent *n.* **pak'alilch'och'**

continuation *n.* **tiqam**

contract *n.* **xaqab'ank aatin**
n. **xaq-aatin**

control *v phr.* **k'ehok eetal**

control tower *n.* **k'aak'aleb'aal**

controller *n.* **tuqb'ametz'ew**

controversial *adj.* **xik' naxye**

convent *n.* **konb'eent**

conventioneer *n agt.* **aj q'unob'tesinel**

convert *n.* **jaltesink**

convex *adj.* **b'uq'**
adj. **b'uq'b'u**

convict *n.* **pereex**
v phr. **raqok aatin chi rix**
v phr. **teneb'ankil sa' xb'een**

cook *n agt.* **aj k'uub'anel tzakahemq**
v. **chiqok**

cooked *adj.* **chiqb'il**
adj. **k'ub'k'u**
adj. **k'uub'aak**

cookhouse *n.* **chi re xam**
n. **k'uub'leb'aal**
n. **xna'aj xam**

cookie *n.* **xujsaa'us**

cooking oil *n.* **kax'olb'**
n. **kaxlanq'ib'**

cool *adj.* **luulu**

cooperation *n.* **komontenq'**
n. **tenq'aal**

cooperative *n.* **komonilk'anjel**

coordinate *n.* **xb'arxukil**

coordinate origin *n.* **xtiklajik xb'arxukil**

copier *n.* **jalam'uuchleb'**
n. **jalam'uuchleb'aal ch'iich'**
n. **puktasib'aalhu**

copper   *adj.* **q'anch'ik'**
          n. **q'an ch'iich'**

copy   *v.* **etalink**

copy machine
          n. **jalam'uuchleb'**
          n. **jalam'uuchleb'aal ch'iich'**
          n. **puktasib'aalhu**

cord   *n.* **jusk'aam**

cordless phone   *n.* **mak'aam b'oqleb'**

coriander   *n.* **kulantr**

corkscrew   *n.* **isib'aal tapon**
             n. **teeleb' meet**

corn   *n.* **ixim**

corn (cutaneous)   *n.* **pat**

corn (prepared for grinding)
          n. **b'uch**

cornea   *n.* **xlemtz'iil u**

corner   *n.* **jech'xuk**
          n. **loot'**
          n. **xuk**
          n. **xxuk b'e**

cornfield   *n.* **k'al**
             n. **waj**

cornmeal   *n.* **q'em**

cornmeal drink   *n.* **q'em ha'**

cornstalk   *n.* **roq waj**

coroner   *n agt.* **aj ilol kamenaq**

corpse   *n.* **kamenaq**

corral   *n.* **xna'aj ketomq**
          n. **xoralwakax**

correcting fluid   *n.* **tuqleb'**

corrections   *n.* **xk'ub'laal tojb'a maak**
               n. **xk'uub'laltojb'ama ak**

cosmetics   *n.* **sunob'resiil**

cosmology   *n.* **suutalnawom**

cosmos   *n.* **choxach'och'**

costume   *n.* **eetz'aal**
           n. **k'utb'aatal**
           n. **uutz'u'ujinb'il eetz'unk**

cot   *n.* **ch'ina ch'aat**

cotton   *n.* **noq'**

cotton candy   *n.* **ki'tuux**

cotton candy vendor   *n agt.* **aj k'ay ki'tuux**

cotton swab   *n.* **tuxil noq'**

cotton tree   *n.* **xche'el noq'**

couch   *n.* **potztem**
         n. **soq'il chunleb'**

cough   *n.* **katzkatz kux**
         n. **kuxb'ej**
         n. **ojb'**
         v. **ojb'ak**

cough drops   *n.* **b'an re ojb'**

cough please   *phr.* **ojob'an b'aanu usilal**

cough syrup   *n.* **uk'b'il b'an**

counselor   *n agt.* **aj chi'resilnel**
             n agt. **aj k'ehol na'leb'**

count   *v.* **ajlank**

country   *n.* **nimla tenamit**

countryside   *n.* **k'aleb'aal**

courageous *adj.* **kaw rib'**
   adj. **naxyoob' rib'**

course *n.* **ru tzolom**
   n. **tzolomil**

court *n.* **neb'aal**
   n. **poopol**
   n. **raqleb'aatin**

court case *n.* **ch'a'jkilal**

cousin *n.* **as e**

cousin (younger) *n.* **iitz'in'e**

covenant *n.* **sumwank**

cover *v.* **lepok**
   n. **ruhil**
   n. **tz'apleb'**
   v. **tz'apok**

cover page *n.* **ruhil**
   n. **xoy**

covet *v.* **tzemok**

cow *n.* **b'aak**
   n. **na'wakax**
   n. **wakax**
   n. **xa'n wakax**

cowardly *adj.* **aj xiw**
   adj. **aj yop**

cowboy *n agt.* **aj ilol wakax**

coyote *n.* **tz'i' pim**
   n. **tz'i' tzuul**
   n. **xojb'**

CPU *n.* **ch'olk'anjelob'aal**

crab *n.* **tap**
   n. **xtap palaw**

cracker *n.* **kaxk'oyem**

cradle *n.* **tz'alamch'aat**
   n. **xkoral k'ula'al**

   n. **xwaresib'aal k'ula'al**

craftsman *n agt.* **aj k'anjel re k'a' re ru**

cramp *n.* **muchkej**

cranium *n.* **xb'aqel jolom**

crate *n.* **kaxon**

crawl *v.* **jukunk**
   v. **k'achiik**

crayfish *n.* **tap re nima'**

crayon *n.* **b'onleb'**

cream *n.* **uq'unil b'an**

crease *n.* **xb'asb'al sa' xyi**

credential *n.* **huraqb'atzolok**

creek *n.* **ch'ina nima'**

creeper vine *n.* **k'aamal pim**

crescent wrench
   n. **q'otleb'ch'iich'**

crevice *n.* **xtz'iral ch'och'**

crib *n.* **tz'alamch'aat**
   n. **xkoral k'ula'al**

cricket *n.* **chili'**
   n. **sij**
   n. **tz'iray**

crime *n.* **maak**

crippled *adj.* **yeq**

crockery *n.* **k'ila sek'**

crocodile *n.* **mama' ayin**
   n. **xyuwa'il ayin**

crooked *adj.* **b'ach'b'o**
   adj. **b'ech'**
   adj. **jech'**
   adj. **k'onk'o**

          adj. **liq'lo**
          adj. **rok'ox**
          adj. **siq'il**
          adj. **yokos**

cross   *n.* **krus**
          v. **nume'k**
          v. **q'axok**
          v. **raqok**
          n. **xukup**

crossroads *n.* **xxaal b'e**

crosswalk *n.* **xb'eleb'aal poyanam**
          n. **xnumik poyanam**

crouch *v.* **chok'laak**
          v. **chok'ob'ank**
          v. **k'ukub'ank**

crow   *n.* **ch'ejej**
          n. **qoch**

crowbar *n.* **b'oq'leb'ch'iich'**

crowd   *n.* **aj ab'ine'leb'**
          n. **amaq' tenamit**
          n. **k'ehal**
          n. **k'ila poyanam**
          n. **naab'alil**

crown   *n.* **ajawilxoy**

crown (dental)
          n. **ruutz'u'ujinkil**

crucifix *n.* **ch'ina xukup**

crude   *adj.* **chaq re ru**

cruelty *n.* **numlab'al**

crush   *v.* **sob'ok**
          v. **tenok**
          v. **yab'ok**

crutch *n.* **kuutiil**

cry   *n.* **yaab'**
          v. **yaab'ak**

cry out (in pain) *v.* **aylok**

cubby *n.* **xna'aj k'a re ru**

cube   *v.* **oxwahink**
          n. **waqxukuut**

cubit   *n.* **chumay**

cucumber *n.* **pepiin**

cuff   *n.* **ruq'm aq'**
          n. **sa' ruq' aq'**

cultivate *v.* **k'anjelank**

cultural identity *n.* **oxloq' ilob'**

cultural values *n.* **loq'alil na'leb'**

culture *n.* **ch'och'el sululel**
          n. **oxloq'il na'leb'**

cup   *n.* **sek'**
          n. **taas**
          n. **uk'leb'lem**
          n. **wa'leb' sek'**

cupcake *n.* **xelexkaxlanwa**

cure   *v.* **k'irtesink**
          v. **b'anok**

curious *adj.* **aj kayanel**
          adj. **nakayan**

curriculum *n.* **nimk'uub'tzolok**
          n. **xk'ub'laltzolok**

curriculum vitae *n.* **esilnawom**

cursive *n.* **q'inixtz'iib'**

cursor *n.* **eetal**
          n. **numch'o**

curtain *n.* **nimla ramleb'aal t'ikr**

curve   *n.* **ramleb'**
            n. **ramleb' saqen**
curve   *n.* **q'oot**
curved   *adj.* **q'otq'o**
            adj. **q'oot**
curved line *n.* **k'onoljuch'**
cushion   *n.* **sok jolom**
custody   *n.* **kolok**
custom   *n.* **na'leb' xe'toon**
customs   *n.* **yu'aminb'il**
cut   *v.* **kuruk**
            v. **setok**
            v. **yok'ok**
            n. **yok'ol**
cut down   *v.* **jachok**

cut in strips *v.* **jisok**
cutlery   *n.* **kok' ch'iich' re wa'ak**
cutting board *n.* **tz'alamche' re setok**
CV   *n.* **esilnawom**
cyclist   *n agt.* **aj ch'e'ol b'aqlaq ch'iich'**
cylinder   *n.* **b'aral**
            n. **b'olb'o**
cylindrical *adj.* **b'olb'o**
cypress   *n.* **k'isis**
            n. **sipres**
cyst   *n.* **saqijoj**
cytoplasm   *n.* **xya'alna'yu'am**

D - d

daisy   *n.* **markariit**
damn it   *phr.* **ay xkux na'**
damp   *adj.* **t'aqt'aq**
dance   *n.* **xajleb'**
            v. **xajok**
dancer   *n agt.* **aj xajonel**
dandruff   *n.* **salb'a**
danger   *n.* **xiwxiw**
dangerous   *adj.* **xiw xiw**
dark   *adj.* **aak'ab'**
            adj. **moymo**
            adj. **q'ojyin**
            adj. **tuh**
dark green *adj.* **rax moyin**

darkness   *n.* **aak'ab'**
darn   *v.* **xiitink**
dash   *n.* **ch'inaaljuch'**
            n. **ch'inq'ejuch**
dashboard   *n.* **xna'aj eetalil**
date   *n.* **xb'e li po**
date of birth *n.* **xkutankil yo'lajik**
daughter   *n.* **ko'**
            n. **rab'in**
daughter-in-law (of a man or woman) *n.* **alib'**
dawn   *n.* **priim**
day   *n.* **kutan**

day after tomorrow *n.* **kab'ej**

day before yesterday
    n. **kab'ejer**

day of rest *n.* **hilob'aal kutan**

dead *adj.* **kamenaq**

deaf *adj.* **tz'apxik**
    adj. **tz'apyaab'il**

death penalty *n.* **kamk tojb'a maak**
    n. **teneb'anb'ilkamk**

debone *v phr.* **isink b'aq**

debt *n.* **b'ayom**
    n. **k'as**

decade *n.* **lajeeb' hab'**

deceit *n.* **b'alaq'**

December *n.* **tisyemr**
    n. **xkab'aljuhilpo**

decipher *v.* **nawyaalalink**

decipherment *n.* **nawyaalal**

decongestant *n.* **aj tuqub'anel sa'**

decorate *v.* **uutz'u'ujink**

decoration *n.* **ruutz'u'ujil aq'**
    n. **xoy**

decorator *n agt.* **aj uutz'u'ujinel**

decree *n.* **ruq'b'chaq'rab'**

deductive *adj.* **nimajel**

deep *adj.* **cham**

deer *n.* **kej**

defeat *n.* **t'ane'k**
    n. **tz'eqok**

defecate *v.* **k'otak**
    v phr. **tz'eqok ib'**

defend *v.* **kolok**

defendant *n.* **jitb'il**
    n. **q'ab'anb'il**

definitely *adv phr.* **jo'kan b'i'an**

defrost *v phr.* **isink xkehil**

degrees *n.* **b'isketiiq**
    n. **xteram**

degrees Fahrenheit
    n. **parenheitil b'iis**

dejected *adj.* **ch'ina xch'ool**

dejection *n.* **kamenaq xch'ool**

delay *n.* **b'ayjik**
    v. **b'ayok**

delayed *adj.* **xb'ay chaq**

delegate *n.* **ruuchilawab'ej**

delicious *adj.* **sa**

delight *n.* **sahilank**

delighted *adj.* **twulaq chi ru**

delinquent *n agt.* **aj maak chi ru chaq'rab'**

delivery truck *n.* **xraqilal xsa'**

democracy *n.* **junajch'oolej**
    n. **sahilwank**

demon *n.* **anum**
    n. **maa'us**
    n. **tza**

demonstrate *v.* **k'utb'esink**

dendrite *n.* **xchaqijik**

denim *n.* **t'ikr loon**

denominator *n.* **jarjek'il**

dent *v.* **sob'ok**
    n. **sob'olal**

dental assistant *n agt.* **aj tenq'anel risihom uuch e**

dental chair *n.* **chunleb'aal**

dental clinic *n.* **uuch eleb'aal**

dental floss *n.* **noq' re uuch e**

dental instrument *n.* **k'anjeleb'aal ruuch e**

dentist *n agt.* **aj ilol'uuch-e** *n agt.* **aj isihom ruuch e**

dentist office *n.* **uuch eleb'aal**

denture *n.* **pak'b'il ruuch e**

deny *v phr.* **ink'a' xsumenkil** *v.* **jalmuqank**

deodorant *n.* **xsununkil sa' tel**

departing flights information *n.* **esilal re elk**

department store *n.* **mama' rochochil aq'ej** *n.* **nimla k'ayib'aal**

departmental government *n.* **rochoch ruuchilawab'ej**

departure *n.* **elk**

departures *n.* **na'elk**

deposit receipt *n.* **xhuhil li k'uulank**

depressed *adj.* **kamenaq xch'ool**

depression *n.* **lub'k ch'oolej**

depth *n.* **chamal**

descendants *n.* **ralal xk'ajol**

describe *v.* **wech'ok**

description *n.* **wech'ok**

desert *n.* **chaqi ch'och'**

desire *n.* **ajok**

desk *n.* **chunleb'aal** *n.* **tz'iib'leb'meex**

desk mat *n.* **ru meex**

despair *n.* **sapsapink ib'**

dessert *n.* **xtz'aqob' wa'**

destroy *v.* **juk'uk** *v.* **po'ok** *v.* **sachok**

detain *v.* **xaq'ab'ank**

detective *n agt.* **aj tz'ilonel**

detergent *n.* **poqxab'on**

develop photos *v.* **kutanob'resink**

development *n.* **usaak wakliik**

devil *n agt.* **maa'us aj winq** *n.* **tza**

dew *n.* **chu' ke** *n.* **chu'ke** *n.* **k'ajob'**

dextrine *n.* **latztz'in**

diadem *n.* **nat'leb'ismal**

diagnose *v.* **nawrub'elalink**

diagonal *adj.* **salam**

diagram *n.* **raqaxinkil**

dialect *n.* **jalb'esiil'aatin** *n.* **ralab'aatinob'aal**

311

dialectal variety *n.* **xcha'alil aatinob'aal**

dialectology *n.* **nawralab'aatinob'aal**

diameter *n.* **xsa'kotko**

diamond *n.* **lemtz'pek** *n.* **salsookil kaaxukuut** *n.* **xaqamkaaxuk**

diamond-shaped *adj.* **b'arxuk**

diaper *n.* **panyal**

diarrhea *n.* **nume' sa'** *n.* **sa'ej**

diastolic blood pressure *n.* **metz'ew ich'mulej okik'**

dice *n.* **q'aqt** *v phr.* **setok chi kaaxukut**

dicotyledonous seed *n.* **lut-al iyaj**

dictate *v.* **yaab'asink**

dictator *n agt.* **aj taqlanel**

dictionary *n.* **molob'aal aatin** *n.* **sik'leb' aatin** *n.* **xtusulal aatin**

die *v.* **kamk**

dieresis *n.* **luttz'uqyaab'**

diesel *n.* **qishumha'** *n.* **ruk'a ch'iich'** *n.* **xya'al b'eleb'aal** *n.* **xya'al ch'iich'**

difficult *adj.* **ch'a'aj** *adj.* **raasa**

difficulty *n.* **ch'a'ajkil** *n.* **rahilal**

dig *v.* **aq'ink** *v.* **b'ekok** *v.* **pikok**

digestive system *n.* **sooto'y**

digging stick *n.* **awleb'**

digital camera *n.* **ch'eb'il jalam'uuchil**

dignitary *n.* **loq'al**

dignity *n.* **loq'alil**

diligence *n.* **sak'ahil**

diligent *adj.* **sak'a**

dilute *v.* **yuulink**

dime *n.* **lajeb' senta**

dimension *n.* **xnimal**

diner *n.* **wa'leb'aal**

dining room *n.* **wa'leb'aal**

dinosaur *n.* **ayin kaaq**

Dionisio *nick.* **Nich**

diphthong *n.* **kajunajink xna'tz'iib'**

diploma *n.* **eetalhu** *n.* **huraqb'atzolok** *n.* **reetalil tzolom**

dipstick *n.* **xche'el kaxolb' ch'iich'**

direct *v.* **jolomink**

direction *n.* **jayal** *n.* **tiikal**

director *n agt.* **aj k'amolb'e** *n agt.* **aj k'utunel b'e** *n.* **xb'eenil tijonel** dirigible *n.* **pamb'eeresinb'il**

dirt *n.* **tz'ajn**

dirt path *n.* **ch'och'il b'e**

dirt road *n.* **pekilnimb'e**

dirty *adj.* **b'alak'**
    adj. **b'ulux**
    adj. **pes**
    adj. **tz'aj ru**
    adj. **yib'ob'aal ru**

dirty words *n.* **xik' aj aatin**

disappear *v.* **muqunk**
    v. **sachk**

disappointed *adj.* **kosa xch'ool**

disappointment *n.* **rahob'k**

disaster prevention *n.* **kawalil chi ru raaxiik'**

disco *n.* **xajleb'aal**

discover *n.* **na'ok**
    n. **ta'ok**
    n. **tehok ru**

discovery *n.* **na'lenk**

discus throw *n.* **kutuk suriil**

disdain *n.* **xik' ilok**

disease *n.* **yajel**
    n. **yajelil**

disease onset *n.* **xtiklajik li yajel**

disguise *n.* **eetz'aal**
    n. **k'utb'aatal**
    n. **uutz'u'ujinb'il eetz'unk**

disgust *n.* **xik' ilok**

disgusting *adj.* **xa'wil ru**

dish *n.* **pulaat**
    n. **sek'**

dishonest *adj.* **ink'a' us xna'leb'**

dishwasher *n.* **ch'ajleb'aal sek**
    n. **ch'ajleb' sek'**

disillusioned *adj.* **kosa xch'ool**

disinfectant *n.* **re chajok tiqil**
    n. **saqleb'**

disk *n.* **surchoch**
    n. **sur chapleb'aal**

diskette *n.* **chochtz'iib'**

dismay *n.* **yot'ek ch'oolej**

disorganized *adj.* **hirook**
    adj. **tzukinb'il ru**

display *n.* **kaxmu'eetalil**

display case *n.* **xlemul k'ayib'aal**

display shelves *n.* **xna'aj k'ay**

displease *v phr.* **po'ok ch'ool**

disposable *adj.* **tz'eeqel**

disrespectful *adj.* **ink'a' na'oxloq'in**

dissolve *v.* **ha'ob'resink**

distance *n.* **najtil**

distance education *n.* **tijb'ajunesal**

distance or motion particle *part.* **chaq**

distract *v phr.* **jahok u**

distress *n.* **ok k'a'uxl**

distribute *v.* **jek'ok**

distributor *n.* **jek'inel**

district   *n.* **teep**

               n. **xteepal tenamit**

ditch   *n.* **cho'ok jul**

               n. **jul**

               n. **pahok jul**

               n. **roq ha'**

dive   *v.* **muqa'lik**

diverse   *adj.* **k'ilpoyanimil**

diversion   *n.* **ajsink-u**

diversity   *n.* **k'iilayehom b'aanuhom**

divide   *v.* **jachok**

               v. **jek'ink**

divided by   *adj.* **jachinb'il chi**

diving board   *n.* **pisk'leb'aal**

division   *n.* **tas**

               n. **xjek'inkil**

               n. **xtasalal**

division symbol (/)

               n. **reetaljek'ajl**

               n. **reetal jach'ajl**

divisor   *n.* **jeb'ib'aal**

divorce   *n.* **jachkab'al**

               n. **jachok-ib'**

dizziness   *n.* **lub'ik**

dizzy   *adj.* **moymo ru**

do   *v.* **b'aanunk**

do you know each other?

               phr. **ma ak nakenaw eeru**

do you speak English?   *phr.* **ma nakat-aatinak sa' inkles**

do you speak Q'eqchi'?   *phr.* **ma nakat-aatinak sa' q'eqchi'**

dock   *n.* **xaqleb'jukub'**

               n. **xxaqleb'aal jukub'**

doctor   *n agt.* **aj b'anonel**

               n. **loktor**

doctrine   *n.* **tij**

               n. **tzoleb'**

document   *n.* **taqlhu**

               n. **tz'iib'anb'ilhu**

dodge   *v.* **kolok**

dog   *n.* **tz'i'**

doll   *n.* **pak'b'il k'uula'al**

               n. **poy'al**

dolphin   *n.* **q'olxulkar**

domestic departures   *n.* **elk yal sa' xteep tenamit**

dominant   *adj.* **nataqlan**

Domingo   *nick.* **Ku'**

don't forget   *phr.* **mi sach sa' laach'ool**

don't mention it

               phr. **matk'a'uxlak**

don't worry about it

               phr. **matk'a'uxlak**

donkey   *n.* **b'uur**

               n. **xul iiqanel**

door   *n.* **okeb'aal**

               n. **pweert**

               n. **re kab'**

door lock   *n.* **rokeb' xlaawil kab'l**

doorbell   *n.* **b'oqleb'aal**

door-bolt *n.* **k'aan**
    n. **nat'leb'**
doorpost *n.* **champa**
dormitory *n.* **warib'aal**
dormouse *n.* **k'iche' ch'o**
dose *n.* **xb'iisul b'an**
double bed *n.* **nimla ch'aat**
doubt *n.* **kiib'ank ch'ool**
doubt particle *part.* **ta**
dough *n.* **q'em**
dove *n.* **mukuy**
down *adj.* **chi rub'el**
    prep. **taq'a**
downpour *n.* **kawil hab'**
downtown *n.* **xyi tenamit**
dozen *n.* **jun toseen**
dragonfly *n.* **tuulux**
drain *n.* **ha'ha'**
    n. **releb'tz'ajha'**
    n. **roq ha'il tzaj**
drape *n.* **ramleb' saqen**
draw *v.* **jalam'uuchink**
draw water *v.* **lekok**
drawer *n.* **k'uulchob'**
    n. **ralmeex**
drawers *n.* **kaax**
drawstring (for a skirt)
    n. **xk'aamal uuq**
dread *n.* **xiw**
dream *n.* **matk'**
    v. **matk'ek**
    v. **na'uuchik**

dress *n.* **b'estiiy**
    n. **jut-aq'**
    n. **tiqb'al**
dresser *n.* **xna'aj aq'**
dribble *v.* **leeleb'ak**
    n. **xya'al e**
drill *n.* **hopleb'**
    n. **hopleb'che'**
    n. **hopleb'tz'ak**
    v. **hopok**
    n. **k'ob'leb'**
drink *n.* **uk'a'**
    v. **uk'ak**
drinking fountain *n.* **uk'leb'aal**
drinking glass *n.* **b'aas**
    n. **uk'leb'lem**
drip *v.* **okesink**
    v. **rachrotk**
    v. **tz'iltz'otk**
    v. **tz'uqluk**
drive *v.* **b'eeresink**
drive belt *n.* **xk'aamal**
driver *n agt.* **aj
b'eresinelch'iich'**
    n agt. **aj ch'e'ol
ch'iich'**
driver's license *n.* **liseens**
driveway *n.* **rokeb'aal
b'eleb'aal ch'iich'**
drizzle *n.* **kok' ruhil hab'**
drool *n.* **xya'al e**
drop *v.* **b'alq'usink**
    v. **koq'ok**
dropcloth *n.* **mokooch**

drought   *n.* **saq'ehil**
drown   *v.* **jaq'e'k**
  v phr. **ok chi ha'**
  v. **paq'e'k**
  v. **xolk'ok**
drowning   *n.* **paq'e'k**
drug   *n.* **kaanilb'an**
drug dealer   *n agt.* **aj k'ay yib' aj b'an**
drug trafficker   *n agt.* **aj naark**
drug trafficking   *n.* **b'eeresink yib' aj k'ay**
drugstore   *n.* **k'ayib'aal b'an**
  n. **loq'leb'aal b'an**
drum   *n.* **job'wajb'**
  n. **moor**
  n. **nimla tun**
  n. **tamb'or**
  n. **tuntun**

drumstick   *n.* **ruq'wajb'**
drunk   *adj.* **kalajenaq**
dry   *adj.* **chaqi**
  v. **chaqob'resink**
  adj. **xujxuj**
dry cough   *n.* **katzkatz aj ja'aj**
dry skin   *n.* **chaqi ix**
dry spell   *n.* **saq'ehil**
duck   *n.* **patux**
dull   *adj.* **chupchu**
dust   *n.* **poqs**
duty   *n.* **kok'anjel**
duty free shop   *n.* **tiikil k'ayib'aal**
dwarf   *adj.* **met**
dye   *v.* **b'onok**
dysentery   *n.* **kik'sa'**

E - e

eagle   *n.* **t'iw**
ear   *n.* **xik**
ear of corn   *n.* **k'ux**
earache   *n.* **rahil sa' xik**
eardrum   *n.* **xulel xikej**
earlier   *adv.* **toj eq'la**
early   *adj.* **eq'la**
early morning   *n.* **hik'o**
  n. **ik'ek'**
  n. **priim**

earn   *v.* **echanink**
  v phr. **sik'ok ib'**
  v. **tzakink**
earn a living   *v phr.* **numsink kutan**
earphones   *n.* **ab'ib'aal**
  n. **xikelyaab'**
earring   *n.* **ka'xik**
Earth   *n.* **ruuchich'och'**
earthen   *adj.* **pak'b'il**
earthenware   *n.* **ch'och' uk'al**

earthquake *n.* **hiik**

earthworm *n.* **lukum**

earwax *n.* **xk'ot xik**

easel *n.* **xna'aj xhu b'ich**

east *n.* **releb' saq'e**

Easter *n.* **rahil kutan**

easy *adj.* **ink'a' ch'a'aj**
adj. **moko ch'a'aj ta**

easy chair *n.* **nimla tem**

easy-going *adj.* **tuqtu ru**

eat *v.* **tiwok**
v. **tzakank**
v. **wa'ak**
v. **wa'ok**

ebony tree *n.* **q'eqi che'**

ebullience *n.* **woqxeel**

echo *n.* **chaq'om**
n. **sumyaab'**

eclipse *n.* **moyk ru li saq'e**
n. **muqlaak kutan**
n. **naxtiw rib' li saq'e ut li po**
n. **tiwok posaq'e**
n. **xyalojikeb' li saq'e ut li po**

ecological preserve *n.* **kolb'il che'k'aam**

ecological values *n.* **loq'alil sutam**

ecology *n.* **nawyu'amilsutaal**
n. **wanjik**

economics *n.* **sachomj**

ecosystem *n.* **k'uub'wank**

edge *n.* **e**
n. **tzelam**
n. **xmar**

edgy *adj.* **yo xsik**

edit *v phr.* **na'leb'ank tz'iib'**
v. **puktasink**

edition *n.* **xpuktasinkil**

editorial *n.* **k'a'uxlal**

educate *v.* **tijok**

educated *adj.* **tijb'il**

education *n.* **xtijb'al**

educational aims *n.* **xjayalihom tijok**

educational process
n. **ch'olk'anjel tijok**

educators *n.* **xmolamil aj k'utunel**

eel *n.* **k'anti' kar**

effervescent salts *n.* **k'aj atz'am b'an**

effort *n.* **yalok q'e**

egg *n.* **mol**

eggplant *n.* **tzaksu**

egocentrism *n.* **pixilk'a'uxl**

eight *num.* **(8.) waqxaqib'**

eighteen *num.* **(18.) waqxaqlaju**

eighteenth *num.* **(18th.) xwajxaqlajuil**

eighteen-wheeler
n. **motzo'ch'iich'**

eighth *n.* **jun xwaqxaqil**
num. **(8th.) xwajxaq**

eightieth *num.* **(80th.)**
xkaak'aalil

eighty *num.* **(80.) kaak'aal**

eighty-eight *num.* **(88.)**
waqxaqib' ro'k'aal

eighty-five *num.* **(85.) oob'**
ro'k'aal

eighty-four *num.* **(84.) kaahib'**
ro'k'aal

eighty-nine *num.* **(89.) b'eleb'**
ro'k'aal

eighty-one *num.* **(81.) jun**
ro'k'aal

eighty-seven *num.* **(87.) wuqub'**
ro'k'aal

eighty-six *num.* **(86.) waqib'**
ro'k'aal

eighty-three *num.* **(83.) oxib'**
ro'k'aal

eighty-two *num.* **(82.) wiib'**
ro'k'aal

ejaculate *n.* **b'ub'**
v phr. **isink xya'al**
tz'ejwal
n. **lal**

elastic *adj.* **q'ochq'och**
adj. **rinrin**

elastic band *n.* **rinrin**

elation *n.* **anchal xmetzew**

elbow *n.* **ch'uukum**
n. **rit telb'**
n. **rit uq'b'**

elder *n.* **tiix**

elder (male) *n.* **cheekel winq**
n. **mama'**

elect *v.* **xaqab'ank**

election *n.* **b'oot**
n. **sik'ok-u**

electric bill *n.* **xhuhil li saqen**

electric current
n. **metz'ewilxaml**
n. **roqkaxlan xam**

electric energy *n.* **metz'ew**
kaxlan xaml

electric light *n.* **kaxsaqenk**

electric meter
n. **b'isb'ametz'ew**

electric saw *n.* **sirk'arch'iich'**
n. **surjachleb'che'**

electric switch
n. **raqb'ametz'ew**

electric tower *n.* **roqechil k'at**

electrical resistance *n.* **kawsik**
kaxaml
n. **k'uyum k'at**

electrician *n agt.* **aj yiib'om**
saqen

electricity *n.* **elektrisidad**
n. **metz'ewilxaml**
n. **raqmetz'ew**
n. **xaml**

electrocuted *adj.* **xrepomkaaq**

electrode *n.* **latzleb'ch'iich'**

electron *n.* **tiikil kaxlanxaml**

elementary school *n.* **tzoleb'aal**
xb'een na'aj

elements *n.* **xcha'al**

Elena *nick.* **Len**

elephant *n.* **ch'em samxul**
    n. **elepaant**
    n. **samxul**

eleven *num.* **(11.) junlaju**

eleventh *num.* **(11th.) xjunlajuil**

elf *n.* **kok' xul**
    n. **ranumal q'ojyin**
    n. **xilik'**

ellipsis *n.* **oxtz'uq**
    n. **tz'uqux**

elliptical galaxy *n.* **k'on tzoqchahim**

email *n.* **muhiltaql**

email address *n.* **reetalil tz'iib'aal**

embarrassed *adj.* **xutaanal**
    adj. **xutaanaq**

embarrassment *n.* **xutaan**

embassy *n.* **rochochil ab'lil tenamit**

embers *n.* **ruuxam**

embrace *v.* **mek'onk**
    v. **q'alunk**

embryo *n.* **ralyu'amej**

emergency exit *n.* **elkleb'aal sa' junpaat**

emergency preparedness *n.* **kawalil chi ru raaxiik'**

emotion *n.* **numsach'ool**
    n. **sachb'ach'ool**

emotional *adj.* **numsaxch'ool**

emphasis particle *part.* **a'**

emphasize *v.* **ka'jultikank**

empty *adj.* **job'**
    adj. **maak'a' xsa'**
    v. **yamresink**
    adj. **yamyo**

empty set *n.* **yamch'uut**
    n. **yamyookil ch'uut**

enchilada *n.* **k'orkik'xe'**

encounter *n.* **ch'utamil**

encyclopedia
    n. **ch'olob'aalna'leb'**
    n. **na'leb'aal tasal hu**

end *v.* **choyok**
    v. **oso'k**
    v. **raqok**

end (spatial) *n.* **xmar**

end (temporal) *n.* **ch'otonik**
    n. **oso'jik**
    n. **raqik**

end piece *n.* **roq**

ending *n.* **raqtz'aqob'l**

endocrine gland *n.* **jek'cha'alil chi sa'**

endoplasmic reticulum
    n. **k'ub'lb'eeleb'aal na' yu'am**

endorsement *n.* **k'ehok juch'**

enemy *n.* **rajtziil**
    n. **xik'onel**

energetic *adj.* **kaw rib'**

energy *n.* **metz'ew**

engineer *n agt.* **aj seeb'alk'anjel**

engineering *n.* **nawk'anjel**

English *lang.* **inkles**

enjoy *v phr.* **ajsink u**

enjoyment *n.* **sahilank**

enough *pron.* **naab'al**
  adj. **tz'aqal**
  adj. **yo'oon ru**

enter *v.* **ok**

entertain *v phr.* **ajsink u**
  v phr. **jahok u**

entertaining *adj.* **sa' xse'enkil**

entertainment *n.* **ajsink-u**

enthusiasm *n.* **anchal ch'oolej**

entrance *n.* **okeb'aal**

entrust *v.* **ab'enank**
  v. **payok**

entry *n.* **okeb'aal**

entry platform *n.* **ne'b'aal**

envelope *n.* **rix esilhu**
  n. **rix taqlhu**

envious *adj.* **aj kaqal**

environment *n.* **sutam**

envy *n.* **kaqal**
  n. **kaqi atawank**

enzyme *n.* **xpaayil kawub'l**

eon *n.* **q'e**
  n. **q'ekutan**

epidemic *n.* **yajel nab'onok**
  n. **yajel naxb'on rib'**

epidemiologist *n agt.* **aj nawkomonyajel**

epidemiology
  n. **nawkomonyajel**

equality *n.* **juntaq'eetil**

equation *n.* **juntaq'eetin k'anjel'ajl**
  n. **sumch'a'ajkilal**

equator *n.* **q'eq'ookil eetalil**

equilibrium *n.* **tuqtuukil**

equinox *n.* **xtuqlajik q'e**

equity *n.* **juntaq'eetil**

equivocal particle *part.* **na**

era *n.* **q'e**
  n. **q'ekutan**

erase *v.* **b'orok**
  v. **sachok**

erased *adj.* **b'orb'il**

eraser *n.* **b'orleb'**
  n. **masleb'**
  n. **sachleb'**

erection *n.* **roq tz'ik**

erode *v.* **ju'e'k**
  v. **uq'e'k**

erosion *n.* **uq'e'k**
  n. **xch'ajom**

errand *n.* **taqlil**

error *n.* **paaltil**
  n. **sachalkil**
  n. **sachk**

eruption *n.* **xa'awilk'u**

escalator *n.* **metz'ewil'eeb'**
  n. **raqmetz'eweb'**
  n. **raq'metz'ewanb'il eeb'**

etc. *adv.* **utwchx**

etcetera *adv.* **utwchx**

eternity *n.* **chalen q'e kutan**

ethics   *n.* **tiikalil**
           n. **tiikil loq'alil**
ethnic group   *n.* **poyanamilal**
           n. **xpaayil tenamitil**
ethnicity   *n.* **ralch'och'il**
           n. **xch'uutulal ilob'**
ethnolinguistics
           n. **nawpoyaatinob'aa**
           l
etymology   *n.* **xxe'ilal**
eukaryote   *n.* **tz'aqalna'yu'am**
Europe   *n.* **junpak'alpalaw**
Eustachian tube   *n.* **numleb'**
           yaab'ej
evening   *n.* **chi q'eq**
           n. **q'ojyin**
ever   *adv phr.* **sa' jun sut**
every week   *adv phr.* **rajlal**
           xamaan
everything   *adj.* **chi junil**
everywhere   *prep.* **yalaq chi b'ar**
evidence   *n.* **eetalil maak**
evolutionary psychology
           n. **nawk'iijikch'ool**
ewe   *n.* **karneer**
exactly   *adv phr.* **jo'kan tz'aqal**
exam   *n.* **tz'ilb'a'ix**
           n. **tz'ilool'ix**
           n. **yalb'a'ix**
examination   *n.* **tz'ilb'a'ix**
           n. **tz'ilool'ix**
           n. **yalb'a'ix**
examine   *v.* **ilok**
           v. **tz'ilok-ix**

example   *n.* **reetalil**
exchage (gifts)   *v.* **sumsihink**
exchage (words)   *v.* **sumchi'ib'k**
excited   *adj.* **rataw chi us**
excitement   *n.* **anchal ch'oolej**
exclamation point (!)
           n. **reetalsachb'ach'o**
           olej
excuse me   *phr.* **chinaakuy**
execution   *n.* **xb'aanunkil**
executive power   *n.* **xwankilal**
           b'aanunel
exercise   *v phr.* **ajsink u li**
           tib'elej
           v. **kawresink**
exhaust pipe   *n.* **releb'aalsib'**
exhort   *v phr.* **patz'ok**
           b'aanunk
exist   *v.* **yo'laak**
exit   *n.* **elkleb'aal**
exocrine gland   *n.* **jek'cha'alil**
           chi rix
exosphere   *n.* **raq xtasalil'iq'**
expand   *v.* **yu'uk ru**
expense   *n.* **sachom**
expensive   *adj.* **terto xtz'aq**
export   *v.* **ab'lilk'ayink**
           n. **taqlilk'ay**
exportation   *n.* **taqlilk'ay**
extension   *n.* **ruq'il**
extension cord   *n.* **xk'aamal**
           saqen

extensive   *adj.* **b'ayk**
            adj. **makach'in**
exterior   *adj.* **chi rix**
extinguish   *v.* **chupuk**
extortionist   *n agt.* **aj b'alaq'**
extracter   *n.* **tz'ob'leb'**
extraterrestrial
            n. **maaruuchich'och'**
            n. **maawa' re**
            ruchich'och'
extrovert   *adj.* **nache'ch'ot**

eye   *n.* **sa' u**
      n. **xnaq' u**
      n. **xnaq' uhej**
eye drops   *n.* **b'an re naq' u**
            n. **tz'uqb'il b'an re sa'**
            u
eye inflammation   *n.* **xkuntz'i'**
eyebrow   *n.* **maatzab' u**
eyedropper   *n.* **tz'uqleb' b'an**
eyelash   *n.* **rismal u**
eyelid   *n.* **rix u**
eyewear shop   *n.* **sa' uleb'aal**

F - f

fable   *n.* **eek'anb'iltz'iib'**
face   *n.* **u**
       n. **uhej**
       n. **xnaq' u**
facing   *prep.* **chi ru**
facing up   *prep.* **pak'po**
factor   *n.* **roqel**
faculty   *n.* **xmolamil aj**
          k'utunel
fail   *v.* **tz'eqok**
faint   *v.* **saqb'yino'k**
fainting spell   *n.* **lub'k**
               n. **saqb'yino'k**
fair   *n.* **nimq'e**
fairy   *n.* **kok' xul**
        n. **ranumal q'ojyin**
        n. **xilik'**

faith   *n.* **paab'aal**
faithful   *adj.* **aj paab'anel**
           adj. **tiik xch'ool**
fake   *v phr.* **b'aanunk ib'**
fall   *v.* **sob'e'k**
       v. **tob'b'ak**
       n. **t'ane'k**
       v. **t'ane'k**
fall (season)   *n.* **otoony**
               n. **xraqik hab'alq'e**
fall in love   *v.* **payok**
fall sick   *v.* **t'anliik**
fallopian tube   *n.* **xnumleb'**
               iyajiil
false ceiling   *n.* **kaxlankaq'**
falsehood   *n.* **tik'ti'**
fame   *n.* **ka'xaqab'aal**

familiar   *adj.* **na'no ru**
family   *n.* **junkab'al**
family chores   *n.* **teneb'anb'il sa' junkab'lal**
family services   *n.* **xkolb'al rix junkab'al**
family tree   *n.* **reetalil iyajil**
famine   *n.* **we'ej**
fan   *n.* **apusinel na'ajej**
    n. **apuul**
    n. **kaxwaal**
    n. **waal**
    v. **waalesink**
fan belt   *n.* **xtaab'il xsa'**
far   *adj.* **najt**
far from   *adv phr.* **najt xk'atq**
fare   *n.* **pasaaj**
farewell   *n.* **chaq'rab'ink**
farm   *n.* **loq'b'ilch'och'**
    n. **rochoch ketomq**
farm animals   *n.* **ketomq**
farmer   *n agt.* **aj awinel**
    n agt. **aj ilol xna'aj ketomq**
    n agt. **aj k'aleb'aal**
    n agt. **aj k'alom**
farming   *n.* **xk'anjelankil li ch'och'**
fart   *n.* **kis**
    v. **kisik**
fashion designer   *n agt.* **aj yib'anel eetalil aq'**
fast   *v phr.* **ayuunink rix**
    v phr. **kuyuk sa'**

    n. **kuyuk sa'**
    adj. **paynum**
fastener   *n.* **jit'leb'**
    n. **kotoxch'iich'**
fat   *n.* **manteek**
    adj. **nim xtib'el**
    n. **olb'**
    adj. **t'inis**
    adj. **t'onos**
    n. **yolq'em**
fat tissue   *n.* **ch'utq'ooq cha'al**
father   *n.* **taat**
    n. **yuwa'**
    n. **yuwa'b'ej**
father's sister   *n.* **ranab' xyuwa'**
father-in-law (of a man)
    n. **xyuwa' ixaqil**
father-in-law (of a woman)
    n. **xyuwa' b'eelom**
fathom   *n.* **moqoj**
    n. **q'aal**
fatty meat   *n.* **k'ook'**
faucet   *n.* **teeleb'ha'**
    n. **xlaawil ha'**
    n. **xteeb'al ha'**
    n. **yaaw**
fault   *n.* **maak**
fault (geologic)   *n.* **uq'e'k**
fauna   *n.* **ch'uuxul**
    n. **puukalxul**
favor   *n.* **usilal**
fax   *n.* **anum ch'iich'**
    n. **muhil'esil**
    n. **num'esil**
fax machine   *n.* **anum ch'iich'**

fear   *n.* **xiw**

feather   *n.* **k'uuk'um**
            n. **rismal xul**
            n. **rismal xxik'**
            n. **xik'**

February   *n.* **pewreer**
            n. **xkab'ilpo**

Federico   *nick.* **Liik**

feed   *v.* **tzakank**

feed tray   *n.* **b'ateey**

feel   *v.* **ch'e'ok**

feeling   *n.* **eek'ahom**
            n. **eek'aal**
            n. **eek'ob'aal**

feet   *n.* **oq**
            n. **oqej**

felines   *n.* **aj ixi'jeb'**

female   *adj.* **ixq**

females   *n.* **ixqilal**

femininity *n.* **ixqilal**

femur   *n.* **b'aq'el'a'**

fence   *n.* **koral**

fence gate *n.* **re b'e**

ferment   *v.* **ch'amok'**

fermented drink   *n.* **b'oj**

fermented mush drink
            n. **ch'amb'ul**

fern   *n.* **xxaq pim**

ferocity   *n.* **k'utuk josq'il**

Ferris wheel   *n.* **kotkookil
            b'atz'uul**

ferry   *n.* **aj iiqom**
            n. **jukub'iiq**

fertilizer *n.* **q'em**
            n. **raxonb'an**
            n. **xq'emal ru li
            ch'och'**
            n. **xq'emulch'och'**
            n. **xtzakahemq
            ch'och'**

fetus   *n.* **alk'uula'al**

fever   *n.* **kaqi yajel**
            n. **k'ehok tiq**
            n. **tiq**

few   *pron.* **ink'a' k'i**
            adj. **kach'in**

field   *n.* **awib'aal**
            n. **awleb'aal**
            n. **k'al**
            n. **k'aleb'aal**
            n. **neb'aal**
            n. **xoral**

fieldworker   *n agt.* **aj k'aleb'aal**

fifteen   *num.* **(15.) o'laju**

fifteenth   *num.* **(15th.) ro'lajuil**

fifth   *num.* **(5th.) ro'**

fifth grade   *n.* **ro' na'aj**

fiftieth   *num.* **(50th.) xlajee
            roxk'aalil**

fifty   *num.* **(50.) lajeeb'
            roxk'aal**

fifty cents   *n.* **jun tuxtun**

fifty-eight   *num.* **(58.)
            waqxaqlaju roxk'aal**

fifty-five   *num.* **(55.) o'laju
            roxk'aal**

fifty-four   *num.* **(54.) kaalaju
            roxk'aal**

fifty-nine *num.* **(59.) b'elelaju roxk'aal**

fifty-one *num.* **(51.) junlaju roxk'aal**

fifty-seven *num.* **(57.) wuqlaju roxk'aal**

fifty-six *num.* **(56.) waqlaju roxk'aal**

fifty-three *num.* **(53.) oxlaju roxk'aal**

fifty-two *num.* **(52.) kab'laju roxk'aal**

fig *n.* **iko**

fight *v.* **ch'e'ok**
v. **yalok**

fighter *n agt.* **aj pleet**

figure *n.* **eetalil**

figures *n.* **eetalilatq**

filament (flower) *n.* **roq xwinkil atz'um**

file *n.* **ji'leb'**
n. **ji'leb'ch'iich'**
n. **k'uulhu**
n. **xokleb'**
v. **xokok**
v. **ji'ok**

fill *v.* **b'utuk**
v. **nujab'resink**

filling (dental) *n.* **b'utb'il uuch e**

film *n.* **eek'mu**
n. **jalam'uuch**
n. **q'och-eetalil**

filth *n.* **tz'ajn**

fin *n.* **xik'**

final *adj.* **ch'otonel**

finally *adv.* **retal**
adv phr. **toj reetal**

find *v.* **tawok**

fine *n.* **muult**
adj. **q'unq'un ru**
n. **tojl**
n. **tojmaak**

finger *n.* **ru'uj uq'**

fingernail *n.* **ixi'ij**

fingerprint *n.* **ru'uj uq'b'**

finish *v.* **choyok**
v. **raqok**

fire *n.* **xam**

fire brigade *n agt.* **aj ch'upul xaml**

fire extinguisher *n.* **chupleb'xaml**

fire truck *n.* **pujha'nel ch'iich'**
n. **tz'ub'pajha'**

firearm *n.* **puub'**

firefly *n.* **mams**
n. **xamxul**

fireman *n agt.* **aj chupulxam**
n agt. **aj tenq' sa' li raxiik'**

fireplace *n.* **k'ub'**
n. **xna'aj xam**

firewood *n.* **kaqcha**
n. **si'**

fireworks *n.* **jutzutzu**

first *num.* **(1st.) xb'een**

first aid *n.* **ramb'al ru yajel**

325

first aid kit *n.* **xna'aj b'an**

first grade *n.* **xb'een na'aj**

first of all *adv phr.* **xb'een wa**

first-born *n.* **xb'een alal**

fish *v phr.* **chapok kar**
n. **kar**
v. **karib'k**
n. **karil**
v. **karink**

fish for shrimp *v.* **k'oxib'k**

fish net *n.* **ch'antun**
n. **soq' re karab'k**
n. **xsokilkar**
n. **yooy**

fish scale *n.* **pati kar**

fish tank *n.* **nimla xna'ajkar**

fish trap *n.* **ra'l kar**
n. **traamp**

fishbowl *n.* **xna'ajkar**

fisherman *n agt.* **aj kar**

fishhook *n.* **chapleb' kar**
n. **kuux re karab'k**
n. **ra'leb'kar**

fishing line *n.* **kordel**
n. **k'aam**

fishing net *n.* **yooy**

fishmonger *n agt.* **aj k'ay kar**

fist *n.* **moch'**

five *num.* **(5.) oob'**

five cents *n.* **oob' senta**

five hundred *n.* **o'k'aal xkab' roq'ob'**

five quetzals *n.* **oob' ketzal**

fix *v.* **k'uub'ank**
v. **yiib'ank**

flag *n.* **lakaam**
n. **q'uq'il t'ikr**

flagpole *n.* **roqechal q'uq'il t'ikr**

flame *n.* **raq'xam**

flamingo *n.* **kaxjukin**
n. **kaxsaq eknil**

flannel *n.* **q'unil t'ikr**

flash *n.* **repsaqenk**

flashlight *n.* **kaxchaj**

flat *adj.* **perpo**
adj. **ruutaq'a**
adj. **tach'to**

flat figures *n.* **helhookil eetalilatq**

flattering compliment
n. **xulil'aatin**

flatulence *n.* **kis**

flavor *n.* **sahil**

flea *n.* **k'aq**
n. **uk'**

flee *v.* **eelelik**

flesh *n.* **tib'**
n. **tib'elej**
n. **tz'ej**

flight attendant *n agt.* **aj k'anjel sa' so'sol ch'iich'**

flint *n.* **tok'**

flip *v.* **suurisink**

flipchart *n.* **b'alq'hu**

flirtatious remark *n.* **xulil'aatin**

float   v. **pamamnak**

flood   n. **b'ut**

floor   n. **ch'och'**
           n. **ru ch'och'**
           n. **ru tz'ak**

floppy disk   n. **chochtz'iib'**
           n. **ululil xokleb'**
           n. **xna'aj xokleb'**

flora   n. **puukalche'k'aam**

florist   n. **k'ayib'aal uutz'u'uj**

floss   n. **noq' re uuch e**

flour   n. **k'aj**
           n. **k'ajil kaxlanwa**
           n. **xpoqsil kaxlanwa**

flour (wheat)   n. **xk'aj ariin**

flow   v phr. **yo i roq**

flower   n. **atz'um**
           v. **atz'umak**
           n. **uutz'u'uj**

flower bed   n. **ruutz'uujil kab'l**

flower bouquet   n. **junq'aal uutz'u'uj**

flower carpet   n. **ruutz'u'ujil ru b'e**

flower garden   n. **xna'aj uutz'u'uj**

flower petal   n. **xcha'al uutz'u'uj**
           n. **xxaq xcha'al uutzu'uj**

flower shop   n. **k'ayib'aal uutz'u'uj**

flower vase   n. **na'aj uutz'u'uj**

flowerbed   n. **xna'aj uutz'u'uj**

flowerpot   n. **xna'aj uutz'u'uj**

flu   n. **jolomb'ej**
           n. **ojb'**

fluorescent marker
           n. **lemtz'juch'leb'aal**

flute   n. **xolb'**

fly   v. **purik**
           v. **rupik**
           v. **waalunk**

fly (insect)   n. **b'ujl**
           n. **saqxul**
           n. **suq**
           n. **utz'**

fly (of pants)   n. **re xch'ool wex**

flyer   n. **esilhu**

flying serpent   n. **rax k'aj**

flying squirrel   n. **rupkuk**

foal   n. **ral kawaay**

foam   n. **woqx**

fog   n. **sujew**
           n. **tuntunkil choq**

foggy   adj. **choq ru**

fold   v. **b'asok**
           v. **mochok**
           n. **xb'asb'al**

folder   n. **tahu**
           n. **xna'aj hu**
           n. **xokleb' hu**

follow   v. **taaqenk**

fondness   n. **q'unal**

food   n. **tib'el wa**
           n. **tzakahem**
           n. **wa'al**

foolish   adj. **jip**

foolishness *n.* **eetil**

foosball table *n.* **b'olotz meex**

foot   *n.* **oq**
           n. **oqej**

footballer *n agt.* **aj b'atz'unel
           b'olotz oq**
           n agt. **aj b'olotz**

footboard *n.* **roq ch'aat**

footbridge *n.* **q'axleb'aal**

footprint *n.* **nums**
           n. **oqej**
           n. **oqil**

for   *adv.* **choq' re**
           adv. **re**

for a long time *adj.* **naab'al
           honal**

for what? *interr.* **k'a'ru aj e**

force   *n.* **metz'ew**

forearm   *n.* **xnaq' telb'**
           n. **xtoon telb'**

forehead *n.* **peekem**
           n. **u**

foreign   *adj.* **mu'us**

foreign language *n.* **ab'lil
           aatinob'aal**
           lang. **kaxlanchi'**
           lang. **kaxlan aatin**

foreign particle *part.* **kax**

foreigner *n.* **ab'lil poyanam**
           n. **aj mu's**
           n. **kaxlan winq**

forest   *n.* **k'iche'**
           n. **ninqi che'**

forge   *v phr.* **jalok ru yaal**

forger   *n agt.* **aj jalonel**

forgery   *n.* **jalok ru yaal**

forget   *v phr.* **sachk sa'
           ch'ool**

forgetful *adj.* **nasach sa'
           xch'ool**

forgive   *v phr.* **kuyuk maak**

forgive me *phr.* **chaakuy
           inmaak**

fork   *n.* **chikleb'**
           n. **orkeet**
           n. **pikleb'**
           n. **rastriiy**
           n. **xokleb'**

forked branch *n.* **ra' che'**
           n. **xaal che'**

form   *n.* **chankatq ru**
           n. **jultikaal**
           v. **pak'ok**
           n. **rilb'al**

former times *n.* **najter q'e
           kutan**

formula   *n.* **b'ehul**
           n. **k'ucha'alk'anjel**

formulation *n.* **xjultikankil**

fornicate *v.* **yumb'eetak**

fornicator *n agt.* **aj yumb'eet**

fortieth   *num.* **(40th.)
           xka'k'aalil**

fortune teller *n agt.* **aj q'e**

forty   *num.* **(40.) ka'k'aal**

forty-eight *num.* **(48.)
           waqxaq'ib' roxk'aal**

forty-five *num.* **(45.) oob' roxk'aal**

forty-four *num.* **(44.) kaahib' roxk'aal**

forty-nine *num.* **(49.) b'eleb' roxk'aal**

forty-one *num.* **(41.) jun roxk'aal**

forty-seven *num.* **(47.) wukub' roxk'aal**

forty-six *num.* **(46.) waq'ib' roxk'aal**

forty-three *num.* **(43.) oxib' roxk'aal**

forty-two *num.* **(42.) wiib' roxk'aal**

fountain *n.* **pak'yu'amha'**
n. **releb'aal ha'**
n. **yo'leb'aal ha'**
n. **yo'lejeb'ha'**

four *num.* **(4.) kaahib'**

four days ago *n.* **kaajer**

four hundred *n.* **jun oq'ob'**

four thousand *n.* **lajeeb' oq'ob'**

fourteen *num.* **(14.) kaalaju**

fourteenth *num.* **(14th.) xkaalajuil**

fourth *num.* **(4th.) xka**

fourth grade *n.* **xka na'aj**

fowl *n.* **ketomq**
n. **tz'ik**

fox *n.* **aj ow**
n. **yak**

fraction *n.* **jachb'il'ajl**

fractional *n.* **jachlil'ajl**

fractionally *adv.* **chi jachal**

fracture *n.* **toqol**

fragment *v.* **murink**

fragrant *adj.* **k'ajo' sununkil**
adj. **sununk**

fraud *n.* **b'alaq'**

freckle *n.* **k'inich**

free *v.* **ach'ab'ank**

free agency *n.* **xch'ool nataqlank re**
n. **xtaql xch'ool**

free will *n.* **xch'ool nataqlank re**
n. **xtaql xch'ool**

freeze *v.* **keho'k**

freezer *n.* **kehob'resib'aal**
n. **saqb'achleb'aal**
n. **xna'aj elaat**

French bread
n. **atz'aminb'ilkaxlan wa**
n. **siip kaxlan wa**

french fries *n.* **kilinb'il paaps**

French toast *n.* **tz'aab'il kaxlan wa**

frequency *n.* **kok'ajil xsa'**
n. **xjartawahil**

frequently *adv phr.* **junes yo**
adv phr. **rajlal rajlal**

fricative *n.* **jilb'il yaab'**
n. **nut'b'il yaab'**

Friday *n.* **b'yers**

fridge *n.* **kehob'resilb'aal**
    n. **keeleb'aal**
    n. **reepri**
fried *adj.* **kilinb'il**
fried chicken *n.* **kilinb'il kaxlan**
friend *n.* **amiiw**
    n. **lo'y**
friendly *adj.* **sa na'aatinak**
friendship *n.* **lo'yil**
fright *n.* **xib'esink**
    n. **xiw**
frog *n.* **amoch**
    n. **kaq ra'**
    n. **pelpel**
from *prep.* **chalen**
    prep. **re**
    part. **aj**
from now on *adv.* **chalen anaqwan**
front yard *n.* **neb'aal kab'l**
frost *n.* **sujen**
fruit *n.* **ki'il q'een**
    n. **ru**
    n. **ru che'**
    n. **saa'us**
    n. **u**
fruit of the cactus *n.* **ru peetaq**
fruit shop *n.* **k'ayib'aal saa'us**
fruit slices *n.* **tz'aab'il ki'ik q'een**
frustration *n.* **ch'inaak ch'ool**
fry *v.* **k'ilink**
    v. **pomok**
    v. **sisank**

frying pan *n.* **k'ileb'aal**
    n. **k'ilolb'**
    n. **xartin**
fuel *n.* **ruk'a ch'iich'**
    n. **xya'al b'eleb'aal**
    n. **xya'al ch'iich'**
full *adj.* **b'ut'**
    adj. **b'uuy**
    adj. **nujenaq**
    adj. **tz'ajtz'otk**
full moon *n.* **tiixil po**
    n. **xoronikpo**
fumigation pump *n.* **xkukil li puutzink**
fumigator *n.* **xkukil li puutzink**
fun *n.* **ajsib'aal'u**
    n. **hoonalhilaal**
    n. **xhoonal asjsink-u**
function *n.* **xk'anjel**
fundamental *n.* **k'ub'el**
funnel *n.* **b'ut'leb'**
funny *adj.* **sa' xse'enkil**
fur *n.* **ta**
fur coat *n.* **tz'uumil chakeet**
furious *adj.* **yo xjosq'il**
furrow *n.* **ch'ol**
    n. **cho'ok jul**
    n. **pahok jul**
    n. **qeer**
    n. **suurk**
    n. **suut**
    n. **tzol**
fury *n.* **josq'il**
fussy *adj.* **wech' re**

future   *n.* **chaalel**   future tense *n.* **moqonil'uxk**
           n. **moqon**

G - g

galaxy   *n.* **saqonaqilchahim**   garlic   *n.* **anx**
          n. **tzoqchahim**   *n.* **jolom q'een**

gallery   *n.* **chinamiit**   Garífuna *lang.* **karifuna**

gallon   *n.* **ch'inapuum**   gas   *n.* **humb'ookilha'**
          n. **ho'meet**   *n.* **jumha'elch'iich'**
          n. **kalon**   *n.* **ruk'a ch'iich'**
          n. **yook**   *n.* **xya'al b'eleb'aal**

gambling *n.* **b'uulik**   *n.* **xya'al ch'iich'**

game   *n.* **b'atz'uul**   gas dispenser *n.* **ralpuub'**
          n. **xul k'iche'**   gas pump *n.* **xkumb'il ruk'a'**

gangway   *n.* **q'axleb'aal**   **poych'iich'**

garage   *n.* **xna'aj b'eleb'aal** gas station
          ch'iich'   *n.* **k'ayib'aalhumb'oo**
                                               kilha'
garbage   *n.* **mul**   *n.* **rochochil ruk'a'**
          n. **mulel**   **poych'iich'**

garbage can *n.* **xchakachil**   gaseous   *adj.* **b'ookil**
          mul
          n. **xna'aj mul**   gases   *n.* **b'ookatq**

garbage collector *n agt.* **aj xokol** gasoline *n.* **humb'ookilha'**
          mul   *n.* **jumha'elch'iich'**
                                             n. **ruk'a ch'iich'**
garbanzo beans *n.* **karwans**   *n.* **xya'al b'eleb'aal**
                                             n. **xya'al ch'iich'**
garden   *n.* **kok'awinq**
          n. **xna'aj kok'awinq** gate   *n.* **okeb'aal**

garden shed *n.* **na'aj re**   *n.* **pweert**
          muhenk   *n.* **re kab'**

gardener *n agt.* **aj ilol uutz'u'uj** gather *v.* **molob'ank**

garden-house *n.* **tz'alam**   *v.* **molok**
                                               n. **xyuch'inkil xsa'**

gauze   *n.* **kok' t'ikr**
           n. **k'aj sut**
           n. **k'aj t'ikr**
gearshift *n.* **k'ub'**
gender   *n.* **chankilal**
gender equality *n.* **xjuntaq'eetil xwinqul**
generalize *v.* **junajink**
generation *n.* **puukalil**
generosity *adj.* **usilalch'ool**
genitals *n.* **cha'alil**
genitals (female) *n.* **b'o**
           n. **b'uuy**
           n. **k'oopopo'**
genitals (male) *n.* **tz'ejwal**
genius   *n.* **numseeb'**
genre   *n.* **chankilal**
gentle   *adj.* **q'un xch'ool**
geography
           n. **k'utleb'ruuchich'och'**
           n. **xcha'alil ruuchich'och'**
geometric figure *n.* **b'isb'il eetalil**
geometric shape *n.* **b'isb'il eetalil**
get   *v.* **k'uluk**
           v. **tawok**
get better *v.* **usaak**
get dressed *v phr.* **k'ehok aq'**
get drunk *v.* **kaltesink**
get lost   *v.* **sachk**

get ready *v.* **kawresink**
get sad   *v phr.* **raho'k xch'ool**
get sick   *v.* **yajerk**
get tired *v.* **lub'k**
get undressed *v phr.* **isink aq'**
get up   *v.* **wakliik**
ghost   *n.* **anumal**
giant   *adj.* **nimnim**
           adj. **tutz'tu**
           adj. **yak'ach**
gift   *n.* **maatan**
           n. **si**
gill   *n.* **xoob'**
gills   *n.* **pospo'ykar**
ginger   *n.* **xanxiiwr**
giraffe   *n.* **yak'achkej**
girl   *n.* **ch'ina ixqa'al**
           n. **saaj ixqa'al**
girlfriend *n.* **suunal**
           n. **suunuhom**
           n. **xsum aam**
           n. **xsum ch'ool**
give   *v.* **k'ehok**
           v. **q'axtesink**
give alms *v phr.* **k'ehok limoox**
give back *v.* **q'ajsink**
give birth *v.* **alank**
           v. **yo'laak**
give it a shot *v phr.* **yalok ch'ool**
give one's opinion *v phr.* **aatinak chi rix**
give up   *v phr.* **q'axtesink ib'**
give way   *v phr.* **k'ehok numik**

glacial erosion *n.* **xch'ajom saqb'ach**

glacial zone *n.* **keehil siraal**

glacier *n.* **pekilha' ch'och'**

glad *adj.* **sa xch'ool**

gladiola *n.* **karayool**
n. **xb'aar li qaawa'**

gland *n.* **xtz'aqob'cha'al**

glass *n.* **b'otb'okilsek'**
n. **lem**
n. **meet**
n. **saqenlem**
n. **uk'leb'lem**

glass cabinet *n.* **xlemul k'ayib'aal**

glasses *n.* **anyooj**
n. **lem'u**

globalize *v.* **junajink**

globe *n.* **reetalil ru chi ch'och'**
n. **xt'oram ruuchich'och'**

gloom *n.* **rahil ch'oolejil**

gloomy *adj.* **ra xch'ool**

glossary *n.* **ch'olob'aal'aatin**
n. **tusleb' aatin**

glottal *n.* **nat'yaab'**

glottalization *n.* **nat'yaab'**

glove *n.* **b'atb'a uq'**
n. **xta uq'**

glue *n.* **letzleb'**
v. **letzok**

glyph *n.* **eetaltz'iib'**
n. **mayertz'iib'**

gnat *n.* **k'uxuk**
n. **suq**

gnaw *v.* **hot'ok**

go *v.* **xik**

go astray *v.* **sachk**

go broke *v.* **neb'a'o'k**

go down *v.* **kub'eek**

go home *v.* **q'ajk**

go horseback riding *v phr.* **taqe'k chi rix kawaay**

go hungry *v.* **we'ejink**

go out *v.* **elk**

go up *v.* **taqe'k**

goal *n.* **ahom**
n. **jayalihom**
n. **k'as**

goalie *n agt.* **aj ramonel b'olotz**

goalkeeper *n agt.* **aj ramonel b'olotz**

goalposts *n.* **okeb'aal b'olotz**

goat *n.* **chib'aat**
n. **yuk**

god *n.* **qaawa'**
n. **tyox**

god's will *n.* **xtaql xch'ool li tyox**

goddaughter *n.* **waltatyox ixq**

goddess *n.* **qaana'**

godfather *n.* **yuwa'chinb'ej**

godmother *n.* **na'chinb'ej**

godson *n.* **waltatyox winq**

goiter   *n.* **b'uq' ja'aj**

gold   *n.* **ka'xik**
            n. **q'anich'iich'**
            n. **q'an pwaq**

golden   *adj.* **nalemtz'un**
            adj. **q'anjorin**

gonorrhea   *n.* **pojkun**

good   *adj.* **chaab'il**
            adj. **q'axal us**
            adj. **us**

good luck   *n.* **rax muhel**

good luck! *phr.* **us chat-elq**

good night (plural)
            phr. **chexwarq**

good value *n.* **chaab'il xtz'aq**

goodbye   *v.* **chaq'rab'ink**
            phr. **inwan b'i'**

goods   *n.* **k'alomal**

goose   *n.* **ch'onpatz**
            n. **kaans**
            n. **t'int'ookil patux**

gopher   *n.* **b'a**

gored   *adj.* **xeq'el**

gorge   *n.* **xyanq tzuul**

gorilla   *n.* **mama' max**

gossip   *n.* **yoob'ank aatin**

gourd   *n.* **joom**
            n. **k'um**
            n. **seel**

govern   *v.* **awab'ejink**
            v. **poopirk**
            v. **taqlank**

government *n.* **awab'ej**
            n. **awab'ejilal**

government identification
            n. **huxaqalil**
            n. **hu chi ru chaq'rab'**
            n. **xaaqalhu**
            n. **xhuhul tenamit**

governor   *n.* **ruuchilawab'ej**

grade   *n.* **rajlil ketom**
            n. **xtz'aq**

grain   *n.* **t'orol**

gram   *n.* **xna'b'iisaalob'**

grammar
            n. **xtuqlal'aatinob'aal**

granary   *n.* **rochochil hal**
            n. **xna'aj hal**

grandchild *n.* **iib'ej**

grandchildren *n.* **wiheb'**

granddaughter *n.* **ixqi i**
            n. **ii**

grandfather *n.* **mama'**
            n. **mel**
            n. **yuwa'chin**

grandmother *n.* **ixa'an**
            n. **na'chin**

grandparents *n.* **mel**
            n. **yuwa'chinb'ejeb'**

grandson   *n.* **ii**
            n. **teelom i**

grape   *n.* **kaxlant'usub'**
            n. **t'usub'**
            n. **uuw**

grapefruit *n.* **toronj**

graph paper
            n. **kaxukuutinb'ilhu**

grasp   *v.* **chapok**

grass   *n.* **aq**
          n. **ichaj**
          n. **pach'aya'**
grasshopper   *n.* **aj pitz'**
          n. **chili'**
          n. **raxq'een**
          n. **saak'**
grate   *v.* **jichok**
grater   *n.* **jisleb'**
grave   *n.* **julel kamenaq**
gravel   *n.* **k'ajpek**
          n. **k'uhilpek**
gravestone   *n.* **eetalkamenaq**
gravity   *n.* **xmetz'ew raalal**
          n. **xmetz'ew xyi li ruchich'och'**
gravy   *n.* **xya'al tib'**
gray   *adj.* **chaacha**
gray hairs   *n.* **saqi ismal**
grease   *n.* **manteek**
          n. **olb'**
          n. **yolq'em**
greasy   *adj.* **b'ik'b'ik'**
great grandchild   *n.* **mam**
great grandfather   *n.* **mel**
great!   *phr.* **chaaab'il**
great-grandchild   *n.* **xikin i**
great-grandfather   *n.* **xikin mama'**
          n. **xna'chin inyuwa'**
great-grandmother   *n.* **xikin xa'an**
          n. **xna'chin inna'**
greatness   *n.* **nimal**

greedy   *adj.* **aj atawanel**
green   *adj.* **rax**
green bean   *n.* **k'aam keenq'**
          n. **q'ap**
greengrocer   *n.* **k'ayib'aal xaq ut xe' pim**
greenish   *adj.* **raxmo'in**
greet   *v phr.* **k'ehok sahil ch'ool**
          v phr. **sahil ch'oolib'k**
greeting   *n.* **sahil ch'oolej**
grid   *n.* **kaxukutinb'il**
grief   *n.* **k'a'uxl**
          n. **rahil ch'oolej**
grill   *n.* **pomleb'**
          v. **pomok**
grilled   *adj.* **pomb'il**
grilled meat   *n.* **sisanb'iltib'**
grime   *n.* **tz'ajn**
grind   *v.* **ke'ek**
          v. **ke'ok**
          v. **sob'ok**
          v. **tenok**
          v. **yab'ok**
grinding stone   *n.* **ka'**
grip   *n.* **roq**
groan   *v.* **tz'uyink**
grocer   *n agt.* **aj k'ay xxe' pim**
grocery store   *n.* **nimla k'ayib'aal**
ground floor   *n.* **xb'een tasal kab'l**

ground meat *n.* **ke'b'il tib'**
            n. **setinb'il tib'**

group   *n.* **ch'uut**

group of three *n.* **oxichal**

grove   *n.* **ch'ina k'iche'**

grow   *v.* **k'iik**
            v. **nimank**
            v. **ninqank**

growl   *v.* **q'urq'utk**
            v. **tz'uytz'utk**

growth   *n.* **k'i**

grumpy   *adj.* **ch'ich'i re**

grunt   *v.* **q'urq'utk**
            v. **tz'uytz'utk**

guard   *n.* **taaqinel**

guayaba   *n.* **pata**

guess   *v.* **eek'ank**
            v. **q'ehink**

guest   *n.* **ula'**
            n. **waril**

guicoy   *n.* **ik'oy**

guide   *n agt.* **aj k'amolb'e**
            n agt. **aj k'utunel b'e**

guideline   *n.* **esilal**

guilt   *n.* **maak**

guilty   *adj.* **aj b'aanun re**
            adj. **maakonel**

guinea hen *n.* **kokech**

guinea pig *n.* **q'an tu'lay aj
            imul**

guisquil   *n.* **ch'ima**

guitar   *n.* **kitaar**
            n. **suwajb'**
            n. **tzintzin**

gulf   *n.* **nimla rokeb'
            palaw**

gullible   *adj.* **jun chi aatin**

gully   *n.* **uul**
            n. **xiik'**

gum   *n.* **k'oy**
            n. **toq'**

gum seller *n agt.* **aj k'ay
            kok'toq'**

gum tissue *n.* **xtib'el xtoon
            ruuch e**

gums   *n.* **sa' e**
            n. **xtib'el xtoon
            ruuch e**

gun   *n.* **puub'**

gunpowder   *n.* **poqsxaml**

guts   *n.* **k'amk'otej**
            n. **sooyom**

gym   *n.* **q'ochleb'aal**

gymnasium   *n.* **q'ochleb'aal**

gynecologist *n agt.* **aj
            nawcha'al'ixq**

gynecology *n.* **nawcha'al'ixq**

H - h

habitation *n.* **ochochil**

hacksaw *n.* **ch'ina k'arch'iich'**

haggle *v phr.* **xwech'b'al xtz'aq**

hail *n.* **saqb'ach**

hair *n.* **ismal**
  n. **rismal jolom**

hair band *n.* **yutleb'**

hair part *n.* **b'e jolom**

hair pin *n.* **chapleb'ismal**
  n. **yut'ismal**

hair tie *n.* **yutleb'**

hairband *n.* **nat'leb'ismal**

hairbrush *n.* **xiyab'**

hairdresser *n agt.* **aj b'esonel**

hairnet *n.* **mochleb' ismal**

hairy *adj.* **tun is**

half *n.* **jun jachal**
  n. **yi**
  n. **yijach**
  n. **yijachal**

half dollar *n.* **jun tuxtun**

half dozen *n.* **waqib'**

hall *n.* **jaleb'aal**

hallucination *n.* **wax'ilom**

hallway *n.* **xmu kab'l**

halve *v.* **jachok**

ham *n.* **jamon**
  n. **xorb'il tib'**

hamburger *n.* **kaxlan xut'**

hamlet *n.* **kok'k'aleb'aal**

hammer *n.* **ruq'wajb'**
  n. **tenleb'**
  n. **t'ojleb'**
  v. **t'ojok**

hammock *n.* **ab'**
  n. **t'uuyleb'**

hand *n.* **uq'm**

hand towel *n.* **t'ikr re chaqob'resink uq**

handcuffs *n.* **xkux uq'b' ch'iich'**

handful *n.* **jun mooch'**

handgun *n.* **kach'in puub'**

handicapped *n.* **yo'rahil**

handkerchief *n.* **kok' sut**
  n. **sut**

handle *v.* **b'iqok**
  v. **jilok**
  n. **k'ub'**
  n. **roq**
  n. **xxik**

handsaw *n.* **ch'ina k'arch'iich'**

hang   *v.* **lukub'ank**

hang on a second
   phr. **chinaawoyb'en b'ayaq**

hang out (clothing)   *v.* **heleb'ank**
   v. **helok**

hang up   *v.* **t'uyub'ank**

hangar   *n.* **xna'aj so'sol ch'iich'**

hanger   *n.* **xlokochil t'ikr**

happen   *v.* **uxk**

happiness   *n.* **sahil ch'oolejil**

happy   *adj.* **k'ojk'o xch'ool**
   adj. **maausilanb'il**
   adj. **sahil ch'ool**
   adj. **sa xch'ool**
   adj. **usilanb'il**

happy birthday   *phr.* **sahil ch'oolejil choq' aawe sa' laakutan**

happy to hear it   *phr.* **sa inch'ool chi rab'inkil**

hard   *adj.* **ch'a'aj**
   adj. **kaw**
   adj. **yotyot**

hard disk   *n.* **rululil**

harden   *v.* **pekark**

hardware store   *n.* **k'ayib'aal k'anjelob'aal**

hard-working   *adj.* **aj k'anjel**

hare   *n.* **k'iche' imul**
   n. **xa'an imul**

harm   *n.* **toch'ok**

harmony (musical)
   n. **sahilyaab'**

harmony (social)   *n.* **sahil wank**

harp   *n.* **rinwajb'**

harvest   *n.* **ch'oqom**
   v. **q'olok**
   n. **q'olom**
   n. **xokok**

hat   *n.* **punit**

hate   *v.* **jatz'uuchink**
   v. **xik'uchink**
   n. **xik' ilok**

hatred   *n.* **xik' ilok**

hauler   *n agt.* **aj kelonel**

have   *v phr.* **wank e**

have a nice day
   phr. **chaanumsi chi us li kutan**

have a nice week
   phr. **chaanumsi chi us li xamaan**

have a seat   *phr.* **chunlan**

have difficulty breathing at night
   v. **aakanak**

have nightmares   *v.* **aakanak**

have sexual relations
   v. **aatinank**

have you got a minute?   *phr.* **ma wan b'ayaq aahoonal**

hawk   *n.* **k'uch**
   n. **liklik**

hay   *n.* **aq**

        n. **k'im**

        n. **tam**

he   *pron.* **a'an**

he who knows *n.* **na'ol**

        n. **na'onel**

head   *n.* **jolom**

head pad *n.* **b'itool**

        n. **xsok b'itom**

head strap *n.* **taab'**

headache *n.* **jolomb'ej**

        n. **rahil jolom**

        n. **xtib' jolom**

headband *n.* **t'upuy**

headboard *n.* **jolom ch'aat**

headdress *n.* **t'upuy**

headphones *n.* **ab'ib'aal**

        n. **xikelyaab'**

headstone *n.* **eetalkamenaq**

heal   *v.* **b'anok**

health   *n.* **kawilal**

health center *n.* **b'anleb'aal**

health education *n.* **tijok chi rix kawilal**

health problems *n.* **yajel qatib'el**

healthy *adj.* **kawal**

heap   *n.* **jun tuub'**

hear   *v.* **ab'ink**

hearing *n.* **ab'ib'aal**

        n. **ab'ink**

heart   *n.* **ch'ool**

        n. **ch'oolej**

heart attack *n.* **xlub'ik li ch'ool**

        n. **xxaqliik aamej**

heat   *n.* **q'ixnal**

        v. **tiqwasink**

heater *n.* **luhasib'aal**

heaven *n.* **choxa**

heavy *adj.* **aal**

heavyset person *n.* **t'inis**

heel   *n.* **rit oq**

heel (of a shoe) *n.* **rit xaab'**

height *n.* **nim xteram**

        n. **xmajolil**

heir   *n agt.* **aj maatan**

helicopter *n.* **tulux ch'iich'**

hell   *n.* **tojleb'aal maak**

        n. **xb'alb'a**

hello   *phr.* **chan xaawil**

helmet *n.* **kolb'ajolom**

        n. **uk'alpunit**

help   *phr.* **chineetenq'aaaq**

        v. **kamab'k**

        v. **tenq'ank**

        n. **tenq'aal**

        n. **xtenq'ankil**

help yourself *phr.* **chap aawe**

hemmorhage *n.* **pujkik'**

hemoglobin *n.* **b'onkik'**

        n. **kaqkik'**

hemp   *n.* **kawil k'aam**

hen   *n.* **tux kaxlan**

        n. **xa'an kaxlan**

hendecagon *n.* **junlajuxuk**

hepatitis   *n.* **q'anil**
             n. **q'anyajel**

heptagon   *n.* **wuqxuk**

her   *pron.* **a'an**

herbicide   *n.* **b'anpim**

herbs   *n.* **sununkil pim**

herd of cattle   *n.* **k'ila wakax**

herder   *n agt.* **aj ilol wakax**
            n agt. **aj k'aak'alehom ketomq**

herdsman   *n agt.* **aj ilol wakax**
            n agt. **aj k'aak'alehom ketomq**

here   *adv.* **arin**
            adv. **ayi'**
            adv. **sa'in**

here it is   *phr.* **wahi'**

hero   *n agt.* **aj kolom**
            n. **xnimal winq**

heron   *n.* **jotz**
            n. **patux ha'**
            n. **saqikil**

hexagon   *n.* **waqxuk**

hi   *phr.* **chan xaawil**

hiccough   *n.* **chuq'ub'**
            v. **chuq'ub'ak**
            v phr. **k'ehok chuq'ub'**

hiccup   *n.* **chuq'ub'**
            v. **chuq'ub'ak**
            v phr. **k'ehok chuq'ub'**

hide   *v.* **jalmuqank**
            v. **muquk**
            n. **rix xul**
            n. **tz'uumal**

hide one's shame   *v phr.* **moyok xutaan**

hieroglyphic   *n.* **mayertz'iib'**

high   *adj.* **najt xteram**
            adj. **nim xteram**
            adj. **yak'ach**

high school   *n.* **xkab' na'aj tzoleb'aal**

highlight   *v.* **ka'jultikank**

hill   *n.* **tzuul**

hills   *n.* **kelkookil tzuul**
            n. **tzoltzookiltzuul**

him   *pron.* **a'an**

hip   *n.* **k'onx a'**
            n. **xko it**

hippopotamus   *n.* **aaqha'**
            n. **kax aaq**

hire   *v phr.* **k'ehok k'anjel**

historian   *n agt.* **aj yehomb'aanuhem**

history   *n.* **jultik uxk**
            n. **resilal b'aanuhom**
            n. **resilal wank**
            n. **uxb'il b'aanunb'il**
            n. **yehom'uxb'il**

hit   *v.* **b'ujuk**
            v. **ketok**
            v. **potz'ok**
            v. **tenok**
            v. **wojok**

hit the road   *v phr.* **chapok b'e**

hoarse   *adj.* **nim sa' xkux**

hoe   *n.* **asaron**
            n. **jookleb'**

hog　　*n.* **aaq**

hold　　*v.* **chapok**

　　　　v. **q'unuk**

hold up　　*v.* **b'ayok**

hole　　*n.* **hopolal**

　　　　n. **jul**

　　　　n. **k'ob'b'il**

　　　　n. **xk'ob'lal**

hole punch　*n.* **hopleb'**

　　　　n. **hopleb'che'**

　　　　n. **hopleb'hu**

hollow　　*adj.* **hopo**

hollow out　*v.* **job'enk**

holster　　*n.* **xna'aj puub'**

holy　　*adj.* **osob'tesinb'il**

　　　　adj. **wankil**

holy image　*n.* **jalam'uuch**

holy spirit　*n.* **santil musiq'ej**

holy week　*n.* **rahil kutan**

home economics　*n.* **sachomj junkab'lal**

　　　　n. **tzolomilk'uub'**

homeostasis

　　　　n. **hilhookilna'yu'am**

homework　*n.* **k'anjel**

homicide　*n.* **kamij winq**

homonym　*n.* **juneetilk'ab'a'**

honest　*adj.* **maak'a' naxch'e'**

honesty　*n.* **tiikilal**

honey　　*n.* **xya'al kab'**

hood　　*n.* **lep ch'iich'**

hood support　*n.* **xche'el lep ch'iich'**

hoof　　*n.* **ixi'ij**

hook　　*n.* **lokoch**

hope　　*n.* **ch'ool re**

　　　　v. **yo'nink**

horizontal　*adj.* **q'e'q'o**

horizontal line　*n.* **q'eq'ookil juch'**

horn　　*n.* **jayaab'wajb'**

　　　　n. **kaxxuxb'**

　　　　n. **q'anch'iich'**

　　　　n. **trompeet**

　　　　n. **xukub'**

hornet　　*n.* **ch'ub'**

horse　　*n.* **kawaay**

　　　　n. **tzimitz**

hortensia　*n.* **orteens**

hose　　*n.* **hoyal**

　　　　n. **simb'tz'uum**

　　　　n. **xb'eleb'aal ha'**

hospital　*n.* **nimlab'anleb'aal**

　　　　n. **rochochil yaj**

hospital bed　*n.* **kaxch'aat**

hospital gown　*n.* **raq' aj b'anonel**

hospital robe　*n.* **raq' yaj**

hostage　*n.* **chapb'il**

hot　　*adj.* **q'ix**

　　　　adj. **tiq**

　　　　adj. **tiqwal saq'e**

hot chocolate　*n.* **tiqwal kakaw**

hot climate　*n.* **tiqwalch'och'**

hot dog　*n.* **salchiich**

hot sauce　*n.* **putz'b'il pix ik**

hot water   *n.* **q'ix ha'**
     n. **tiqwal ha'**

hotel   *n.* **ochochnaal**

hot-water bottle *n.* **xb'ooxil tiqwal ha'**

hour   *n.* **hoonal**
     n. **oor**

house   *n.* **kab'l**
     n. **ochoch**

housepainter *n agt.* **aj b'ononel kab'l**

housewife *n agt.* **aj k'anjel sa' kab'l**

how are you? *phr.* **chan ru wankat**
   phr. **ma sa laach'ool**

how do you pronounce [ ]?
   phr. **chan ru nakaayaab'asi [ ]**

how do you say [ ]? *phr.* **chan ru nayehman [ ]**

how far? *interr.* **jo' najtil**

how long ago? *interr.* **jarmayer**

how many times? *interr.* **jarsut**
   interr. **jarwa**

how many? *interr.* **jarub'**

how much each time?
   interr. **jarjartk**

how much for each? *interr.* **jarjar**

how much? *interr.* **jar**
   interr. **jo' k'ihal**
   interr. **jo' nimal**

how old are you? *phr.* **jarub' chihab' wan aawe**

how's the weather? *phr.* **chan ru li kutan**

how? *interr.* **chan ru**

however *conj.* **a' chik ut**
   conj. **ab'anan**
   conj. **yalaq chan ru**

howl   *v.* **oq'lok**
   v. **tz'uyte'ek**
   v. **wote'ek**

hug   *v.* **mek'onk**
   v. **q'alunk**

hug each other *v phr.* **q'alunk ib'**

human *n.* **poyanam**

human biology *n.* **poyanimil nawyu'am**

human rights
   n. **xk'ulub'poyanam**

human skeleton *n.* **yolojilb'aq**

humanity *n.* **poyanimil**

humble *adj.* **q'un**
   adj. **tuulan**

humid *adj.* **lan lan**
   adj. **t'aqt'aq**

humidity *n.* **xlanlanil**

humiliated *adj.* **tz'eqtananb'il**

humiliation *n.* **maajewank**

humility *n.* **xtuulanil**

hummingbird *n.* **tz'unun**

hundred *n.* **ok'aalil**

hundredth *num.* **(100th.) ro'k'aalil**

hunger	n. **ch'um**
	n. **we'ej**
hungry	adj. **tz'okaaq**
hunt	v. **tzakib'k**
	v. **yohob'k**
hunter	n agt. **aj yo**
hurricane	n. **kaqsut-iq'**
hurry	v. **seeb'ank**
hurt	v. **raho'k**
	n. **toch'ok**
	adj. **toch'ool**
husband	n. **b'eelom**
husk	n. **rix**
husk (grain)	n. **sol**
hut	n. **paapa'x**
	n. **po'lem kab'l**

hydrogen	n. **ha'il**
hydrology	n. **nawha'il**
hydrosphere	n. **ruuchiha'**
hymen	n. **ranq'**
hymnal	n. **b'ichleb'**
hypertension	n. **numt'ikt'ot-aam**
hyphen	n. **ch'inaaljuch'**
	n. **ch'inq'ejuch**
hypocritical	adj. **ka'pak'al u**
hypotension	n. **yalaalt'ikt'ot-aam**
hypothermia	n. **keho'ktib'elej**
hypothesis	n. **k'a'uxlanb'il**
hypothetical	adj. **k'a'uxlanb'il**

I - i

I pron. **laa'in**
I am lost phr. **sachsookin**
I disagree phr. **ink'a' naxk'ul inch'ool**
I don't feel very well phr. **ink'a' jwal sa naweek'a**
I don't know phr. **ink'a' ninnaw**
I don't like [ ] phr. **ink'a' nahulak chi wu [ ]**
I don't mind phr. **maak'a' ink'as chi rix**
I don't speak English phr. **ink'a' nin'aatinak sa' inkles**

I don't speak Q'eqchi' phr. **ink'a' nin'aatinak sa' q'eqchi'**
I feel sick phr. **yo inyajel**
I hope so phr. **maare jo'kan**
I know phr. **ninnaw**
I like [ ] phr. **nahulak chi wu [ ]**
I miss you phr. **nakatinjultika**
I only speak a little Q'eqchi' phr. **yal b'ayaq nin'aatinak sa' q'eqchi'**

I only speak a little Spanish *phr.* **yal b'ayaq nin'aatinak sa' kastiiy**

I understand *phr.* **xintaw ru**

I'd love to *phr.* **us raj**

I'm at home *phr.* **wankin sa' wochoch**

I'm bored *phr.* **xintitz'**

I'm exhausted *phr.* **lub'luukin**

I'm fine thanks *phr.* **us wankin b'antyox**

I'm full *phr.* **nujenakin**

I'm going out *phr.* **ok we chi elk**

I'm in a bad mood *phr.* **ch'ich'i' we**
phr. **yo wix**

I'm in a hurry *phr.* **twaj ru**

I'm looking forward to it *phr.* **yo inch'ool chi royb'eninkil**

I'm not sure *phr.* **ink'a' ch'olch'o**

I'm sorry *phr.* **chaakuy inmaak**

I'm thirsty *phr.* **chaqiq we**

I'm tired *phr.* **tawajenaqin**

I'm worried *phr.* **yo ink'a'uxl**

I've been busy *phr.* **jwal laatz' wu**

I've got to go *phr.* **tento tinxik**

ice *n.* **ke**
n. **pekb'ach**
n. **pek ha'**
n. **saqb'ach**

ice bag *n.* **xb'ooxil saqb'ach**

ice cream *n.* **ki'b'ach**
n. **ki'ilsaqb'ach**
n. **ki'il saqb'ach saa'us**

ice cream cart *n.* **xtoltolil ki'il saqb'ach saa'us**

ice cream vendor *n agt.* **aj k'ay ki'ilsaqb'ach**

icepack *n.* **xb'ooxil saqb'ach**

icon *n.* **eetaltaql**

iconography *n.* **ch'utub'eetalil**
n. **sik'ok-eetalil**

ICU *n.* **xna'aj nimqal yaj**

ID *n.* **huxaqalil**
n. **hu chi ru chaq'rab'**
n. **xaaqalhu**
n. **xhuhul tenamit**

idea *n.* **k'a'uxl**
n. **na'leb'**

ideal *n.* **sik'mank'a'uxl**

identity *n.* **loq'al wankilal**
n. **loq'-ilok**

ideograph *n.* **tz'iib'uuchil**

ideological imposition *n.* **minb'ilna'leb'**

idiolect *n.* **raatinul**

idiomatic *adj.* **aatinob'aalil**

idiot *n.* **yajti'ox**

idol *n.* **jalam'uuch**

if *conj.* **wi**

iguana *n.* **iwaan**

ill *adj.* **yaj**

illness   *n.* **yajel**
       n. **yajelil**
ill-tempered   *adj.* **yo rix**
illustration   *n.* **xsahob'resinkil**
imagination
      n. **k'a'uxlanb'ilna'leb'**
imitate   *v phr.* **ech ajaatink**
immediately   *adv.* **aka'**
      adv phr. **anaqwan tz'aqal**
      adv. **koko**
      adv phr. **sa' jumpaat**
      adv. **tikto**
immoral   *adj.* **tz'i'ej**
immoral practices   *n.* **tz'i'ej na'leb'**
impatient   *adj.* **ch'ich'i re**
      adj. **ch'iq' rik'in k'a re ru**
important   *adj.* **aajel**
impressed   *adj.* **nasach xch'ool**
imprint   *n.* **puktasib'aalhu**
imprison   *v phr.* **k'ehok sa' tzalam**
improve   *v.* **usaak**
improvization   *n.* **yoob'kink**
impulsive   *adj.* **yal naxkuti rib'**
in   *prep.* **sa'**
in a moment   *adv phr.* **ake' hoon**
in accordance with   *adv phr.* **jo' chan ru**
in four days   *n.* **ko'ej**
      adv. **wej**

in front   *prep.* **u**
in front of   *prep.* **chi ru**
      prep. **sa' xka'yab'aal**
in love   *adj.* **xikenaq xch'ool**
in order to   *adv.* **choq' re**
in peace   *adv.* **kalkab'**
in seven days   *adv.* **wuqub'ix**
in the afternoon   *adv phr.* **chi ru li ewu**
in the early morning   *adv phr.* **chi ru li saqewk**
in the evening   *adv phr.* **chi ru q'oqyin**
in the first place   *adv phr.* **xb'een wa**
in the morning   *adv phr.* **chi ru li eq'la**
in thirds   *adj.* **oxjach**
in three days   *adv.* **oxej**
in three parts   *adj.* **oxjach**
in-box   *n.* **k'uulb'ahu**
incense   *n.* **kaxlan pom**
      n. **pom**
      n. **sununkil k'ol**
incense burner   *n.* **k'atleb'aal pom**
inclining   *adj.* **an'o**
incomplete   *adj.* **ink'a' tz'aqal**
incubator   *n.* **kaxsuk**
indefinite or future particle   *part.* **aq**
independence   *n.* **junesalil**
independent   *adj.* **junesalil**

index   *n.* **tusna'leb'**

index finger   *n.* **k'utunel ru'uj uq'**

indicate   *v.* **k'utuk**

indictment   *n.* **jitom**

indifferent   *adj.* **maak'a' naraj wi'**

indigenous   *n.* **yaal winq**
   n. **ralch'och'**
   n. **tzaqal winq**

individual   *n.* **junaqlil**

individually   *adv.* **chi junaqlil**

indoctrinate   *v.* **tijok**

induce   *v.* **aalenk**

inductive   *adj.* **taqb'eetil**

inductively   *adv.* **sa' taqb'eet**

industrial   *adj.* **k'uub'k'ay**

industrial arts   *n.* **tzolyiib'ahom**

inexpensive   *adj.* **kub'enaq xtz'aq**

infarct   *n.* **xlub'ik li ch'ool**

infatuation   *n.* **jipo'k**

infection   *n.* **q'aak**

inference   *n.* **jo'kanil**

infinite
   adj. **maachoyb'ach'uut**

infinite set   *n.* **maalajkch'uut**

infix   *n.* **sa'iltz'aqob'l**

inflamed   *n.* **kaqpech'in**

inflammation   *n.* **sipook**
   n. **siipilal**

inflate   *v.* **apusink**

inform   *v.* **ch'olob'ank**

information   *n.* **esilal**

information office   *n.* **xna'aj aj k'ehol esil**

information technology   *n.* **esilal nawk'anjelahom**

infrared light   *n.* **xche' kaqixaml**

inhabitant   *n.* **echkab'al**

inhaler   *n.* **jiq'leb'aal b'an**

initial side (of an angle)   *n.* **xk'atq xtiklajik**

inject   *v.* **kutuk**

injection   *n.* **b'akuun**
   n. **kutb'il b'an**
   n. **yeksyon**

injure   *v.* **jot'ok**
   v. **tawasink**

injured party   *n.* **toch'ol**

injury   *n.* **yok'olal**

ink   *n.* **xya'al puktasiilhu**

ink pad   *n.* **xb'onilkaaxt**

inner cell components
   n. **kok'cha'al**

inner ear   *n.* **numleb'yaab' xik**

inner tube   *n.* **homtol'iq'**
   n. **iq'ob'aal**

innocent   *adj.* **maak'a' xmaak**

inquire   *v.* **patz'ok**

insect   *n.* **inseekt**
   n. **kok' xul**
   n. **k'ajxul**

insect bite   *n.* **xtiwom xul**

insecticide *n.* **b'antz'ipxul**
   n. **lajtesib'aalxul**
   n. **xb'anil xxulil**
   awimq
   n. **xb'anol suq**

insecure *adj.* **yal yalok re**

insecurity *n.* **ink'a' tuqtu**
   xch'ool
   n. **xiwxiwil**

insensitive *adj.* **maak'a' naraj**
   wi'

inside *prep.* **chi sa'**
   prep. **sa'**

insistence particle *part.* **pe'**

insole *n.* **xsa' xaab'**

insolent *adj.* **maak'a' xxutaan**

insomnia *n.* **maak'a'il wara**

instep *n.* **ru oq**

instrument *n.* **k'anjelob'aal**

insult *n.* **hob'ok**

intelligence *n.* **na'leb'**

intelligent *adj.* **ch'ukch'u**
   xk'a'uxl
   adj. **wan xna'leb'**

intensive care unit *n.* **xna'aj**
   nimqal yaj

intention *n.* **rajb'al**

intercultural *adj.* **sa' k'ilawank**

interculturality
   n. **wotzb'aanuhem**

interest *n.* **raltumin**

interference *n.* **ch'ik-ib'**

interjection *n.* **xyikutb'il aatin**

intermediate point *n.* **yanqil**

international *adj.* **ab'liltenamit**

international check-in
   n. **na'ilman xhuhil re**
   najtil tenamit

international departures *n.* **elk**
   sa' najtil tenamit

internationalize
   v. **sutruuchich'och'in**
   k

internationally
   adv. **sutruuchich'och'**

internet *n.* **muhilsik'leb'**

interpretation *n.* **jalok-aatin**

interrogate *v.* **patz'ok**

interrogative *n.* **patz'leb' aatin**

interrogative particle *part.* **ma**

interrupt *v.* **jot'ok**

interruptor *n.* **raqb'ametz'ew**

interval *n.* **yanq**

interview *n.* **titz'ok**

interviewer *n.* **aj pech'onel**

intestines *n.* **k'amk'otej**
   n. **sooyom**

intonation *n.* **xyaab'kuxil**

intone *n.* **yaab'kuxink**

intransitive (verb)
   n. **junesal'uxk**

intravenous line *n.* **kawub'l kik'**

intravenous solution *n.* **sweer**

introverted *adj.* **ink'a'**
   na'eek'an

invent *v.* **yoob'ank**

invented *adj.* **yoob'anb'il**

invention *n.* **yoob'**

inventor *n.* **yoob'k'a'aq**

investigate *v.* **tz'ilok-ix**

investigator *n agt.* **aj tzilol'ix**
    n agt. **aj tzilonel**

invite *v.* **b'eenink**
   v. **b'oqok**

invoice *n.* **huhil-loq'om**
   n. **xhuhilk'uluk**
   n. **xhuhil loq'om**

involuntary reflex *n.* **seeb'al rib'**

iodine *n.* **mertyolaat**

ionosphere *n.* **xamlt'or**

IOU *n.* **hu xaqb'anb'il
xwankil**
   n. **xhuhiltoj**

iris (eye) *n.* **xlem u**

iron *n.* **ch'iich'**
  n. **ji'leb'aal**
  n. **ji'leb't'ikr**

iron (clothing) *n.* **ji'leb' t'ikr**
     v. **ji'ok**

iron bars *n.* **tz'alam**

ironing board *n.* **ji'leb'aal**
   n. **tz'alam re ji'ok aq'**

ironmonger *n agt.* **aj k'ay
ch'iich'**

irrealism *n.* **k'a'uxlanb'ilal**

irresponsibility *n.* **ninqilwank**

irresponsible *adj.* **maak'a' xk'as
chi rix**
   adj. **ninqiwank**

irresponsibly *adv.* **ninqilwankil**

irrigate *v.* **hoyok**
   v. **t'aqresink**

irritation *n.* **josq'ok**

is anything wrong? *phr.* **ma ra
xk'ul**

island *n.* **ch'ina ochoch**
   n. **ch'och'ilha'**
   n. **ch'och' sutsu chi
ha'**
   n. **muhul**
   n. **neb'a ha'**
   n. **xch'och palaw**
   n. **xyampi ha'**

isolation *n.* **junesal**

it *pron.* **a'an**

it doesn't matter *phr.* **maak'a'
naxye**
   phr. **moko wan ta
xloq'al**

it is not *phr.* **maawa'**

it will be that (him, her, it)
   pron. **a'anaq**

it will be this *pron.* **a'aq**

it's not important *phr.* **moko
wan ta xloq'al**

it's not worth it *phr.* **maak'e
xloq'al**

it's OK *phr.* **us maak'a naxye**
   phr. **us naq nawil**

it's up to you *phr.* **a' yaal aawe**

itch   *n.* **katz**
            n. **katzkatz**
            n. **wotz'ok**
            n. **wotz'okil**

Itza   *lang.* **itza'**
IV   *n.* **kawub'l kik'**
            n. **sweer**

J - j

jack   *n.* **taqsiil**
jacket   *n.* **chakeet**
            n. **q'ixleb'aq'**
            n. **q'ixt'ikr**
jaguar   *n.* **b'alam**
            n. **hix**
jail   *n.* **tz'alam**
jail cell   *n.* **xraqlil xsa' tz'alam**
Jakaltek [aka Popti]
            lang. **jakalteka**
janitor   *n agt.* **aj ilol okeb'aal**
January   *n.* **eneer**
            n. **xb'eenilpo**
jasmine   *n.* **jasmin**
javelin throw *n.* **kutuk q'e'che'**
jaw   *n.* **rub'el e**
            n. **xkaalam e**
jealous   *adj.* **sowen**
jealousy   *n.* **kaqal**
            n. **sowenal**
            n. **sowenk**
jeans   *n.* **loonil wex**
            n. **wex re loon**
Jeep   *n.* **k'aleb'aal poy ch'iich'**
jersey   *n.* **b'atz-aq'**

Jew   *n.* **juliis**
jewel   *n.* **q'ol**
jeweller   *n agt.* **aj tenol ch'iich'**
            n agt. **aj yiib'om q'ol**
jewelry   *n.* **kok' tenb'il ch'iich'**
jewelry store *n.* **k'ayib'aal kok' tenb'il ch'iich'**
Jewish   *adj.* **aj juliis**
job   *n.* **kub'siil**
            n. **k'anjel**
            n. **tenq'**
job orientation *n.* **xna'leb'ankil k'anjel**
join   *v.* **ch'utub'ank**
            v. **laq'ab'ank**
joint (bones) *n.* **k'ulb'ab'aq**
joke   *v.* **ch'uch'ib'k**
journalist *n agt.* **aj k'ehol esil**
            n agt. **aj molol'esil**
Juan   *nick.* **Xiwan**
judge   *n agt.* **aj raqol'aatin**
            n agt. **aj raqol chaq'rab'**
            v phr. **raqok aatin**
judgment   *n.* **raqb'a' aatin**

judicial power   *n.* **xwankilal raqonel**

judicial system   *n.* **xk'uub'lalraqleb'a atin**

jug   *n.* **puk'xaar**
    n. **xaar**

juice   *n.* **xya'al**

juice press   *n.* **pitz'leb'**
    n. **yatz'leb'**

juicer   *n.* **yatz'leb'**

July   *n.* **juul**

jump   *v.* **pisk'ok**
    v. **pitzok**

June   *n.* **juun**

jungle   *n.* **k'iche'b'aal**

Jupiter   *n.* **ro' ralsaq'e**

jury   *n.* **raqonel chaq'rab'**

just   *adj.* **tiik xch'ool**

just joking   *phr.* **yal ch'uch'ib'k we**

just kidding   *phr.* **yal ch'uch'ib'k we**

just now   *conj.* **toja'**

justice   *n.* **chaq'rab'**
    n. **raqok aatin**
    n. **tiikilwank**
    n. **tz'ilok maak**

K - k

K'iche   *lang.* **k'iche'**

kangaroo   *n.* **k'unuch imul**

Kaqchikel   *lang.* **kaqchikel**

keep   *v.* **k'aak'alenk**
    v. **xokok**

keeper   *n agt.* **aj k'aak'anel**

kerosene   *n.* **b'ookhumha'**
    n. **humb'ookilha'**

ketchup   *n.* **keb'il pix**

kettle   *n.* **ak'ach**

key   *n.* **alpek'iich'**
    n. **jaqleb'**
    n. **laaw**
    n. **teeleb'**

key (of keyboard)   *n.* **ru tz'iib'leb'**

keyboard   *n.* **ru ululch'iich'**
    n. **tz'iib'leb'**
    n. **xche'e'b'al**

keychain   *n.* **chapteeleb'**

kick   *v.* **lapok**
    v phr. **lapok chi oq**
    v. **t'i'ok**
    v. **xaab'ank**
    v. **yeq'ok**

kid   *n.* **ral chib'aat**
    n. **ral yuk**

kidnapper   *n agt.* **aj elq'**

kidnapping   *n.* **muquk poyanam**

kidney   *n.* **kenq'**

kill   *v.* **kamsink**

kilo   *n.* **kiil**
kilometer *n.* **hiil**
kind   *adj.* **chab'il xch'ool**
kinesiology *n.* **naw'q'och**
kinetic energy *n.* **xmetz'ew tiik**
king   *n.* **ajaw**
kingdom   *n.* **wankilal**
kiosk   *n.* **ja'leb'aal**
          n. **wakax kab'l**
kiss   *v phr.* **tz'ub'uk u**
          v phr. **utz'uk u**
kitchen   *n.* **chi re xam**
          n. **k'uub'leb'aal**
kite   *n.* **rupelhu**
Kleenex   *n.* **huhil sut**
knead   *v.* **q'emrasink**
          v. **yoq'ok**
knee   *n.* **xb'een aq**
knee guard *n.* **b'atb'een'aq**

knee pad *n.* **b'atb'een'aq**
          n. **b'een'aqej**
          n. **sok xb'een'aq**
          n. **xlanb'al xb'een'aq**
knee patch *n.* **b'een'aqej**
          n. **sok xb'een'aq**
          n. **xlanb'al xb'een'aq**
knee-high stocking *n.* **xta a'**
kneel   *v.* **wiq'laak**
knife   *n.* **b'itzilch'iich'**
          n. **ch'ina ch'iich'**
          n. **sekch'iich'**
knit   *v.* **kemok**
knot   *n.* **t'oklal**
          n. **t'ok'**
          n. **xtok'**
know   *v.* **na'ok**
          v. **nawink**
know how to act *v phr.* **eek'aj ib'**
knowledge *n.* **nawom**
Kool-Aid *n.* **b'onb'ilha'**

L - l

lab   *n.* **tz'ileb'aal**
          n. **tz'ileb' rix yajel**
laboratory *n.* **tz'ileb'aal**
          n. **tz'ileb' rix yajel**
laborer   *n agt.* **aj k'anjel**
lace   *n.* **re t'ikr**
ladder   *n.* **eskaleer**
          n. **eeb'**
          n. **taqleb'aal**

Ladino   *n.* **aj mu's**
          n. **kaxlan winq**
ladle   *n.* **lekleb'**
          n. **nimla lek**
lady   *n.* **qana'**
ladybug   *n.* **kokxul**
lagoon   *n.* **kaq'naab'**
          n. **pumpuukil ha'**

lake   *n.* **kaq'naab'**
            n. **nimla kaqnab'**
            n. **palaw**
            n. **pumpuukil ha'**

lamb   *n.* **b'oreeg**
            n. **chib'aat**
            n. **kordeer**
            n. **ob'eja**

lame   *adj.* **sik**
            adj. **yeq**

lamp   *n.* **kanxam**
            n. **lampr**
            n. **saqenb'aal**
            n. **xam**

land   *n.* **ch'och'**
            v. **k'ochlaak**

landing strip *n.* **k'ochleb'aal ch'iich'**

landslide   *n.* **uq'ul**
            n. **uul**

language   *n.* **aatinob'aal**
            n. **yehom**

language policy *n.* **xna'leb'il nawaatinob'aal**

lantern   *n.* **kanxam**
            n. **lampr**
            n. **xam**

lard   *n.* **k'ook'**
            n. **olb'**
            n. **yolq'em**

large bag   *n.* **iiq**

large hummingbird *n.* **pap tz'unun**

lasso   *n.* **laas**

last   *v.* **b'ayk**
            adj. **ch'otonel**
            adj. **marilb'ej**
            adj. **raqik**
            adj. **roso'jik**
            adj. **rosob'**

last month *n.* **li po ak xnume'**

last night *n.* **ewer chi q'eq**

last son   *n.* **ch'i'p**

last week   *adv phr.* **chi ru li xamaan xnume'**

last year   *adv phr.* **chi ru li hab' xnume'**

latch   *n.* **k'aan**
            n. **nat'leb'**

latchkey   *n.* **ralteeleb'**

late   *adj.* **ewu**
            adj. **najt kutan**

later   *adv.* **jo' wanaq**
            adv. **moqon**

latex   *n.* **kik'che'**

latitude   *n.* **xhelam**
            n. **xk'atqil**

latrine   *n.* **k'otleb'aal**

laugh   *v.* **se'ek**

launch   *n.* **much' jukub'**

laundress   *n agt.* **aj puch'unel**

laundromat *n.* **xpuchleb'aal tenamit**

laundry   *n.* **aq' re puch'e'k**

laundry basket *n.* **xchakachil aq'**

laundry room *n.* **cha'jleb'aal**

lava   *n.* **woqxkum**
        n. **xa'awku**

law   *n.* **chaq'rab'**

lawn   *n.* **pach'aya'**

lawnmower   *n.* **setleb' pach'aya'**

lawyer   *n agt.* **aj na'onel chaq'rab'**

laziness   *n.* **q'emkunal**

lazy   *adj.* **aj q'em**
       adj. **jip**
       adj. **jok**
       adj. **q'emkun**

lead   *v.* **jolomink**
       v phr. **k'amok b'e**
       v phr. **k'utuk b'e**

lead (metal)   *n.* **rax ch'iich'**

leaf   *n.* **q'een**
       n. **xaq**

lean   *v.* **kuutunk**

leaning   *adj.* **an'o**

leap   *v.* **pisk'ok**
       v. **pitzok**

learn   *v.* **tzolok**

learning   *n.* **xtzolb'al**

leather   *n.* **tz'uumal**

leave   *v phr.* **chapok b'e**
       v. **elk**

leave me alone   *phr.* **mi naach'ich'i**

leaves   *n.* **xxaq**
       n. **xxaqeb'**

left   *adj.* **sa' tz'e**
       adj. **tz'e**

leg   *n.* **a'**

leg pain   *n.* **rahil ruuch a'**

legal adult   *n.* **tz'aqalil hab'**

legend   *n.* **seeraq'**

legibility   *n.* **xch'olch'ookilal**

legislation   *n.* **nawchaq'rab'ik**

legislative power   *n.* **xwankilal chaq'rab'inel**

legislative system
       n. **xk'ub'leb'aalchaq'r ab'**

legislator   *n.* **aj k'uub'anelchaq'rab'**

lemon   *n.* **lamuunx**

lemon tea   *n.* **k'isk'im**

lemonade   *n.* **xya'al lamunx**

lend   *v.* **jalb'eetink**
       v. **jalok**
       v. **to'nink**

length   *n.* **nimroq**
       n. **xnimal roq**

leopard   *n.* **cho'hix**
       n. **hix**

leper   *n.* **saqleb'**

leprotic   *adj.* **saqleb' rix**

lesson   *n.* **tzolom k'anjel**

let go   *v.* **ach'ab'ank**
       v. **tob'ok**

let me know   *phr.* **chaayehaq we**

let through   *v phr.* **k'ehok numik**

let's go   *phr.* **yo'o**

letter   *n.* **esilhu**
           n. **tz'iib'**

letter body   *n.* **nayeeman sa' li esilhu**

letter carrier   *n agt.* **aj kanab'om esilhu**

letterhead   *n.* **k'uut**

lettuce   *n.* **lechuuk**
          n. **woch ichaj**

leukemia   *n.* **xyajel kik'**

level   *n.* **tas**
        n. **tuqb'iis**
        n. **tuqleb'**

lever   *n.* **k'ub'**

lexicographer   *n agt.* **aj nawtus'aatin**

lexicography   *n.* **nawtus'aatin**

lexicon   *n.* **molob'aal aatin**
          n. **sik'leb' aatin**
          n. **xtusulal aatin**

liar   *n agt.* **aj tik'ti'**

liberalism   *n.* **ach'ab'ilal**

liberate   *v.* **ach'ab'ank**

librarian   *n agt.* **aj ilol k'ila tasal hu**

library   *n.* **rochochil tasal hu**
          n. **xna'aj tasal hu**

license   *n.* **ach'ab'alhu**

license plate
          n. **rajlilb'eleb'ch'iich'**
          n. **reetalil b'eleb'aal ch'iich'**
          n. **xaqch'iich'**

lick   *v.* **req'ok**

lid   *n.* **tz'apleb'**

lie   *n.* **tik'ti'**

lie (tell falsehoods)   *v.* **b'alaq'ik**
          v phr. **pak'ok aatin**
          v. **tik'ti'ink**
          v. **yik'ti'ink**

lie down   *v.* **sotlaak**
          v. **yoklaak**
          v. **yokob'ank**

life   *n.* **yu'am**
       n. **yu'amej**

life expectancy   *n.* **yu'amil**

life sentence   *n.* **tzapliik junelik**

lift   *v.* **paqonk**
       v. **waklesink**

light   *v phr.* **k'ehok xam**
        v. **lochok**
        adj. **saqen**
        n. **saqen**
        v. **tz'ab'ok**

light (in weight)   *adj.* **poy**
          adj. **seeb'**

light (not dark)   *adj.* **raxk'urin**
          adj. **saqen**

light airplane   *n.* **ch'ina so'sol ch'iich'**

light bulb   *n.* **b'omb'iiy**
          n. **sulem**
          n. **xnaq' saqen**

light refraction   *n.* **jalb'ehil saqen**

light switch   *n.* **chupleb' saqen**
          n. **raqleb' saqen**

lighter   *n.* **lechleb'**

light-hearted   *adj.* **se'se' ru**

lightning   *n.* **raq'kaaq**
             n. **repom**
lightning bolt   *n.* **lemskaaq**
             n. **xrepom kaaq**
lightning bug   *n.* **mams**
like   *adj.* **chanchan**
             adj. **jo'**
             adj. **xchaq'**
like that   *adv phr.* **chi kama'an**
             adv. **kama'an**
like this   *adv phr.* **chi kama'in**
             adv. **kama'in**
likeness   *n.* **taq'eetil**
liking   *n.* **sahil**
lily   *n.* **asuseen**
limbs   *n.* **roq ruq'm**
lime (stone)   *n.* **chun**
limp   *v.* **yeqo'k**
line   *n.* **juch'**
             n. **jusk'aam**
             n. **tzol**
             n. **tzolil**
linear function   *n.* **junaj k'anjel**
lined up   *adj.* **tzoltzo**
linguistic borrowing   *n.* **to'chi'**
linguistic community
             n. **xmolamil aatinob'aal**
linguistic development
             n. **waklesink naw'aatinob'aal**
linguistic norms   *n.* **xtz'iib'ul aatinob'aal**

linguistics   *n.* **naw'aatinob'aal**
             n. **nawchi'**
link (in a chain)   *n.* **tiqilal**
linkage of syllables
             n. **k'ulb'atz'iib'**
lion   *n.* **xyuwa'il xul**
lips   *n.* **tz'uumal e**
lipstick   *n.* **laasp re xtz'uumal e**
liquify   *v.* **putz'ink**
             v. **uq'unink**
liquor   *n.* **traaw**
listen   *v.* **ab'ink**
listless   *adj.* **maak'a' naraj wi'**
liter   *n.* **liitr**
             n. **meetilsu**
literacy   *n.* **nawtzoltz'iib'**
             n. **tzoltz'iib'ank**
litter   *n.* **mul**
little   *adv.* **ch'in**
little bell   *n.* **ral punitch'iich'**
little by little   *adv.* **ch'inqal**
             adv phr. **chi ch'inqil**
live   *v.* **na'ajink**
             v. **wank**
liver   *n.* **ch'och'**
             n. **saaseb'**
livestock   *n.* **ketomq**
living room   *n.* **hilaal**
lizard   *n.* **tolokok**
loan   *n.* **k'asib'k**
             n. **to'**
             v. **to'nink**

location   *n.* **na'ajej**
lock   *n.* **kantaaw**
           n. **nat'leb' okeb'aal**
           n. **pek'iich'**
           n. **tz'apleb'**
lock up   *v.* **tz'apok**
locker   *n.* **xna'aj k'a re ru**
logic   *n.* **tuqtuukil k'a'uxl**
           n. **tusnaw**
Lola   *nick.* **Lool**
loneliness *n.* **juntaalil**
lonely   *adj.* **junesal**
long   *adj.* **jukuch**
           adj. **lujuch**
           adj. **najt roq**
           adj. **nim roq**
           adj. **nim xkelam**
long jump *n.* **najtil pisk'ok**
long vowel *n.* **sum na'tz'iib'**
longaniza *n.* **b'utb'il paayil tib' aaq**
longing   *n.* **atawank**
longitude *n.* **kelam**
           n. **xnajtil roq**
look   *v.* **ka'yank**
look for   *v.* **sik'ok**
look out   *phr.* **k'e reetal li taab'aanu**
look!   *phr.* **iliii**
loom   *n.* **kemleb'**
           n. **k'uub'ch'iich'kem**
loop   *n.* **xxik aq'**

loose   *adj.* **yotzotznak**
           adj. **yootzan**
loosen   *v.* **kotzok**
loot   *v.* **min'isink**
           v. **minyamtesink**
lord   *n.* **ajaw**
           n. **qaawa'**
loroco (edible herb)
           n. **tz'aktz'um**
lose   *v.* **sachok**
lose (a game) *v.* **tz'eqok**
lose (a possession) *v.*
           phr. **tz'eqok ib'**
lose your train of thought *v.*
           phr. **b'orok na'leb'**
loss of blood *n.* **tz'eqok kik'**
lot   *n.* **waqlajuk'aam**
lotion   *n.* **sununkil b'ook**
lottery   *n.* **b'uuleb'**
           n. **b'uuleb'aal**
           n. **b'uulik**
           n. **b'uuluk**
           n. **pumb'uul**
           n. **yalok hu**
loud   *adj.* **kaw**
           adj. **kaw xyaab'**
           n. **yaab'il**
loudspeaker *n.* **chajb'a'e**
           n. **puktasib'aal aatin**
louse   *n.* **uk'**
love   *v.* **oxloq'ink**
           n. **rahok**
           v. **rahok**
           n. **rahom**

low   *adj.* **kach'in xteram**
low neck   *n.* **xtehelal xkux**
lower case letter   *n.* **itz'intz'iib'**
lubricant   *n.* **kax'olb'**
Lucas   *nick.* **Kax**
luggage   *n.* **iiq**
luggage tram   *n.* **b'elahom iiq**
lukewarm   *adj.* **luulu**
lullaby   *n.* **b'ich k'uula'al**
lunar capsule   *n.* **k'achleb'aal sa' po**

lunar eclipse   *n.* **muqlaak po**
           n. **muqpo**
lunar module   *n.* **k'achleb'aal sa' po**
lunch   *n.* **wa re wa'leb'**
lung   *n.* **pos**
           n. **pospo'oy**
Luz   *nick.* **Lus**
lynx   *n.* **yak**
lyre   *n.* **tusch'iich'wajb'**
Lázaro   *nick.* **Las**

M - m

macaw   *n.* **mo'**
machete   *n.* **tz'alamch'iich'**
machine   *n.* **k'uub'ch'iich'**
          n. **maak**
machine gun   *n.* **k'ilapotz' puub'**
          n. **paraq'aq'a**
macro competencies   *n.* **ninqi seeb'alil**
mad   *adj.* **kaan ru**
           adj. **look**
           adj. **wax ru**
made of clay   *adj.* **pak'b'il**
magazine   *n.* **ch'ina tashu'esil**
           n. **xnaq' puub'**
magic   *n.* **nawalil**
           n. **tuul**
magical   *adj.* **sachb'ach'oolej**

magician   *n agt.* **aj eek'**
           n agt. **aj nawal**
magician's hat   *n.* **xpunit aj eek'**
magnet   *n.* **tz'ub'ch'iich'**
magnetic resonance imaging
           n. **tz'ub'ch'iich'b'il eek'ch'iich'**
magnetism   *n.* **metz'kelob'**
magnolia   *n.* **k'onop**
mahogany   *n.* **sutz'ujl**
maid   *n.* **aj k'anjel sa' kab'l**
mail   *n.* **taql**
mailbag   *n.* **xchampa aj kanab'om esilhu**
           n. **xkoxtalil li esilhu**
mailbox   *n.* **xna'aj esilhu**
           n. **xna'aj taql**
           n. **xkaxonil esilhu**

mailman *n agt.* **aj kanab'om esilhu**

mainland *n.* **kontineent**

maize *n.* **ixim**

make *v.* **b'aanunk**
 n. **paak'ilal**
 v. **yiib'ank**

make an offering *v.* **mayejak**

make clear *v phr.* **xtawb'il li manawb'il**

make the sign of the cross *v phr.* **k'utuk eetalil**

make tortillas *v.* **xorok**

make war *v.* **katunink**

malaria *n.* **raxkihob'**

male (of animals) *adj.* **k'ol**

male (of birds) *adj.* **tzo'**

male (of humans) *adj.* **teelom**

males *n.* **winqilal**

mall entrance *n.* **xmu mama' k'ayib'aal**

mallet *n.* **tenleb'**

Mam *lang.* **mam**

mammal *n.* **tu'unel**

mammalian *n.* **tu'unel**

man *n.* **teelom**
 n. **winq**

mandate *n.* **taqlankil**

mango *n.* **mank**
 n. **q'unixholob'oob'**

manhood *n.* **winqilal**

manioc *n.* **tz'in**

manioc bread *n.* **tz'in**

manner *n.* **naraj**

manservant *n agt.* **aj tenq'**

manuscript *n.* **uq'miltz'iib'**

many *adj.* **k'ihal**
 pron. **k'ila**
 adj. **mayalok**

map *n.* **reetalil ch'och'**

maracas *n.* **jook'**
 n. **tzujtzuj**

marble *n.* **saqi pek**

marbles *n.* **mitz' b'olotz**
 n. **mitzt'orotz**
 n. **t'orlemtz'**

Marcelina *nick.* **Liin**

Marcelino *nick.* **Liin**

March *n.* **maars**
 n. **roxilpo**

marchant *n agt.* **aj yakonel**

Marcos *nick.* **Kux**

mare *n.* **xna' kawaay**

margarine *n.* **xxeeb'ul pim**

marimba *n.* **tusb'ilche'wajb'**
 n. **tusb'il che' son**
 n. **tusche'wajb'**

marines *n.* **rampalaw**

marionette *n.* **poyb'atz'uul**

mark *v.* **eetalink**
 v. **jalam'uuchib'k**

marker *n.* **b'onleb'**

market *n.* **k'ayiil**

marmot *n.* **kaxmis**

married man   *n.* **sumsuukil**

married woman   *n.* **sumsuukil**

marrow   *n.* **sulutz**
 n. **xsulutzil b'aq**

marry   *v.* **sumlaak**

marsh   *n.* **saab' ha'**

María   *nick.* **Mar**

masculine particle   *part.* **aj**

masculinity   *n.* **winqilal**

mashed potatoes   *n.* **puq'b'il paaps**

mask   *n.* **k'oj**

mason   *n agt.* **aj tz'ak**

masonry   *n.* **tz'akkab'l**

mass   *n.* **miix**

masterly   *adj.* **xaaqilalk'utuk**

mat   *n.* **aj**
 n. **poop**

match   *n.* **kaxtok'**
 n. **lochleb' xaml**
 n. **poos**
 n. **tokxaml**

maternity ward   *n.* **alab'tesib'aal**

math   *n.* **naw'ajl**
 n. **nawom chi rix ajl**

mathematically   *adv.* **chi'ajlil**

mathematician   *n agt.* **aj naw'ajl**

mathematics   *n.* **naw'ajl**
 n. **nawom chi rix ajl**

Matilde   *nick.* **Mat**

mattress   *n.* **ru ch'aat**
 n. **xsokel ru ch'aat**

mature   *adj.* **aj cheek**

mauve   *adj.* **kaq moyin**

May   *n.* **maay**
 n. **ro'ilpo**

Maya   *adj.* **maayil**
 n. **aj mayab'**
 adj. **mayab'**
 adj. **maay**
 n. **yaal winq**
 n. **ralch'och'**
 n. **tzaqal winq**

Maya calendar   *n.* **ch'olq'e maayab'**

Maya culture   *n.* **na'leb' mayab'**

Maya priest   *n agt.* **aj k'atol mayej**

Maya pyramid   *n.* **ox'ukab'l mayab'**

Maya spiritualist   *n.* **aj mayej**

Maya tradition   *n.* **na'leb' mayab'**

Mayan   *adj.* **maayil**

Mayan glyph   *n.* **mayertz'iib' maay**

Mayan languages   *n.* **aatinob'aal maay**

Mayan numbers   *n.* **eetalil ajl mayab'**

maybe   *adv.* **maare**
 adv. **tana**

mayo   *n.* **mayonees**
 n. **t'oqtzak**

mayonnaise   *n.* **mayonees**
 n. **t'oqtzak**

mayor   *n.* **aj jolominel k'aleb'aal**
       n. **xb'eenil poopol**

me too   *phr.* **laa'in ajwi'**

meadow   *n.* **potreer**

meal   *n.* **tib'el wa**
       n. **tzakahem**
       n. **wa**

mean   *adj.* **kaq ru xch'ool**

meaning   *n.* **xyaalalil**

means of communication
       n. **aatinab'aal**
       n. **puktasib'aal esil**

measles   *n.* **kaqlamj**
       n. **sarampyon**

measure   *v.* **b'isok**
       v. **ch'ikok**

measure (by one hundred)
       n. **ok'aalil b'isleb'**

measuring cup   *n.* **b'isleb' sek'**

measuring tape   *n.* **b'isleb'**
       n. **eetaal**

meat   *n.* **tib'**

meat grinder   *n.* **ke'leb'aal tib'**

meatballs   *n.* **t'ort'ookil tib'**

mechanic   *n agt.* **aj k'uub'anel poych'iich'**
       n agt. **aj xiitinelch'iich'**
       n agt. **aj yiib'om ch'iich'**

media   *n.* **aatinab'aal**
       n. **puktasib'aal esil**

medical examiner   *n agt.* **aj ilol kamenaq**

medical professional   *n agt.* **aj nawk'anjel yajel**

medical record   *n.* **resilal yajel**

medicine   *n.* **b'an**
       n. **k'iila b'an**
       n. **nawb'anok**

medicine cabinet   *n.* **xna'aj b'an**

medicine cart   *n.* **xtoltolil b'an**

Mediterranean Sea
       n. **q'otch'och'ilpalaw**

medlar   *n.* **nispr**

meek   *adj.* **q'axal q'un**
       adj. **tuulan**

meet   *v phr.* **k'uluk ib'**
       v phr. **tawok u**

meeting   *n.* **ch'utamil**

meeting hall   *n.* **ch'uutleb'aal**
       n. **ch'uutleb'aalkab'l**

meeting place   *n.* **ch'uutleb'aal**
       n. **ch'uutleb'aalkab'l**

meiosis   *n.* **jek'muriil**
       n. **jek'pojk'ok**

melody   *n.* **kuxil**
       n. **yaab'ich**

melon   *n.* **melon**

melt   *v.* **ha'ob'resink**

member   *n.* **komonil**

memorize   *v.* **k'uulank**
       v. **tuub'ank**

mend   *v.* **xiitink**

meninges   *n.* **kolb'a'ich'mulej**

menses   *n.* **kaqlak**

menstruate   *v.* **puch'uk**

menstruation *n.* **kaqlak**

menudo *n.* **xkok' xch'al xul**

merchant *n agt.* **aj k'ay**
　n agt. **aj k'ayinel**
　n agt. **aj loq'onel**
　n. **yakonel**

Mercury *n.* **xb'een ralsaq'e**

meridian *n.* **numlentz' saqen**

Merry Christmas *phr.* **sahil ch'oolejil choq' aawe sa' ralankil**

Mesoamerica *n.* **xyi ab'yayala**
　n. **yiib'ejilch'och'**

mesosphere *n.* **rox tasal'iq'**

Mesozoic era *n.* **xka q'ekutan**

message *n.* **seeraq'**

message (written) *n.* **esil nayehman sa' li hu**

messenger *n agt.* **aj b'eetaql**

metal *n.* **ch'iich'**
　n. **pu'ak**

metal bars *n.* **koral ch'iich'**

metal beam *n.* **oqechch'iich'**

metal carriage insert
　n. **kuukb'eleb'ch'iich'**

metal door
　n. **tz'apokeb'ch'iich'**

metal pipe *n.* **b'olb'okiil ch'iich'**

metal tube *n.* **b'olb'okiil ch'iich'**
　n. **homch'iich'**

metaphysics *n.* **xe'k'a'uxl**

metasphere *n.* **xkab't'or**

meteor *n.* **chahimpek**
　n. **k'ajchahim**

meteorite *n.* **xk'otchahim**

meteorology *n.* **nawq'ehil**

methane *n.* **b'ookha'**

method *n.* **b'ehil**
　n. **xb'ehul**

methodological steps
　n. **tusb'ehul**

methodology *n.* **nawb'ehil**

meticulous *adj.* **natz'ilok chi us**

Mexico *n.* **meej**

microorganism *n.* **mitz'k'icha'al**

microphone *n.* **aatik'uul**
　n. **aatinob'aal**
　n. **pukyaab'**

microscope *n.* **ileb'aalmitz'**

microscopic *adj.* **mitz'cha'al**

microwave oven *n.* **mikro oont**
　n. **pomleb'aal tzakahemq**

midday *n.* **jun wa'leb'**

middle *n.* **sa' xyi**
　n. **yi**
　n. **yiib'ej**

middle finger *n.* **xyihil ru'uj uq'**

midge *n.* **k'uxuk**
　n. **suq**

midnight *n.* **tuqtu q'ojyin**

midwife *n agt.* **aj xokol'al ixq**

migraine *n.* **rahil jolom**

migrant *n agt.* **aj b'e**

Miguel   *nick.* **Mek**

mild   *adj.* **luulu**
         adj. **q'axal q'un**
         adj. **tuulan**

milk   *n.* **leech**
         n. **xya'al tu'**
         v. **yatz'ok**

milkshake   *n.* **puq'b'il**

Milky Way   *n.* **saqb'e**
              n. **xtzoq saq'e**

mill (grain)   *n.* **keleb'aal**
                 n. **k'uub'poch'leb'**
                 n. **poch'leb'**

miller   *n agt.* **aj poch'onel**

millet   *n.* **kok' ixim**

millimeter   *n.* **mitz'jisb'ilis**

million   *n.* **oob' chuy xwaq
                 k'alab'**

mime   *n.* **sa' memil**

mimeograph   *n.* **pukleb'hu**

mince   *v phr.* **setok tib'**

mind   *n.* **k'a'ux**

mini tamale   *n.* **kok' poch
                    ob'en**

minimal pair   *n.* **xsumalil**

miniskirt   *n.* **ch'ot b'estiiy**

minivan   *n.* **saajil poy ch'iich'**

mint   *n.* **isk'i'ij**

minus sign (-)   *n.* **reetaljeb'ok-
                         ajl**

minute   *n.* **k'asal**

miracle   *n.* **sachb'ach'oolej**

miraculous
         adj. **sachb'ach'oolej**

mirror   *n.* **lem**

miscarriage   *n.* **numsink-al**
                n. **tz'eqok k'ula'al**

mischievous   *adj.* **xulil**
                adj. **xul aj al**

misdemeanor   *n.* **kok' maak**

mission   *n.* **rajom**
            n. **taqlankil**

mist   *n.* **musmus hab'**
         n. **sujew**

mistake   *n.* **sachjik**

mitochondria   *n.* **alab'metz'ew**

mitosis   *n.* **pojk'ok**
            n. **xmurinkil rib'**

mix   *v.* **junajink**
        n. **yuul**

mixed number   *n.* **jachlil'ajl**

mixer   *n.* **b'ukleb'aal**
          n. **kaxkojl**
          n. **puq'leb'**
          n. **yuuleb'**

model   *n.* **paak'ilal**

modern warfare   *n.* **ak'il
                      xb'aanunkil raaxiik'**

module   *n.* **xch'uutulal**
           n. **xtasalil**

mojarra   *n.* **chakti'**

molar   *n.* **ka'**
          n. **ka' e**

mold   *v.* **pak'ok**

mole   *n.* **chut**

moment   *n.* **hoonal**
      n. **junpaatil**
Monday   *n.* **luuns**
      n. **xb'een kutan**
money   *n.* **loq'leb'**
      n. **pu'ak**
      n. **tumin**
money box   *n.* **k'ohaal**
monitor   *n.* **kaxmu'eetalil**
monja blanca   *n.* **saqihix**
monkey   *n.* **b'atz'**
      n. **max**
monocotyledonous seed
      n. **jun'al iyaj**
monologue   *n.* **aatinak-ib'**
monomial   *n.* **junajeetalb'irok**
month   *n.* **po**
      n. **pohol**
monthly pay   *n.* **po**
monument   *n.* **eetalil jalam u**
      n. **eetalil patz'e'k**
moods   *n.* **ru ch'oolej**
moody   *adj.* **yo rix**
moon   *n.* **po**
moon landing   *n.* **k'ochlaak sa' li po**
mop   *n.* **masleb'tz'ak**
Mopan   *lang.* **mopan**
moral (to a story)   *n.* **xcha'al seeraq'**
moral principle   *n.* **chaq'rab'**
morality   *n.* **oxloq'ilal**

more   *adv.* **chik**
      adv. **q'axal**
      adj. **toj**
more and more   *adv phr.* **rajlal naab'al**
morgue   *n.* **kamna'aj**
      n. **xna'aj kamenaq**
Mormon   *adj.* **aj mormon**
morning   *n.* **eq'la**
morning star   *n.* **kaqchahim**
      n. **kutan chahim**
morpheme   *n.* **k'ajyaab'aatin**
morphology
      n. **nawk'ajyaab'aatin**
mortgage
      n. **xchapliikroqruq'b'**
mosquito   *n.* **ch'een**
      n. **kok' utz'**
      n. **suq**
      n. **utz'**
moth   *n.* **max**
mother   *n.* **na'**
mother tongue   *n.* **xb'een aatinob'aal**
mother's brother   *n.* **ikan**
mother's milk   *n.* **xya'al tu'**
mother's sister   *n.* **xchaq'na' na'**
mother-in-law   *n.* **xna' wechb'een**
mother-in-law (of a man)   *n.* **xna' ixaqil**
mother-in-law (of a woman)
      n. **xna' b'eelom**

mother-of-pearl *n.* **jutz'un pemech**

motivate *v.* **k'utb'esink**

motivating *adj.* **waklesinelch'ool**

motor *n.* **ch'oolmetz'ew** *n.* **eek'metz'ew** *n.* **motor** *n.* **xch'ool ch'iich'**

motor oil *n.* **kax'olb' poych'iich'** *n.* **xkax'olb' poych'iich'**

motorboat *n.* **kaxjukub'**

motorcycle *n.* **kawaaya ch'iich'** *n.* **moot** *n.* **paattzim**

motorist *n.* **aj kawaayach'iich'**

motorized *adj.* **kawaayach'iich'i nb'il**

motto *n.* **k'a'uxlil**

mount *v.* **taqe'k**

mount a horse *v phr.* **taqe'k chi rix kawaay**

mountain *n.* **k'iche'** *n.* **tzuul**

mountain lion *n.* **kaqkoj**

mountain range *n.* **kelkookil tzuul** *n.* **tzoltzookiltzuul**

mountain ridge *n.* **kelkookil tzuul** *n.* **tzoltzookiltzuul**

mountain spirit *n.* **tzuultaq'a**

mouse *n.* **uch ch'o** *n.* **xa'nch'o**

mouse pad *n.* **ch'ohib'aal**

mousetrap *n.* **xra'al ch'o**

mouth *n.* **e**

mouthful *n.* **jun nub'uk**

move *v.* **eek'asink**

movie *n.* **eek'mu** *n.* **eek' jalam'uuch** *n.* **jalam'uuch**

movie screen *n agt.* **xlemul kaxmuhel**

movie theater *n.* **eetalmu** *n.* **ileb'aalmu** *n.* **rochochil ilob'aal mu**

moving picture *n.* **eek' jalam'uuch**

mow *v.* **setok**

MRI machine *n.* **tz'ub'ch'iich'b'il eek'ch'iich'**

much *adj.* **jwal** *pron.* **naab'al** *pron.* **xiikil**

muck *n.* **tz'ajn**

mud *n.* **sulul**

mug *n.* **xaar**

mugger *n agt.* **aj maq'onel**

mugging *n.* **maq'ok**

mulberry *n.* **tokan**

mule *n.* **muul**

multicellular *adj.* **k'ilana'yu'am**

multicultural *adj.* **k'ilana'leb'**

multiculturality *n.* **k'iilayehom b'aanuhom**

multiethnic *adj.* **k'ilpoyanimil**

multilingual *adj.* **k'ila'aatinob'aal**

multiple *n.* **puktaal**

multiplication *n.* **puktahil'ajl** *n.* **puktasiil**

multiplication sign (x) *n.* **eetalpuk-ajl** *n.* **reetal puktasiil**

multiplication symbol (x) *n.* **eetalpuk-ajl** *n.* **reetal puktasiil**

multiplied *adj.* **puktasinb'il**

multiplied by *phr.* **puktasink chi**

multiplier *n.* **puktasinel**

multiply *v.* **puktasink** *v.* **puktasink ajl**

mumble *v.* **hasb'ak**

mummy *n.* **b'atxaqam**

mumps *n.* **b'uq' kux** *n.* **papeer**

municipality *n.* **teepalpoopol**

murder *v.* **kamsink** *n.* **kamsiik**

murderer *n agt.* **aj kamsinel**

murmurs *n.* **sak'ok aatin**

muscle tear *n.* **yu'uk ichmul**

muscles *n.* **tib'elej**

mush *n.* **matz'** *n.* **saqjuy** *n.* **uq'un**

mushroom *n.* **okox**

music *n.* **son** *n.* **wajb'ak**

music education *n.* **tijb'ab'ich**

music stand *n.* **xna'aj xhu b'ich**

musical group *n agt.* **ch'uut aj wajb'**

musical instrument *n.* **wajb'**

musical note *n.* **xyaab' b'ich**

musician *n agt.* **aj wajb'**

Muslim *n.* **musulman**

mustache *n.* **xmach u**

mute *adj.* **mem**

mutual help *n.* **kamab'k**

my *adj.* **in**

mysterious *adj.* **muqmuukil**

mysteriously *adv.* **muqb'aanunb'il**

mystery *n.* **muqmuukilal**

myth *n.* **yoob'k'a'uxl**

N - n

nail   *n.* **chapleb'**
            n. **klaawx**
            n. **sub'inch'iich'**
            n. **t'ojom**
            n. **ixi'ij**

nail clippers   *n.* **setleb' ixi'ij**

nail polish   *n.* **yulb'ilb'on**

naive   *adj.* **maak'a' xna'leb'
            naxk'ut rib'**

naked   *adj.* **mich'mo**
            adj. **moq'mo**
            adj. **t'urt'u**
            adj. **t'ust'u**
            adj. **yach'yo**

nakedness   *n.* **t'usam**

name   *n.* **k'ab'a'**
            n. **k'ab'a'ej**
            v. **k'ab'a'ink**
            v. **xaqab'ank**

name of recipient   *n.* **xk'ab'a' li
            taak'ulu'q re**

name of sender   *n.* **xk'ab'a' li
            nataqlan re**

nameplate   *n.* **eetalil**

namesake   *n.* **eeqaj**
            n. **tz'ob'ay**

nametag   *n.* **ch'ina eetalil**

nape of the neck   *n.* **rix ja'aj**
            n. **rix kux**

napkin   *n.* **lanb'alwa**
            n. **lanleb'**
            n. **xt'ikrul wa**

narcotic   *n.* **kaanilb'an**

narrate   *v.* **seeraq'ik**

narration   *n.* **yehom**

narrator   *n agt.* **aj yehonel**

narrow   *adj.* **kach'in ru**
            adj. **kok' ru**
            adj. **laatz'**

nasal   *n.* **ujinb'ilyaab'**

nasal mucus   *n.* **sam**

nasalization   *n.* **ujinb'ilyaab'**

national identity   *n.* **xtenamitil
            ilob'**

national palace   *n.* **rochochil
            awa'b'ejink**

nationality   *n.* **xtenamitil**

native country   *n.* **ch'och'el**

Natividad   *nick.* **Nat**

natural resources   *n.* **eechej
            che'k'aam**
            n. **rawimal ch'och'**
            n. **eechej ch'och'**

natural sciences
            n. **tzolomilchoxach'o
            ch'**

naturally   *adv.* **jo'kan**
            adv. **jo' chanru**

nature   *n.* **choxach'och'**

naughty   *adj.* **xulil**
            adj. **xul aj al**

navel   *n.* **ch'up**

navigator   *n agt.* **aj b'ehenel**

navy blue   *adj.* **rax moyin**

near   *adj.* **nach'**
            adv phr. **nach' xk'atq**
            adj. **rik'in**

nearly   *adv phr.* **kach'in chik
            (ma)**

nebulizer   *n.* **puutz'leb'aal**

nebulous galaxy   *n.* **choqlil tzoqchahim**

necessity   *n.* **rajb'al ru**

neck   *n.* **ja'aj**
     n. **kux**

necklace   *n.* **q'ol**

necktie   *n.* **b'eq**
     n. **yutkux**

need   *n.* **rajb'al ru**

needle   *n.* **kuux**

needle (hypodermic)
     n. **jutz'kutleb'**

needle (of a tree)   *n.* **xaqchaj**

needle (sewing)   *n.* **b'ekleb' k'ix**
     n. **jutz'b'ojleb'**

negation particle   *part.* **ma**

negative   *adj.* **q'etq'etil**
     adj. **yiib'na'leb'**

negative electric charge
     n. **xsak'om tiikil kaxlanxaml**

neighbor   *n.* **as itz'in**
     n. **echkab'al**

neighborhood   *n.* **teep**
     n. **xteepal tenamit**

neither   *conj.* **chi moko**

neologism   *n.* **ak'aatin**
     n. **yoob'aal aatin**

nephew   *n.* **ral chaq'na'**
     n. **ral we**

Neptune   *n.* **xwaqxaq ralsaq'e**

nerve   *n.* **ich'mej**

nerve tissue   *n.* **ch'ut-eek' cha'al**

nervous system   *n.* **ch'uut ich'mul**

nest   *v.* **sokink**
     n. **sok xul**
     n. **suk**

net   *n.* **champa**
     n. **kelkookil soq'**
     n. **keelsoq'**

net bag   *n.* **soq'**

nettle   *n.* **la**
     n. **panchool**

neuron   *n.* **xyihil xk'ub'lal ich'mulej**

neutron star   *n.* **kehil chahim**

never   *adv phr.* **ma jun wa**
     adv. **maajaruj**
     adv. **maajoq'e**

nevertheless   *conj.* **ab'anan**

new   *adj.* **ak'il**
     adj. **ak'**

new moon   *n.* **al po**

news   *n.* **yehol'esilal**

newspaper   *n.* **b'anb'alil esil**
     n. **esilhu**
     n. **nawil hu**
     n. **periood**
     n. **tz'iib'anb'il esil**
     n. **xhuhul esil**

newspaper boy   *n agt.* **aj jek'ol preens**

newsprint   *n.* **nut'leb'hu**

next   *adj.* **sa' jun chik**

next month *n.* **li po chalk re**

next to *prep.* **chi xk'atq**

    prep. **nach' rik'in**

next week *adv phr.* **chi ru li xamaan chalk re**

next year *n.* **li hab' chalk re**

nice to meet you *phr.* **nasaho inch'ool xnawb'al aawu**

nickel *n.* **oob' senta**

nickname *n.* **yoob'k'ab'a'**

niece *n.* **ralal ikan**
    n. **ral chaq'na'**
    n. **xrab'in we**

niece (from a younger sibling) *n.* **xrabin iitz'in**

niece (from an older sibling) *n.* **xrab'in as**

night *n.* **chi q'eq**
    n. **q'ojyin**

night stand *n.* **ch'ina meex warib'aal**

night table *n.* **ch'ina meex**
    n. **ch'ina meex warib'aal**

nightclub *n.* **xajleb'aal**

nightgown *n.* **jur aq'**

nine *num.* **(9.) b'eleeb'**

nineteen *num.* **(19.) b'eleelaju**

nineteenth *num.* **(19th.) xb'ele'lajuil**

ninetieth *num.* **(90th.) xlajee ro'k'aalil**

ninety *num.* **(90.) lajeb' ro'k'aal**

ninety-eight *num.* **(98.) waqxaqlaju ro'k'aal**

ninety-five *num.* **(95.) o'laju ro'k'aal**

ninety-four *num.* **(94.) kaalaju ro'k'aal**

ninety-nine *num.* **(99.) b'elelaju ro'k'aal**

ninety-one *num.* **(91.) junlaju ro'k'aal**

ninety-seven *num.* **(97.) wuqlaju ro'k'aal**

ninety-six *num.* **(96.) waqlaju ro'k'aal**

ninety-three *num.* **(93.) oxlaju ro'k'aal**

ninety-two *num.* **(92.) kab'laju ro'k'aal**

ninth *num.* **(9th.) xb'elee**

nipple *n.* **ru'uj tu'**

nit *n.* **k'ot uk'**

nitrate
    n. **ratz'amilq'olch'iich'**

nitroglycerine *n.* **ha'ilyol**

no *adv.* **i'**
    adv. **ink'a'**
    adv phr. **moko [   ] ta**

no entry *phr.* **maak'a' nume'k**

no one *pron.* **maani**

nod off *v.* **xiiqank**

noise   *n.* **eek'ank**
           n. **xkuxb'il**
           n. **yaab'**
noisy   *adj.* **xik' naxye**
nominate   *v.* **xaqab'ank**
nonagon   *n.* **b'eleexuk**
nonperishable   *n.* **yo'yookilal**
noodles   *n.* **tayarin**
noon   *n.* **tuqtu waleb'**
norm   *n.* **xtz'iib'ul**
north   *n.* **releb' iq'**
North America   *n.* **xjolom
           ab'yayala**
           n. **xye ab'yayala**
north pole   *n.* **xtaqe'qil
           ruuchich'och'**
nose   *n.* **u'uj**
           n. **u'ujej**
nostril   *n.* **sa' u'uj**
nosy   *adj.* **nakujkut**
not   *adv.* **ink'a'**
           adv phr. **moko [ ] ta**
not at all   *phr.* **maak'a'**
not bad   *phr.* **wan b'ayaq
           rusilal**
not even   *adv phr.* **ma chan
           naxye**
not guilty   *adj.* **maak'a' xmaak**
not so well   *phr.* **ink'a' jwal us**
not yet   *adv.* **maaji'**
notch   *v phr.* **isink sa' re che'**
note   *n.* **esilhu**
           n. **xyaab' b'ich**

notebook   *n.* **tz'iib'leb'aalhu**
nothing   *pron.* **maajun**
           pron. **maak'a'**
           pron. **maalay**
           pron. **yal ta k'a'**
nothing at all   *adv phr.* **maak'a'
           chi junwaakaj**
nothing more   *phr.* **ka'aj wi a'an**
nothing of the kind   *adv*
           phr. **moko a'an ta**
notice   *n.* **esilal**
           v phr. **k'ehok eetal**
noun   *n.* **k'ab'a'atq**
           n. **k'ab'a'ej**
nova   *n.* **ak'chahim**
November   *n.* **nowyemr**
           n. **xjunlajuhilpo**
now   *adv.* **anaqwan**
nowadays   *n.* **anaqwan q'e
           kutan**
nowhere   *adv.* **maab'ar**
nucleus   *n.* **xch'ool**
           n. **xyich'ool
           xna'yu'am**
number   *n.* **ajl**
numeracy   *n.* **nawajlil**
numeral   *n.* **ajl**
numeration   *n.* **ajlil**
numerator   *n.* **jek'iil**
nun   *n.* **mayr**
           n. **rixkil paab'aal**
nurse   *n agt.* **aj ilolyaj**
           n agt. **aj tenq' re
           b'anok**

v. **tu'resink**

n agt. **xtenq' aj b'anonel**

nursing home *n.* **xna'ajeb' cheek**

nut   *n.* **nwes**

nut (fastener) *n.* **jit'leb'**
          n. **kotoxch'iich'**

nylon   *n.* **nayl**

O - o

oak   *n.* **arkute'**
          n. **ji**

oar   *n.* **kanaleet**
          n. **paleet**

oasis   *n.* **hilob'aal k'iche'**

oath   *n.* **somenkil**
          n. **sumenk aatin**

obedient *adj.* **napaab'an**

obey   *v.* **ab'ink**
          v. **paab'ank**

object of a suitor's affection
          n. **payom**

objective *n.* **ahom**

obligation *n.* **teneb'aal**

obscenity *n.* **tz'i'ej aatin**

obscure *adj.* **ink'a' ch'olch'o**

observe *v.* **ka'yank**
          v phr. **k'ehok eetal**

obsidian *n.* **xmar choxa**
          n. **xmaal kaaq**

obstetrician *n agt.* **aj xokonel**

obstetrics *n.* **nawxokok**

obstinate *adj.* **jip**

occlusive *n.* **tz'apyaab'**

occupation *n.* **laatz'al**

ocean   *n.* **palaw**
          n. **xnimalpalaw**

octagon *n.* **waqxaqxuk**

octahedron *n.* **waqxaqxuk-u**

October *n.* **oktuuwr**
          n. **xlajehilpo**

octopus *n.* **moch'kar**

odd numbers *n.* **maasumal'ajl**

of   *prep.* **re**

of course *phr.* **usaq b'i'**

of course not *phr.* **ink'a' b'i'**

offended *adj.* **hob'il**

offense *n.* **nimlamaak**

offensive words *n.* **sak'ok aatin**

offer   *v.* **yeechi'ink**

office   *n.* **rochochilmolam**
          n. **tz'iib'leb'aal**

often   *adv phr.* **kok'atq xsa'**
          adv. **kok'sa'**

oil   *n.* **aseet**
          n. **olb'**
          n. **olb'il b'an**
          n. **q'olch'och'**

n. **xkax'olb' poych'iich'**

n. **yolq'em**

oil filter   *n.* **tz'ilb'akax'olb'**

n. **tz'ileb' olb'**

ointment   *n.* **b'anol u**

n. **b'iqb'ilb'an**

n. **olb'il b'an**

n. **pomaat**

n. **sununkil b'an**

n. **t'oq't'ookil b'an**

n. **uq'unil b'an**

old   *adj.* **junxil**

adj. **mama'**

adj. **najter**

adj. **qeel**

adj. **q'eel**

adj. **tiix**

old man   *n.* **tiix**

old woman *n.* **tiix**

olden days *n.* **najter q'e kutan**

older sibling *n.* **anab'ej**

n. **asb'ej**

n. **chaq'na'b'ej**

older sister *n.* **chaq'na'**

olive   *n.* **asetuun**

omen   *n.* **xq'ehinkil**

on parole *adj.* **wank sa' ilb'il**

on probation *adj.* **wank sa' ilb'il**

on top   *prep.* **sa' xb'een**

on trial   *adj.* **wank sa' raqb'a aatin**

once   *adv.* **junsut**

adv. **junwa**

once more *adv phr.* **jun sut chik**

oncilla   *n.* **k'amb'olay**

one   *num.* **(1.) jun**

one cent   *n.* **jun senta**

one fourth *n.* **jun xka**

one hundred *n.* **(100.) o'k'aal**

one hundred quetzals *n.* **o'k'aal ketzal**

one million *n.* **kiib' oq'ob' xkab' xchuy**

one more   *adv.* **jun chik**

one time   *adv.* **junwa**

onion   *n.* **seb'ooy**

n. **tuxim**

only   *adj.* **ka' aj wi'**

adj. **yal**

only child *n.* **junaatal alalb'ej**

onomatopoeia *n.* **yaab'k'ab'a'il**

onwards   *adv.* **chi ru**

open   *v.* **jaqok**

adj. **pahpo**

v. **tehok**

adj. **tehto**

open syllable *n.* **jap yahiil**

opener   *n.* **jaqleb'**

n. **teeleb'**

opening   *n.* **pahal**

n. **xhopolal**

operating system *n.* **xk'ub'lal xsa'**

operating table *n.* **xmesul cho'ok**

operation *n.* **cho'ok**

opine   *v phr.* **aatinak chi rix**

opossum *n.* **aj b'oox uch**
         n. **aj uch**
         n. **b'aqlaq xul**
opportunity *n.* **okenk**
opposite *prep.* **xjunpak'alil (li...)**
optic nerve *n.* **eek'al uhej**
optimism *n.* **kawil ch'ool**
or   *conj.* **malaj**
         conj. **malaj ut**
oral rehydration solution
         n. **ich'mulb'an**
         n. **k'uub'anb'il b'an**
         n. **uk'metz'ewilb'an**
orange   *n.* **chiin**
         adj. **chiin**
         adj. **kaqiq'an**
         adj. **q'an kaqin**
orange juice *n.* **xya'al chiin**
orange tree *n.* **chiin**
orbit   *n.* **suutilal**
         n. **xb'e'chahim**
         n. **xb'e ruuchich'och'**
orchard *n.* **kok'awinq**
         n. **xna'aj kok'awinq**
order   *n.* **ruq'b'chaq'rab'**
         v. **taqlank**
         v. **tusub'ank**
         v. **tusuk**
ordinary *adj.* **chaq re ru**
oregano *n.* **oreek**
organ   *n.* **cha'al**
         n. **tz'uywajb'**
organelle *n.* **kok'cha'al**

organized *adj.* **ch'olch'o**
           nak'anjelak
           adj. **tustu ru**
           adj. **tusul**
organizer *n agt.* **aj b'uub'anel**
organs   *n.* **cha'alil**
orientation *n.* **ch'olna'leb'**
origin   *n.* **roqel**
         n. **xtiklajik**
origin particle *part.* **aj**
orphan   *n.* **neb'a'**
ORS   *n.* **ich'mulb'an**
         n. **k'uub'anb'il b'an**
         n. **uk'metz'ewilb'an**
orthodontist *n agt.* **aj**
           tiikob'resinel'uuch-e
orthography *n.* **nawtz'iib'ak**
           n. **tuqlaaltz'iib'**
           n. **tuqtutz'iib'**
ostrich *n.* **najtil t'uru' ak'ach**
other   *adj.* **jalan**
other people's *adj.* **ab'l**
otoscope *n.* **kaxkukay**
           n. **kaxlan xam**
ounce   *n.* **ons**
our abandoned house
           phr. **qapo'lem**
our ruins *phr.* **qapo'lem**
our rustic abode *phr.* **qapo'lem**
out of order *phr.* **moko us ta**
outcome *n.* **xraqik**

outlet   *n.* **chapleb'metz'ew**
            n. **nub'leb'aal**
            n. **ruq'il**
outlet (electrical)   *n.* **chapleb'**
            saqen
outrigger   *n.* **jukub'**
outside   *prep.* **chi rix**
outskirts   *n.* **re tenamit**
outstanding   *adj.* **us'elk**
oval   *adj.* **b'aq'**
            n. **b'aq'al**
            adj. **b'aq'b'o**
ovary   *n.* **xn'aj alaal**
oven   *n.* **joor**
            n. **pomleb'aal**
oven vent   *n.* **rokeb'l sib'**
over   *prep.* **sa' xb'een**
over there   *adv phr.* **sa' a'an**
            adv phr. **toj le'**
overcast   *adj.* **muqb'il**
overcoat   *n.* **jut aq'**
            n. **jut t'ikr**

overhead projector
            n. **kutleb'mu**
            n. **repolmu**
            n. **repom**
owe   *v.* **k'asok**
owl   *n.* **joob'aq**
            n. **warom**
own   *v.* **eechanink**
owned   *adj.* **wan aj eechal re**
ox   *n.* **b'ooyx**
            n. **kapuninb'il wakax**
            n. **kapunwakax**
            n. **pakun wakax**
oxidation   *n.* **mo'**
oxidize   *v.* **mo'onk**
oxygen   *n.* **b'ook-iq'**
            n. **b'ookol**
            n. **xb'ook iq**
oxygen tank   *n.* **xna'aj iq'**
oxygenation   *n.* **xb'ookil-iq'**
ozone   *n.* **jal'iq'**

P - p

Pablo   *nick.* **Lo**
Pacific Ocean   *n.* **tuulan palaw**
pacifist   *n agt.* **aj tuqtuukilnel**
pack   *v.* **b'atok**
package   *n.* **ab'en**
packet   *n.* **k'amom**

paddle   *n.* **kojl**
            n. **paleet**
paddock   *n.* **potreer**
padlock   *n.* **nat'leb' okeb'aal**
pail   *n.* **b'oot**
            n. **ch'inkumb'**

pain   *n.* **q'oq**
            n. **rahil**
            n. **rahilal**

painful   *adj.* **ra**

painkiller *n.* **re xkotzb'al xrahil**
            n. **re xkub'sinkil xrahil**

paint   *n.* **b'on**
            v. **b'onok**

paintbrush *n.* **b'onleb'**

painted face *n.* **b'onb'il u**

painted house *n.* **b'onb'il ochoch**

painter   *n agt.* **aj b'ononel**

paintgun   *n.* **puub'b'on**

painting   *n.* **b'omb'il eetalil**
            n. **kaaxukuut**

pair   *n.* **alab'**
            n. **jun suumal**
            n. **sumal**

palace   *n.* **rochochil'awab'ej**

palatal   *n.* **xb'een'e yaab'**

palate   *n.* **xb'een'e**

pale   *adj.* **saqb'etin**
            adj. **saqkirin**

Paleozoic era *n.* **rox q'ekutan**

pall   *n.* **paqleb'**

palladium   *n.* **saqmuch'iich'**

pallbearer *n agt.* **aj iiqanel**

pallor   *n.* **saqb'et**

palm (of the hand) *n.* **sa' uq'**
            n. **xsa' uq'b'**

palm tree   *n.* **b'ob'**
            n. **kala'**
            n. **xeek'**

pamphlet   *n.* **b'asb'il tasalhu**

pan   *n.* **k'ileb'aal**
            n. **xartin**

pancreas   *n.* **maal**

pans   *n.* **chiqleb'**

pant cuff   *n.* **xb'asalal**

pant leg   *n.* **roq wex**

panther   *n.* **aj b'oob'**
            n. **hix**

panties   *n.* **kok' aq' re ixq**

pantry   *n.* **xna'aj tzakahemq**

pants   *n.* **wex**

panty   *n.* **yach'**

papaya   *n.* **putul**

paper   *n.* **hu**
            n. **huhil**

paper bag   *n.* **ch'ina huhiljelool**

paper clip *n.* **chapleb'hu**
            n. **nat'leb'hu**

paper collator *n.* **tusleb'hu**

paper punch *n.* **hopleb'hu**

paper roll *n.* **b'otb'il hu**

paper towel dispenser
            n. **xche'el li b'otb'il hu**

papyrus   *n.* **xche'elhu**

parable   *n.* **jaljookil ru aatin**

parabola   *n.* **q'ot-eetalil**

parade   *v phr.* **b'eek chi tustu**
   n. **tusilb'eek**

paradigm   *n.* **chaab'ilob'resink**

paradise   *n.* **choxahil wank**

paragraph   *n.* **ch'ol'aatin**
   n. **raqalk'a'uxl**

parakeet   *n.* **puyuch'**

parallel line   *n.* **laq'juch'**
   n. **laq'lookil juch'**

paralytic   *n.* **sik**

paralyzed   *adj.* **sik**

paramedic   *n agt.* **aj ilom yaj**

paraphrase   *v.* **ch'ool'aatin**
   n. **yu'yuukil k'a'uxl**

parasol   *n.* **mu**

parasympathetic autonomic
   nervous system
   n. **xk'ub'lal ich'mul**
   ak re

parcel   *n.* **ab'en**
   n. **k'amb'il esilhu**

pardon me   *phr.* **chinaakuy**

parentheses   *n.* **k'ontz'uq**
   n. **nimaljuch'**
   n. **nimaljuch'**

parents   *n.* **yuwa'b'ejeb'**

parents (my)   *n.* **inna' inyuwa'**

parents-in-law   *n.* **hi'om e**
   n. **xyuwa' b'eelomej**
   n. **xyuwa' ixaqilb'ej**

park   *n.* **ajsib'aal u**
   n. **ja'leb'aal'u**
   n. **ja'leb'ch'ool**

parking lot
   n. **hiltasib'aalch'iich'**

parking meter   *n.* **xhilob'aal**
   b'eleb'aalch'iich'

parrot   *n.* **chocho'**
   n. **loor**

parsley   *n.* **perejil**

part   *n.* **ch'ol**
   n. **raqal**
   n. **teep**
   n. **xjachalal**

particle   *n.* **k'aj'aatin**
   n. **k'ajtz'iib'**

particle physics   *n.* **k'aj**
   nawcha'al

partner   *n.* **echaalal**
   n. **komon**

partridge   *n.* **kormaach**

parts of speech   *n.* **xraqilal li**
   aatinob'aal

party   *n.* **nimq'e**
   v. **nimq'ehink**

pass   *v.* **nume'k**

pass gas   *v.* **kisik**

passage   *n.* **numleb'aal**

passenger   *n agt.* **aj b'eenel**

passer-by   *n agt.* **aj b'e**

passion   *n.* **anchal xch'ool**

passive   *adj.* **ink'a' na'oken**

passive voice   *n.* **nume'k'uluk**

passport   *n.* **numilhu**

past tense   *n.* **numenaqil'uxk**

pasta   *n.* **paast**

pastor   *n.* **pastor**

pastor (animals)   *n.* **aj ilolketomq**

pastor (religious)   *n agt.* **aj k'ehol kuult**

pasture   *n.* **koral wakax**
     n. **potreer**
     n. **rax ch'och'**
     n. **wa'lem**

patch   *n.* **letzb'il b'an**

path   *n.* **ch'ina b'e**
     n. **jalb'e**
     n. **numleb'aal**
     n. **ruqb'e**

pathological   *adj.* **xyajelil**

pathology   *n.* **nawyajel**

patient   *n.* **yaj**

patient chart   *n.* **eetalil yaj**

patio   *n.* **neb'a**

patriotic   *adj.* **aj raholtenamit**

patriotic symbols
     n. **reetaltenamit**

patrol   *n.* **b'eetak'aak'alenel**
     v. **b'eetak'aak'alenk**

pattern   *n.* **reetalil**

pattern (clothing)   *n.* **ru aq'**

pavement   *n.* **tz'akalb'e**

paw   *n.* **roq**

pay   *v.* **tojok**

payment plan   *n.* **xhuhil tojok**

payphone   *n.* **tojb'il b'oqleb'**

payroll   *n.* **xhuhil tojok**

PC   *n.* **ulul ch'iich'**

pea   *n.* **arb'eej**
     n. **kaxche'kenq'**

peace   *n.* **sahil ch'oolej**
     n. **tuqtuukilal**

peaceful   *adj.* **q'un xch'ool**
     adj. **tuulan**

peach   *adj.* **turans**
     n. **turans**

peach fuzz   *n.* **q'ol is**

peacock   *n.* **tzo' pu'**

peak   *n.* **ru'uj tzuul**
     n. **xb'een tzuul**

peanut   *n.* **maniiy**

pear   *n.* **peer**
     n. **raxki'**

pearl   *n.* **q'ol**

peas   *n.* **arb'eej**
     n. **kaxche'kenq'**

peasant   *n agt.* **aj se' k'al**

pedagogue   *n agt.* **aj nawtijok**

pedagogy   *n.* **nawtijok**

pedal   *v phr.* **ek'asink chi oq**
     n. **leplepb'aal**
     v. **perperink**
     n. **tiikisib'aal**

pedestrian   *n agt.* **aj b'eenel**
     n agt. **aj numelb'e**

Pedro   *nick.* **Lu'**

pee   *v.* **chu'uk**

peel   *v.* **b'ich'ok**
     v. **jotzok**
     v phr. **mich'ok ix**

peeler   *n.* **jotzleb'**

peep   *v.* **yaab'ak**

peg   *n.* **kapoteer**
      n. **lokoch**
      n. **lukub'al**

pegboard *n.* **lukleb'**

pen   *n.* **ha'il tz'iib'leb'**
      n. **kik' tz'iib'**
      n. **k'uk'umtz'iib'**
      n. **tz'iib'leb'**
      n. **tz'iib'leb'on**

penal code *n.* **raschaq'rab' chi rix tojb'amaak**

penalty   *n.* **tojleb'aal maak**

pencil   *n.* **tz'iib'leb' che'**

pencil sharpener *n.* **jotzleb' tz'iib'leb' che'**

penguin   *n.* **kaxpatz xul**

penicillin *n.* **chunilb'an**

peninsula *n.* **ru'uj ch'och'**
      n. **ruq'b'ich'och'**

penis   *n.* **b'irich**
      n. **kun**
      n. **kunutz'**
      n. **pirich**
      n. **pur**
      n. **tz'ejwal**
      n. **tz'ik**
      n. **xche'el ab'aj**

penitentiary system *n.* **xk'uub'laltojb'amaak**

penny   *n.* **jun senta**

pentagon *n.* **o'xukuut**

penultimate *adj.* **rub'elal xraqik**

people   *n.* **kristian**
      n. **poyanam**
      n. **tenamitil**

pepper   *n.* **kaxlan q'een**
      n. **pens**

pepper shaker *n.* **xna'aj k'aj pens**

peppercorn *n.* **t'orol pens**

per capita income *n.* **junq eechej**

perform   *v.* **k'utb'esink**

perform rituals *v.* **wa'tesink**

perfume   *n.* **jaq'b'ab'**
      n. **sunob'l**
      n. **sununkil b'ook**

perhaps   *adv.* **maare**
      adv. **tana**

period   *n.* **raqleltz'uq**
      n. **raqtz'uq**
      n. **tiiqeltz'uq**
      n. **tz'uq**

permanently open *adj.* **jaqam**

permit   *v.* **k'ehok**

perpendicular line *n.* **raqro juch'**

person   *n.* **kristian**
      n. **poyanam**

personal values *n.* **rehil loq'alil**

perspire *v.* **tiqob'ak**

pessimism *n.* **k'ahil ch'oolej**

pessimistic *adj.* **aj sik'onel xyib'al ru**

pestle   *n.* **ruq' ka'**

petroleum *n.* **petrool**
   n. **q'olch'och'**

Petrona *nick.* **Pet**

petticoat *n.* **xta-uuq**

petty *adj.* **aj pix**

pew *n.* **hilaal**

pharmacist *n agt.* **aj k'ayinel b'an**

pharmacologist *n agt.* **aj nawb'an**

pharmacy *n.* **k'ayib'aal b'an**
   n. **loq'leb'aal b'an**

pheasant *n.* **chakmut**

philosopher *n agt.* **aj tz'ilom k'a'uxl**

philosophically *adv.* **xe'nawomil**

philosophy *n.* **xe'nawom**

phone *n.* **aatinob'aal ch'iich'**
   n. **b'oqleb'**
   n. **b'oqleb'aal**
   n. **b'oqleb'aal ch'iich'**
   n. **teleef**

phone card *n.* **tarjeet re b'oqleb'**

phone charger
   n. **metz'ewib'aalb'oqleb'**

phone line *n.* **xk'aamal b'oqleb'aal**

phone number *n.* **rajlil b'oqleb'**

phoneme *n.* **ch'oolyaab'**

phonetics *n.* **yaab'aatin**
   n. **yaab' kux**

photo *n.* **jalam'uuch**

photo album
   n. **k'uuleb'jalam'uuch**

photocopier *n.* **jalam'uuchleb'**
   n. **jalam'uuchleb'aal ch'iich'**
   n. **puktasib'aalhu**

photocopy *v.* **jalam'uuchink**
   n. **jalam'uuchu**

photographer *n agt.* **aj isihom jalam'uuch**

photosynthesis *n.* **xrajikraxil**

phrase *n.* **kok'raq aatin**
   n. **raqal'aatin**

physical education
   n. **q'ochleb'tzolom**
   n. **tijb'a'ajsiil**

physician *n agt.* **aj b'anonel**
   n. **loktor**

physics *n.* **nawcha'al**

piano *n.* **meexwajb'**

picante sauce *n.* **putz'b'il pix ik**

pick up *v.* **xokok**

pickaxe *n.* **pikleb'**

pickpocket *n agt.* **aj elq' karteer**

pickup truck *n.* **ch'ina iiqob'aal ch'iich'**

picture *n.* **jalam u**

piece *n.* **ch'iil**
   n. **ch'otolal**
   n. **ch'uyul**
   n. **jachal**
   n. **tolche'**
   n. **wechelal**

pig   *n.* **aaq**
      n. **kuy**

pigeon   *n.* **mukuy**

piggy bank   *n.* **k'ohaal**

pigpen   *n.* **rochoch aaq**

pile up   *v.* **b'uyuxink**

pilgrim   *n agt.* **aj b'e**

pill   *n.* **ch'ina b'an**
      n. **nuq'b'ilb'an**
      n. **pastiiy**

pillar   *n.* **roqechal xmukab'l**

pillow   *n.* **sok jolom**

pillowcase   *n.* **rix sok jolom**

pilot   *n agt.* **aj b'eresinelch'iich'**
      n agt. **aj ch'e'ol ch'iich'**

pimple   *n.* **tzelek**

pin   *n.* **kok' kuux**
      n. **xukub'k'ix**

pin cushion   *n.* **xna'aj kuux**

pincer   *n.* **yax**
      n. **k'uxch'iich'**

pinch   *v.* **ch'epok**
      v. **ch'uyuk**
      v. **jochok**
      v. **xeb'ok**

pine   *n.* **chaj**

pineapple   *n.* **ch'op**

pineapple juice   *n.* **xya'al ch'op**

pink   *adj.* **kaq saqin**
      adj. **saqikaq**

pinkie finger   *n.* **xch'i'pul uq'mej**

pinwheel   *n.* **ch'ina ral simaj**

pipe   *n.* **kachiimp**

pipe (metal)   *n.* **simb'ch'iich'**

pipe (plastic)   *n.* **simb'plaast**

piss   *v.* **chu'uk**

pistol   *n.* **kok' puub'**

pit   *n.* **jul**

pitcher   *n.* **puk'xaar**
      n. **xaar**

pitchfork   *n.* **orkeet**
      n. **rastriiy**

pituitary gland   *n.* **k'uub'aal sam**

pity   *n.* **toq'ob'al u**

pizza   *n.* **piitza**

piñata   *n.* **puk'um**
      n. **uutz'u'ujinb'il saa'us**

place   *v.* **kanab'ank**
      v. **k'ehok**
      n. **na'aj**
      n. **na'ajej**

placenta   *n.* **riiqk'uula'al**

plain   *n.* **helo**
      n. **roq taq'a**
      n. **taq'a**

plaintiff   *n.* **jitonel**

plait   *v.* **kemok**
      n. **tz'uluk**

plan   *n.* **tusk'anjel**
      v. **tusk'anjelank**

plane   *n.* **ji'leb'che'**
       v. **ji'ok**

plane figures   *n.* **helhookil eetalilatq**

plane ticket   *n.* **xhuhil purik**

planet   *n.* **nimlachahim**
       n. **ralsaq'e**
       n. **xtumb'choxa**

plant   *n.* **awinq**
       v. **awok**

plantain   *n.* **ch'ol tul**
       n. **saqi tul**
       n. **sayi'**

plantain chip   *n.* **k'orechtul**

plantation   *n.* **loq'b'ilch'och'**

planted   *adj.* **awo**

plants   *n.* **kok' che'**

plaque   *n.* **sol**

plaster   *n.* **yees**

plastic   *n.* **plastiik**

plastic arts
       n. **tzoljalam'uuch'ink**

plastic bag   *n.* **kaxtzuychampa**

plastic tube   *n.* **hompaq'**

plate   *n.* **ch'och' sek'**
       n. **helhokil sek'**
       n. **wa'leb' sek'**

platform   *n.* **taqleb'**
       n. **taqleb'aal**

play (instruments)   *v.* **toch'ok**

play bill   *n.* **eetalil hu**

play instruments   *v.* **wajb'ak**

play sports   *v phr.* **ajsink u li tib'elej**

play the flute   *v.* **xolb'ak**
       v. **xolib'k**

playful   *adj.* **aj b'atz'unel**

playground   *n.* **neb'aal**

playing field   *n.* **b'atz'ub'aal**
       n. **jomal**

plaza   *n.* **xnimal neb'aal**

plead   *v.* **patz'ok**

plead guilty   *v phr.* **yehok maak**

please   *phr.* **b'aanu usilal**
       v phr. **sahob'resink ch'ool**

please say that again
       phr. **b'aanu ye jun sutaq chik**

please speak slowly   *phr.* **b'aanu usilal aatinan chi timil**

please write it down   *phr.* **b'aanu usilal tz'iib'a**

pleased   *adj.* **k'ojla xch'ool**

pleasing   *adj.* **sa**

pleasure   *n.* **sahilank**

pleat   *n.* **xtusb'al xsa'**

pledge of allegiance   *n.* **xtij tenamit**

pliers   *n.* **k'atzleb'**
       n. **yaxch'iich'**
       n. **k'uxch'iich'**

plot   *n.* **waqlajuk'aam**
       n. **xoral**

plowed land *n.* **cho'leb' ch'och'**

plug *n.* **chapleb'metz'ew**
n. **chapleb' saqen**
n. **nub'leb'aal**

plum *n.* **ab'aal**
n. **sirweel**

plumb *n.* **alalch'iich'**
n. **tiikalxaqab'aal**

plumb line *n.* **jiileb'**

plumber *n agt.* **aj letzolsimb'ha'**
n agt. **aj yiib'om ha'**

plunder *v.* **min'isink**
v. **minyamtesink**

plural *adj.* **k'ihalatq**

pluralization particle *part.* **eb'**

pluricellular *adj.* **k'ilana'yu'am**

plus sign (+) *n.* **reetaltamok-ajl**
n. **reetal molam ajl**

plush toy *n.* **kaxtzukxul**

Pluto *n.* **xb'ele' ralsaq'e**

PO Box *n.* **xkaxonil esilhu**

pocket *n.* **b'oox**

poem *n.* **uutz'u'jinb'il aatin**

poet *n agt.* **aj uutz'u'ujinel aatin**

poetry *n.* **uutz'u'jinb'iltz'iib'**

poetry collection *n.* **xhuhul uutz'u'jinb'il aatin**

point *v.* **jayalink**
n. **tz'uq**

pointed *adj.* **jutz'**
adj. **jutz' ru'uj**
adj. **q'es**

poison *v phr.* **kamsink chi uk'b'il**
n. **may**

pole *n.* **oqech**

police *n agt.* **aj chaponel**
n agt. **aj iloltenamit**
n agt. **aj k'aak'alenel**

police car *n.* **k'aak'aleb'aal ch'iich'**

police officer *n agt.* **aj chaponel**
n agt. **aj iloltenamit**
n agt. **aj k'aak'alenel**

police station *n.* **xna'aj aj ilol tenamit**

policeman *n agt.* **aj chaponel**
n agt. **aj iloltenamit**
n agt. **aj k'aak'alenel**

policeman's belt *n.* **xk'aamal sa' aj puub'**

policy *n.* **xna'leb'il**

polio *n.* **luqaak**

polish *v.* **mesok**

political party *n.* **ch'uut awab'ejilal**

politician *n agt.* **aj yalol u chi awab'ejink**

pollen *n.* **poqsiyaal**

pollination *n.* **poqsiyajink**

polyglot *n agt.* **aj ka'aatin**
n agt. **aj k'ila'aatin**

polygon *n.* **k'ila'u**

polynomial *n.* **k'ila eetalb'irok**

polysyllable *n.* **k'ilayehiil**

pomade *n.* **yulb'ilb'an**

pomegranate *n.* **kranaa**

poncho *n.* **isb'**

pond *n.* **pumpuukil ha'**

pony *n.* **ch'ina kawaay**

pool *n.* **atib'aal**
    n. **numxib'aal**

poor *adj.* **kaqcha**
    adj. **neb'a'**
    adj. **toq'ob' ru**

poorly *adv phr.* **moko chaab'il ta**

popcorn *n.* **moqx**

pope *n.* **paap**

poppy *n.* **amapool**

Popti [aka Jakaltek] *lang.* **popti**

Poqomam *lang.* **poqomam**

Poqomchi *lang.* **poqomchi'**

porcelain *n.* **porselaan**

porcupine *n.* **k'ix uch**

pork *n.* **xtib'el aaq**

pork rind *n.* **chiron**

pork rinds *n.* **xujanb'iltib'**

pork sausage *n.* **choriis**

porridge *n.* **matz'**
    n. **saqjuy**
    n. **uq'un**

port *n.* **hilob'jukub'**
    n. **xaqleb'jukub'**

porter *n agt.* **aj k'amol iiq**

positive *adj.* **tz'aqal ru**
    adj. **us li naraj**

positive electric charge
    n. **xsak'om tiqkaxlanxaml**

possess *v.* **eechanink**

possessions *n.* **eechej**

possessive *n.* **eechaninb'il**

post *n.* **oqech**
    n. **taql**

post office *n.* **nums'esilb'aal**
    n. **rochochil esilhu**

post office box *n.* **xkaxonil esilhu**

postage *n.* **eetaltoj**
    n. **tiimbr**
    n. **xtojb'al relik**

postage stamp *n.* **eetal**

postcard *n.* **jalam'uuchil taql**
    n. **tarjeet postal**

poster *n.* **esilhu**
    n. **k'utleb'hu**
    n. **ninqiperhu**

posture *n.* **xaqal**
    n. **xaaqalil**

pot *n.* **joomuk'al**
    n. **uk'al**

potato *n.* **kaxlan is**
    n. **paaps**

potential energy *n.* **xmetz'ew k'a'aq ru**

potter *n agt.* **aj pak'ol**
    n agt. **aj pak'onel**

pottery *n.* **pak'b'il**

pound   *n.* **b'iis'aal**
         n. **liiwr**
         v. **t'i'ok**
pour   *v.* **hoyok**
         v. **pajink**
         v. **xulub'ank**
poverty *n.* **neb'a'il**
powder   *n.* **poqsxaml**
power   *n.* **ruhan**
         n. **wankil**
power switch *n.* **chupleb'
         saqen**
         n. **raqleb' saqen**
powerstrip *n.* **jekb'ametz'ew**
practice *v.* **b'aanunk**
         n. **xb'aanunkil**
pragmatism *n.* **oksinb'il na'leb'**
prairie *n.* **roq taq'a**
         n. **taq'a**
praise   *n.* **nimank u**
         n. **terq'usink k'ab'a'**
prawns   *n.* **jit**
         n. **k'ox**
pray   *v.* **tijok**
prayer   *n.* **tij**
prayer book *n.* **oxloq'il hu**
praying mantis *n.* **tz'upq'een**
preach   *v.* **k'eelenk**
Precambrian era *n.* **xb'een
         q'ekutan**
precious metal *n.* **chaab'il
         ch'iich'**
precipice *n.* **chamal jul**
         n. **uul**

precipitation *n.* **rachhab'**
predicate *n.* **ch'olob'ihom**
predict *v.* **q'ehink**
prediction *n.* **xq'ehinkil**
prefix   *n.* **tiktz'aqob'l**
pregnancy *n.* **yu'amil**
pregnant *adj.* **sa' yu'am**
         adj. **yaj aj ixq**
preoccupation *n.* **xtib' jolom**
prepaid phone card *n.* **tojhuil
         b'oqleb'**
prepare *v.* **kawresink**
preposition *n.* **q'inolaatin**
         n. **xtiqb'al aatin**
preschool *n.* **k'aytesiil**
prescription *n.* **reetalil b'an**
         n. **xhuhul b'an**
present *v.* **k'utb'esink**
         v. **q'axtesink**
         adj. **wan**
present tense
         n. **anaqwankil'uxk**
presenter *n agt.* **aj xaqab'anel**
preserve *v.* **kolb'eetank**
president *n.* **awab'ej**
         n. **xb'eenil awab'ej**
press   *n.* **nat'leb'**
         v. **nat'ok**
         v. **pitz'ok**
pressing machine *n.* **nat'leb'**
pressure cooker *n.* **nat'b'il uk'al**
         n. **tz'aptz'ookil uk'al**

pretty   *adj.* **ch'ina us**
       adj. **chaq'al ru**

prevent   *v.* **ramok**
       v. **romok**

prey   *n.* **tzak**

price   *n.* **xloq'al**
       n. **xtz'aq**

pride   *n.* **wankil**

priest   *n agt.* **aj k'ehol miix**
       n. **chimam**
       n. **payr**
       n. **xb'eenil aj tij**

primate   *n.* **aj maxxul**

prince   *n.* **xch'ajom ajwal**

princess   *n.* **rab'in ajwal**

principal   *n.* **xb'eenil tzoleb'aal**
       n. **xjolomil tzoleb'aal**

principal's office   *n.* **jolomilal tzoleb'aal**
       n. **jolomnib'aal**
       n. **xna'aj xb'eenil**

print house   *n.* **pukhub'aal**

printer   *n.* **pukleb'hu**
       n. **puktasib'aalhu**
       n. **puktasiil**

printer cartridge   *n.* **na'aj b'onhu**

printer ink   *n.* **xya'al puktasiilhu**

printer's   *n.* **pukhub'aal**

prison   *n.* **tz'alam**

prison system   *n.* **xk'ub'laal tojb'a maak**

n. **xk'uub'laltojb'amaak**

prisoner   *n agt.* **aj tz'alam**
       n. **preex**

private   *adj.* **wan aj eere**

prize   *n.* **maatan**

probably   *adv.* **maare**

problem   *n.* **ch'a'ajkil**

process   *n.* **ch'olk'anjel**

processor   *n.* **ch'olk'anjelob'aal**

prodigy   *n.* **numseeb' xch'ool**

product   *n.* **na'el**
       n. **x'el**

productivity   *n.* **ruuch**

profession   *n.* **k'anjel**

professional   *n agt.* **aj nawk'anjel**
       n. **nimru'ajk'anjel**
       n. **tz'aqal'ajk'anjel**

professionalism   *n.* **nawk'anjelil**

prognosticate   *v.* **q'ehink chi ru**

program (TV)   *n.* **k'uub'anb'il k'anjel**
       n. **k'uub'ank**

progress   *n.* **wakliik**
       v. **wakliik**
       v. **yu'k**

progressive particle   *part.* **yo**

progressivity   *n.* **wakliikil**

projector   *n.* **kutleb'mu**
       n. **repolmu**
       n. **repom**

prokaryotic cell
n. **ch'emna'yu'am**

promise *v phr.* **sumenk ru aatin**

promissory note *n.* **hu xaqb'anb'il xwankil** *n.* **xhuhiltoj**

prompter *n agt.* **aj jultikahonel**

pronoun *n.* **ruuchik'ab'a'ej** *n.* **uuchilk'ab'a'ej**

pronounce *v.* **yaab'asink**

pronunciation *n.* **xyaab'asinkil**

proof *n.* **k'utb'esil**

propaganda *n.* **pukta'esil**

propane *n.* **b'ookilxaml** *n.* **iq'xaml**

propeller *n.* **sururu**

proper noun *n.* **xk'ab'a'il**

property line *n.* **nub'aal**

prophase *n.* **xb'een pojk'ok**

propose *v.* **xaqab'ank**

prostitute *n.* **kaan ru ixq** *n.* **k'ayihom rib'** *n.* **puut**

prostitution *n.* **puutink**

protagonist *n agt.* **aj b'aanunel**

protect *v.* **kolok** *v.* **tenq'ank**

protection *n.* **kole'k**

protein *n.* **ajsiil** *n.* **kawub'l**

Protestant *n.* **kapiiy**

proton *n.* **tiqkaxlan xaml**

protractor *n.* **b'isxuk**

proud *adj.* **kaw xch'ool** *adj.* **numtaak** *adj.* **q'etq'et**

proverb *n.* **jaljookil'aatin** *n.* **tawilna'leb'**

pruning shears *n.* **setleb' uutz'u'uj**

psychologically *adv.* **nawtuqch'oolil**

psychologist *n agt.* **aj nawtuqch'ool**

psychology *n.* **nawtuqch'ool**

psychotherapist *n agt.* **aj aatinanel rik'in yaj**

psychotherapy *n.* **aatinak rik'in yaj**

pubis *n.* **peekem kun**

public *adj.* **re tenamit**

public services *n.* **k'a'aq re ru li tenamit**

public telephone
n. **raatik'aamch'iich' tenamit**

publication *n.* **xpuktasinkil**

publish *v phr.* **puktasink esil**

published *adj.* **puktasinb'il**

publisher *n.* **pukhub'aal**

pull *v.* **jukunk** *phr.* **kelo** *v.* **kelonk**

pumice *n.* **maqs**

pumpkin *n.* **k'um**

pumpkin seed *n.* **sakil k'um**

punctuation mark *n.* **reetalil tz'aqob'tz'iib'**

punish *v.* **k'ajtesink**

punishment *n.* **tojb'a maak** *n.* **tojleb'aal maak**

pupil *n.* **tijom** *n.* **tzolom**

pupil (eye) *n.* **xtehelem'u**

puppet *n.* **poyb'atz'uul**

purchase *v.* **loq'ok** *n.* **loq'om**

purple *adj.* **q'eqmoyin**

purse *n.* **b'ools** *n.* **xna'aj tumin**

pursue *v.* **taaqenk**

pus *n.* **pojel** *n.* **pojk**

push *v.* **minok** *v.* **miikisink**

v. **tiikink**
phr. **tiikis**

put *v.* **kanab'ank** *v.* **k'ehok**

put off *v.* **b'ayok**

put on *v phr.* **tiqok ib'**

puzzled *adj.* **sachenaq ru**

PVC *n.* **simb'plaast**

pyjamas *n.* **aq' re wark** *n.* **warib'aq** *n.* **warib'aal aq**

pyramid *n.* **jutz'-eetalil** *n.* **ox'u**

pyramid (four-sided) *n.* **jutz' kaaxukuut**

pyramid (monument) *n.* **jutz'il na'aj** *n.* **jutz'ochochilpek** *n.* **ox'ukab'l**

pyramid (three-sided) *n.* **jutz' oxxukuut**

Q - q

Q'eqchi' *lang.* **q'eqchi'**

Qanjobal *lang.* **q'anjob'al**

quail *n.* **tonq'** *n.* **turunhut tz'ik**

quantity *n.* **nimal**

quarrel *n.* **raaxiik'**

quarter *n.* **jun kaajachal** *n.* **jun xka**

n. **o'laju xk'ak'aal senta**

queen *n.* **ixajaw** *n.* **xoq'jaw**

question *n.* **patz'om**

question mark (?) *n.* **reetalil patz'omq**

questionnaire *n.* **raqalyalb'a'ix**

quetzal	*n.* **jun ketzal**
	n. **q'uq'**
quickly	*adv phr.* **sa' jumpaat**
quiet	*adj.* **ink'a' na'aatinak**
	adj. **kulku**
	adj. **k'irnak**
	adj. **tuulan**
quince	*n.* **mem'riiy**

quite	*adv.* **chi xjunil**
	adv. **us**
quiz	*n.* **yalok ix**
quotation marks	
	n. **ka'muluq'utiltz'uq**
quotes	*n.* **ka'muluq'utiltz'uq**
quotient	*n.* **xjek'iil**

R - r

rabbit	*n.* **imul**
	n. **xa'an imul**
rabies	*n.* **wax ru**
raccoon	*n.* **ow**
radiation	*n.* **xnumsinkil**
radiator	*n.* **tuqtiq**
	n. **wosleb'**
radio	*n.* **ray**
radio (receiver)	*n.* **ab'ib'aalson**
	n. **ab'ib'aal aatin**
radio (transmitter)	
	n. **puktasib'aal**
radio antenna	*n.* **xmisik' puktasib'aal**
radio studio	*n.* **xtoonal li ab'ib'aal aatin**
radio tower	*n.* **puktasib'aal kab'l najt xteram**
radio transmitter	*n.* **numsib'aal esil**
radioactivity	*n.* **numsiilk'anjel**
radish	*n.* **kaqxe'**

Rafael	*nick.* **Rap**
raffle	*n.* **b'uuleb'**
	n. **b'uulik**
	v. **b'uulink**
	n. **pumb'uul**
raffle a prize	*v phr.* **b'uulink maatan**
raffle money	*v phr.* **b'uulink tumin**
raft	*n.* **poyte'**
	v. **poyte'ib'k**
rafter	*n.* **b'aqsotz'**
	n. **xb'e ch'o**
rag	*n.* **sut**
	n. **xputz't'ikr**
railing	*n.* **ramleb'**
rain	*n.* **hab'**
	n. **hab'al**
rain with hail	*n.* **b'achal hab'**
rainbow	*n.* **kaqlaaq'**
	n. **xokaq'ab'**
rainfall meter	*n.* **b'isleb'hab'**

rainy	*adj.* **kutankil hab'**
	adj. **yo hab'**
raise	*v.* **paqonk**
	v. **taqsink**
	v. **waklesink**
	v. **xaqab'ank**
raise to the fifth power	
	v. **ro'wahink**
rake	*n.* **jochleb'**
	n. **jochleb'mul**
	n. **rastriiy**
ram	*n.* **karneer**
rancid	*adj.* **ch'am**
range	*n.* **kelkookil tzuul**
	n. **tzoltzookiltzuul**
ransom	*n.* **tumin re uuchil**
rape	*v.* **muxuk**
	n. **muxuk**
	n. **xminb'al ru**
rapids	*n.* **xkawil roq ha'**
rapist	*n agt.* **aj muxunel**
rare	*adj.* **toj rax**
rash	*n.* **porha'**
	adj. **yal naxkuti rib'**
rasp	*n.* **ji'leb'**
	n. **ji'leb'ch'iich'**
rat	*n.* **ch'o**
	n. **uch ch'o**
rate	*n.* **aj b'isonel na'leb'**
rather	*adv.* **chi xjunil**
	adv. **us**
ratio	*n.* **aj b'isonel na'leb'**
rattle	*n.* **luk'luk' che'**
raven	*n.* **tuntz'oq**

ravine	*n.* **uul**
	n. **xiik'**
raw	*adj.* **rax**
raw materials	*n.* **usil k'a'aq re ru**
ray	*n.* **perkar**
razor	*n.* **johob'a mach**
	n. **jooleb'**
	n. **jooleb'mach**
	n. **nawaaj**
razor blade	*n.* **xileet**
read	*v phr.* **ilok ru hu**
ready	*adj.* **k'ub'k'u**
realistic	*adj.* **sa' yaal na'aatinak**
reality	*n.* **xyaalalil**
realize	*v phr.* **k'ehok eetal**
really	*adv phr.* **elik chi yaal**
really?	*phr.* **ma yaal**
rear-view mirror	*n.* **ilb'a'ixlem**
	n. **ka'yab'aal ixkej**
	n. **lemaal'ix**
reason	*v.* **na'leb'ank**
rebar	*n.* **b'aqch'iich'**
rebellious	*adj.* **ink'a' na'ab'in**
rebirth	*n.* **rajikab'aal**
reborn	*v.* **rajikru**
	v phr. **yo'laak xka'wa**
receipt	*n.* **huhil-loq'om**
	n. **xhuhilk'uluk**
	n. **xhuhil loq'om**
receive rites	*v.* **wa'tesiik**
receive visitors	*v.* **ula'anink**

receiver *n agt.* **aj k'ulul re**

recent *adj.* **toje'**

reception *n.* **k'uleb'aal**

receptionist *n agt.* **aj k'ulul ula'**

recess *n.* **ajsib'aal'u**
n. **hoonalhilaal**
n. **xhoonal asjsink-u**

recipe *n.* **reetalil k'uub'ank**

recipe book *n.* **xhuhuil'esil**

recipient *n agt.* **aj k'ulul re**
n. **xk'ab'a' li
taak'ulu'q re**

reciprocal *adj.* **sumenk-ib'**

recital *n.* **kawyehink**

recitation *n.* **kawyehink**

recite *v.* **yaab'asink**

recline *v.* **salab'ank**

reclined *adj.* **salso**

recognize *v.* **na'link**

recompense *n.* **k'ajk'amunkil**

record *v phr.* **chapok aatin**
n. **surb'ich**

record a video *v.* **chapokmu**

record player
n. **surb'ichleb'aal**

recording studio *n.* **xna'aj aj
aatinanel**

recreation *n.* **ajsib'aal'u**
n. **hilaal**
n. **hoonalhilaal**
n. **xhoonal asjsink-u**

recreation center *n.* **xna'aj
ajsink u**

rectangle
n. **kelkookilkaaxuku
ut**

rectangular *adj.* **kelkookil
kaaxukuut**

rectum *n.* **mam**

recyclable *adj.* **ak'oresiil**

recycle *v.* **ka'oksink**

recycling *n.* **xka'oksinkil**

red *adj.* **kaq**

red blood cells *n.* **kaqkil
mitz'kotkik'**
n. **xxulel kik'el**

red face *n.* **kaqxot'ink**

red wine *n.* **q'eqil b'iin**

redact *v phr.* **na'leb'ank tz'iib'**

reddish-gray *adj.* **tz'ib'**

reduce *v.* **k'osok**

reed *n.* **aj**

reef *n.* **pekil ha'**

referee *n agt.* **aj tuqub'anel**

refine *v.* **hesok**

refinement *n.* **xhesb'al**

reflect *v.* **k'oxlank**

reflection (light) *n.* **xk'utum
xaml**

reflection (thought)
n. **xk'a'uxlankil**

reflexive particle *part.* **ib'**

reforest *v.* **ka'awk**

reforestation *n.* **ka'awb'il**

reforested *adj.* **xka'awb'il**

reform   v. **tuqub'ank**
          n. **xtuqub'ankil**
refraction n. **jalb'ehil saqen**
refrain   n. **jaljookil'aatin**
           n. **tawilna'leb'**
refreshment n. **kolb'ach'ool**
refrigerator n. **kehob'resilb'aal**
           n. **keeleb'aal**
           n. **reepri**
refuse   v phr. **ink'a'**
          xq'ulub'ank
register   v. **poqlenk**
regret   v phr. **ch'inank ch'ool**
          v. **kiib'ch'oolink**
          v phr. **yot'ok ch'ool**
regulator n. **tuqb'ametz'ew**
rehearse   v. **yalb'ek**
          v. **yalok**
rehydration n. **xka'ha'resinkil**
reign   v. **poopirk**
reject   v. **tz'eqtaanank**
rejected adj. **tz'eqtananb'il**
rejection n. **tz'eqtanaank**
relative   n. **cha'al**
          n. **komon**
          n. **ruk'**
relatives n. **amaq'il tenamit**
relaxed vowel n. **jayaab' na'tz'iib'**
release   v phr. **k'ehok sa' sahilal**
religion   n. **paab'aal**

reluctantly adv phr. **kab' rix ch'ool**
remain   v. **kanaak**
remainder n. **jeb'ok**
remains   n. **ela'**
          n. **rela'**
          n. **xb'een**
          n. **xeel**
remedy   n. **b'an**
remember   v. **jultikank**
          v phr. **naqk sa' ch'ool**
remove   v. **isink**
          v. **sote'k**
rename   v. **ka'k'a'b'aink**
rendition n. **t'ane'k**
renew   v. **ak'o'k**
          v. **ak'ob'resink**
renewable adj. **ak'ob'resink**
renown   n. **ka'xaqab'aal**
repatriate n. **sutq'isinb'il**
          v. **sutq'iik**
repeat that phr. **ye wi'chik**
repent   v phr. **ch'inank ch'ool**
          v. **yot'o'k**
repentance n. **ek'ank ib'**
repetition n. **ka'sutink**
          n. **ka'wahink**
reply   v. **chaq'ok**
          v. **sumenk**
report   n. **esilk'anjel**
reporter n agt. **aj k'ehol esil**
          n agt. **aj molol'esil**
          n agt. **aj tz'iib'anel esil**

represent *v.* **eeqajink**
v. **uuchilink**

representative *n.* **aj k'uub'anelchaq'rab'**
n. **uuchilej**

representativity *n.* **uuchininkil**

reprimand *v.* **q'usuk**

reproduce *v.* **alab'tesink**
v. **ka'sutink**

reptile *n.* **ahin jukxul**
n. **jukxul**

request *n.* **ajb'il**
n. **patz'b'il**

rescue *v.* **kolok**

rescue unit *n.* **xmolam aj kolonel**

research *v.* **tz'ilok-ix**

researcher *n agt.* **aj tzilol'ix**
n agt. **aj tzilonel**

reseed *v.* **ka'awk**

reside *v.* **wank**

resonant *n.* **yaab'il**

resource *n.* **eechej**

resource conservation *n.* **xkolb'al rix li loq'laj che'k'aam**

respect *n.* **oxloq'il**
v. **oxloq'ink**

respected *adj.* **oxloq'inb'il**

respectful *adj.* **na'oxloq'in**

respiration *n.* **musiq'**

respiratory system *n.* **musiq'ab'aal**

respire *v.* **musiq'ak**

respond *v.* **chaq'ok**
v. **sumenk**

responsibility *n.* **k'amch'oolanink**

responsible *adj.* **aj ch'oolanel**

rest *v.* **hilank**
n. **hiil**
n. **rela'**

restaurant *n.* **nimlawa'leb'aal**
n. **nimla k'ayib'aal tzakahemq**
n. **wa'leb'aal**

restless *adj.* **yal k'a' naxb'aanu**

result *n.* **na'el**
n. **x'el**

resumé *n.* **esilnawom**

resurrection *n.* **kab'yo'lajik**

retina *n.* **jayiltz'uumal'u**
n. **xyi**

retreat *v.* **eelelik**

retribution *n.* **eeqaj**

return *v.* **q'ajk**
v. **q'axtesink**
v. **sutq'iik**

reuse *v.* **ka'oksink**
n. **xka'oksinkil**

reversed *adj.* **xsal**

reversible *adj.* **junpak'alil**
adj. **xsutq'isinkil chi rix**

revert *v.* **sutq'iik**

revolting *adj.* **yib' yib'**

revolution   *n.* **sutrix**

revolver   *n.* **kok' puub'**

revolving drum   *n.* **pumb'uul**

reward   *v.* **k'ajk'amunk**
     n. **k'ajk'amunkil**

rewrite   *v.* **ka'tz'iib'ank**

rhinoceros   *n.* **kaxchixl**

rhodium   *n.* **q'anmuch'iich'**

rhomboid   *adj.* **b'arxuk**

rhombus   *n.* **salsookil kaaxukuut**
     n. **xaqamkaaxuk**

rhubarb   *n.* **rub'aarb'**

rhyme   *n.* **uutz'u'jinb'ilraq**

rhythm   *n.* **roqil**

rib   *n.* **poolok'il**
     n. **xb'aqel xukuy**
     n. **xchakachil b'aq**
     n. **xukuy**

ribbon   *n.* **jisil t'ikr**
     n. **tz'uleb'**

ribosome   *n.* **mitz'k'amk'ot**

ribs   *n.* **kostiiy**

Ricardo   *nick.* **Rik**

rice   *n.* **aros**

rice paddy   *n.* **xna'aj aros**

rich   *adj.* **b'ihom**
     adj. **sa**

riches   *n.* **b'ihomal**

rickets   *n.* **chaqi'oqil**
     n. **numay**

riddle   *n.* **jorb'ana'leb'**

ride   *v phr.* **taqe'k chi rix kawaay**

ride (a horse)   *v.* **kawaayink**

ridgepole   *n.* **tz'amb'a**

rifle   *n.* **puub'**

right (correct)   *adj.* **q'axal chaab'il**

right (spatial)   *adj.* **sa' nim**

right away   *adv phr.* **ak anaqwan**

right here   *adv phr.* **arin tz'aqal**

right there   *adv phr.* **aran tz'aqal**

righteous   *adj.* **tiik xch'ool**

righteousness   *n.* **yaalal**

rights   *n.* **k'ulub'**
     n. **k'ulub'em**
     n. **xk'ulub'poyanam**

ring   *n.* **b'ot**
     n. **ch'ina sursukil ch'iich'**
     n. **matq'ab'**
     v. **tzinb'ak**

ring (phone)   *n.* **yaab'aal**

rinse   *v.* **nub'resink**

ripe   *adj.* **chaq'**
     adj. **q'an**
     adj. **yuq'uq'nak**

rise   *v.* **taqsink**
     v. **wakliik**
     v. **xaqliik**

river   *n.* **nima'**
     n. **roq ha'**

river rock   *n.* **pekil nima'**

rivet   *n.* **ka't'oj**

roach   *n.* **paachach**

road   *n.* **b'e**
             n. **nimb'e**
             n. **nimla b'e**
             n. **numleb'aal**

roadrunner   *n.* **rak'ach tzuul**

roar   *v phr.* **chajok e**

roast   *v.* **pomok**
             v. **sisank**

roast beef   *n.* **pomb'il tib'**

roasted   *adj.* **pomb'il**

roasting pan   *n.* **pomleb'**

Roberto   *nick.* **Rob'**

robot   *n.* **yolojch'iich**
             n. **yu'am ch'iich**

robust   *adj.* **kaw rib'**

rock   *n.* **pek**
             n. **pekal**

rodents   *n.* **aj k'oyoneleb'**
             n. **aj setoneleb'**

roll   *v.* **b'arb'arink**
             n. **q'ooch**

roll out   *v.* **helok**

roll paper dispenser   *n.* **xche'el li b'otb'il hu**

rolling pin   *n.* **b'ola**
             n. **kok'poli'n**

rolls   *n.* **kok' kaxlan wa**
             n. **potzkaxlanwa**

roof   *n.* **xb'een kab'l**

rooftop terrace   *n.* **xb'een ochoch**

room   *n.* **kwaart**
             n. **sa' kab'l**

rooster   *n.* **tzo'xul**
             n. **tzo' kaxlan**

root   *n.* **xe'**

roots   *n.* **xxe'il**

rope net   *n.* **soq'**

rosary   *n.* **rajleb' tij**

rose   *n.* **k'ix'atz'um**
             n. **roos**

rose bush   *n.* **roos**

rosemary   *n.* **romeer**

rotation   *n.* **sutrib'**

rotten   *adj.* **q'aaneq**

rough   *adj.* **b'urux**
             adj. **chaq re ru**
             adj. **k'urux**
             adj. **purux**
             adj. **q'es ru**
             adj. **turux**

round   *adj.* **kotko**
             adj. **q'otq'o**
             adj. **sursu**
             adj. **t'ort'o**

roundabout   *n.* **k'ulb'aq'qax'ib'**

route   *n.* **numleb'aal**

row   *v phr.* **b'eeresink jukub'**
             v. **juyuk**
             v. **kojlenk**
             n. **tzol**
             n. **tzolil**

rower   *n agt.* **aj b'eresinel jukub'**

rub	*v.* **b'iqok**	rules	*n.* **xchaq'rab'il**
	v. **jilok**	ruling	*n.* **ruq'b'chaq'rab'**
rubber	*n.* **kik'che'**	rum	*n.* **ron**
	n. **rin**	rumor	*n.* **yoob'ank aatin**
rudder	*n.* **xik'jukub'**	run	*v.* **aanilak**
rude	*adj.* **maak'a' xxutaan**		*v.* **chak'chotk**
rug	*n.* **alfoombr**	run out	*v.* **oso'k**
	n. **ruhiltz'ak**	runner	*n agt.* **aj aanilanel**
	n. **xta ru ch'och'**	runway	*n.* **k'ochleb'aal**
ruins	*n.* **po'lem**		**ch'iich'**
	n. **xtz'akeb' xe'toon**	Ruperto	*nick.* **Rup**
rule	*v.* **awab'ejink**	rust	*n.* **mo'**
	v. **poopirk**		*v.* **mo'onk**
	v. **taqlank**	ruthless	*adj.* **maak'a' xkuyum**
	n. **xtz'iib'ul**	Rómulo	*nick.* **Room**
ruler	*n.* **juch'leb'**		
	n. **ruuchilawab'ej**		
	n. **tikil che'**		
	n. **tiikal juch'leb'**		

S - s

sack	*n.* **koxtal**	sadness	*n.* **q'oq**
	v. **min'isink**		*n.* **rahil ch'oolejil**
	v. **minyamtesink**	safe	*n.* **pak'b'il tz'ak**
sacred	*adj.* **oxloq'**	safety	*n.* **wank sa' xyaalal**
sacrifice	*n.* **mayej**	safety pin	*n.* **xukub'k'ix**
sacristan	*n agt.* **aj ilol tijob'aal**	saffron	*n.* **asapran**
	n. **pixcal**	sail	*v phr.* **b'eek chi ru ha'**
sad	*adj.* **k'uul ru**		*n.* **b'eel**
	adj. **rahil ch'ool**	sailor	*n agt.* **aj b'eresinel**
	adj. **ra xch'ool**		**jukub'**
sadden	*v phr.* **raho'k xch'ool**		

saint   *n agt.* **aj santil**
          paab'anel
          n agt. **aj tiikilal**
          n. **saant**

salad   *n.* **ichaj tzakahemq**

salad bowl   *n.* **xna'aj murinb'il**
          sa us

salamander   *n.* **paqmaal**
          n. **xna' k'anti'**

sale   *n.* **kotzko xtz'aq**
          n. **kub'enaq xtz'aq**

sales clerk   *n agt.* **aj k'ay**

salesman   *n agt.* **aj k'ay**
          n agt. **aj k'ayinel**

saliva   *n.* **chuub'**

salsa   *n.* **putz'b'il pix ik**
          n. **xya'al pix**

salt   *n.* **atz'am**

salt shaker   *n.* **xna'aj atz'am**

salty   *adj.* **k'ipitz'in**
          adj. **pitz'pitz'**

same   *adj.* **junaj**
          adj. **juneet**
          adj. **juntaq'eet**
          adj. **na'ajil**

same as usual   *phr.* **jo' junelik**

same to you   *phr.* **jo'kan ajwi'**
          tinye aawe

sand   *n.* **samahi'**
          v. **ji'ok**

sandal   *n.* **perxaab'**

sandfly   *n.* **k'uxuk**
          n. **suq**

sandpaper   *n.* **ji'leb'**
          n. **k'arhu**
          n. **q'unleb'**

sap   *n.* **q'ol**
          n. **ya'al**

sardines   *n.* **saqi kar**

sash   *n.* **k'aamal sa'**

satellite   *n.* **aj b'e chahim**
          n. **b'eenelchahim**
          n. **chahimch'iich'**

satellite dish   *n.* **esilsek'**
          chahimch'iich'

satisfied   *adj.* **k'ojkookilch'ool**
          adj. **saasa xch'ool**

Saturday   *n.* **saaw**
          n. **xwaqkutan**

Saturn   *n.* **satuurn**
          n. **xwaq ralsaq'e**

sauce   *n.* **putz'b'il**

saucepan   *n.* **mansek'**
          n. **per'uk'al**

saucer   *n.* **platiiy**

sausage   *n.* **b'utb'iltib'**
          n. **salchiich**

savannah   *n.* **sabaan**

save   *v.* **kolok**
          v. **k'uulank**
          v. **xokok**

savings   *n.* **k'o'al**

savings account   *n.* **ch'uut**
          tumin

savings passbook   *n.* **xtasal**
          xhuhil tumin

savor   *v.* **yalok**

saw   *n.* **jachleb'**
           n. **kelk'arch'iich'**
           n. **k'ixsetleb'**
           n. **seruch**
           v. **setok**
           n. **xeer**

sawdust   *n.* **k'ajche'**

saxophone *n.* **ch'ere'wajb'**

say   *v.* **yehok**

say again *phr.* **ye wi'chik**

saying   *n.* **jaljookil'aatin**
           n. **tawilna'leb'**

scabbard   *n.* **rixch'iich'**

scabies   *n.* **tuxl**

scaffolding *n.* **k'ochkaq'l**
           n. **lochte'b'aal**
           n. **taqleb'**
           n. **taqleb'aal**

scale   *n.* **b'isleb'**
           n. **b'isleb'aal**
           n. **peex**
           n. **rep'ix**
           n. **solel**
           n. **tuqb'isleb'**
           n. **xsol rix**

scale (reptilian) *n.* **pat**

scan   *v.* **k'atok-eetalil**

scanned   *adj.* **k'atb'il-eetalil**

scanner   *n.* **k'atleb'-eetalil**
           n. **numjalam'uuch**

scar   *n.* **eetalil yok'ol**
           n. **reetalil tiq'ilal**
           n. **xna'aj tiiq'**
           n. **yotolal**
           n. **yotom**

scarce   *adj.* **majel**
           adj. **we'ej**

scarcity   *n.* **we'ejil**

scarecrow *n.* **xxib'enkil k'al**

scared   *adj.* **xiwajenaq**
           adj. **yo xiw**

scarf   *n.* **lanb'aja'aj**
           n. **xb'aatal ja'aj**

scarlet   *adj.* **kaq kaq**

scene   *n.* **raqalilk'utb'esink**

schedule   *n.* **hoonalil**
           n. **q'eqhilk'anjel**
           n. **xhoonalil**

scholarship *n.* **tenq'**

school   *n.* **tzoleb'aal**

school bag *n.* **sukhu**

science   *n.* **nawom chi rix k'a**
           re ru
           n. **nawsutam**

scientist *n agt.* **aj**
           chamalnawom

scissors   *n.* **ka'lach'**
           n. **setleb'**
           n. **tixeer**

scold   *v.* **ch'iilank**
           v. **q'usuk**

scoop   *v.* **jokok**

scooter   *n.* **nuchkawaay**
           ch'iich'

score   *n.* **rajlil ketom**
           n. **tusb'ich**

scorpion   *n.* **xook'**

scrambled eggs *n.* **yulenb'il**
                molb'

scrap of cloth   *n.* **rela' t'ikr**
scrape   *v.* **jichok**
         v. **jochok**
         n. **jochol**
         v. **jokok**
         v. **jot'ok**
         v. **qirok**
         v. **q'oyok**
scraper   *n.* **jotzleb'**
scratch   *v.* **ch'uyuk**
          v. **jochlenk**
          v. **jochok**
          n. **jochol**
          v. **parok**
          v. **q'oyok**
          n. **q'oyol**
screen (dividing)   *n.* **tasl**
screen (TV)   *n.* **ileb'**
              n. **lemaal**
              n. **xlemul kaxmuhel**
screw   *n.* **b'alent'ojiil**
        n. **b'arch'iich'**
        n. **jit'iil**
        v phr. **jit'ok kotox ch'iich'**
        n. **torniiy**
screwdriver   *n.* **b'otz'leb'**
              n. **hitb'arch'iich'**
              n. **hitleb' kotox ch'iich'**
              n. **k'ixleb'**
scribe   *n agt.* **aj tz'iib'**
scrotum   *n.* **ab'aj**
scrub   *v.* **ji'lenk**
        v. **kich'kich'ink**
        n. **kok' pim**
        n. **k'atk'al**

scuba dive   *v.* **muqa'lik**
sculptor   *n agt.* **aj pak'onel**
           n agt. **aj pech'onel**
scythe   *n.* **k'onk'ookil ch'iich'**
sea   *n.* **palaw**
      n. **xnimalpalaw**
sea shell   *n.* **xpemechil palaw**
sea snail   *n.* **soch**
seafood   *n.* **xxulel palaw**
seagull   *n.* **xtz'ik ha'**
seahorse   *n.* **xch'ina kawaay palaw**
seal   *n.* **kaxt**
       v. **kaaxtink**
       v. **latzok**
       n. **tz'i'ha'**
seam   *n.* **b'ojom**
seamstress   *n agt.* **aj b'ojonel ixq**
search   *v.* **tziib'aak**
seashore   *n.* **re palaw**
season   *n.* **estasion**
         v. **tiikob'resink**
         n. **xq'ehil**
seasoning   *n.* **xb'anol**
            n. **xsahob' tzakahemq**
            n. **xyuutzakahemq**
sebaceous gland   *n.* **k'uub'aal xeeb'**
Sebastián   *nick.* **B'ex**
second   *num.* **(2nd.) xkab'**
second grade   *n.* **xkab' na'aj**

second language
  n. **xkab'aatinob'aal**

second language acquisition
  n. **xb'ehul k'utuk xkab'aatinob'aal**

second to last *adj.* **rub'elal xraqik**

secret *n.* **muqmukilna'leb'**
  n. **muqmukil aatin**

secretary *n agt.* **aj k'ulul ula'**
  n agt. **aj tz'iib'**

section *n.* **ch'uutal**

sector *n.* **teep**
  n. **xteepal tenamit**

security *n.* **ch'oolch'oolkilal**

security camera
  n. **chapleb'jalam'u**

security door *n.* **k'ulb'lem**
  n. **tz'apokeb'ch'iich'**

security guard *n agt.* **aj k'aak'alom**
  n agt. **aj puub'**

sedative *n.* **re kubsink rahil**

see *v.* **ilok**

see you later *phr.* **chi qilaq qib'**

see you soon *phr.* **jo' wan chik**

seed *n.* **iyaj**
  n. **sakil**
  n. **xnaq'**

seedbed *n.* **iyajiil**
  n. **mu'**

seek *v.* **sik'ok**

segment *n.* **xch'uylal**

segregate *v.* **murink**

seismologist *n agt.* **aj nawhiik**

seismology *n.* **nawhiik**

seldom *adv phr.* **naj xyanq**

self-absorbed *adj.* **k'uul ru**

self-esteem *n.* **kawresil-ib'**

selfish *adj.* **kaq ru xch'ool**

self-test *n.* **tz'ilok ib'**
  v phr. **tz'ilok ib'ink**

sell *v.* **k'ayink**

semen *n.* **b'ub'**
  n. **lal**

semester *n.* **xwaq po**

semi truck *n.* **motzo'ch'iich'**

semicircle *n.* **jachsirso**
  n. **yiisirso**

semicolon *n.* **raqyanq**
  n. **xjolom muluq'util tz'uq**

semiconductor *n.* **numleb' kaxlanxaml**

send *v.* **taqlank**

sender *n agt.* **aj taql'esil**
  n agt. **aj taqlanel re**
  n. **xk'ab'a' li nataqlan re**

sensational *adj.* **xik' naxye**

sense of hearing *n.* **ab'ib'aal**

sense of humor *n.* **se'se'il ch'oolej**

sense of sight *n.* **ileb'aal**
  n. **ilob'aal xsa'u**

sense of smell *n.* **utz'leb'aal**

sense of taste *n.* **yaleb'aal**

sense of touch *n.* **eek'ob'aal**
    n. **ixkej**

sensitive *adj.* **yal maatoch'**

sentence *n.* **ch'ol'aatin**
    n. **raqal'aatin**
    n. **tojok maak**
    n. **xhuhultojb'amaak**

sentiment *n.* **eek'ahom**
    n. **eek'aal**

sepal *n.* **xxaq atz'um**

separate *adv.* **jach'bil**
    v. **jachok**
    v. **jilosink**
    v. **murink**
    v. **raqaxink**

separated *adv.* **jach'bil**

September *n.* **sektiyemr**
    n. **xb'elehilpo**

serenade *n.* **ajsi'baalb'ich**
    n. **aj si'b'ich**

serious *adj.* **tiik ru**

servant *n.* **moos**

serve *v.* **k'ehok**

serve a sentence *v phr.* **tojok maak**

service window *n.* **ch'ina k'uleb'aal**

sesame seeds *n.* **jonjoli**

set *n.* **ch'uut**
    n. **sahob'k'utleb'aal**
    n. **xyik'utb'esink**

set up *v.* **k'uub'ank**

seven *num.* **(7.) wuqub'**

seventeen *num.* **(17.) wuqlaju**

seventeenth *num.* **(17th.) xwuqlajuil**

seventh *num.* **(7th.) xwuq**

seventieth *num.* **(70th.) xlajee xkaak'aalil**

seventy *num.* **(70.) lajeeb' xkaak'aal**

seventy-eight *num.* **(78.) waqxaqlaju xkaak'aal**

seventy-five *num.* **(75.) o'laju xkaak'aal**

seventy-four *num.* **(74.) kaalaju xkaak'aal**

seventy-nine *num.* **(79.) b'elelaju xkaak'aal**

seventy-one *num.* **(71.) junlaju xkaak'aal**

seventy-seven *num.* **(77.) wuqlaju xkaak'aal**

seventy-six *num.* **(76.) waqlaju xkaak'aal**

seventy-three *num.* **(73.) oxlaju xkaak'aal**

seventy-two *num.* **(72.) kab'laju xkaak'aal**

sew *v.* **b'ojok**
    v. **kuuxink**

sew buttonholes *v phr.* **yiib'ank sa' ru t'ikr**

sew eyelets *v phr.* **yiib'ank sa' ru t'ikr**

sew on buttons *v phr.* **k'ehok b'otonx**

sewing machine *n.* **b'ojleb'**
    n. **b'ojleb' ch'iich'**
    n. **k'uub'ch'iich'b'ojle**
    b'

sewing workshop *n.* **b'ojleb'aal**

sex (gender) *n.* **chankilal**

sexual assault *n.* **muxuk**

shackle *n.* **q'otol**

shade *n.* **mu**

shade (under trees) *n.* **xmu**
    che'

shadow *n.* **mu**

shadow (of animate being)
    n. **muhej**

shake *v.* **chiq'chiq'ink**
    v. **chiq'ok**
    v. **puxink**

shallow *adj.* **ink'a' cham**

shame *n.* **xutaan**

shampoo *n.* **sasalxab'on**
    n. **xampu**

shape *v.* **pak'ok**

share *v.* **jek'ok**
    v. **sihink**
    v. **wotzok**

shark *n.* **ayin kar**
    n. **mama' kar**
    n. **tiburon**

sharp *adj.* **q'es**

sharpen *v phr.* **jotzok ru'uj**
    v phr. **k'ehok q'esnal**

sharpen (a point) *v phr.* **xjotzb'al**
    ru'uj

sharpness *n.* **xq'esnal**

shave *v.* **johok**

shave (wood) *v.* **ji'ok**

shaved ice *n.* **saqb'ach ha'**

shaving *n.* **xhumalilche'**

shaving cream *n.* **woqx re**
    joohok

shawl *n.* **peeraj**

she *pron.* **a'an**

shears *n.* **ka'lach'**
    n. **setleb'**
    n. **tixeer**

sheath *n.* **rix**
    n. **rixch'iich'**

sheep *n.* **karneer**
    n. **tzukxul**

sheet *n.* **jayil'isb'**

sheet music *n.* **tusb'ich**

shelf *n.* **tasal**
    n. **t'anruche'**

shell *n.* **pemech**
    n. **rixnaq'puub'**
    n. **soch**

shelves *n.* **tusleb'aal k'ay**

shepherd *n.* **aj ilolketomq**

shield *n.* **lak'am**

shin *n.* **ru tzelek**
    n. **xmap oq**

shin guard *n.* **ramtzelek**

shine *v.* **lemlotk**
    v. **mesok**

shiny *adj.* **nalemtz'un**

ship *n.* **b'aark**
    n. **mama' jukub'**

shirt   *n.* **ch'otlepon**
    n. **kamiis**
    n. **yaalt'ikr**
shirt (woman's) *n.* **lepon**
shirt cuff *n.* **xkux ruq' aq'**
shiver *v.* **parpotk**
    v. **siksotk**
    n. **xsik ke**
shoe *n.* **xaab'**
shoe brush *n.* **mesleb' xaab'**
shoe mold *n.* **reetalil xaab'**
shoe polish *n.* **b'onxaab'**
    n. **xlemtz' xaab'**
shoe store *n.* **k'ayib'aal xaab'**
shoe workshop *n.* **rochochil li yiib'leb'aal xaab'**
shoelace *n.* **xk'aamal xaab'**
shoemaker *n agt.* **aj yiib'om xaab'**
shoemaker's *n.* **rochochil li yiib'leb'aal xaab'**
shoeshiner *n agt.* **aj b'onol xaab'**
    n agt. **aj mesol ru xaab'**
shoeshiner kit *n.* **xkaxon aj b'onol xaab'**
shoetree *n.* **reetalil xaab'**
shoot *v.* **kutuk**
    v. **puub'ak**
    v. **puub'ank**
    n. **xtuxmel**
shooting star *n.* **jus chahim**

shop *n.* **kayib'aal**
    n. **loq'leb'aal**
shopkeeper *n agt.* **aj yakonel**
shore *n.* **chi re ha'**
short *adj.* **ch'ot**
    adj. **ka'ch'in roq**
    adj. **ka'ch'in xteram**
    adj. **tupus roq**
short vowel *n.* **junil na'tz'iib'**
shorten *v.* **k'olok**
shorthand *n.* **seeb'altz'iib'**
shortly *adv.* **ake'**
shorts *n.* **ch'otwex**
    n. **mut aq'**
    n. **wex ch'ot roq**
shot *n.* **b'akuun**
    n. **kutb'il b'an**
    n. **traaw**
    n. **yeksyon**
shotgun *n.* **toqb'ilpuub'**
shoulder *n.* **xb'een tel**
shoulder blade *n.* **b'aqel xb'een tel**
shout *v phr.* **chajok e**
    v phr. **q'ichok e**
shovel *n.* **lekleb'**
    n. **lekleb'ch'och'**
    n. **paal**
show *v.* **k'utuk**
show off *v.* **wenb'enk ib'**
shower *n.* **atib'aal**
    n. **kawil hab'**
shriek *v.* **yaab'ak**

shrimp   *n.* **jit**
          n. **k'ox**
          v. **k'oxib'k**
shrink   *v.* **k'osok**
shrub   *n.* **chik che'**
          n. **pim**
shudder   *n.* **xsik ke**
shut   *v.* **tz'apok**
shut up! (singular)
          phr. **matchoqin**
shutters *n.* **ramch'iich'**
shy   *adj.* **aj xiw**
Siamese twins *n.* **latzlut**
sibling-in-law *n.* **b'alk**
          n. **ech alalb'ej**
sibling's child *n.* **ikaq'b'ej**
sick   *adj.* **yaj**
sicken   *v.* **yajerk**
sickle   *n.* **k'onk'ookil ch'iich'**
sickness *n.* **yajel**
          n. **yajelil**
side   *n.* **k'atq**
          n. **pak'al**
          n. **ru**
sideboard *n.* **xn'aj sek'**
sidewalk *n.* **reb'e**
sieve   *n.* **tz'ileb'**
          v. **tz'ilok**
sight   *n.* **ileb'aal**
          n. **ilob'aal xsa'u**
sign   *n.* **eetal**
          n. **eetalil**
          n. **k'utleb'hu**

signal   *v.* **k'utb'esink**
signature *n.* **juch'**
signature of sender *n.* **xjuch' li**
          nataqlan re
silence   *n.* **ch'anaak**
          n. **ch'anch'o**
silent   *adj.* **kulku**
silhouette *n.* **kootal**
          n. **muhelil**
silk   *n.* **lemtz'ti'kr**
          n. **seet**
silver   *n.* **plaat**
          n. **saqi ch'iich'**
          n. **saqi pwaq**
          adj. **saqpotz'in**
silver screen *n agt.* **xlemul**
          kaxmuhel
silverware *n.* **kok' ch'iich' re**
          wa'ak
similar   *adj.* **chanchan**
          adj. **chanchan aj wi'**
          a'an
          adj. **jo'**
          adj. **ru**
similar figures *n.* **chanchanil**
          eetalilatq
simmer   *v phr.* **woqxink chi**
          timil
sin   *n.* **maak**
          v phr. **sik'ok maak**
since   *adv.* **chalen**
          adv. **tojaq**
since then *adv.* **chalen chaq**
sinew   *n.* **ich'**
          n. **ich'mul**

sing   *v.* **b'ichank**

singer   *n agt.* **aj b'ichanel**

single bed   *n.* **ch'aat re junesal**

singular   *adj.* **junaatalil**

sink   *n.* **ch'ajleb'**
     n. **ch'ajleb'aal uq'b'**
     v. **muqunk**
     v. **nuq'unk**
     v. **sob'e'k**
     v. **sub'e'k**

sinner   *n agt.* **aj maak**

Sipakapa   *lang.* **sipakapense**

sir   *n.* **qawa'**

siren   *n.* **yaab'aal**

sister (older, of a female)
     n. **chaq'na'**

sister (older, of a male)   *n.* **anab'**

sister (younger, of a male or
     female)   *n.* **itz'in ixq**

sister-in-law   *n.* **b'alk ixq**

sit   *v.* **chunlaak**
     v. **woq'laak**

six   *num.* **(6.) waqib'**

six-pack   *n.* **waqib' ru**

sixteen   *num.* **(16.) waqlaju**

sixteenth   *num.* **(16th.)**
     xwaqlajuil

sixth   *num.* **(6th.) xwaq**

sixth grade   *n.* **xwaq na'aj**

sixtieth   *num.* **(60th.) roxk'aalil**

sixty   *num.* **(60.) oxk'aal**

sixty-eight   *num.* **(68.)**
     waqxaqib' xkaak'aal

sixty-five   *num.* **(65.) oob'**
     xkaak'aal

sixty-four   *num.* **(64.) kaahib'**
     xkaak'aal

sixty-nine   *num.* **(69.) b'eleb'**
     xkaak'aal

sixty-one   *num.* **(61.) jun**
     xkaak'aal

sixty-seven   *num.* **(67.) wuqub'**
     xkaak'aal

sixty-six   *num.* **(66.) waqib'**
     xkaak'aal

sixty-three   *num.* **(63.) oxib'**
     xkaak'aal

sixty-two   *num.* **(62.) wiib'**
     xkaak'aal

size   *n.* **nimal**
     n. **ninqal**
     n. **xnimal**

skeleton   *n.* **b'aqel**
     n. **yolojilb'aq**

sketch   *v.* **jalam'uuchink**

sketch artist   *n agt.* **aj jalom**
     uuchinel

skin   *v.* **b'ich'ok**
     v. **mich'ok**
     n. **rix xul**
     n. **tz'uumalej**

skin cream   *n.* **b'an re ixkej**

skin infection   *n.* **joj**

skin rash   *n.* **chachib'**

skin spots (white)   *n.* **saqlep**

skirt   *n.* **b'otb'il aq'**
             n. **chet-aq'**
             n. **kaxlanuuq**

skirt (typical indigenous)   *n.* **uuq**

skull   *n.* **xjolom kamenaq**
             n. **xb'aqel jolom**

skunk   *n.* **aj paar**

sky   *n.* **choxa**

sky blue   *adj.* **raxjo'in**
             adj. **raxpotz'in**
             adj. **saqirax**

skylight   *n.* **rokeb'aal saqen**
             n. **saqenk'im**

slave   *n.* **moos**

sledgehammer   *n.* **jorleb'pek**

sleep   *v.* **wark**

sleep well   *phr.* **chexwarq**

sleep well (singular)
             phr. **chatwarq chi us**

sleepiness   *n.* **wara**

sleeping pills   *n.* **b'an re wark**

sleepy   *adj.* **yo xwara**

sleeve   *n.* **ruq'b'**

slice   *n.* **jun surul**
             v. **k'okok**

sliced bread   *n.* **setb'ilkaxlanwa**

slick   *adj.* **yolyol**

slide   *v.* **b'alok**
             v. **jole'k**
             n. **jolool**
             v. **yole'k**
             v. **yolk'ok**

sling   *n.* **jok'**
             v. **jok'ib'k**
             n. **oont**
             n. **rant'in**
             n. **sut**

slip   *n.* **aq' re sa' aq'ej**
             v. **b'alok**
             v. **jole'k**
             n. **xta-uuq**
             v. **yole'k**
             v. **yolk'ok**

slipper   *n.* **pere'xaab'**

slippery   *adj.* **yolyol**

slippery place   *n.* **jolool**

sloping   *adj.* **an'o**

slow   *adj.* **elajik**
             adj. **k'ooq**
             adj. **leb'eb'nak**
             adj. **riil**
             adj. **timil**

slowly   *adv.* **chi timil**

slowly go broke   *v.* **neb'a'irk**

slurs   *n.* **sak'ok aatin**

small   *adj.* **kach'in**
             adj. **kok'**
             adj. **mitz**
             adj. **ch'ina**

small boat   *n.* **ch'ina jukub'**

small intestine   *n.* **kok' k'amk'ot**

small village   *n.* **kok'k'aleb'aal**

smaller than   *adv phr.* **ka'ch'in chi ru**

smallpox   *n.* **ninqixox**

smart   *adj.* **wan xna'leb'**

404

smell   *n.* **utz'leb'aal**
     n. **utz'leb'aal**
     n. **utz'uk**
     v. **utz'uk**

smelly   *adj.* **chu**

smile   *n.* **se'**
     v. **se'ek**

smock   *n.* **ramb'atz'aj**

smoke   *v.* **mayib'k**
     n. **sib'**
     v. **sib'tehenk**
     v. **sik'lik**

smooth   *adj.* **ji'ji'**
     adj. **q'un**
     adj. **tiik**
     adj. **yolyol**
     v. **ji'ok**

snack   *n.* **kolb'ach'ool**

snail   *n.* **pemech**
     n. **pur**
     n. **t'ot'**
     n. **tziitzib'**

snake   *n.* **k'anti'**

sneakers   *n.* **kok' xaab'**

sneeze   *v.* **at'isb'ak**

sniff   *v.* **utz'uk**

snore   *v.* **jilq'ank**
     v. **joq'ank**
     v. **qoorank**
     v. **q'uusank**

snout   *n.* **ru'uj**

snow   *n.* **xchu' ke**

snowcone   *n.* **saqb'ach ha'**

so   *adv.* **jo'kan**

soak   *v.* **tz'ahok**
     v. **tz'uqresink**

soap   *n.* **xab'on**

soap dish   *n.* **xna'aj xab'on**

soccer   *n.* **b'olotz oq**

soccer ball   *n.* **b'olotz oq**

soccer player   *n agt.* **aj b'atz'unel b'olotz oq**
     n agt. **aj b'olotz**

social equality   *n.* **juntaq'eetil amaq'il**

social security
     n. **xch'olch'ookil amaq'il**

social studies   *n.* **amaq'il loq'alil**
     n. **naw'amaq'il**
     n. **tzolomilkomon**

social values   *n.* **amaq'il loq'alil**

social worker   *n agt.* **aj waklesihom ch'uut**

socialism   *n.* **komonilwank**

society   *n.* **amaq'il**

socio constructivism
     n. **amaq'kab'lk'a'uxl**

sociolinguistics
     n. **naw'amaq'ilchi'**

sociologist   *n.* **aj nawkomonil**

sociology   *n.* **naw'amaq'il**
     n. **nawkomonil**

sock   *n.* **b'atb'al oq**
     n. **tz'apb'al oq**
     n. **xta oq**
     n. **xta xaab'**

socket   *n.* **chapleb' saqen**

soda   *n.* **kaxlanha'**

sofa   *n.* **potztem**
             n. **soq'il chunleb'**

soft   *adj.* **potzpotz**
             adj. **q'ochq'och**
             adj. **q'un**
             adj. **roq'roq'**
             adj. **yab'yab'**
             adj. **yuq'yuq'**

soft drink   *n.* **kaxlanha'**
             n. **kaxuk'a'**

soft palate   *n.* **xb'een'e**

soil   *n.* **ch'och'**

solar eclipse   *n.* **muqlaak saq'e**
                n. **muqsaq'e**

solar system   *n.* **wankilal saq'e**
               n. **xtusulal ruuchich'och'**

soldering iron   *n.* **xiitleb'ch'iich'**

soldier   *n agt.* **aj kookox**
             n agt. **aj puub'**
             n. **soldaa**

sole   *n.* **sa' oq**
             n. **xsa' oq**

sole (footwear)   *n.* **sa' roq xaab'**

solid   *adj.* **kaw ru**

solidarity   *n.* **junajil**

solution (to a problem)
             n. **yiib'ank ch'a'ajkilal**

solve equations   *v phr.* **yiib'ank ch'a'ajkilal**

solvent   *n.* **aj ha'resinel**

some   *pron.* **b'ayaq**
             adj. **junaq**
             adj. **ka'b'ayaq**
             adj. **k'a'na**

somebody else's   *adj.* **jalan aj e**
                  adj. **ab'l**

sometimes   *adv.* **ramro'**
             adv phr. **sa' junq sut**
             adv phr. **wan naq**

son   *n.* **al**
             n. **alal**

son (of a mother)   *n.* **yum**
                    n. **yumej**

son (of god)   *n.* **k'ajolb'ej**

song   *n.* **b'ich**

songbook   *n.* **b'ichleb'**

son-in-law (of a man or woman)
             n. **hi'**

soon   *adv.* **ake'**
             adv phr. **chi seeb'**
             adv. **tikto**

sorcerer   *n.* **awasinel**
             n. **tuulanel**

sore   *n.* **saan**
             n. **tiq'ilal**
             n. **yok'olal**

sorghum   *n.* **kok' ixim**

sorrow   *n.* **k'a'uxl**

sorry I'm late   *phr.* **chinaakuy xib'ayon chaq**

sorry to keep you waiting
             phr. **chinaakuy xatink'e chi oyb'enink**

soul   *n.* **aamej**
            n. **ch'oolej**

soul mate   *n.* **xsum aam**

sound   *v.* **tzinb'ak**
            v. **tzinb'ank**
            n. **xkuxb'il**
            n. **yaab'**
            n. **yaab'kuxink**

sounds good *phr.* **sa naxye**

soup   *n.* **kaalt**
            n. **soop**
            n. **ya'al**

sour   *adj.* **ch'am**
            adj. **k'a**
            adj. **remrem**
            adj. **rub'rub'**

south   *n.* **rokeb' iq'**

South America   *n.* **roq ab'yayala**

south pole *n.* **xtaq'ahil ruuchich'och'**

sow   *v.* **awok**
            v. **hirok**
            n. **ixqi aaq**
            n. **xa'an aaq**

sown   *adj.* **awo**

space   *n.* **yanq**

space capsule   *n.* **b'oq'ch'iich' iq'**

space shuttle
            n. **choxahilb'eeleb'**
            n. **jukub' iq'**

space station   *n.* **na'leb'aal ch'iich' iq'**

space suit *n.* **puraq'**
            n. **purik aq' aj b'eenel sa' po**
            n. **raq' aj b'eenel sa' po**

space travel   *n.* **b'eek xb'aan choxach'och'**

spaceship   *n.* **jukub' iq'**

spade   *n.* **paal**

Spanish   *lang.* **kastiiy**
            lang. **kaxlanchi'**
            lang. **kaxlan aatin**

sparrow   *n.* **tz'unun**
            n. **wilix**

speak   *v.* **aatinak**
            v. **aatinamank**
            v. **seeraq'ik**

speak slowly   *phr.* **ye chi timil**

speaker   *n.* **meexwajb'**
            n. **pukyaab'**
            n. **yaab'aal**

spear   *n.* **jutz'che'**
            n. **jutz'leb'**
            n. **topleb'**

spearmint   *n.* **isk'i'ij**

species   *n.* **ch'uutulal**

spectacles *n.* **anyooj**
            n. **lem'u**

spectator   *n agt.* **aj ilonel**

speech   *n.* **aatinom**

speech impairment   *n.* **tos e**

speed   *n.* **metz'ewil**
            n. **raanil**

spend   *v.* **sachok**

sphere   *n.* **t'ort'o**

spherical   *adj.* **t'ort'o**

    adj. **t'ort'ookil**

sphygmomanometer

    n. **ich'leb'ch'iich'**

spice   *n.* **k'ay**

    n. **xb'anol**

    n. **xsahob'**

    tzakahemq

    n. **xyuutzakahemq**

spider   *n.* **aj am**

    n. **x'am**

spider web   *n.* **xkem aj am**

spin   *v.* **k'aamak**

    v. **sutisink**

spinach   *n.* **espinaak**

spinal column   *n.* **juruch'**

spindle   *n.* **peteet**

spine   *n.* **juruch'**

    n. **k'ix**

spiral galaxy   *n.* **kototiil**

    tzoqchahim

spirit   *n.* **aamej**

    n. **ch'oolej**

    n. **mu**

    n. **muhel**

    n. **musiq'ej**

spirits   *n.* **kaxlan b'oj**

spiritual guide   *n agt.* **aj q'e**

spit   *n.* **chuub'**

    v. **chuub'ak**

spiteful   *adj.* **naxk'uula ra sa'**

    xch'ool

splash   *v.* **pach'lenk**

    v. **pach'ok**

    v. **rachok**

    v. **repok**

split   *v.* **jachok**

    v. **kiib'ank**

    v. **kuruk**

    v. **toqok**

    v. **xerok**

spoiled   *adj.* **q'aajenaq**

sponge   *n.* **sob'sob'k'uub'**

spool   *n.* **xche'el noq'**

spoon   *n.* **jokleb'**

    n. **kuchaar**

    n. **lekleb'**

spoonful   *n.* **jun kuchaar**

sport utility vehicle   *n.* **ch'ina**

    poy ch'iich'

sportsman   *n agt.* **aj b'atz'unel**

sportswear   *n.* **aq' re b'atz'unk**

spot   *n.* **xox**

spotless   *adj.* **t'uj**

sprain   *n.* **b'ach'al**

spray   *n.* **puutz'leb'aal**

    v. **puutzink**

spread out   *v.* **chirok**

    v. **helok**

spring   *n.* **uk'leb'aal**

    n. **ch'ina ha'**

    n. **kumb'**

    n. **k'ak'naab'**

    n. **tuq**

spring (metal)   *n.* **pitzk'**

spring (season) *n.* **primab'eer**
n. **tikkehil kutan**

sprout   *n.* **xtuxmel**

spy   *v phr.* **lemaank sa' muqmu**

square   *n.* **eswaayr**
n. **kaaxukuut**
adj. **kaaxukuut**
n. **kaaxukuutleb'**
v phr. **puktasink ib'**
n. **xnimal neb'aal**

squash   *n.* **k'um**
n. **seel**

squeejee   *n.* **mesol lem**

squeeze   *v.* **pitz'ok**
v. **yatz'ok**

squirrel   *n.* **kuk**

stab   *v phr.* **k'ob'ok chi ch'iich'**
v. **xeq'ok**

stable   *n.* **xna'aj wakax**

stadium   *n.* **b'atz'unleb'aal**

stage   *n.* **k'utb'esib'aal**
n. **xyik'utb'esink**

staging   *n.* **sahob'k'utleb'aal**

stain   *v.* **b'onok**

stained glass   *n.* **ramleb'aal lem**

staircase   *n.* **eeb'**

stake   *n.* **awleb'**

stalk   *n.* **xche'el pim**

stall   *n.* **xna'aj wakax**

stallion   *n.* **kawaay**
n. **kranyon**

stammer   *v phr.* **lotz re**
v phr. **tat re**

stamp   *n.* **eetaltoj**
n. **kaxt**
v. **kaaxtink**
n. **tiimbr**
n. **xtojb'al relik**

stamp pad   *n.* **xb'onilkaaxt**

stand   *v.* **xaqliik**

standing   *adj.* **xaqam**

stands   *n.* **tusb'il chunleb'al**

stanza   *n.* **raapal**

staple   *v.* **chapokhu**

stapler   *n.* **k'achleb'**
n. **k'atz'leb'hu**
n. **k'axleb'hu**

star   *n.* **chahim**

start   *n.* **xtiklajik**

starting today   *adv.* **chalen anaqwan**

state capital   *n.* **rochoch ruuchilawab'ej**

state house   *n.* **rochoch ruuchilawab'ej**

statue   *n.* **jalam'uuch**
n. **pak'b'il poyanam**
n. **poyanamb'iltz'ak**

steak   *n.* **kilinb'il tib'**

steal   *v.* **elq'ak**
v. **ixi'jink**
v. **jochok**
v. **uq'mink**

steam   *n.* **b'ook**
n. **tiqwal**

steamer trunk *n.* **mama' kaax**

steel *n.* **kulb'ch'iich'**

steel nail *n.* **kulb't'ojom**

steering wheel *n.* **jayab'aalb'e**
    n. **xch'e'b'al**
    n. **xche'el tiikob'aal b'e**

stela *n.* **tz'ak-eetalil**

stem *n.* **roq'**
    n. **xche'el pim**

stenography *n.* **seeb'altz'iib'**

step *n.* **eeb'**
    n. **yok**

stepdaughter *n.* **ka' ralal**
    n. **xkab' rab'in**
    n. **xka' alalb'ej**

stepfather *n.* **ka'yuwa'**
    n. **xkab' yuwa'**

stepmother *n.* **ka'na'**
    n. **xkab' na'**

steps *n.* **taqleb'aal**

stepson *n.* **kab' alal**
    n. **xkab' alal**

stereo *n.* **pumleb'yaab'**

sterile (man) *n.* **maa'alwinq**

sterile (woman) *n.* **maa'al'ixq**

sterilized water *n.* **b'an ha'**

stethoscope
    n. **ab'ib'leb'aal'ch'ool**
    n. **ab'ib'leb'aal aam**
    n. **ab'ib'leb'aal yajel**

stew *n.* **chiqb'il tib'**

sticker *n.* **eetalil**
    n. **latz-eetal**
    n. **letzelhu**

stiff *adj.* **chek'**

stigma (flower) *n.* **ru'uj atz'um**

still *conj.* **toj**

still life *n.* **xaqxo jalam'uuch**

stimulant *n.* **kawresinel ch'ool**

stimulate *v.* **kawresink ch'ool**

stimulus *n.* **kawresil**

stingray *n.* **perkar**

stingy *adj.* **aj pix**
    adj. **pix**

stinking *adj.* **chu**

stir *v.* **junajink**
    v. **yuuk'ink**

stitch *v phr.* **ranok chi noq'**

stocking *n.* **b'atb'al oq**
    n. **tz'apb'al oq**
    n. **xta oq**
    n. **xta xaab'**

stomach *n.* **job'nil**
    n. **sa'**

stomach ache *n.* **rahil sa'ej**
    n. **sa'ej**

stomach acid *n.* **yib'onik sa' sa'ej**

stone *n.* **pek**
    n. **pekal**

stop *v.* **xaq'ab'ank**

stop it! *phr.* **xxaqlin**

stopper *n.* **tapon**

storage battery
    n. **k'uulmetz'ew**
store   *n.* **kayib'aal**
    n. **loq'leb'aal**
storm   *n.* **kaqsut-iq'**
    n. **kaaq**
story   *n.* **seeraq'**
stove   *n.* **chiqleb'**
    n. **estuuf**
    n. **kaxlan chiqleb'**
    n. **kaxxaml**
    n. **q'ixaml**
straight   *adj.* **tiik**
straight line   *n.* **tiikaljuch'**
    n. **tiikil juch'ul**
strain   *v.* **tz'ilok**
strainer   *n.* **tz'ileb'**
strait   *n.* **laatz'**
strange   *adj.* **xik' ru**
stranger   *n.* **najtil poyanam**
    n. **najt xtenamit**
stratosphere   *n.* **xkab' tasal iq'**
straw   *n.* **k'im**
    n. **tz'ub'leb'**
straw hut   *n.* **k'imal kab'l**
strawberry   *n.* **met' tokan**
    n. **pechtokan**
    n. **perees**
stream   *n.* **nima'**
    n. **roq ha'**
streamer   *n.* **milmich' hu**
street   *n.* **numleb'aal**
    n. **roqb'e**
street corner   *n.* **xxuk b'e**

street sweeper   *n agt.* **aj mesunel**
streetlight   *n.* **ch'ina kaaxukuutil lem**
strength   *n.* **metz'ew**
stress   *n.* **ch'ich'i'il**
    v. **kawyaab'ink**
    n. **yaab' aatin**
stress on last syllable   *n.* **xmaril kawil yaab'**
stress on second to last syllable
    n. **xkab' kawil yaab'**
stress on third to last syllable
    n. **rox kawil yaab'**
stressed vowel   *n.* **kawyaab' na'tz'iib'**
stretch   *v.* **rinok**
    v. **yu'uk**
stretcher   *n.* **ch'ina ch'aat**
strict   *adj.* **tz'aqal re ru naraj**
strike   *v.* **b'ujuk**
    v. **ketok**
    v. **potz'ok**
    v. **tenok**
    v. **wojok**
string   *n.* **k'aam**
string bean   *n.* **q'ap**
strip   *n.* **xk'aamal**
    n. **xtaab'il**
strong   *adj.* **kaw**
    adj. **kaw xmetz'ew**
structural geology
    n. **nawk'uub'tzuul**
structure   *n.* **rilb'al**

stubborn *adj.* **jip**
    adj. **numjip**

student *n.* **tijom**
    n. **tzolom**

student desk *n.* **meexil tz'iib'**

study *v phr.* **ilok chi us**
    v. **tzolok**
    n. **xna'aj tzolok**

study guide *n.* **xb'ehulk'utuk**

stuff *v.* **b'ut'uk**

stuffed animal *n.* **kaxtzukxul**

stump *n.* **toon**

stupid *adj.* **jip**
    adj. **jok**

stutter *v phr.* **lotz re**
    v phr. **tat re**

style (flower) *n.* **roq-atz'um**

sub ceiling *n.* **kaxlankaq'**

subconscious
    n. **rub'elal'aj'ookil**

subject *n agt.* **aj b'aanunel**
    n. **b'aanunel**
    n. **nak'ab'a'iik**
    n. **ru tzolom**

submarine *n.* **jukub' re rub'elha'**

substitute *n.* **eeqaj**

subtract *v.* **jeb'ok**

subtraction *n.* **jeb'ok**
    n. **jeb'ok-ajl**

succeed *v.* **elab'k**

success *n.* **elab'k**

suck *v.* **tz'ub'uk**

suddenly *adv.* **maare**

suffer *v.* **raho'k**

sufficient *adj.* **tz'aqal**

suffix *n.* **raqtz'aqob'l**

sugar *n.* **asuukr**
    n. **k'ajkab'**

sugar bowl *n.* **xna'aj k'aj kab'**

sugarcane *n.* **asuukr utz'ajl**
    n. **utz'ajl**
    n. **utz'aal**

suggest *v.* **sihokna'leb'**

suit *n.* **junxaqalil t'ikr**

suit case *n.* **iiq**

sullen *adj.* **moymo ru xtib'el**

sulphur *n.* **rarehilpoq**

sum *n.* **ch'utub'ank**
    n. **molool**
    n. **tamok-ajl**
    n. **xmola**

summarize *v.* **k'osok**

summarized *adj.* **k'osb'il**

summary *n.* **xk'oslal**

summer *n.* **saq'ehil**

summit *n.* **ru'uj tzuul**
    n. **xb'een tzuul**

summon *v.* **b'oqok**

sun *n.* **saq'e**

sun belt *n.* **tiqwal siraalch'och'**

sun dry *v phr.* **k'ehok chi ru saq'e**

sun god *n.* **b'alamq'e**

sunburn *n.* **k'atom saq'e**

sunburn lotion *n.* **b'an xk'atom saq'e**

Sunday *n.* **tomiin**

sunflower *n.* **k'onon**

sunglasses *n.* **moyileb'**

sunny *n.* **saq'ehil kutan**

sunrise *n.* **eq'laaho'k**

sunset *n.* **ewuuk**

sunshade *n.* **mu**

sunshine *n.* **roq saq'e**

sunstroke *n.* **lub'k chi ru saq'e**

supermarket *n.* **nimla k'ayib'aal**

supernova *n.* **pukchahim**

supersonic *adj.* **numkawyaab'**

supervisor *n agt.* **aj ilolk'anjel** *n agt.* **aj ilom aj k'anjel**

supper *n.* **wa re ewu**

suppository *n.* **b'aqil b'an** *n.* **ch'ikb'ilb'an**

supreme court *n.* **nimalraqb'leb'aati n** *n.* **xnimal raqb'a chaq'rab'**

sure *phr.* **jo'kan tz'aqal**

surface *n.* **xb'een**

surface area *n.* **xsa' ruhil**

surgeon *n agt.* **aj cho'onel**

surgical instruments *n.* **xk'anjelob'aal aj b'anonel**

surgical scar *n.* **cho'b'ol**

surprise *n.* **maatan**

surprised *adj.* **nasach xch'ool** *adj.* **sachaamil xch'ool**

surrender *v phr.* **q'axtesink ib'** *v phr.* **xe'xke rib'**

surround *v.* **sutuxink**

survey *n.* **ka'ch'olob'ank** *v.* **patz'ok** *n.* **raqalyalb'a'ix**

suspect *v.* **k'a'uxlak** *n.* **poyanam wan aatin chirix**

suspender *n.* **riiqankil** *n.* **xk'aamal**

suspension points *n.* **oxtz'uq** *n.* **tz'uqux**

sustainability *n.* **ilok ib'**

suture *n.* **b'ojok tiq'il** *n.* **xiitink tiq'il**

SUV *n.* **ch'ina poy ch'iich'**

swallow *v.* **nuq'uk**

swamp *n.* **k'anha'** *n.* **saab'** *n.* **saab' ha'**

swan *n.* **kaxkatras** *n.* **yenyookil patux**

swear (an oath) *v.* **ch'olob'ank**

sweat *n.* **tiqob'**

sweater *n.* **q'ixt'ikr**

sweatpants *n.* **potzwex**

sweats *n.* **potzwex**

413

sweep   *v.* **mesunk**

sweet   *adj.* **ki'**

sweet corn   *n.* **al ixim**

sweet potato   *n.* **is**
    n. **paaps**

sweet roll   *n.* **kab'il kaxlan wa**

sweets   *n.* **kab'**

swelling   *n.* **sipook**
    n. **siipilal**
    n. **teb'elal**

swim   *v.* **numxik**

swimmer   *n agt.* **aj muqa'l**
    n agt. **aj numxinel**

swimming   *n.* **numxik**

swimming pool   *n.* **atib'aal**
    n. **numxib'aal**

swimsuit   *n.* **aq' re atink**
    n. **atiyach'**

swindle   *n.* **maq'ok sa' b'alaq'**

swindler   *n agt.* **aj maq'onel**

swine   *n.* **aaq**

swing   *n.* **ab'**
    n. **t'uuyleb'**

switch   *n.* **raqb'ametz'ew**

swollen   *n.* **kaqpech'in**

sword   *n.* **makaan**
    n. **nimla ch'iich'**

swordfish   *n.* **jutz' kar**

syllabary   *n.* **xhuhul raq**
    n. **yehiileb'**

syllable   *n.* **yehiil**

symbol   *n.* **eetal**

symbolism   *n.* **eetalilul**

symmetric figure   *n.* **juntaq'eetil**
    eetalil

symmetry   *n.* **tiik-uhil**

symptoms   *n.* **xtiklajik li yajel**

synaleph   *n.* **k'ulb'atz'iib'**

synonym   *n.* **juneetil'aatin**
    n. **juntaq'eetil'aatin**
    n. **juntaq'eetyaalalil**

syntax   *n.* **nawtus'aatin**

synthesis   *n.* **xb'ehul k'osok**

syphilis   *n.* **b'ux**

syringe   *n.* **jerink**
    n. **kutleb'**

syrup   *n.* **b'an uk'b'il**

systolic blood pressure
    n. **metz'ew ich'mulej elkik'**
    n. **xmetz'ew ich'mulej elkik'**

T - t

tab   *n.* **sachom**

table   *n.* **meex**

tablecloth   *n.* **ru meex**
    n. **xtameex**

tablet   *n.* **ch'ina b'an**
              n. **nuq'b'ilb'an**
              n. **pastiiy**
taboo   *n.* **awas**
tack   *n.* **ch'int'ojiil**
              n. **tachweel**
taco   *n.* **b'otwa**
tact   *n.* **eek'ob'aal**
              n. **ixkej**
tail   *n.* **ye**
tail wing   *n.* **xye so'sol ch'iich'**
tailor   *n agt.* **aj b'ojonel**
take   *v.* **chapok**
take (an amount of time)
              v. **b'aayk**
take communion *v.* **loq'oniik**
take note of *v phr.* **k'ehok eetal**
take notes   *v.* **tz'iib'ak**
take out   *v.* **isink**
take pictures *v.* **jalam'uuchib'k**
take possession of *v.* **eechank**
take your time *phr.* **b'aanu sa'
              xyaalal**
talc   *n.* **poqb'an**
              n. **poqilsunob'l**
              n. **putzputzb'an**
talcum powder *n.* **poqb'an**
              n. **poqilsunob'l**
              n. **putzputzb'an**
tale   *n.* **seeraq'**
talk   *v.* **aatinak**
              v. **aatinamank**
              v. **seeraq'ik**

talkative   *adj.* **aj num aatin**
              adj. **yal sa' re naxik**
tall   *adj.* **najt roq**
              adj. **najt xteram**
              adj. **nimnim**
              adj. **nim roq**
              adj. **nim xteram**
              adj. **tutz'tu**
              adj. **yak'ach**
talon   *n.* **nimqi ixi'ij**
tamale   *n.* **ob'en**
tamarind   *n.* **wach'iil**
tambourine   *n.* **kottzuj**
              n. **tzojtzojch'iich'**
tan   *v phr.* **chiqok tz'uum**
tangerine   *n.* **mandariin**
tangle   *v.* **pixlenk**
              v. **tzuklenk**
tap   *n.* **yaaw**
tape   *n.* **letzleb'**
              v. **letzok**
tape player   *n.* **chapleb'aal
              aatin**
              n. **chapleb'aatin**
              n. **taab'leb'aal b'ich**
tape recorder *n.* **chapleb'aal
              aatin**
              n. **chapleb'aatin**
              n. **chapleb' aatin**
tapir   *n.* **tixl**
tar   *n.* **q'eqitz'aakalb'e**
tarantula   *n.* **q'eq aj am**
target shoot *v phr.* **b'atz'unk
              puub'ak**

tarp   *n.* **mokooch**

task   *n.* **kub'siil**

            n. **tenq'**

taste   *v phr.* **hulak chi uhej**

            n. **yaleb'aal**

            v. **yalok**

            v phr. **yalok xsahil**

tasty   *adj.* **sa**

            adj. **saasa**

tattoo   *n.* **eetalil xtz'uumal**

tax   *n.* **toj**

tax identification number
            n. **ajlilkomontoj**
            n. **rajliltoj**

taxes   *n.* **toj chi ru awab'ej**

taxi   *n.* **taks**

taxi stand *n.* **xna'aj taks**

TB   *n.* **xyajel pospo'oy**

tea   *n.* **te**

teach   *v.* **k'utuk**

            v. **tzolok**

teacher   *n agt.* **aj k'utunel**
            n. **aj tzolonel**
            n. **q'usunel**

teaching   *n.* **nawk'utuk**

teaching methods *n.* **xb'ehul
            k'utuk**

teaching module *n.* **xtasalil
            tzolok**

teaching staff *n.* **xmolamil aj
            k'utunel**

team   *n.* **aj b'atz'uneleb'**
            n. **xmolamil b'atz'unk**

team jersey *n.* **b'atz-aq'**

teapot   *n.* **xxaaril te**

tear   *v.* **pejok**
            v. **q'ichok**
            v. **q'irok**
            v. **re'ok**
            n. **xya'al u**

teat   *n.* **ru'uj tu'**
            n. **tu'**

technology *n.* **nawk'anjelahom**

technology use *n.* **oksink
            nawk'anjelahom**

tectonic plates *n.* **tasal
            ruuchich'och'**

teeth   *n.* **ruuch e**

Tektitek   *lang.* **tektiteko**

telegram   *n.* **junpaatil'esil**
            n. **k'aj'esil**

telegraph   *n.* **pitz'leb'taql**

telegraph machine
            n. **numsib'aal k'aj'
            esil**

telegrapher *n agt.* **aj numsihom
            k'aj' esil**
            n. **nums'esilb'aal**

telephone   *n.* **aatinob'aal
            ch'iich'**
            n. **b'oqleb'**
            n. **b'oqleb'aal**
            n. **b'oqleb'aal ch'iich'**
            n. **teleef**

telephone bill *n.* **xhuhil li
            aatik'aam ch'iich'**

telescope   *n.* **ilob'aal chahim**
            n. **najt-ileb'**

television *n.* **kaxmu**
　　n. **kaxmu helleb'**
　　n. **lemaal'esil**
　　n. **teleb'ision**
television antenna *n.* **xmisik' kaxmu**
tell stories *v.* **seeraq'ik**
teller *n agt.* **aj xokol tumin**
telophase *n.* **xka pojk'ok**
temperate zone *n.* **keekehil siraalch'och'**
temperature *n.* **tiqkehil**
　　n. **xtiqwalil**
temple *n.* **ermiit**
　　n. **kapiiy**
　　n. **tijob'aal**
temples *n.* **k'atq jolom**
　　n. **toon xik**
tempt *v.* **aalenk**
temptation *n.* **atawank**
ten *num.* **(10.) lajeeb'**
ten cents *n.* **lajeb' senta**
ten quetzals *n.* **lajeb' ketzal**
tender *adj.* **q'un**
tenderness *n.* **q'unil**
tendon *n.* **ich'**
　　n. **ich'mul**
tennis shoes *n.* **aanilxaab'**
　　n. **potzxaab'**
tent *n.* **kaxmuheb'aal**
tenth *num.* **(10th.) xlajee**
terminal *n.* **hilob'eleb'aal ch'iich'**

terminal side (of an angle)
　　n. **xk'atq xraqik**
termites *n.* **k'ams**
terrace *n.* **tz'akal'ochoch**
terrain *n.* **waqlajuk'aam**
　　n. **xoral**
terrified *adj.* **naxiwak**
test *n.* **tz'ilb'a'ix**
　　v. **tz'ilok-ix**
　　n. **tz'ilool'ix**
　　n. **yalb'a'ix**
　　n. **yalok ix**
testicles *n.* **ab'aj**
　　n. **molb'**
　　n. **naq' it**
　　n. **naq' kun**
testify *v phr.* **yehok aatin sa' chaq'rab'**
testimony *n.* **yehom**
tetrasyllable *n.* **kaayehiil**
text message *n.* **esil sa' tz'iib'**
thank *v.* **b'antyoxink**
thank you *phr.* **b'antyox**
thank you very much
　　phr. **naab'alwa b'antyox**
thankful, grateful
　　adj. **nab'anyoxin**
thanks *phr.* **b'antyox**
thanks for your help
　　phr. **ninb'anyoxi laa tenq'**

that   *pron.* **a'an**
          pron. **naq**
          pron. **wan le'**

that depends *phr.* **toja' yaal**

that one *pron.* **a'an a'an**
          pron. **a'wa'ran**
          pron. **wan le'**

that one (over there)
          pron. **a'wanle'**

that's all *phr.* **ka'aj wi a'an**

that's enough *phr.* **tz'aqal**

that's interesting *phr.* **us raj**

that's it *phr.* **ka'aj wi a'an**

that's life *phr.* **jo'kan li wank**

that's true *phr.* **yaal**

that's why *conj.* **a' ajb'an**
            conj. **jo'kan**
            conj. **jo'kan naq**

thatch *n.* **k'imal kab'l**

the (plural) *art.* **eb' li**

the (singular) *art.* **li**

the day before *n.* **jun kutan rub'elaj**

the day before a party
          n. **mixpirik**

theater *n.* **k'utb'esib'aal**

theatrical *adj.* **k'utb'il**

theatrical production
          n. **k'utb'ahom**

theft *n.* **elq'**

them *pron.* **eb' a'an**

thematic *adj.* **xna'leb'il**

theme *n.* **xna'leb'il**
        n. **na'leb'**

then *adv phr.* **jo'kan b'i'**

there *adv.* **aran**
        adv. **le'**
        adv phr. **sa' a'an**

there is no more *phr.* **maak'a' chik**

there still are... *phr.* **toj ruch...**
                    phr. **toj wan...**

thermometer *n.* **b'isleb'tiq**
             n. **re b'isok tiq**

thermos *n.* **kaxsu**
         n. **k'uuleb'aaltiq**

thermosphere *n.* **xka tasal'iq'**

thermostat *n.* **tuqb'ametz'ew**

thesaurus *n.* **xch'oolaatin juntaq'eetil**

these *pron.* **a'ineb'**
        pron. **eb' a'in**

they *pron.* **a'aneb'**
      pron. **eb' a'an**

thick *adj.* **b'urux b'urux**
        adj. **leb'lo**
        adj. **nim xsa'**
        adj. **pim**
        adj. **sas**
        adj. **teb'es**
        adj. **t'ikt'o**

thicken *v.* **sasob'resink**

thief *n agt.* **aj elq'**
        n. **jochonel**
        n. **piyok**

thigh   *n.* **ru a'**
             n. **tib'elej**
             n. **tz'ej**
thimble   *n.* **xkolb'al ru'uj uqb'**
thin   *adj.* **b'aq xtib'el**
             adj. **b'arich'**
             adj. **jay**
thing   *n.* **k'a'aq re ru**
             n. **k'a'atq ru**
thing to be weighed *n.* **aalom**
think   *v.* **k'a'uxlak**
             v. **k'oxlak**
think nothing of it
             phr. **matk'a'uxlak**
thinker   *n agt.* **aj k'a'uxl**
third   *n.* **oxjachal**
             num. **(3rd.) rox**
third grade *n.* **rox na'aj**
third to last *adj.* **roxch'otonel**
thirst   *n.* **chaqi'el**
thirsty   *adj.* **chaqiq re**
thirteen   *num.* **(13.) oxlaju**
thirteenth   *num.* **(13th.) roxlajuil**
thirtieth   *num.* **(30th.) xlajee**
             xka'k'aalil
thirty   *num.* **(30.) lajeeb'**
             xka'k'aal
thirty-eight *num.* **(38.)**
             waqxaqlaju
             xka'k'aal
thirty-five *num.* **(35.) o'laju**
             xka'k'aal
thirty-four *num.* **(34.) kaalaju**
             xka'k'aal

thirty-nine *num.* **(39.) b'elelaju**
             xka'k'aal
thirty-one   *num.* **(31.) junlaju**
             xka'k'aal
thirty-seven *num.* **(37.) wuqlaju**
             xka'k'aal
thirty-six   *num.* **(36.) waqlaju**
             xka'k'aal
thirty-three *num.* **(33.) oxlaju**
             xka'k'aal
thirty-two   *num.* **(32.) kab'laju**
             xka'k'aal
this   *pron.* **a'in**
this evening *adv phr.* **chi ru li**
             q'oqyin a'in
this month   *n.* **li po a'in**
this one   *pron.* **a'an a'in**
             pron. **a'in**
this week   *n.* **li xamaan a'in**
thorax   *n.* **maqab'**
             n. **polook'**
thorn   *n.* **k'ix**
             n. **xk'ix**
though   *conj.* **us ta**
thought   *n.* **k'a'uxl**
thoughtful   *adj.* **tk'a'uxlaq**
thousand   *n.* **lajeeb' syent**
             n. **lajeek'aal rox**
             oq'oob'
thread   *n.* **noq'**
thread a needle *v*
             phr. **xnoq'inkil li**
             akuux
threat   *n.* **k'ehok xiw**

threaten *v phr.* **k'ehok xiw**
    v. **seb'esink**
    v. **xib'enk**
three   *num.* **(3.) oxib'**
three by three *adv.* **ox ox**
three days ago *adv.* **oxejer**
three hundred *n.* **o'lajuk'aal**
three thousand *n.* **lajeek'aal**
    xwaqxaq roq'ob'
three times *adv.* **oxsut**
    adv. **oxwa**
thresh   *v.* **ch'epok**
    v. **iximaak**
throat   *n.* **sa' kuxej**
    n. **xolol**
    n. **xsa' ja'aj**
throne   *n.* **k'ojarib'aal**
through *prep.* **rik'in**
    prep. **sa'**
    prep. **sa' xk'ab'a'**
    prep. **sa' xmaak**
    prep. **xb'aan**
throw   *v.* **kutuk**
    v. **pumuk**
    v. **puulesink**
    v. **rumuk**
    v. **tz'eqok**
thumb   *n.* **na' uq'm**
    n. **xmama'il uq'mej**
thumbnail photo *n.* **mitz'jalam'u**
thumbtack *n.* **ch'int'ojiil**
    n. **tachweel**
thunder *n.* **kaaq**
    n. **xyaab' kaaq**
thunderstorm *n.* **repom kaaq**

Thursday *n.* **jweews**
    n. **xkakutan**
thus   *adv phr.* **chi kama'an**
    adv phr. **chi kama'in**
tiara   *n.* **nat'leb'ismal**
tick   *n.* **sip**
ticket   *n.* **tojl**
ticket office *n.* **k'ayib'aal**
    b'oleet
ticket taker *n agt.* **aj k'aak'anel**
ticket window *n.* **tojleb'aal**
tickle   *n.* **katzkatz**
    n. **wotz'otz'**
    v. **wotz'otz'ink**
tie   *v.* **b'ak'ok**
    n. **b'eq**
    v. **jit'ok**
    n. **korb'aat**
    n. **yutkux**
tiger   *n.* **hix**
tiger cat *n.* **k'amb'olay**
    n. **saq b'alam**
tighten *v.* **nat'ok**
tightrope walker *n agt.* **aj**
    b'eenel chi ru
    b'aqb'il k'aam sa iq'
tile   *n.* **ch'ejej**
    n. **lemtz'un xan**
tilled land *n.* **cho'leb' ch'och'**
time   *n.* **kutan**
    n. **q'iil**
    n. **sut**
    n. **taqik**
time particle *part.* **chaq**

times   *n.* **eetalpuk-ajl**
          n. **reetal puktasiil**
tin   *n.* **laat**
tin cup   *n.* **ch'iich' sek'**
tin plate *n.* **ch'iich' sek'**
tin roofing sheet
          n. **k'imalch'iich'**
tire   *v.* **lub'k**
          n. **roq poy ch'iich'**
          n. **tolb'ech'iich'**
          n. **tool**
tired   *adj.* **lub'lu**
          adj. **tawajenaq**
tissue   *n.* **tz'uumal**
tissues   *n.* **huhil sut**
tithing   *n.* **lajetqil**
title   *n.* **huraqb'atzolok**
          n. **jolomil na'leb'**
          n. **k'ajk'amontzolok**
to   *prep.* **chi**
          adv. **choq' re**
          prep. **sa'**
to feel itchy   *v.* **amamnak**
to grow old   *v.* **tixk**
to the left   *adv phr.* **chi tz'e**
to the right   *adv phr.* **chi nim**
to your left   *adv phr.* **sa' laatz'e**
to your right   *adv phr.* **sa' laanim**
toad   *n.* **amoch**
          n. **k'oopopo'**
toast   *n.* **k'orechkaxlanwa**
          v. **jorank**
toasted   *adj.* **jorinb'il**

toaster   *n.* **jorinkleb'**
          n. **k'ileb'aal**
          n. **k'orechib'aal**
          n. **k'orleb'**
tobacco   *n.* **may**
today   *n.* **anaqwan**
          adv. **hoon**
together *adv.* **ch'utch'u**
          adv. **laq'lo**
          adj. **ochb'eninb'il**
          adj. **sa' komonil**
toilet   *n.* **k'otleb'aal**
          n. **tz'eqleb'aal**
toilet paper   *n.* **hu re li k'otak**
tolerance   *n.* **xk'uyb'al**
tolerate   *v.* **kuyuk**
toll   *v.* **tzinb'ank**
toll booth   *n.* **rochoch aj titz'ol toj**
tomato   *n.* **pix**
tomato juice   *n.* **xya'al pix**
tomato sauce   *n.* **ke'b'il pix**
          n. **puq'b'il pix**
tomorrow   *adv.* **hulaj**
tomorrow afternoon   *adv phr.* **hulaj ewu**
tomorrow evening   *adv phr.* **hulaj chi q'eq**
tomorrow morning   *adv phr.* **hulaj chi eq'la**
Tomás   *nick.* **Max**
ton   *n.* **junmay kintal**
          n. **xyuwa'ilb'iis**

tongs   *n.* **q'esyaxch'iich'**
              n. **yax**
tongue   *n.* **aatinob'aal**
              n. **ru'uj aq'**
              n. **xtib'el ru'uj aq'**
tongue (of a shoe)   *n.* **raq'xaab'**
tongue depresser   *n.* **kub'sib'aal**
              ru'uj aq'
tongue twister   *n.* **t'ilb'a'u'ji'aq**
              n. **t'ilru'uj'aq**
tonight   *n.* **hoon chi q'eq**
tonsillitis   *n.* **xyajelxnaq'ja'aj**
too   *adv phr.* **jo'kan aj wi'**
too bad (for you)!   *phr.* **ink'a' us**
              xat-elq
too much   *adv.* **numtajenaq**
tool   *n.* **k'anjelob'aal**
toolbox   *n.* **xkaxonil**
              k'anjeleb'aal
tooth   *n.* **e**
              n. **ruuch e**
toothache   *n.* **rahil ruuch e**
toothbrush   *n.* **ji'leb'-e**
              n. **re chajok sa' e**
              n. **xji'b'al ruuch e**
toothless   *adj.* **lolom re**
              adj. **t'omt'o re**
toothpaste   *n.* **xq'emal ruuch e**
              n. **xxab'onil ruuch e**
top   *n.* **ru'uj**
              n. **sururu**
              n. **sururub'atz'uul**
              n. **tz'apleb'**
toponym   *n.* **k'ab'a'na'jej**

torch   *n.* **b'eexam**
              n. **kanxam**
              n. **lampr**
              n. **xam**
torso   *n.* **maqab'**
              n. **yiitoq**
tortilla   *n.* **wa**
tortoise   *n.* **kok**
tostada   *n.* **xujwahiltib'**
total   *n.* **tamok-ajl**
total eclipse   *n.* **juntz'ap tiwok**
toucan   *n.* **raxpan**
              n. **seelapan**
touch   *v.* **ch'e'ok**
              n. **eek'ob'aal**
              n. **ixkej**
tourist   *n agt.* **aj ab'l tenamit**
              n agt. **aj b'e**
tow truck   *n.* **xook'il ch'iich'**
toward   *prep.* **chi xk'atq**
towel   *n.* **chaqihob' t'ikr**
              n. **masleb'ix**
              n. **potzt'ikr**
              n. **tuntuukir t'ikr**
              n. **tuwaay**
tower   *n.* **kab'l najt xteram**
              n. **toor**
town   *n.* **tenamit**
town leader   *n.* **aj jolominel**
              k'aleb'aal
toy   *n.* **b'atz'uul**
toy store   *n.* **k'ayib'aal**
              b'atz'uul

trace   v. **jalam'uuchib'k**
      v. **juch'uk**

tractor   n. **b'ekol ch'och'**
      n. **hixch'iich'**

trade   v. **jalok**

tradition   n. **najter na'leb'**

traditional
      adj. **najterilk'utb'esin k**

traffic   n. **xk'ihal b'eleb'aalch'iich'**

traffic circle   n. **k'ulb'aq'qax'ib'**

traffic light   n. **kaxlan xamlel b'e**
      n. **k'utb'a numleb'**
      n. **k'utul numeb'aal**

traffic sign   n. **reetalil b'e**

traffic signal   n. **ilb'anumleb'**
      n. **k'ehol numleb'**

trailer truck   n. **motzo'ch'iich'**

train   v. **jultikank**
      n. **k'anti'ch'iich'**
      n. **tren**

tramp   n. **neb'a'**

transform   n. **jaltesink**

transformer   n. **jalb'a'metz'ew**

transitive (verb)   n. **ka'kab'iluxk**

translation   n. **jalok-aatin**

transmit   v. **numsink**

transparent   adj. **kutaniru**
      adj. **saqen ru**

transparent roof panel
      n. **saqenk'im**

transport   n. **b'eleb'aal**

trap   n. **ch'imb'**
      n. **ch'imb'ul**
      v. **ch'imb'unk**
      n. **ra'al**
      v. **ra'alenk**

trapeze artist   n agt. **aj t'uyanel**

trash   n. **mul**
      n. **mulel**

trash can   n. **xchakachil mul**
      n. **xna'aj hu**
      n. **xna'aj mul**

travel   v. **b'eek**
      v. **b'eenink**

travel allowance
      n. **eeqajsachomj**

travel around   v. **b'eenink**

travel through the forest
      v. **k'iche'b'aalik**

travel through the mountains
      v. **k'iche'b'aalik**

traveler   n agt. **aj b'e**

tray   n. **b'elaal tzakahemq**

treasure   n. **k'o'al**

treatment   n. **b'ane'k**

tree   n. **che'**

tree trunk   n. **roq**
      n. **toon**
      n. **xtoonal ruq'b'**

trees   n. **che'eb'**

tremble   v. **parpotk**

trial   n. **raqok aatin**

triangle   n. **b'alxuk**
      n. **oxxukuut**

tributary   *n.* **ruq' nima'**

tribute   *n.* **toj**

trim   *v.* **k'osok**
　　　v. **setok**

trinomial   *n.* **ox'eetalb'irok**

trip   *v.* **tichk'ok**

tripe   *n.* **k'aamk'ot**

triphthong   *n.* **oxjunajink xna'tz'iib'**

tripod   *n.* **chak'oq**
　　　n. **oxxaala**

trisyllable   *n.* **oxraqyehok**

troglodyte   *n.* **ch'olwinq**

trophy
　　　n. **k'ajk'amonkmetzew**
　　　n. **maatanej**
　　　n. **xmaatanil li yaloku**

Tropic of Cancer   *n.* **taqe'q q'eq'ookot eetalil**

Tropic of Capricorn   *n.* **taq'a q'eq'ookot eetalil**

tropics   *n.* **tiqwal siraalch'och'**

troposphere   *n.* **xb'een tasal iq'**

trough   *n.* **job'che'**

trousers   *n.* **wex**

trowel   *n.* **ji'leb'tz'ak**
　　　n. **tz'akleb'**
　　　n. **xlek aj tz'ak**

truck   *n.* **kamyon**
　　　n. **teken ch'iich'**

true   *adj.* **yaal**

trumpet   *n.* **jayaab'wajb'**
　　　n. **kaxxuxb'**
　　　n. **q'anch'iich'**
　　　n. **trompeet**

trumpeter   *n.* **aj wajb'a'apuul**

trunk   *n.* **kaax**
　　　n. **xna'aj iiq**
　　　n. **xe'**

trunk (fruit bearing)   *n.* **raqan**

truth   *n.* **yaal**
　　　n. **yaalal**

try   *v.* **yalok**

t-shirt   *n.* **ch'otlepon**

tuberculosis   *n.* **kuxb'ej**
　　　n. **xyajel pospo'oy**

Tuesday   *n.* **maarts**
　　　n. **xkab'kutan**

tumpline   *n.* **taab'**

tune in   *v.* **rab'inkil**

turkey   *n.* **ak'ach**
　　　n. **xtib'el ak'ach**

turkey soup   *n.* **kaq ik**

turn   *v.* **b'alq'usink**
　　　v. **q'otok**

turn around   *v.* **b'alq'usink**
　　　v. **q'otonk**

turn red   *v.* **kaq'ok**

turn signal   *n.* **ch'ina elajinel**
　　　n. **patz'num**
　　　n. **patz'numleb'**

turnip   *n.* **naaw**
　　　n. **saqxe'**

turtle   *n.* **kok**

turtle shell   *n.* **rix kok**

tusk   *n.* **tz'i' e**

TV   *n.* **kaxmu**

            n. **lemaal'esil**

twelfth   *num.* **(12th.)**
            xkab'lajuil

twelve   *num.* **(12.) kab'laju**

twentieth   *num.* **(20th.)**
            xjunmayil

twenty   *num.* **(20.) jun may**

twenty-day period   *n.* **k'aal**

twenty-eight   *num.* **(28.)**
            waqxaq'ib' xka'k'aal

twenty-first   *num.* **(21st.) xjun**
            xka'k'aalil

twenty-five   *num.* **(25.) oob'**
            xka'k'aal

twenty-five cents   *n.* **o'laju**
            xk'ak'aal senta

twenty-four   *num.* **(24.) kaahib'**
            xka'k'aal

twenty-nine   *num.* **(29.) b'eleb'**
            xka'k'aal

twenty-one   *num.* **(21.) jun**
            xka'k'aal

twenty-second   *num.* **(22nd.)**
            xkab' xka'k'aalil

twenty-seven   *num.* **(27.) wukub'**
            xka'k'aal

twenty-six   *num.* **(26.) waqib'**
            xka'k'aal

twenty-three   *num.* **(23.) oxib'**
            xka'k'aal

twenty-two   *num.* **(22.) wiib'**
            xka'k'aal

twice   *adv.* **ka'wa**
            adv. **ka'ta**

twig   *n.* **ch'ina ruq'**

twins   *n.* **lut**

twist   *v.* **k'onok**
            v. **siq'ok**
            v. **yokosink**

twisted   *adj.* **q'otq'o**
            adj. **q'oot**

two   *num.* **(2.) wiib'**

two days ago   *n.* **kab'ejer**

two days later   *n.* **kiib' kutan**
            chi rix

two hundred   *n.* **lajeek'aal**

two thousand   *n.* **oob' oq'ob'**

two times   *adv.* **ka'wa**
            adv. **ka'ta**

tympanic membrane   *n.* **xulel**
            xikej

type   *n.* **chankatq ru**
            n. **paay**
            n. **paayil**

typewriter   *n.* **k'uub'tz'iib'leb'**
            n. **tz'iib'leb' ch'iich'**

typhoid   *n.* **kaqi yajel**

typical   *adj.* **ok eechej**

Tz'utujil   *lang.* **tz'utujil**

U - u

udder *n.* **xtu' wakax**

ugly *adj.* **jo'maajo'**
 adj. **xa'b'eetal**
 adj. **yib' ru**

ultraviolet light *n.* **xche' saq'e**

umbrella *n.* **muheel**
 n. **paraaw**
 n. **xik'sotz'**

uncle *n.* **ikan**

uncombed *adj.* **ink'a' t'e'b'il**

uncomfortable *adj.* **ch'a'aj treek'a**
 adj. **kosa**

unconscious *adj.* **ink'a' jultik re**
 adj. **junpaatilsachk**

unconverted (archaic) *n.* **ch'olwinq**

under *prep.* **chi rub'el**
 prep. **rub'el**

underpants *n.* **kok' aq' re winq**

undersea earthquake *n.* **palawhiik**

undershirt *n.* **ch'ot t'ikr**

underskirt *n.* **xta-uuq**

understand *v phr.* **tawok u**
 v phr. **tawok xyaalal**

undertaker *n agt.* **aj ilom kamenaq**

underwear *n.* **kok' aq' re ixq**
 n. **kok' aq' re winq**
 n. **xta b'aatal**
 n. **xyach'winq**
 n. **yach'**

underworld *n.* **xb'alb'a**

undo *v.* **juk'uk**
 v. **po'ok**

undress *v phr.* **isink aq'**

unfortunate *adj.* **kaqcha**

unhappiness *n.* **maasahil wank**

unicellular *adj.* **junilna'yu'am**

uniform *n.* **aq'**

union *n.* **junajihom**
 n. **laq'ab'ank**

unique *adj.* **jun**
 adj. **junrib'**

unit *n.* **junqalil**
 n. **xraqalil**

unit of ten *n.* **lajetqil**

United Nations *n.* **xmolamil k'iila tenamital**

United States *n.* **ch'uutal tenamit**

unity *n.* **junajil**
 n. **junqalil**

universe *n.* **choxach'och'**

university *n.* **nimaltzoleb'aal**
 n. **xnimal ru tzoleb'aal**

university level *n.* **xkaatanal tzolok**

unknown *adj.* **aak'ab'**
 adj. **manawb'il**

unoccupied *adj.* **yamyo ru**

unpaved road *n.* **pekilnimb'e**

unpredictable *adj.* **ink'a' nanawman k'a tb'aanu**

unravel   *v.* **hitok**

unreliable   *adj.* **moko naxsume ta jo'yaal**

unripe   *adj.* **al**
          adj. **rax**
          adj. **toj al**

unroll   *v.* **b'orok**

unsatisfied   *adj.* **ch'iqch'o xch'ool**

untangle   *v.* **hirok**
            v. **hitok**

untie   *v.* **b'orok**
         v. **hitok**
         v. **k'ixok**

until   *conj.* **retal**
         conj. **tixto toj**
         conj. **toj**

until now   *conj.* **toja'**

untrue   *adj.* **moko yaal ta**

unuseful   *adj.* **maak'a' rusil**

unwind   *v.* **b'orok**

up   *prep.* **taqe'q**

upper case   *n.* **astz'iib'**

upset   *adj.* **nach'a'ajko'**

Uranus   *n.* **xwuq ralsaq'e**

urban center   *n.* **tenamitil teepal**

urinary pain   *n.* **ra chu'**

urinate   *v.* **chu'uk**

urine   *n.* **chu'**

Ursa Major   *n.* **wuqchahim**

Ursa Minor   *n.* **nach'ilchahim**

us   *pron.* **laa'o**

use up   *v.* **sachik**

used   *adj.* **lil**
        adj. **qeel**

useful   *adj.* **aajel**
          adj. **wan rusil**

usher   *n agt.* **aj hiltesinel**

uterus   *n.* **alob'aal**
          n. **kub'sa'**
          n. **sa' ixq**

utility room   *n.* **xna'aj k'a'aq re ru**

utterance indicating a close call   *interj.* **uy**

utterance indicating a minor failure   *interj.* **t'**

utterance indicating danger   *interj.* **uyaluy**

utterance indicating hope or a wish   *part.* **taxaq**

utterance indicating lack of interest   *interj.* **i'**

utterance of disapproval   *interj.* **sht!**

utterance of disgust   *interj.* **chix**

utterance of doubt or disagreement   *interj.* **eh**

utterance of pain   *interj.* **ay**

utterance of pain or pity   *interj.* **aaa**

utterance of surprise   *interj.* **eh!**

utterance of understanding   *interj.* **ah**
                             interj. **ih**

utterance seeking recognition   *interj.* **sht**

V - v

vacation *n.* **xq'ehil hilaal**

vaccination *n.* **b'akuun**

vacuole *n.* **julel**
     n. **tz'ilol**

vacuum cleaner *n.* **jiq'leb'mul**

vagina *n.* **mi'**

vain *adj.* **namunta**

validation *n.* **ustaanankil**
     n. **xsumenkil**

valley *n.* **ru taq'a**
     n. **taq'a**

valuable *adj.* **loq'al**

value *n.* **xloq'al**
     n. **xtz'aq**

value-added tax *n.* **komontoj**

values *n.* **loq'alil**
     n. **tiikalil**
     n. **tiikil loq'alil**

variable *n.* **xjalanil**

variant form *n.* **raatinxcha'alil aatinib'aal**
     n. **xjalob'aatinob'aal**

variety *n.* **paay**
     n. **paayil**

varnish *n.* **lemtz'b'on**
     v. **lemtz'b'onik**

vase *n.* **xjaar uutz'u'uj**
     n. **xna'aj uutz'u'uj**

VAT *n.* **komontoj**
     n. **toj**

vegetable *n.* **ruuch che'k'aam**
     n. **xe' ru che'**
     n. **supq'een**

vegetable seller *n agt.* **aj k'ay xe' ru che'**

vegetables *n.* **ru ut xe' pim**

vegetation *n.* **che'k'aam**

veil *n.* **b'eel**

vein *n.* **ich'**
     n. **ich'mul**

velar *n.* **xb'een'e yaab'**

velocity *n.* **metz'ewil**
     n. **raanil**

venison *n.* **xtib'el kej**

Venus *n.* **kaqchahim**
     n. **xulab'**

verb *n.* **xch'oolaatin**

verbal *adj.* **yeeb'il**

verse *n.* **ch'ol'uutz'ujinb'il aatin**
     n. **raqaltz'iib'**
     n. **raapal**
     n. **xtz'iib'ul b'ich**

vertebrate *n.* **b'aqil xuleb'**

vertical *adj.* **xaqxo**

vertical line *n.* **xaqxookil juch'**

vertigo   *n.* **lub'ik**

very   *adv.* **jwal**

very bitter *adj.* **k'aak'a**

very clean *adj.* **ch'aj ch'aj**

very fermented
    adj. **ch'amch'am**

very fine *adj.* **musmus**

very good *adj.* **q'axal us**

very important *phr.* **jwal aajel**

very salty *adj.* **num atz'am**

very stiff *adj.* **chek'chek'**

very white *adj.* **saqpotz'in**
    adj. **saqpuk'in**

vest   *n.* **aq' ch'ot ruq'**

vestment *n.* **nimla t'ikr**
    n. **raq' qaawa'**

veterinarian *n agt.* **aj ilom xul**

veterinary store *n.* **k'ayib'aal**
    b'an re ketomj

vial   *n.* **mitz'meetil b'an**

vice president
    n. **xkab'awa'b'ejil**
    n. **xkab'il awab'ej**

vicious *adj.* **maak'a' xkuyum**

Victor   *nick.* **B'it**

victory *n.* **echanink**
    n. **ketok**

video   *n.* **ilob'aal mu**

video camera
    n. **chapleb'jalam'u**
    n. **xokleb' mu**

videocassette *n.* **xna'aj lemal**
    eetalil

view   *n.* **ilob'aal**

vigorous *adj.* **kaw rib'**

vile   *adj.* **tz'i'b'eetal**

village *n.* **tenamit**

vindictive *adj.* **naxk'e reeqaj**
    naxk'ul

vine   *n.* **aq'**

vinegar *n.* **b'oj ha' tzakahemq**
    n. **b'inaayr**

violate *v.* **muxuk**

violation *n.* **muxuk**

violent *adj.* **ch'impo'**
    adj. **josq'**

violet *adj.* **raxtint**

violin *n.* **jitz'jitz'**

violinist *n agt.* **aj iitz'in**

viper   *n.* **k'anti' ra xmay re**
    n. **xna' k'anti'**

virgin   *n.* **tuq'ixq**

virtual education
    n. **muhilb'atijok**

virus   *n.* **xmaxel**

viscous *adj.* **waa**

vise   *n.* **chapleb'**

vision *n.* **ileb'aal**
    n. **ilob'aal xsa'u**

visit   *n.* **hulak**
    n. **ula'**
    v. **ula'ak**
    v. **ula'ank**

visitor *n.* **ula'**

visitor log *n.* **tasal hu re ula'**

visor   *n.* **ilob'aal**
     n. **lep-punit**

visual arts
     n. **tzoljalam'uuch'ink**

vitamin   *n.* **kawub'lb'an**

vitamin C   *n.* **b'itamin Se**

vocabulary   *n.* **tusleb'aal aatin**

vocalize   *v.* **yaab'ank**

voice   *n.* **ja'ajul**

volcanic   *adj.* **xk'uhil**

volcano   *n.* **k'u**
     n. **puub' tzuul**

volcanology   *n.* **nawk'uhil**

volleyball   *n.* **b'olotz sum uq'ib'k**
     n. **sak'lemb'ilb'olotz**

volunteer work   *n.* **kamab'k**

vomit   *n.* **xa'aw**
     v. **xa'wak**
     n. **xawak**

vote   *v.* **juch'uk**
     v. **xaqab'ank**

voter   *n agt.* **aj juch'unel**

voucher   *n.* **eeqajsachomj**

vowel   *n.* **xna'tz'iib'**

vowels   *n.* **xna'tz'iib'eb'**

vulcanologist   *n agt.* **aj nawk'uhil**

vulgar   *adj.* **lolob'**

vulnerability   *n.* **rahob'tesink wank**

vulture   *n.* **so'sol**

vulva   *n.* **b'irk**
     n. **choy**
     n. **pirk'**

W - w

wages   *n.* **po**

wagon   *n.* **kareton**

waist   *n.* **sa' yi**
     n. **yi**
     n. **yiib'ej**
     n. **yiitoq**

waistband   *n.* **xyi**

wait   *v.* **oyb'enink**

wait a minute
     phr. **chinaawoyb'en b'ayaq**

waiter   *n agt.* **aj k'ehonel tzakahemq**

waiting room   *n.* **na'aj re oyb'enink**
     n. **oyb'eb'aal**

wake up   *v.* **ajk**

walk   *v.* **b'eek**

walkie talkie   *n.* **numsib'aal esil**

walking stick   *n.* **b'axton**
     n. **xuq'**

walkway   *n.* **ch'ina b'e**
     n. **q'axleb'aal**

wall   *n.* **kuuk**
     n. **kuukil tz'ak**

n. ru tz'ak

n. tz'ak

wall clock   *n.* ilob'aal hoonal

wallet   *n.* xna'aj huhil tumin

walnut tree   *n.* nokal

want   *v.* atawank

    v. rahink

war   *n.* kamsink-ib'

    n. pleet

    n. raaxiik'

    n. yalok

wardrobe   *n.* xna'aj aq'

warehouse   *n.* k'uuleb'aal

warm   *adj.* tiq

warn   *v.* q'usuk

warp   *v.* b'atok

warrior   *n agt.* aj yalonel

warship   *n.* jukub' re pleetik

wary   *adj.* sa' xyaalal

wash   *v.* ch'ajok

    v. puch'uk

wash basin (clothing)   *n.* xna'aj puch'um

wash with soap   *v.* xab'onink

washbasin   *n.* kaxemel

    n. kaxjoom

    n. puch'leb'

    n. tamb'aha'

washbowl   *n.* kaxemel

    n. kaxjoom

    n. puch'leb'

    n. tamb'aha'

washing machine

    n. metz'ewilpuch'leb'

n. puch'leb'aal ch'iich'

wasp   *n.* ch'ub'

waste   *v.* tz'eqink

waste time   *v.* b'ayok ib'

wastebasket   *n.* xchakachil mul

    n. xna'aj mul

wastepaper bin   *n.* xna'aj hu

watch   *n.* uq'mil k'uthoonal

watch out   *phr.* k'e reetal li taab'aanu

watch over   *v.* k'uulank

watchmaker   *n agt.* aj yiib'om reloj

water   *n.* ha'

    v. hoyok

water bill   *n.* xhuhil li ha'

water fountain   *n.* uk'leb'aal

water jar   *n.* kukb'

water jug   *n.* xaaril ha'

water meter   *n.* ajleb'ilha'

water pump   *n.* k'uub'kutha'

    n. tzub'pajha'

water tank   *n.* pumleb'ha'

    n. xna'aj ha'

water tap   *n.* teeleb'ha'

    n. xlaawil ha'

    n. xteeb'al ha'

water well   *n.* uk'leb'aal ha'

waterfall   *n.* pach'il ha'

    n. pajaj ha'

    n. rusos

n. **t'anleb'aalha'**
n. **xpisk' ha'**
n. **xulk'ukil nima'**

watering can *n.* **chaab'**
n. **chirleb'**
n. **kira'sleb'**

watering hole *n.* **xna'aj ha'**

watermelon *n.* **kaxq'ooq'**
n. **sandiiy**

watershed *n.* **roqtaq'a**

wave *n.* **b'oolha'**
n. **xrepom palaw**

wax seal *n.* **t'oqb'on**

we *pron.* **laa'o**

weak *adj.* **lub'lu**
adj. **maak'a' xmetz'ew**
adj. **q'un**

weak signal *n.* **jwal kach'in xkutum**

wealth *n.* **b'ihomal**

wealthy *adj.* **b'ihom**

weapons *n.* **kamsib'aal**
n. **kamsiil**

weary *adj.* **tawajenaq**

weasel *n.* **saqb'in**

weather *n.* **kutan**

weather satellite
n. **chahimch'iich' aj na'onel ru li ruchich'och'**

weather vane *n.* **eetalnum'iq**

weave *v.* **kemok**

wedding *n.* **sumlajik**

Wednesday *n.* **miercools**

weeds *n.* **chamal pim**
n. **pim**

week *n.* **wuq'ix**
n. **xamaan**

weevil *n.* **max**
n. **maxel hal**

weigh *v.* **aalank**
v. **b'isok**

weight *n.* **aalal**

welcome *adj.* **usilk'ulunk**

welcome to all of you
phr. **usilk'ulunk cho'q eere**

well *conj.* **b'i'**
adv. **chaab'il**
adv. **us**

well (water) *n.* **ch'ina ha'**
n. **kumb'**
n. **k'ak'naab'**
n. **tuq**

well done *adj.* **chaq' chi us**
adj. **rek'**

well done! *phr.* **chaab'il xaab'anu**

west *n.* **rokeb' saq'e**

wet *adj.* **b'aqx**
adj. **luub'**
adj. **raap**
v. **t'aqresink**
adj. **t'aqt'aq**
adj. **t'oqx**
adj. **tz'uuq**

whale *n.* **b'ayeen**
n. **xna' kar**

what a pity *phr.* **k'a' xja'lenkil**

what a shame *phr.* **k'a' xja'lenkil**

what are you doing? (singular) *phr.* **k'a'ru yookat**

what did you say? *phr.* **k'a'ru xaaye**

what does [ ] mean? *phr.* **k'a'ru naraj naxye [ ]**

what happened? *phr.* **k'a'ru xk'ulman**

what is happening? *phr.* **k'a'ru yo**

what is that? *phr.* **k'a' ru a'an**

what is this? *phr.* **k'a' ru a'in**

what size? *interr.* **jo' ch'inal**

what's the matter? *phr.* **k'a'ru xk'ulman**

what's your email? *phr.* **chan ru la weetalil sa' internet**

what's your phone number? *phr.* **b'ar rajlil laab'oqleb'**

what? *interr.* **k'a'**
interr. **k'a'ru**

whatever *conj.* **yalaq b'ar wan**
conj. **yalaq k'a'ru**

wheat *n.* **riximul kaxlan wa**
n. **triiw**

wheel *n.* **roq**
n. **roq poy ch'iich'**
n. **rueed**
n. **sursu**

n. **tolb'ech'iich'**
n. **xb'eelil**

wheel chair *n.* **b'eleb'aal tem**
n. **kaxlan tem**
n. **toltem**

wheelbarrow *n.* **iiqaal**
n. **karetiiy**
n. **toltol**

wheelchair *n.* **b'eleb'aal tem**
n. **xb'eeleb'aal yaj**

when *pron.* **naq**

when? *interr.* **joq'e**

whenever *conj.* **yalaq joq'e**

where are you from? *phr.* **aj b'arat**
phr. **b'ar wan aatenamit**

where are you? *phr.* **b'ar wankat**

where do you come from? *phr.* **b'ar nakatchal**

where do you live? *phr.* **b'ar wan aawochoch**

where is the toilet? *phr.* **b'ar wan li tz'eqleb'aal**

where? *interr.* **b'ar**

wherever *conj.* **yalaq b'ar**

whetstone *n.* **hux**
n. **ji'leb'**

which? *interr.* **b'ar wan re**
interr. **k'a'ru**

which? (plural) *interr.* **b'ar wankeb'**

which? (singular) *interr.* **b'ar wank**

whichever *conj.* **yalaq**

whip *v.* **juylek**
   n. **tz'uum**

whirlpool *n.* **suut ha'**

whisk *v.* **yulenk**

whiskey *n.* **wiisk**

whisper *v.* **hasb'ak**
   v phr. **jiq'jiq'ink ib'**

whisper sweetly *v.* **payok**

whistle *v phr.* **b'oqok chi yaab'**
   v. **xuxb'ak**

whistle (object) *n.* **b'ololch'iich'**
   n. **kaxb'olol**

whistle (sound) *n.* **xuxb'**

white *adj.* **saq**

white blood cells *n.* **saqkil mitz'kotkik'**

white gold *n.* **saqi pwaq**

white orchid *n.* **saqihix**

White Out *n.* **tuqleb'**

white wine *n.* **saqi b'iin**

white-nosed coati *n.* **sis**

whitish *adj.* **saqjorin**

who? *interr.* **ani**

whoever *pron.* **yalaq ani**

whole *adj.* **tzaqal jun**

whose? (plural) *interr.* **aniheb' aj e**

whose? (singular) *interr.* **ani aj e**

why not? *phr.* **k'a'ut naq ink'a'**

why? *interr.* **k'a'ut**

wide *adj.* **nim ru**

wide open *adj.* **ch'a'ch'o**

widow *n.* **malka'an**

widower *n.* **te'elch'ool**

width *n.* **xnimal ru**

wife *n.* **ixaqil**
   n. **ixaqilb'ej**

wig *n.* **pak'b'il ismal**

wild bee *n.* **aaq kab'**

wild boar *n.* **k'iche' aaq**

wild cardamom *n.* **tz'i' k'iche'**

wild cilantro *n.* **samat**

wild dove *n.* **uut**

wild grass *n.* **pim**

wild horse *n.* **t'initz**

win *v phr.* **k'ehok k'as**
   v. **tzakib'k**

wind *n.* **iq'**

wind erosion *n.* **xch'ajom iq'**

windmill *n.* **ke'leb'aal**

window *n.* **b'entaan**
   n. **ch'uukib'aal**
   n. **rokeb'aal saqen**

window pane *n.* **lem**

windshield *n.* **mesb'a lem**

windshield wiper *n.* **masleb'ha'**

windy *adj.* **iq' xsa'**

wine *n.* **b'iin**

wing *n.* **xik'**

winter   *n.* **hab'al q'e**

wipe   *v.* **mesok**

wiper   *n.* **mesol lem**

wire   *n.* **k'ahamch'iich'**

wise   *adj.* **wan xna'leb'**

witch   *n.* **awasinel**
    n. **tuulanel**

with   *prep.* **rexb'een**
    prep. **rik'in**

with pleasure   *adv phr.* **chi sa xch'oolil**

with what?   *interr.* **k'a'ru aj ik'in**

with whom?   *interr.* **ani aj ik'in**

without   *prep.* **maawa' rik'in**

witness   *n agt.* **aj kuutunel**
    n. **testiig**

witness statement   *n.* **yehok aatin sa' chaq'rab'**

wolf   *n.* **aj xoj**
    n. **loob'**
    n. **tz'i' k'iche'**

woman   *n.* **ixq**

womb   *n.* **alob'aal**
    n. **kub'sa'**
    n. **sa' ixq**

wood   *n.* **che'**

wood drum   *n.* **ch'ina tun**
    n. **che'wajb'**

woodcarver   *n agt.* **aj pech'ol che'**

woodpecker   *n.* **pich'**
    n. **tzentzejer**

woods   *n.* **k'iche'**

woodshop   *n.* **peech'leb'aal**

wool   *n.* **laan**

word   *n.* **aatin**

work   *n.* **k'anjel**

work bench   *n.* **xmeexul li peech'ab'k**

work metal   *v.* **pu'akink**

work of art   *n.* **b'onb'il q'esnalna'leb'**

work out   *v phr.* **xtawb'il li manawb'il**

workbench   *n.* **meex re k'anjelak**

worker   *n agt.* **aj k'anjel**

workplaces   *n.* **xna'aj li k'anjel**

workshop   *n.* **k'uub'leb'aal**
    n. **rochochil k'anjel**
    n. **xna'aj k'anjeleb'aal**
    n. **yiib'leb'aal**

world   *n.* **ruuchich'och'**

world map
    n. **reetalilruuchich'och'**

worm   *n.* **b'itzkiri'**
    n. **chajal**
    n. **chupil**
    n. **hay**
    n. **koton is**
    n. **kuluk**
    n. **k'ixix**
    n. **k'utub'**
    n. **lukum**
    n. **motzo'**
    n. **pirik'**

n. **tin**

n. **tzonok'**

worried   *adj.* **yo xk'a'uxl**

worry   *n.* **xtib' jolom**

worse   *adv phr.* **jwal ink'a us**

worsen   *v phr.* **nimank ru**

worship   *v.* **loq'onink**

v phr. **xb'aanunkil mayejak**

worthiness   *n.* **loq'alil**

worthy   *n.* **loq'al**

would you like a drink?   *phr.* **ma tawaj uk'ak**

wound   *n.* **saan**

n. **tiq'ilal**

n. **yok'olal**

woven shoulder bag   *n.* **champa**

wrap   *v.* **lanok**

v. **q'ochok**

n. **xta**

v. **xut'uk**

v. **yutuk**

wrap-around   *n.* **xta**

wrapped   *adj.* **b'irb'o**

wrath   *n.* **josq'il**

wrench   *n.* **q'otleb'ch'iich'**

wring   *v.* **b'alq'usink**

v. **yatz'ok**

wrinkled   *adj.* **mochmo**

adj. **mochox**

wrinkles   *n.* **yoch**

wrist   *n.* **xkux uq'b'**

wristwatch   *n.* **uq'mil k'uthoonal**

write   *v.* **tz'iib'ak**

write a check   *v phr.* **xk'eb'al xhuhul tojleb'**

write up   *v phr.* **na'leb'ank tz'iib'**

writer   *n agt.* **aj tz'iib'**

writing   *n.* **tz'iib'**

written request   *n.* **hupatz'om**

n. **hutz'aam**

wrong   *adj.* **ink'a' us**

adj. **moko yaal ta**

X - x

Xinca   *lang.* **xinka**

X-ray   *n.* **numsinb'il'eetalil**

n. **xjalam'uuchil**

X-ray machine   *n.* **eek'ch'iich'**

X-ray plate   *n.* **reetalil b'aq**

xylophone   *n.* **xolb'ch'iich'**

Y - y

yamstick *n.* **awleb'**

yard   *n.* **neb'aal**

yawn   *v phr.* **japink e**

year   *n.* **chihab'**
           n. **hab'**

yeast   *n.* **xsiiptz'ub' kaxlan wa**

yellow   *adj.* **q'an**

yellow gold *n.* **q'an pwaq**

yellow hornet *n.* **q'anch'ub'**

yellowish *adj.* **q'anb'uyin**
           adj. **q'anmalaw**
           adj. **q'antzoq'i**

yes   *adv.* **enhe'**
           adv. **heehe'**
           adv. **us**

yesterday *n.* **ewer**

yesterday evening *n.* **ewer chi q'eq**

yesterday morning *n.* **ewer eq'la**

yoke   *n.* **yunta**

yoke (of oxen) *n.* **b'ooyx**

yolk   *n.* **xq'anal mol**

you (plural) *pron.* **laa'ex**

you (singular) *pron.* **laa'at**

you're right *phr.* **yaal laak'a'uxl**

you're welcome *phr.* **maak'a' naxye**

you're wrong *phr.* **moko yaal ta laak'a'uxl**

young   *adj.* **al**
           adj. **ch'ajom**
           adj. **saaj**

young man *n.* **ch'ajom**

young men *n.* **xerek' winq**

young woman *n.* **ixqa'al**
           n. **tuq'ixq**

younger brother *n.* **iitz'in**

younger sibling *n.* **iitz'inb'ej**

younger sister *n.* **iitz'in**

younger than *adv phr.* **ka'ch'in chi ru**

youth   *n.* **ch'ajomal**

Z - z

zeal   *n.* **sowenk**

zebra   *n.* **b'alaq xul**
           n. **jilix kawaay**

zeppelin   *n.* **pamb'eeresinb'il**

zero   *n.* **sero**
           n. **yam**
           num. **(0.) maajun**

zinc   *n.* **sink**

zip drive *n.* **k'osleb'**

zipper   *n.* **k'erex**
           n. **tz'apleb'**

zoo   *n.* **rochoch xul**

      n. **xna'ajleb'aalxul**

      n. **xna'aj k'ila xul**

zoologist   *n agt.* **aj nawxul**

zoology   *n.* **nawxul**

APPENDICES

Xraqikeb' Ch'ol

APPENDICES

Xraqikeb' Ch'ol

NOTES ON Q'EQCHI' LINGUISTIC BORROWING

(Chirixeb' li to'chi' Q'eqchi')

Included in some of the entries in Section II of this reference work are notes on linguistic borrowing taken from the Q'eqchi' loanword database compiled by Søren Wichmann and Kerry Hull. The World Loanword Database (WOLD) is the result of a collaborative effort called the Loanword Typology Project (LWT) coordinated by Uri Tadmor and Martin Haspelmath between 2004 and 2008. As of 2015 the results of this project reside on the World Wide Web at: http://wold.livingsources. org/.

The list of 1,460 meanings on which the vocabularies represented in the WOLD project are based is called the Loanword Typology meaning list, which was in turn based on the list of the Intercontinental Dictionary Series. The Q'eqchi' database constitutes 1,995 Q'eqchi'/English word pairs which were analyzed by Wichman and Hull for evidence of borrowing from other languages (European and Mesoamerican). I have included their conclusions on borrowing and donor language as a note to these entries using the numbers of their classification scheme:

(1) Clearly borrowed
(2) Probably borrowed
(3) Perhaps borrowed
(4) Very little evidence for borrowing
(5) No evidence for borrowing

Many other entries in Section II contain notes on Spanish loanwords which are not a part of the World Loan Word Database—these notes are my own.

In addition to the WOLD notations, I have adapted information on Q'eqchi' surnames from Burkitt's *Notes on the Keckchi' Language* and made notes on the likely or possible origin of Q'eqchi' surnames using the following scheme:

(B1) Clearly borrowed
(B3) Perhaps borrowed

LIST OF ABBREVIATIONS USED

(Xk'osb'al ru li aatin neke'oksiman chi sa')

Abbrev.		Term	Definition
adj	=	adjective	A word that modifies nouns and pronouns, primarily by describing a particular quality of the word they are modifying.
adv	=	adverb	A word that functions as a modifiers of verbs or clauses, and in some languages as a modifier of adjectives.
adv phr	=	adverbial phrase	A group of two or more words that function together as an adverb.
art	=	article	A member of a small class of words found in certain languages that are linked to nouns and that typically have a grammatical function identifying the noun as a noun rather than describing it.
conj	=	conjunction	A member of a small class of words distinguished in many languages by their function as connectors between words, phrases, clauses, or sentences.

interj	=	interjection	A part of speech signifying an emotion or mental state by means of a standardized instinctive utterance.
interr	=	interrogative	A word used in forming or constituting a question.
lang	=	language	The system of communication used by a particular community or geographic region.
n	=	noun	A word that can function as the main or only element of subjects of verbs, or of objects of verbs or prepositions.
n agt	=	agent noun	A noun that denotes an agent that performs the action denoted by the verb from which the noun is derived.
n comp	=	compound noun	A noun that is made with two or more words that acts as a single unit and can be modified by adjectives and other nouns.
nick	=	nickname	A name substituted for the proper name of a person which connotes affection or familiarity.
num	=	numeral	A word, letter, symbol, or figure expressing a number; number.

part	=	particle	A small word of functional or relational use that is neither a verb nor a noun.
phr	=	phrase	A small string of words standing together as a single conceptual unit
prep	=	preposition	Words found in many languages that are used before nouns, pronouns, or other substantives to form phrases functioning as modifiers of verbs, nouns, or adjectives, and that typically express a spatial or temporal relationship.
pron	=	pronoun	Any member of a small class of words found in many languages that are used as replacements or substitutes for nouns and noun phrases, and that have very general reference.
sur	=	surname	A hereditary name given to all members of a family. In English and Q'eqchi' linguistic communities it usually follows the given or first name.

v	=	verb	Any member of a class of words that function as the main elements of predicates, that typically express action, state, or a relation between two things, and that may be inflected for tense, aspect, voice, mood, and to show agreement with their subject or object.
v phr	=	verb phrase	A group of words including a verb and its complements, objects, or other modifiers that functions syntactically as a verb.
Var	=	variant form	A way of writing or pronouncing a word which is used by some people as an alternative to the standard or generally accepted form.

BIBLIOGRPAHY

(Reetalil k'ila tasal hu oksinb'ileb')

Ager, Simon. 2014. Q'eqchi' pronunciation. On: Omniglot: The online encyclopedia of writing systems and alphabets website. (Available on the internet at http://www. Omniglot.com/writing/qeqchi.htm, Accessed on 2014-04-28.)

ALMG, 2004. Xtusulal Aatin Sa' Q'eqchi: Vocabulario Q'eqchi'. Guatemala City: Academia de Lenguas Mayas de Guatemala.

ALMG, 2004(?). Eb' li Ak' Aatin sa' li Aatinob'aal Q'eqchi': Actualización Lexical Q'eqchi'. Guatemala City: Academia de Lenguas Mayas de Guatemala.

ALMG, 2008. Molob'aal Aatin Q'eqchi. Coban (Kob'an xch'och'el tezulutlan) Guatemala: Academia de Lenguas Mayas de Guatemala.

Burkitt, Robert. 1902. Notes on the Kekchi' Language, American Anthropologist, pp 441 - 463.

Caal, Luz Maria and Chub Choc, Pedro. 2015. Q'eqchi' Mayan Words for Mammals. (Available on the internet at http://maya-archaeology.org/mayan-anthropology-ethnography-archaeology-art-history-iconography-epigraphy-ethnobotany/qeqchi-mayan-words-for-animals-mammals-alta-verapaz-guatemala.php, Accessed on 2015-05-28.)

Cahill, Nathan. 2014. Community Cloud Forest Conservation. (Available on the internet at http://www.cloudforest

con-servation.org/community/qeqchi.php, Accessed on 2014-08-10.)

Caz Cho, Sergio. 2007. Xtz'ilb'al rix li aatinak sa' Q'eqchi'. (Informe de Variacion Dialectal en Q'eqchi'.) Antigua, Guatemala. OKMA—Oxlajuuj Keej Maya' Ajtz'iib'. Guatemala, Guatemala: Cholsamaj.

CODISRA. 2010 Fuente Indicadores y Estadísticas por Pueblos y Comunidades Linguísticas de Guatemala, Comisión Presidencial contra la Discriminación y el Racismo contra los Pueblos Indígenas de Guatemala.

Cu Cab, Carlos Humberto. 1998. Q'eqchi' - Kaxlan aatin ut Kaxlan aatin - Q'eqchi'. Guatemala City: Instituto de Lingüística de la Universidad Rafael Landívar.

Haeserijn, Esteban. 1979. Q'eqchi' – Diccionario K'ekchi' Español. Editorial Piedra Santa.

Kaufman, Terrence with John Justeson. 2003. A Preliminary Mayan Etymological Dictionary. Foundation for the Advancement of Mesoamerican Studies. (Available online at http:// www.famsi.org/reports/01051/pmed. pdf, Accessed on 2015-05-28.)

Kockelman, Paul. 2003. The Meanings of Interjections in Q'eqchi' Maya. *Current Anthropolgy*, Vol 44, No 4, August-October.

K'u Kab', Kalich. 2012. Tusleb'aal Aatin Q'eqchi' – Inglés – Español. First ed. Chamelco, Alta Verapaz, Guatemala.

Lewis, M. Paul, Gary F. Simons, and Charles D. Fennig (eds.). 2014. *Ethnologue: Languages of the World, Seventeenth edition.* Dallas, Texas: SIL International. Online version: http:// www.ethnologue.com.

PLFM, 2003. Diccionario Q'eqchi. Proyecto Lingüístico Francisco Marroquín. Antigua, Guatemala.

Redish, Laura. 2014. Q'eqchi' pronunciation guide. On: Native Languages of the Americas website. (Available online at http://www.native-languages.org/kekchi_guide.htm, Accessed on 2014-04-28.)

Romero, Sergio. 2012. "They Don't Get Speak Our Language Right": Language Standardization, Power And Migration among the Q'eqchi' Maya. *Journal of Linguistic Anthropology*, Vol. 22, Issue 2, pp. E21–E41,

Sam Juárez, Miguel, Ernesto Chen Cao, Crisanto Xal Tec, Domingo Cuc Chen, and Pedro Tiul Pop. 1997. Diccionario del idioma q'eqchi'. La Antigua, Guatemala: Proyecto Lingüístico Francisco Marroquín.

Sedat, William. 1955. Nuevo diccionario de las lenguas k'ekchi' y española. Chamelco, Alta Verapaz, Guatemala: Instituto Lingüístico de Verano.

Wichmann, Søren and Hull, Kerry. 2009. Q'eqchi' vocabulary. In: Haspelmath, Martin & Tadmor, Uri (eds.) World Loanword Database. Leipzig: Max Planck Institute for Evolutionary Anthropology, 1995 entries. (Available online at http:// wold.livingsources.org/vocabulary/34, Accessed on 2014-04-28.)

Verdugo de Lima, Lucía (ed). 2004. Palabras: Diccionario Ilustrado Castellano / Q'eqchi' – Eb' li Aatin: K'uub'an-b'il Sik'leb'aal Aatin sa' Kaxlan Aatin / Q'eqchi'. Instituto de Lingüística y Educación, Universidad Rafael Landívar, Guatemala. 3a edición, revisada y aumentada

Xb'epo xb'een xpuktasinkil li k'anjel a'in jo' li
ch'olkutan maayab' (kelkookil ajlank):

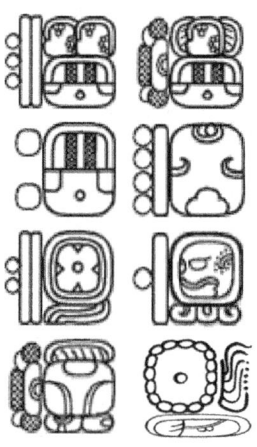

13 baktun   0 katun
2 tun   9 winal
12 kin   6 eb'
0 sek

Made in the USA
Monee, IL
24 August 2020